THE NEW GAMBLER'S BIBLE

HOW TO BEAT THE CASINOS, THE TRACKS, YOUR BOOKIE, AND YOUR BUDDIES

Arthur S. Reber

Crown Trade Paperbacks
New York

♣   ♦   ♥   ♠

The Gambler's Ruin table in chapter 5 is based on material in *Gambling Theory and Other Topics* by Mason Malmuth and is presented with permission of the author and the publisher, Two Plus Two Publishing.

The hold 'em hand rankings presented in chapter 6 are reproduced from *Hold 'em Poker for Advanced Players* by David Sklansky and Mason Malmuth and are presented with permission of the authors and the publisher, Two Plus Two Publishing.

The past performance and results charts in chapter 7 are reproduced by permission of the copyright owner, the *Daily Racing Form*.

The various tables showing hold percentages for sports books and recommended payouts for particular wagers presented in chapter 8 are from *Race and Sports Book Management: A Guide for the Legal Bookmaker* by Michael Roxborough and Mike Rhoden and are reproduced by permission of the authors, who published the book independently.

Published by Crown Trade Paperbacks, 201 East 50th Street, New York, New York 10022. Member of the Crown Publishing Group.

Random House, Inc. New York, Toronto, London, Sydney, Auckland
CROWN TRADE PAPERBACKS and colophon are trademarks of Crown Publishers, Inc.
http://www.randomhouse.com/

Printed in the United States of America

Design by Interrobang Design Studio

Library of Congress Cataloging-in-Publication Data
available upon request

ISBN 0-517-88669-3

10 9 8 7 6 5 4 3 2 1

First Edition

CONTENTS

ACKNOWLEDGMENTS

When I finished this book and sat down to write this section I was struck by how many people I had actually turned to for information, assistance, advice, or just plain support. It was a humbling moment. In fact, there were so many I hope I have not forgotten to thank anyone.

First, of course, there is Bob Silverstein, who worked with me from the very beginning to put the whole project together. Without Bob there would be no book. Danny Montagna, VP for casino operations at TropWorld in Atlantic City, was a steady source of information and insight into the world of casino gambling. I have come to regard Danny as a friend and am pleased that he so regards me. George Mancuso, VP in charge of slots at TropWorld, also gave me his time and expertise, and I am grateful. My son Paul, a pretty good poker player (in addition to being himself a research scientist), made many helpful suggestions. Steve Crist, one of the world's leading handicappers and currently director of communications and development for the New York Racing Association, read over the whole book and provided excellent advice and counsel, especially on the material in chapter 7. Roxy Roxborough and Lem Banker were both extremely helpful, particularly with issues pertaining to sports betting and, in Roxy's case, how a sports book operates. A couple of deeply insightful friends of mine who must be credited anonymously made their mark on my thinking about the material in chapter 8. Howard Schwartz, director of marketing of the Gambler's Book Club of Las Vegas and a transplanted Brooklynite, was a never-ending source of information about gambling and the people associated with it. My colleague and occasional "partner in crime" Buzzy Chanowitz saved me from many sins of omission and commission.

A special note of appreciation goes out to the crew at the track, a marvelous bunch of lowlifes with whom I have spent countless afternoons over the past two decades. In no special order they are: Harry, Giggi, Buzzy, Danny, Pete, Chuck, Bob, Eddie, Ninny, Nick, Jack, Pauly, Joey Blue Eyes, and the gone but fondly remembered Skip. All the rich and varied slices of reality run through these guys, and I will always be grateful for the way in which they shared their own special perspectives on life.

The section on tipping in chapter 11 goes into considerable detail. I have dedicated this section to my mother. A truly spectacular woman, she is a recognized and respected artist and sculptor who, undaunted by age (she's in her middle eighties), trots around the globe routinely visiting the most remote and unreachable places, taking photographs, riding camels, climbing mountains, marching across the Great Wall of China, and totally freaking out if anyone puts her in a situation where she is obliged to tip. In fact, she is so psychologically derailed by having to tip anyone that she will now travel only in groups that have already taken care of all financial aspects. This infirmity of hers is totally out of character, since she has been able to handle with aplomb every other situation that has been placed before her in her long and wondrous life, but there it is.

I also want to give a very special thank-you to Wendy Hubbert, my editor at Crown. First, she was willing to take a shot on a book that is unique in the gambling literature. Second, she was virtually the perfect editor. She cajoled when it was needed and left me alone when that was appropriate. What more could an author ask?

But my deepest thanks go to Mason Malmuth, who is recognized as one of today's leading gambling authorities and whose publishing group, Two Plus Two Publishing, has produced some of the best works in the gambling field. Mason read the entire manuscript with the intelligence and attention to detail for which he is famous. He caught and corrected a number of absolute howlers that I had committed and provided proper advice and direction on innumerable occasions. I cannot thank him enough for his help on this project, and I hope that someday I will be able to play poker as well as he does. Finally, a note of appreciation to my wife, who thinks this whole gambling thing is just plain nuts but manages to tolerate my affection for it.

FOREWORD

Let's face it, people crave action. It's part of the excitement that makes our lives more interesting. If we weren't this way, everything we do would be boring and routine. That's why most of us like to gamble, and thanks to new laws legalizing casino gambling in many localities, most of us will now have the opportunity to do so.

It wasn't always this way. Years ago, if you wanted to visit a casino, you had to go to Nevada, and Nevada is located in the middle of nowhere. However, all that has changed. Not only are casinos legal in many places, but Nevada, and particularly Las Vegas, has become a major vacation destination. One like no other.

In many ways this creates a problem for most people. Even though they want to gamble, they are not knowledgeable enough to do so in any sort of successful manner. That is, the typical casino customer will lose his money if he keeps gambling, and sometimes he will lose it at a very rapid rate.

But there is another trap here. Even if you don't know what you are doing, you can and should have some winning nights. This is because most forms of gambling inherently contain a large short-term luck factor. That is, as we gamblers like to say, the games are highly fluctuating, and someone who doesn't know what he is doing can "run good" for a fairly long period of time. But this doesn't mean that gambling is the future for you. Just because you have done well in the past doesn't mean that your future results won't be just what they should be.

On the other hand, there's a small number of people who have been quite successful at the gambling tables. Of course, they don't play games like craps or roulette, which cannot be beaten. They have become highly skilled at games like poker and blackjack, where an expert can obtain an edge large enough to allow him to make a good living. But it takes a lot of work and effort; very few people achieve this status.

So where does that leave everyone else? In most cases it leaves them not doing so well. Of course, there are available many systems and techniques that claim to beat all sorts of games. But virtually all of them are not worth the paper they are printed on. (And a few of these systems are quite expensive to purchase.) With a small number of exceptions, the typical casino visitor has nowhere to turn. In other words, there has long been a need for a good book that would give someone new to gambling the tools to walk in and have a fighting chance. But until now, an all-encompassing text on gambling that is well done and full of accurate information has not existed.

This has changed with the writing of the book in your hands. Anyone new to casino gambling can read it and get good advice on virtually all forms of gambling. This information won't make you a champion, but it will allow you to maximize your enjoyment in the casino environment, and it will show you the potential that certain forms of gambling have. In addition, you'll be told that not all the games are beatable. Reber correctly explains why certain games can be beaten and why other games should be played for the action they provide.

His advice is accurate, concise, and meaningful. But you won't be overwhelmed with mathematics and esoteric concepts that don't seem to make any sense. And, for those of you who wish to learn more, Reber tells you where you can turn and how to proceed.

I've spent a lot of time going over this material, and I know that this advice is what those of us who write in this field would term "solid and reliable." Now it is your turn to read *The New Gambler's Bible*—and then, of course, to try your luck at the "very exciting gaming tables."

MASON MALMUTH

What you are now holding in your hot little hand is not your typical book on gambling. The initial thing to note is that it is the first book in nearly two decades that covers *all* of the basic forms of modern gambling, from casino table games through slots, keno, and lotteries, and on to horse racing, poker, and sports betting. But more important, it is the first book ever that provides a thorough analysis of each game that is both mathematically and strategically correct, outlining which games can be beaten (what we'll call "Type W" games) and how, and which ones cannot (what we'll call "Type L" games) and why. For those games you can win (like blackjack or poker), I'll explain in detail how to do it. For those you can't win (like roulette or shooting craps), I'll tell you how to lose as little as possible.

The book is divided into four parts. The first covers some basic elements of gaming that anyone who would belly up to a game of chance must understand, including an overview of the probabilities of the various outcomes of each game. The second part examines the many Type L games that are found in casinos and elsewhere, including roulette, baccarat, craps, slot machines, keno, and lotteries. The third section reviews the classic Type W games of blackjack, poker, horse racing, and sports betting. The fourth and final part covers other topics of importance, such as cheating, intuition, and how to manage your bankroll. As we march through these topics there will be interesting stories to tell and more than a few intriguing characters to meet. Also, from time to time, I'll comment on some of the more controversial aspects of gambling.

I'd like to take this opportunity to introduce myself, for I am an unlikely character to be writing a book like this. In my real life, I am what journalists like to call a "research scientist"—although they typically don't think of that term as being applied to people who do research in psychology, which happens to be my field. I am currently Professor of Psychology at Brooklyn College and the Graduate Center of the City University of New York. My research concerns the issue of, to use the layperson's term, intuition. That is, how we come to have a vague feeling that we know what a person is thinking or feeling, what the right answer to a problem is, what the correct move in a game is, and so forth—without really knowing what it is we know. At least, that is, without knowing it consciously. In my scientific writings I've labeled the capacity to acquire this kind of knowledge implicit learning, to distinguish it from explicit learning, which is the situation where we come to know (consciously) what it is we know.

Right about now you might be able to see the link with gambling—an awful lot of good gambling is dependent upon making the right choice at the right time, although, when you question the experts who make such choices routinely, they often cannot tell you what it is that they knew that enabled them to make those choices. As the song says, "you've got to know when to hold 'em, know when to fold 'em." But "knowing" can be a matter of a subtle intuitive sense of right and wrong quite independent of any conscious knowledge. Good gamblers have a lot of intuitive or "implicit" knowledge.

By the way, just in case any of you are thinking that this sense of intuition is really something like ESP and that some "sixth sense" is operating here, forget it. Let me disabuse you of this notion right up front. There is absolutely no evidence whatsoever for any special, paranormal powers here (or, for that matter, anywhere). Implicit or intuitive thinking is perfectly ordinary and fairly well understood—we have no need to consider the weird and the nonsensical to understand what goes on when gamblers make decisions. (We will deal with the general issue of intuition and the related topic of hunches, or feelings that something is about to happen, in more detail in chapter 10. There we will discover that at times your intuition is something to be listened to, particularly when playing games like poker or handicapping the horses. We will also discover that a hunch that a slot machine is ready to give up a jackpot or a sense that the dice are going to get hot at craps is *not* to be listened to.)

The research my colleagues and students and I have carried out over the years clearly shows that in order to build up a solid base of intuitive knowledge—the kind that you should listen to, the kind that makes you a winner rather than a loser—you need to have a lot of experience and a lot of practice. That's okay. It just makes being a good gambler like being a good anything else—from a good commodities broker to a good lawyer, a good homemaker, or a good psychologist. If anyone is the slightest bit curious about this research, feel free to pick up a copy of my book *Implicit Learning and Tacit Knowledge,* published by Oxford University Press. While you're at it, you can also pick up a copy of the new edition of my best-selling *Dictionary of Psychology,* published by Penguin/Viking. I can always use the royalties; I never know when I'm going to run into a nice, soft poker game.

But despite my academic orientation, I've always been interested in and intrigued by gambling. I'm not really sure how or why this came about. My best guess is that it comes from my particular affection for my father's two brothers, Irvin and Leonard, who were inveterate and pretty good horse players (especially Len) and who took me along on many an equine voyage during what we call in my field my "formative years." No one else in the family took much notice of this little perversion, and so I enjoyed immensely those little adventures into what seemed to be a forbidden world. In fact, I enjoyed them so much that I gradually found myself drawn toward games of chance in all of their manifestations. Beginning in high school and then later in college, I spent truly embarrassing numbers of hours playing poker, betting on the horses, and hustling marks at the bowling alley. As the years went by I adopted a strategy of narrowing my madness down to a day (or two— or, at worst, three during the summer when there are no classes) a week. So here I am, in my fifties, modestly successful, a full professor, and still hanging around a couple of days a week with assorted groups of Damon Runyon types at racetracks and casinos.

I am a good amateur gambler. By that I mean I haven't quit my day job. I really like teaching and doing research, so gambling remains a sideline. I am a reasonably big bettor, not what I would call a "high roller," although I've been known to put up serious money when the circumstances called for it. There is, however, one lesson I learned early on that must be understood by anyone who would step up to a game of chance: Never bet "scared money"—Never risk anything that you cannot afford to lose. This message about maintaining control over your bankroll, what is called in the trade "bankroll management" (or "money management"), is perhaps the most important lesson I hope my readers will learn. Bankroll management is also a topic about which an enormous amount of extremely bad advice has been offered. In chapter 11 we will examine it in some, what I believe to be sensible, detail. With this message in mind, let's get down to it!

PART I

THE BARE
NECESSITIES

1

LAYING THE FOUNDATION GAMBLING BASICS

Gambling in America has become almost mind-bendingly popular. According to the results of a recent article in *Gaming and Wagering Business*, an astonishing 65 percent of the adult population engaged in some form of legal gambling activity in 1993. As of this writing, only two states in the nation, Hawaii and Utah, do not have some form of legal gambling. The total number of dollars that went into these enterprises was estimated at $400 billion, and the revenues from this activity were in the neighborhood of $35 billion.

But these numbers, staggering as they are, are clearly serious underestimates. People also engage in a wide variety of forms of gambling that are outside the scope of this analysis. For example, since the survey looked only at legal, organized gaming, it did not consider the enormous amount of money that is wagered through illegal bookmakers. Only four states (Nevada, North Dakota, Montana, and Oregon) have legal sports betting, and only Nevada permits wagers on all forms of sporting events. Hence, virtually all the betting on baseball, basketball, football, hockey, boxing, and occasional other events like golf, tennis, and auto racing, that takes place in the rest of the country is carried out through your friendly local bookie. Also not included in the survey were monies wagered in weekly poker games by the kitchen sink, high-stakes gin rummy games played at country clubs and resorts, bingo games in churches and community halls, Las Vegas nights run as fund-raisers by charities and churches, office pools for the World Series and football playoffs, payoffs for the winners of Rotisserie leagues in baseball, and just good old-fashioned wagers on which raindrop will hit the bottom of the window first. Similarly left out are the monies bet on the numbers; wagers on participant sports like golf, bowling, pool, and billiards; and gambling on pinochle, backgammon, chess, bridge, whist, canasta, dominoes, mah-jongg, and other games that are routinely played for money.

Frankly, I'm not sure how to get a grip on the total number of dollars exchanged among individuals and institutions in one or another form of gambling. Most of the executives in the gambling industry I've spoken with and my own casual estimates based on my research suggest that the $400 billion figure is way short of the mark. Danny Montagna, VP at TropWorld in Atlantic City, and I tried to put a best guess on the total and came up with $600 billion, or about 50 percent above the estimate in *Gaming and Wagering Business*. Who's right? Who knows? All I can tell you is that the amount of money North Americans put into gambling is more that the GNP of roughly half the nations on this planet. And, since recent surveys reveal that all estimates on gambling display dramatic year-by-year increases, all these numbers are undoubtedly even larger today. From 1982 to 1995, revenue from legal gambling increased by over 50 percent. Gambling is one of the fastest growing industries in the country.

With this kind of investment of dollars, not to mention time and energy, it seems pretty clear that there is a need for a book that treats all of the most frequently played forms of gaming, including casino games, sports betting, racehorse handicapping, and poker. It's not that there aren't books on these topics. The Gambler's Book Club in Las Vegas has a catalog with more than a thousand titles in it. However, I've read a lot of these books in recent years, and I can tell you that while some of them are superb, some are just awful. Unfortunately, the ones in the latter category vastly outnumber those in the former.

So, part of what I'm trying to do here is provide some balance against the enormous number of worthless books currently on the shelves that claim to tell players how to win games they cannot win, purport to explain how to make money in situations where coming out ahead in the long run is virtually impossible, and put forward betting systems that are mathematically and logically flawed. This last point is important. Many of the existing works on gambling actually contain good information about the underlying structure of particular casino games—and blow it all by encouraging their readers to use betting systems that not only do not work but have the distinct disadvantage of costing them money in the long run. I am beginning to suspect that more nonsense has been written about gambling than about almost anything else—with the possible exception of astrology, which is appropriate, I guess, since so many gamblers keep consulting their astrologers!

At this point it is surely reasonable for the reader to ask: Why should I believe this guy? Why should I assume that he knows what he's talking about and that all those other authors don't? There is, of course, no knockdown answer to questions like these. The world is full of blowhards and fabricators, and you are within your rights to think that I am another. However, I just happen to be right in my assessment of the various games presented here, and, for now, you're just going to have to take that statement at face value. As we go along I hope you will begin to get a sense of the depth of the interpretations that are provided. The analyses of various gambling situations that will be presented in later chapters are based on sound mathematical reasoning and proper strategy and present what I believe to be the proper assessment in each case. But, being a good scientist, I'm open to suggestion and prepared to change my mind when convincing evidence is presented. If you feel that my analysis of any particular game is incorrect or misleading, feel free to contact me directly at the Department of Psychology, Brooklyn College, Brooklyn, NY 11210. I will be more than happy to publish corrections in future editions and give full credit to those who have spotted the error.

What this book does that is novel, but also absolutely critical for the average gambler, is break down the various forms of gaming along the most basic line of cleavage: (1) those games where the house has an incontrovertible edge and where you must, in the long run, lose (for want of a better name, let's call these Type L games), and (2) those games where, with knowledge and skill, you can, in fact, win (let's call these Type W games). In the first category are all those games where the odds are fixed in advance of your play and whoever is running the game holds a probabilistic advantage over the players. When you play these games you play with negative expectation. In the second category are those games where the odds fluctuate with play and/or are set by the participants as the game develops. In games in this latter category, participants with greater knowledge and skill will win more than those with lesser knowledge and skill. When you play these games it is possible (although not easy) to play with positive expectation. The first category includes almost all casino games, most slot machines, keno, and lotteries. The second category includes a single casino game (blackjack), handicapping the horses, sports betting, and poker.

Most of the existing books on gambling treat in any depth games from only one or the other of these categories. Worse, when the authors whose expertise covers only one of the two take a few pages to say something about the other, they almost invariably give hideous advice. For example, in a recent, otherwise reasonable book on casino games, the author, while correctly advising against playing the "any 7" bet at the craps table, tossed off the line that this was such a stupid bet that making it was nearly as bad as playing the horses, where the player stood to lose in excess of 17 percent of monies wagered. Alas, such a remark rings true in one terribly simpleminded sense in that the average takeout from most bets at the racetrack is in the neighborhood of 17 percent, but it fails to recognize the subtlety in handicapping racehorses. By being consistently more accurate in selecting horses that are undervalued by the public and consistently shrewder in your wagering than the average horseplayer, this 17 percent takeout can be overcome. There are people who make a living playing the horses; no one can make a living shooting craps. Wagering on the horses is a wholly different proposition from wagering on the dice. What statisticians call the "expected value" of the gamble at the craps table is always negative, while at the horses (and other forms of wagering such as sports betting, blackjack, and, of course, poker) it can be made positive.

In addition to failing to appreciate these different categories of games, many people who write about gambling and most of those who engage in the various forms of it know surprisingly little about the underlying statistical structure of the games they play and profess to understand. As a result many gamblers consistently place themselves in situations in which they are at a terrible financial disadvantage. Let me give you a simple example of what I am talking about here. I recently read a book written to teach people how to play craps. It said that they should consider making "place" bets rather than "come" bets and "taking the odds" because in the latter case the proper number had to come up twice in order for them to win while in the former it need only come up once. I have also had players at the tables tell me the same thing, but one would hope that a so-called expert would know better. As we shall see in our discussion of craps in chapter 3, this argument is fundamentally flawed and a simple understanding of probability theory makes this apparent. So, another purpose of this book is to educate average players about the underlying structure of the games they play. What the odds are in each. Which ones can be beaten and which ones cannot. How to go about the game of gambling. How to have fun and not get hurt.

Before we get into the nitty-gritty of probability theory and the actual games themselves, let's begin with a few words of basic advice that are useful no matter what games you are playing, no matter where you are playing them.

A FEW SMALL PIECES OF ADVICE

There are a few things that anyone who ventures in the general direction of a game of chance needs to know, a couple of rules of thumb. These little tidbits are straightforward, but despite their obvious value they are typically ignored by the vast majority of players. I begin with them merely to emphasize their importance.

Alcohol

Most casinos in North America will offer you free drinks. My first and simplest piece of advice is this: Never consume alcohol or any other psychoactive substance to the point that it will compromise your decision-making ability while playing Type W games such as poker and blackjack, or while doing the handicapping required for the horses or sports betting. In fact, it is best not to drink at all when playing these games. On the other hand, if you are so inclined, feel free to have a drink or two while playing Type L games like baccarat, roulette, the slots, or other casino games. Stay within reason, of course; you don't want to go on an alcoholic "tilt" in any game, for it can get very expensive. Clouded judgment can be fatal in some games, in others less so.

Fatigue

The same warning holds for fatigue. Never play Type W games that require serious thinking when you are tired. Fatigue can creep up on you, particularly after you have spent several hours at the tables. Learn to spot the feeling before you lose critical thinking facilities and take a walk, a nap, a meal. Like alcohol, tiredness is quite irrelevant when playing most Type L casino games, since you have no control over the odds or mathematical expectation on any given play. The roulette wheel and its bouncing little ball will follow the same principles of probability whether you are fresh as a daisy or dead on your feet.

However, it's not easy to make recommendations about how to conduct yourself when playing Type W games like poker or blackjack. Fatigue is a kind of personal thing. I read a book recently in which the author suggested that you never play a game that requires some measure of concentration for more than two hours straight. I can't make this kind of strict recommendation. Some people can sit at a poker table for days (literally) and not show the slightest change in the quality of their play, others find their attention wandering after an hour or two. I find that my own stamina shifts dramatically. There are days when I can play for hours and never notice it, others when an hour leaves me feeling groggy and confused. Learn to pay attention to your body. Take a break and come back later. There's always a seat open at a table and there's always another hand being dealt. Don't play any time you feel you are not at your best. The games are tough enough without giving up an edge.

Bankroll Management

Managing your money while gambling is about as important a topic as there is in the game. It is also one of the most difficult skills to learn and one about which enormous amounts of nonsense have been written. Virtually every book on gambling has its obligatory chapter on this topic, although the majority of them provide what is, frankly, stupid advice. In chapter 11, I will try to provide what I believe to be good advice. Here, I simply want to draw your attention to one critical rule of thumb. As was noted above, as a recreational gambler you should never, ever wager money that you cannot afford to lose, never bet "scared money." The hallmark of a gambler who has lost control is the risking of more money than he or she can comfortably afford to lose. You should wager at a level that gives you a kind of "kick." That is, you should risk an amount that would not make you happy should you lose but that will not in any way compromise your or your family's needs. In short, bet amounts that you can afford. Nothing interferes with your judgment like that gnawing sense "I really can't afford to lose this bet." As they say, "Bet with your head, not over it."

Probability Theory

Learn something about probabilities. The complex and abstruse field of probability theory and the study of the mathematics of probabilitics began with the analysis of specific situations in gambling. It quickly became apparent to early gamblers that winning or losing particular wagers was intimately connected with the theoretical likelihood of particular events occurring. If an 11 comes up on the dice on average once in every eighteen throws, it would be to your advantage to know this—and it could be very much to your advantage if others did not. If you could persuade them to wager on the occurrence of an 11 on any given throw by offering them odds of 15 to 1 (as most casinos do), you would quite rapidly become a wealthy individual.

In the next chapter and throughout the book I will present some very simple and basic probabilistic analyses of various games. This information will be of value to anyone who engages in any form of gambling in even the most casual fashion. However, for anyone who gets seriously into various forms of gaming, a deeper knowledge of probability theory is absolutely essential. It may come as a surprise to the uninitiated gambler, but the good players have a rich and subtle knowledge of the probabilities associated with the various outcomes in whatever games they are playing. If you could overhear expert poker players or expert racehorse handicappers discussing the relative strengths and weaknesses of various plays you would likely be quite surprised. The pros know their stuff. Anything less and you are just another sucker. Where appropriate, I will provide guidelines for additional reading for those of you who are serious about playing these games correctly and wish to go beyond the advice given here.

Winning and/or Losing

Since it's all about winning and losing, let's be quite clear about what those terms mean. "Winner" and "loser" can be terribly subjective. Sure, if you take more money out of a casino than you brought in you leave a "winner." But there is more to the game than just cash. If you play in a small-stakes poker game for three hours, have a wonderful time, meet some new and interesting people, and lose $10, are you a loser or a winner? I rather think you are a winner. If you play blackjack for six hours and lose $50 but the casino comps you (see chapter 3 for a discussion of comping) to a dinner that would have set you back $25, are you a loser? I think not. If you spend a glorious summer day at a place like Belmont racetrack, stroll around the grounds, marvel at the beauty of the thoroughbred racehorse, have lunch with good friends in the restaurant, and leave behind $40, are you a loser? This happens to me all the time and I never feel like I lost on days like this. But if you play the slots for three hours, drop $150, and get comped to a cholesterol-laden cheeseburger, fries, and a Coke, you are, I suspect, a loser. If you spend three hours standing at a craps table while watching your once-substantial bankroll dwindle as you repeatedly hope for the "hard 8" or the "horn bet" to come in, you are, alas, a loser. As we progress we will get a better sense of what is involved in gaming and what winning and losing are all about. There is as much psychology here as economics.

But, as Richard Nixon used to say, "Let me be perfectly clear about that." What I have to tell you here will not magically make you a winner. As we shall discuss in some detail, actually winning in the long run at any Type L game cannot be done, and actually winning at a Type W game is a difficult (although not impossible) proposition. My purpose here is to key the reader in on when it is possible to win and when it is not. And, once again, by "win" here I mean win in that delicate sense that combines psychology and cash. I do not mean win in any particular session or even over a couple of sessions of play. I mean win in the long run, win over an extended period of play involving many long sessions, win over the years, indeed, win over a lifetime. It is possible to win in this rather permanent sense, although in order to do so you must restrict your play to particular classes of games and often to particular plays within those games. There are people who do, in fact, make their living at gaming. We will discuss them, the games they play, and how they do it. Be forewarned, these people are professionals like any other, and plying their trade requires the same commitment of time and energy as being, say, a stockbroker or a lawyer—even a college professor. However, while it is not easy to become a winner, it is surprisingly simple to keep from becoming a loser.

Defining "Gambling"

It's interesting to try to understand the meaning of the very term "gambling" and how it tends to be used. Most dictionaries define it in a way that reflects the notion that some risk is taken for the possibility of ultimate gain. This notion, of course, is intriguingly general. In fact, it captures the essence of our capitalist way of life here in America. From this perspective starting a business is a gamble, investing in the stock market is a gamble, buying a house is a gamble—good gracious, getting married is a gamble! Perhaps the ubiquity of these kinds of situations and our close connection with them lies at the heart of the popularity of organized gambling. After all, in some sense what casinos, racetracks, poker rooms, bingo halls, and lotteries do is merely provide a well-structured and semiartificial format within which we can carry out life's little dramas. Surely this is one of the attractions of organized gaming. We enter into life's true gambles with precious little understanding of the ultimate odds, but at a craps table or a roulette wheel the complexity is reduced to a manageable level. The typical gambler may not really understand the probabilistic nuances of the wheel or the dice, but such things certainly seem a good bit more tractable than, say, trying to raise children in this lunatic society of ours.

In any event, this notion that gambling involves the principle of taking an initial risk for the possibility of eventual gain does seem to capture the essence of the enterprise. However, the critical word here is *possibility,* for it ties in directly with our distinction between Type L and Type W games and, interestingly, allows us to provide yet another way of distinguishing between them. Gamblers play Type L games; gamblers and professionals play Type W games. There are no professionals playing Type L games for anything but the fun of it. Games like roulette, craps, baccarat, the typical slot machine, keno, lotteries, and the like are "gambling" games. They are games where, when you sit down to play, you take a certain risk with, of course, the possibility of gain. The house has a statistical advantage and, in the long run, expects to show a profit, but the notion of risk for *possible* gain is there and real.

Those who play Type W games as professionals, those who play them for a living, do not really regard themselves as gamblers. Professional poker players, for example, do not see themselves as gamblers in the sense given above. The risk for the professional is a momentary thing. As time goes by, *they are highly confident that they are going to win.* They are not "risking" money in anything like the sense that someone who sits down at a roulette wheel is "risking" money. A better way to view it is that they are "investing" money. Around the racetrack, for example, it is not uncommon to hear expert handicappers talk not about what they "bet" on a race but about what they "invested" in it.

Does it make sense to view what the layperson regards as gambling in this, perhaps pompous manner? Well, in one sense it does. The professional gambler plays with the long-range expectation of substantial profits, just as someone like a newly minted medical school graduate does. The young physician expects to lay out considerable capital to get an education and then to set up or buy into a practice, but his or her long-range gain is pretty clear (although not guaranteed) and the "risk" is a sensible investment. It is similar for the professional gambler—but with a twist. While the professional poker player or sports bettor approaches the game with positive expectation, these games have *much greater* volatility than something like the practice of medicine. Put another way, the short-term luck factor in the life of a physician is relatively small compared with what it is in the life of a professional poker player. Most doctors are making serious money most of the time. The professional gambler's life has been likened to a roller coaster with dramatic highs and plummeting lows.

But as Mason Malmuth points out, it is this very element of volatility that makes gambling so attractive to so many. While the untrained person could never walk into an operating room and perform surgical procedures, anyone can walk into a casino and win substantial numbers of dollars. Of course, if you do not possess the necessary skills and continue to play the game you will eventually give it all back, but that shot at serious money makes the game utterly seductive.

Nevertheless, for the few folks who manage to survive the volatility of the enterprise and play games like blackjack and poker as professionals, the psychology of the game is very different than it is for the rest of us. Professional poker players sit down to play knowing that they are much more likely to take some of yours than lose some of theirs. They may lose on any given day, in any given game, just as the casino may lose to a particular craps or baccarat player. But the professionals know, just like the house, that in the long run they are going to come out ahead. They are not, in the standard sense of the term, gambling, any more than our medical school graduate is gambling. The point is that there are various games that can be played for profit. It is not easy to do this, but then again it is not easy to graduate from medical school. In the following chapters we will develop this theme in more detail, outlining games that are "true" gambles and games that are gambles only insofar as the knowledge and understanding the individual brings to them are greater or less than what is brought by the other participants. Poker is a gamble for some; it is a source of income for others.

Rational Behavior

Can we really be rational? In fact, does it make sense to speculate, as many have done, that we are the only species that can be? Well, sometimes we seem to be pretty good at it and at other times we're pretty dismal. The gambling arena is one place that will surely test your sense of your own rationality. One thing to keep in mind when gambling is that your sense of rationality, latent though it may be, is going to be your best friend. The games we will discuss are based either on incontrovertible odds that do not favor you (unless you happen to own a casino) or on skill, where the edge goes to, well, the skilled. If you understand this and don't try to fight it you'll be okay. Rationality in a gaming forum really entails little more than knowing and understanding the circumstances you are operating under and making the best and well-reasoned choice of those options available to you. Easy to say, not so easy to do.

Let me tell you about a study done with reasonably intelligent (and, it is hoped, rational) college students a couple of years back by two psychologists named Miller and Gunasegaram. The students were presented with the following: A benefactor approaches three young men and promises to give them $100 each provided that they each toss a coin and all three get heads. If anyone gets a tail no one will be paid. The first two flip their coins and both get heads; the third young man flips and gets a tail. The benefactor, seeing the dismay in all their faces, offers them one more chance. Alas, the same outcome occurs: the first two get heads, the third a tail. The interesting question is: How did the students subsequently react to this third person? Answer—they shunned him. They regarded him as unlucky. They said things like they wouldn't want to go on a junket to Las Vegas with him, since not only was he unlucky himself but clearly he cost other people money! When pressed, respondents acknowledged that these feelings were irrational, that such an outcome could easily happen by chance alone, but (and here's the interesting part) *they held them anyway*. Moreover, they argued that they thought that most people would react the same way. Would they? Well, the results of the study certainly suggest that they would.

Does this mean that we are hopelessly irrational? Yes and no. I suspect that we have a strong tendency toward the irrational, but it can be overcome. It simply takes some reflection about the situation we are in, some knowledge of probabilities, and understanding who we are and what we are about. In short, it takes following each of the little pieces of advice just outlined and adhering to the recommendations made throughout this book. It is not easy to approach a craps table or sit down at a poker game and feel totally rational. It is even harder to roll those dice and play those cards for several hours with all of the ups and downs and bumps and grinds of the game and maintain a sense of rationality. But give it a shot. When you're feeling confused or you're at a loss as to what to do, try turning your mind to the rational and the sensible. It won't always work, but it is good advice.

That's an introduction to the basic issues underlying gambling. What we need to do now is get a feeling for some of the raw mathematical principles that support the whole gambling operation. Chapter 2 will introduce us to these issues.

2

A QUICK AND DIRTY INTRODUCTION TO PROBABILITIES

*M*ost people hate complicated formulas and detailed mathematics—at least, most of the students I've taught over the years do. However, all of gambling just happens to be based on mathematical and statistical considerations. The casinos know all about probabilities, and so do the professional gamblers. Casinos cleverly offer us games like roulette and craps, which have been carefully set up so they have the probabilistic edge. The pros look for games like blackjack and poker, where they have the edge. So, stick with me here, folks. In this chapter I'll give you the basics of probability theory—just enough to level off the playing field but not so much that you will feel intimidated. If you want to play these games with what we call positive expectation, you are going to have to know this stuff.

Gambling and probability theory are inextricably linked—the latter *began* because of the former. The Chevalier de Méré was a seventeenth-century aristocrat with a fondness for games of chance. De Méré, in his search for games in which he felt he had an advantage, had developed a standard wager in which he would offer even odds that he could throw at least one 6 in a series of four throws of a single die. The wager proved rather lucrative, but (no surprise) after a time it became increasingly difficult to find people who would take it. In order to entice new players, he adjusted the gamble, offering even odds that using two dice he could throw at least one 12 (two 6's) in a series of twenty-four throws. In his mind these two wagers were equivalent. He reasoned as follows: "In the first case, since there are exactly six things that can occur when one die is thrown and one of them will win for me, if I multiply this times the number of throws I should win because $1/6 \times 4 = 4/6 = 2/3$. Now, in the second case, if there are exactly thirty-six things that can occur when two dice are thrown and one of them will win for me, if I multiply this times the number of throws I should also win, and at the same rate, because $1/36 \times 24 = 24/36 = 2/3$."

Alas, it turns out that the chevalier was terribly wrong—in both cases. However, what makes his story interesting and relevant for us is that, by a fluke, in the first case he had set up a game in which he actually had a small but real probabilistic advantage—and as a result won more than he lost. It turned out not to be anywhere near the advantage he thought he had, but it was, nevertheless, real. In the second case he had set up a gamble in which he had, as the saying goes, the short end of the stick. He wasn't giving up a terrible statistical edge, but it was enough to cost him money over time.

Confused and beginning to hurt in the pocket, the chevalier turned to the great French mathematician, logician, and philosopher Blaise Pascal for help. Pascal examined the games that the chevalier had set up and quickly realized that he had been using the wrong formulas for calculating the probabilities of the various outcomes. Actually, the formulas were more than just wrong, they were totally nonsensical. To see how irrational they were, extend the reasoning the chevalier used to establish his first game. He was multiplying the likelihood of the outcome he was interested in (throwing a 6) by the number of times that he would actually throw the die; multiplying one-in-six (1/6) by 4. Now suppose the gamble involved rolling the die ten times. Following his formula, he would now multiply 1/6 by 10. However, $1/6 \times 10 = 10/6 = 1.67$, which is nonsensical. Probabilities are always between 0 and 1.0. If something cannot possibly happen, its probability of occurrence is 0; if something is certain to happen, its probability of occurrence is 1.0.

Pascal pointed out that the proper way to determine the number of winning outcomes is to calculate the number of *losing* outcomes and subtract that number from the total number of possible outcomes. Pascal was operating from the most basic of premises. As we shall see, this basic principle will go a long way to help us analyze a variety of games in which the calculation of probabilities can get rather complex.

Let's look at the chevalier's first game using Pascal's technique. The winning number is a 6, hence there are five losing numbers. Thus, the likelihood of failing to win the wager on the first roll is 5/6. Similarly, the likelihood of losing on each of the next three rolls is also 5/6. The only way the chevalier could lose his gamble was to fail to throw a 6 on any of these four rolls. Since each roll of the die is an independent event (more on this term below), the probability of throwing the die four times in a row without getting a 6 is $5/6 \times 5/6 \times 5/6 \times 5/6 = .482$—by the way, this is usually written as $(5/6)^4 = .482$, which is a lot less cumbersome. Put simply, the chevalier would, in the long run, lose his wager roughly 48 percent of the time—which means he would win it about 52 percent of the time. A pretty good edge for the chevalier; it is no surprise that he won handsomely on the wager.

But what was happening with the second game? Well, here he was betting on an outcome that could be expected to occur only once in every thirty-six throws of two dice, hence his chances of failing to throw a winning combination on the first throw was 35/36. Since he was making a total of twenty-four throws, the only way he could lose his wager was if he threw one of these losing tosses on every single throw. Following the logic from the first case, we know the probability of this to be $(35/36)^{24}$. You don't really want to work this one out, since it requires multiplying 35/36 times itself twenty-four times, so you are going to have to trust me that it turns out to be .509, a proposition of a very different kind. In this case our aristocratic friend was offering his compatriots a wager that he must, in the long run, lose. No wonder that after a time he turned with a lighter purse to his mathematician friend.

Is there a moral to this story? I sure hope so. Know the probabilities of the outcomes in a wager before you put your money on the line. As we shall see, most gamblers are, to their financial peril, painfully ignorant of the probabilities of winning and losing most of the wagers that are available to them. The typical casino gambler is prone to risking his or her hard-earned cash on wagers with much poorer mathematical prognoses than the one de Méré got himself into. His second wager put him at what may appear to have been a small disadvantage, but in fact, it was nearly 2 percent. Consider what would have happened to the chevalier if he'd made the bet one hundred times at $1 per try. Since the probability of winning is .491, he would have an expected win of $49.10 and an expected loss of $50.90. Hence, the expected value of the gamble is $50.90 − $49.10 = −$1.80 for each $100, or −1.8 percent of the money wagered. This may appear to be a small loss to the untutored gambler, but it is not. It is larger than the house edge in baccarat, for example. It is no surprise that, in time, he clearly felt the losses. Always know the odds before you open your wallet. So, on to a more careful discussion of probabilities and how they play out in gaming situations.

Probabilities

Let's begin the more formal part of this chapter with a short discussion about the concept of probability itself. Put simply, the probability that any particular event will occur is the likelihood of that event (let's call it x) relative to all possible events that could possibly occur (let's call this y). Put another way, a probability is expressible as a ratio, a fraction expressed as x/y where y will always be a number as large as or larger than x. Moreover, since you can always divide a fraction out, any probability can also be stated as a number between 0 and 1.0. Lest this sound a bit too hairy for the average reader, do not despair. A simple example will clarify matters.

Assume we have a fair coin (one with no bias) with a "head" and a "tail." We can easily calculate the probability that a head will come up on any given flip. First, determine how many ways the event we are interested in (getting the head) can occur. Answer: 1. There is only one way to get a head with a fair coin. Now determine the total number of possible events. Answer: 2. There are two possible outcomes here, a head and a tail. Take the ratio: 1/2. Convert the ratio to a probability by carrying out the division: $1/2 = .5$. Voilà! We have formally calculated the probability of getting a head on the flip of a fair coin (and found the answer to be exactly what everyone knew it was, which is comforting).

Notice that when dealing with probabilities we can use fractions or decimals. It doesn't matter, since one is merely a version of the other. In this book I'll go back and forth, depending on which one is easiest to calculate or understand. It is also okay to express probabilities by the proportions they represent. In fact, this is the way most people think of them. For example, if you ask average people on the street the chances of getting a head when flipping a coin, they will tell you "Fifty-fifty."

Another couple of examples: Assume we have a normal deck of fifty-two cards out of which we will select a single card at random. What is the probability that this card is a spade? Well, there are thirteen cards that are spades and a total of fifty-two cards that could be drawn, so the likelihood of drawing a spade is given by the ratio $13/52 = 1/4 = .25$. Now, what is the probability of drawing any ace? Engaging the same operations leads us to the conclusion that it must be $4/52 = 1/13 = .077$. See how easy this is? One last example: What's the probability of drawing the ace of spades? Answer: $1/52 = .019$. Before we leave this set of examples I'd like to draw your attention to the fact that the answer to the last question could also have been calculated by multiplying the probability of drawing an ace by the probability of drawing a spade: $.25 \times .077 = .019$. If you want, try working all this out for yourself to get a sense of how to calculate probabilities.

That's enough formal stuff on probabilities. Let's now turn to the way in which probabilistic analyses enter into gambling situations, let's look at the concept of "odds." In gambling, probabilistic situations are always given in terms of the odds of a particular wager. As we do this we will, of course, continue to learn about probability theory.

Odds

The term "odds" refers to the likelihood that particular events will or will not occur under particular circumstances relative to the payoff you will receive should those particular events, in fact, occur. That is, odds links the probabilities of events to the payoffs for wagering on those events. In our discussion of odds it is going to be important to distinguish between the true or fair odds and the payoff odds. True odds reflect the actual, real-world odds against some event's occurring; payoff odds reflect the rate at which you will be paid if this event occurs. Casinos and other organizations that control gambling make their money by setting the payoff odds below the true odds. All this technical lingo is easy to understand with an example.

Suppose you and a friend are tossing a fair coin and you are wagering $1 on each flip that the coin will come up heads. Since there are but two outcomes here, and each is equally likely, the odds that heads will occur is expressed as "1–1," "1 to 1" (or "even odds"). This is what is known as a fair wager—the payoff corresponds to the actual probabilities. That is, when you win you will receive $2 (you are up $1), and when you lose you will receive $0 (you have lost $1). Since you should win half the time, the expected value of the gamble is 0. Notice that the odds on this gamble are determined by the probabilities that the events will occur. The odds are "even" because each event has the same probability.

However, in actual play a gambler has to be sensitive to the distinction in phrasing between a bet that will pay "*x to* 1" and one that will pay "*x for* 1." The replacement of one one-syllable word for another here can cost you serious money if you don't pay attention. Let's look at the difference to the player when a wager is listed as paying out "15 *to* 1" compared with when it is listed as paying out "15 *for* 1." If you win a $1 bet at "15 to 1" you will get back $16—the $15 win plus your original wager. If you win one at "15 for 1" you will get back only $15. In some casinos, the payoff at craps on wagers like the single-roll bet on 11 will be paid at "15 *for* 1," at others "15 *to* 1." Now, a mere $1 may not seem like a lot given the size of the payoff, but it turns out that playing at a table with the former payoff will, in the long haul, cost the average player slightly more than an additional 5 percent. When we get into analyzing individual games it will turn out that figures like 5 percent of money wagered are very large figures indeed.

Some more examples. Suppose you are tossing a fair die and wagering $1 that it will come up 4 on each toss. The die has six sides, so the chances of a 4 are one in six (phrased another way, the probability of a 4 on any single roll is $1/6 = .167$). The odds payoff for a fair wager in this situation would be given as "5 to 1" or "6 for 1." That is, since 4's come up on average only once every six throws, you would win once and lose five times in the average run of six throws. On your five losses you would be out $5, but on your one win you would take $6 out of the game (the $5 win plus your $1 wager). Hence, at the end of the typical series of six tosses of the die you will have $6 in your pocket. An even game.

Now let's make the situation a bit more complicated. Suppose you want to work out the probability that 4's will come up on two dice when you throw them and determine the proper odds for such a wager. There are two ways to calculate the probability here. One, the simplest way, is to recognize that each roll of a die is an *independent* event. This notion of independent events is important. It means that what happens in one case has nothing whatsoever to do with what will happen in the other—a 4 on one die has no effect at all on whether or not a 4 will appear on the other die. Probability theory tells us that whenever you have two independent events, the probability of an outcome involving *both of them* is the probability of the first multiplied by the probability of the second. Since the likelihood that a 4 will come up on the first die is 1 out of 6, or $1/6$, and the probability of a 4 on the second is similarly $1/6$, the likelihood of getting 4's on both dice is $1/6 \times 1/6 = 1/36$. The other way to calculate the probability of this kind of outcome is to examine all possible outcomes and determine what proportion of them fit the conditions that have been specified (that is, do the kind of analysis that Pascal did for his friend the chevalier some three hundred and fifty years ago). We know that there are 36 total outcomes (6 possible outcomes for the first die and 6 for the second, and $6 \times 6 = 36$), and since there is only one way to make two 4's, the likelihood of this occurring must be 1 out of the full set, or $1/36$. Hence, fair odds for such a wager would be "35 to 1" or "36 for 1."

One more. What's the probability of getting a hand of twenty made up of two ten-valued cards at blackjack when dealing out exactly two cards? This case is like the previous one—but with a twist, an important twist. As before, we have two events, getting a ten-valued card on the first card and getting another on the second. But these are *not independent events*, so we cannot carry out the kind of simple multiplication we used in the case of the two dice. Here we have to determine the impact the occurrence of the first event has on the likelihood of the second. Let's look at the situation closely. The probability of getting a ten on the first card is straightforward and easily calculated. There are sixteen ten-valued cards in a deck of fifty-two cards (four each of tens, jacks, queens, and kings). Hence the probability of being dealt the first ten-valued card is $16/52 = .308$. But the likelihood of getting the second ten-valued card is affected by the fact that one appeared as the first card. There are only fifteen ten-valued cards left and there are only fifty-one cards left to draw from. The probability of getting a ten on the second card is $15/51 = .294$. Now that we have calculated the probability of each of the events in our example, we can carry out the multiplication operation. Hence, the probability of a hand of two ten-valued cards in blackjack when dealing exactly two cards is $.308 \times .294 = .0905$, or roughly 9 percent of the time.

Could we calculate this outcome using the other technique of figuring out how many possibilities there are and how many satisfy our conditions? Sure. It goes like this. There are fifty-two cards in the deck. Since order doesn't matter (a jack plus a 10 gives twenty no matter which one was dealt first) we divide by 2; the formula is $(52 \times 51)/2 = 1,326$ possible hands. Of this total, 120 of them $[(16 \times 15)/2 = 120]$ satisfy our conditions. Hence, of the 1,326 possible hands, 120 will total twenty. Dividing 120 by 1,356 gives us .0905—the same answer, roughly 9 percent of the time. The professor in me insists that before we leave this topic I give a problem to be solved by the student, er . . . reader. So here it is. Note that there are other ways to get a hand of twenty in blackjack with two cards—specifically, an ace and a 9. Your homework assignment is to calculate the probability of getting *any* hand of twenty in blackjack drawing *exactly* two cards. The answer is given on page 39 at the end of the chapter.

This distinction between independent and nonindependent events is very important. Many gamblers fail to appreciate both the fact that some events are independent of each other (like the rolls of dice) and the fact that the likelihood that independent events will actually take place has no relationship to whether or not they have occurred before. We'll discuss this issue in more detail later but for now take it on face value that the likelihood that someone will throw a 7 in craps is exactly the same for a first-time shooter as it is for one who's just thrown three, four, five, or twenty straight 7's. Each of these events is independent of the others, and the probabilities of occurrence do not change. If you do not understand this (or do not believe it) you are never going to be able to play games of chance with any measure of success.

These cases were pretty straightforward. Now let's look at examples where the situation is not so simple. You are playing five-card stud poker against three other players and need a king to fill a straight on the last card. You can see thirteen cards, the three upcards for each of the four players and your hole card. One of your opponents shows a king. That leaves three kings somewhere among the remaining thirty-nine cards. Hence, your chances of filling your straight are 3 in 39 or .077—and you should play accordingly. That is, you should make and call bets only when you expect to win at least thirteen times your bet in the event that you make your straight. If there isn't enough money in the pot to provide you with such a gain (what are called "pot odds"), and there's no hope of getting it from your opponents on the last round of betting (what David Sklansky has called "implied odds"), then it would not be a good bet. You may draw your straight (and, of course, you can be pretty sure that in the long run you will about 7 percent or 8 percent of the time), but if you continue to make such plays at less than proper odds (about which we will have more to say in the chapter on poker), you will slowly but inexorably go broke.

Notice that this poker example is fundamentally different from the examples using coins and dice. While we were able to specify what the odds of a particular outcome were, we were not able to specify what the payoff would be should that particular outcome occur. That is, we were not able to calculate the specific odds. In poker the expected value of a wager is determined not simply by pure probabilities but by these probabilities adjusted by the amount of money in the pot and how you expect your opponents to play if you happen to catch your card. This feature is one of the reasons for the fundamental difference between Type L and Type W games. Tossing dice is a Type L game, poker is a Type W game.

Moreover, you can catch your straight and still lose! Someone else at the table may have a higher hand and beat you. The point is that there are occasions where simply knowing the probability of a particular outcome does not guarantee a win. In craps it's pretty clear: Bet on a "hard 8" (both dice coming up 4—a bet that, by the way, you should never make), and if it shows up you will win; you can even calculate the expected value of the gamble. In games like poker all this is not so clear.

You can calculate the probability of drawing a straight in a given situation, but you are not necessarily guaranteed winning with that hand.

Beating the Odds

One of the more common phrases used in the titles of books and articles on gambling is "beat the odds." The frequent use of the term indicates that authors are aware of the need to take probabilities into account. Indeed, there must be at least a dozen books that use this phrase in their titles, and recently *Esquire* magazine featured an article titled "Gambling: How to Beat the Odds." These titles may help sell books and magazines, but they are, at the very least, false advertising, misrepresenting the situation. The point is simple: *You cannot beat the odds!* Sorry, folks, you just can't. In fact, *by definition*, you can't beat the odds—since the odds merely specify what the payoffs will be relative to the probabilities of the several outcomes, and in virtually every game of chance the house sets the payoff odds below the true odds. The phrase "beat the odds" is an oxymoron. In the long run, whoever holds the probabilistic upper hand is going to win. Whenever you play any Type L game for any extended period of time you are going to lose, and your loss will approximate the difference between the true odds on that wager and the odds that the casino is offering.

Percent of Money Wagered

Casinos like to calculate their profits in terms of monies wagered. They think of profit as the percent of the drop (money in the drop box at each table in the form of cash, counter checks, or markers) they keep after they've paid winning players. Since these profits come from their probabilistic edge, the more that is wagered, the more they will profit. As a result, casinos have developed a variety of techniques to attract the so-called high roller—as well as to increase the number of dollars wagered by the typical player. To get a feel for this, try stopping by at an Atlantic City casino on the July Fourth weekend or visit one of the big casinos on the Las Vegas Strip on the Saturday before the Super Bowl. If you are looking for a friendly $2 or $5 blackjack game, forget it. In a stroll around three different casinos in Atlantic City this past summer on our nation's birthday, I was hard-pressed to find a blackjack table with a minimum under $25. And I rarely saw an open seat.

In any event, when it comes to getting a feeling for what the laws of probability are going to do to you in any given session of gambling, it is important to get some feel for how much money you will be wagering. For example, if you're playing roulette, on average you are going home with 5.26 percent less—*not of what you came with but of what you wagered!* It may come as a surprise to many players just how much money they actually wager in a typical session at the tables. It may come as even more of a surprise just how devastating the house advantage can be when it is looked at in terms of percent of monies wagered. However, in the spirit of total honesty that underlies this book, let's take some examples and explore the painful truth. Let's begin, not with a casino game, but with one of today's all-time favorites, a state-run lottery. In New York, the standard lottery is based on a game in which the player picks six numbers out of fifty-four. If the player hits all six he or she hits the jackpot. If the player hits it alone he wins it all; if others have the same numbers on their tickets, they split the prize. No matter, the odds are the same in all cases, and the payout, in terms of percentage of monies wagered, is the same. In New York, 50 percent of monies wagered is returned to the winners. That's it, that's all. From the point of view of the player there are not many games with a worse outcome. We will discuss lotteries and their allure in more detail in chapter 4.

I got a laugh from the recent series of ads that were run in New York promoting the state lottery. In one, people on a busy street are jockeying with each other for an open traffic lane. One guy yells out "Hey, lady, get that Jaguar out of my way, I'm coming through in my Ferrari." A woman sticks her head out the window of her Rolls and complains about someone in a Mercedes who is trying to steal a parking place from her. A voice-over intones something like: "We won't be happy till everyone's a millionaire." Well, they might eventually make everyone a winner of a one-million-dollar prize, but, on average, each winner would have to have wagered two million dollars.

That was pretty clear—and pretty painful. Let's now go into the casino and look at a seemingly benign situation. Suppose you are playing blackjack at $5 a hand—which is about the smallest game you can find these days in Atlantic City, although there are still a few $1 and $2 tables in Nevada and elsewhere. When you sit down, there are three other players at the table and the cards are being dealt from an eight-deck shoe.

Experience has shown that in these situations you will play about fifty to sixty hands an hour. Moreover, if you are playing the game correctly (see chapter 5), you will be either doubling down or splitting your cards on roughly 15 percent of these hands. Hence, in the typical hour you will make roughly sixty-three wagers of $5 each, a total of $315. If you play for a total of ten hours on a two-day sojourn to the casino, you will be wagering a total of roughly $3,150! Quite a bit for a low-stakes player. Most $5 blackjack players have no idea how much money they have actually put on the line.

If you are a good blackjack player who plays what is known as "basic strategy," the expected value of your wagering (your theoretical expectation based on money bet) is likely to be in the neighborhood of −.3 or −.4 percent of monies wagered, or roughly $11. That doesn't sound so bad; $11 is not an unreasonable amount of money to expect to spend for two days of bloody good fun. But note that this is the minimum number of dollars that will be wagered by a "low roller" in a "mere" ten hours of play. Many players play for much larger stakes, play more than one hand at a time, look for tables where there are few or no other players, and sit for hours on end. For them, the total amount of money wagered can quickly creep up to astonishing levels.

Another example. You are playing craps at a $10 minimum table and, since you have read the material in chapter 3, your approach to the game is clear. You are betting the pass line and taking maximum odds on the point, and because you like a little action, you also are making two additional come bets and taking maximum odds on both. Craps is, to put it mildly, a very fast game. A roll of the dice takes place approximately once every thirty seconds or so. If you are betting as described, you'll be making an additional wager roughly every two minutes. If you are playing in a casino that allows double odds, each of these wagers is for a total of $30 and you will have as much as $90 on the table at any given moment. You are wagering something in the neighborhood of *$1,000 per hour*. Spend ten hours at the craps tables and you will likely have wagered in excess of $10,000. By the way, as we will outline later in the chapter on craps, the player who is making these wagers is not playing a bad game at all and is at roughly a −.6 percent disadvantage. However, such a player can be expected to lose $60 in ten hours of play—which is still well within reason for a couple of days of pumped adrenaline. Many craps players, however, are at a much worse disadvantage; depending on the kinds of bets made, the disadvantage may be more like −5 percent to −7 percent or even higher. With an expected loss of −6 percent of monies wagered, the anticipated loss for $10,000 wagered is $600. Now it's starting to get expensive.

This example is particularly important to understand. Just because you are playing a game that has a minimal negative expected value does not mean that you cannot lose virtually your entire bankroll on an average day. The following are the PCs for 1994 for the four basic table games from a popular casino in Atlantic City (PC is the casino's shorthand for the percentage of money wagered at a particular table or game that stays at the table).

Table Game	Annual PC
Roulette	25%
Baccarat	18%
Craps	15%
Blackjack	14%

What this means is that the roulette wheels kept, on average, 25 percent of the money that was brought by the players to those tables. The other table games ranged from 14 to 18 percent. Yet, and here's the important part, the worst of these games (roulette) has an expected value for the player of only −5.26 percent of monies wagered. But clearly this percentage can be devastating. What happens is known as "churning." That is, you, the small bettor, come to the table with a mere $100. But over the course of an hour or so of play you will bet a total of $500, since you will "recycle" the chips that come your way on winning wagers. If you end up wagering a total of $500 on a game with a 5.26 percent advantage over you, your expected loss, in the long run, is $26, or 26 percent of the money you brought to the table with you. And that, sports fans, is how the casino can hold a quarter of the money brought in with a "mere" 5.26 percent edge.

Understand also that the way in which these small negative percentages become serious cash losses operates the other way. If you play a game in which you have a small *positive* percentage you can win serious money in the long run. Expert blackjack players may enjoy only a small positive edge (perhaps 1 percent or a tad above for the very best of them), but this tiny statistical advantage can be turned into significant profits when making large wagers over extended periods of play.

These kinds of calculations give the term "percent of monies wagered" new meaning to most gamblers—who typically have precious little appreciation of the magnitude of their betting. I have discovered that when I tell some of my friends who like to shoot craps for serious money how much they will actually have wagered over a two- or three-day period of rolling the cubes, they look at me like I'm nuts. But it does mount up—and rather quickly. In the chapters to follow we will analyze casino games in terms of this notion of percent of monies wagered. It is the only logical way to approach these games of chance—that is, the Type L games.

Expected Value

Here we have yet another phrase that gets tossed around in discussions of the probabilistic nature of games; indeed, I've been using it freely in the above discussions. Its meaning is pretty straightforward. It refers to what a player can anticipate winning or losing on an extended series of wagers, or, in simple terms, what the player expects to happen to his or her money. From a mathematical point of view the expected value (EV) of a gamble is given by an analysis of the probabilities of the several outcomes contained in that gamble. That is, the expected value of a particular wager is given, as was noted above, as a percent of monies wagered. Wager $100 in a game where the house has a 5 percent edge and the EV of the wager is –$5; wager $1,000 in the same game and it is –$50.

However, the expected value of a gamble can be calculated only when there are specifiable probabilities associated with that game. While it is possible to calculate the EV of every play in games such as craps, roulette, and baccarat, it is not possible to carry out such calculations in other games such as poker, blackjack, or sports betting, where the odds either shift with the play of the game or are determined by the pattern of betting that takes place. The notion of expected value is still important in these games; it just must be approached from a different, somewhat more empirical perspective. For example, a poker player or racehorse handicapper can derive a sense of what his or her expected gain or loss is for an individual session by analyzing the gains and losses from previous sessions. The player can calculate his or her average (or mean) win or loss and then use one of the most basic of all statistical principles: The mean of a set of scores is the best predictor of future scores. A player's average win or loss provides the best estimate of future wins and/or losse.s. The serious player of Type W games needs to keep honest records of play. It is from such records that a player can get a true sense of how the games are going, whether particular patterns of play are success-ful, and what the impact of specific strategies of betting has been on the old bottom line. In chapter 11, where we will take a look at the issue of bankroll or money management, we'll explore this factor in more detail.

Variability

While the EV of a gamble basically tells us what the player's average bottom line will be when playing that particular game, from a proba-bilistic point of view we also need to know something about variability of play. The point is deadly obvious. If your average win/loss at poker turns out to be +$100 per four-hour session of play, it surely does not mean that you win exactly $100 each and every time you play for four hours. Sometimes you will win a great deal more and sometimes you will lose a substantial amount. In order to get a proper understanding of the statistical nature of your play you must be able to estimate variability. Statisticians have a straightforward way of measuring this. It is known, appropriately, as the standard deviation (or SD). The SD provides a measure of how much the observed scores in a distribution of scores vary from the mean or, in our case, how much a player's session-to-session wins and losses vary from his or her average outcome.

I've been teaching long enough to know that most students hate for-mulas. I've also been teaching long enough to know that in order to understand basic statistical and probabilistic principles they have to learn the damnable things. So, here are the formulas for calculating the mean and standard deviation, respectively:

$$M = \frac{\Sigma X}{N}$$

$$SD = \sqrt{\frac{\Sigma(M\text{-}X)^2}{N}}$$

Where X stands for each score (an individual session outcome); Σ is the summation sign meaning "add up all the cases that follow" (ΣX means "add up all of the individual scores or individual session outcomes"); N is the number of scores (sessions of play); $\hbar$ is the sign for the square root; M is the mean; and SD is the standard deviation. You can immediately see the parallel between these two statistics. The mean is simply the sum of all the scores divided by the number of scores. The standard deviation is the square root of the sum of all the individual deviations from the mean, squared and divided by the number of scores. The reason for squaring the difference between each score and the mean is simple. If we didn't do this the sum of the deviations would be zero, since in a normal distribution (or the good old bell-shaped curve) the numbers above and below the mean would cancel each other out. By the way, statisticians also like to talk about "variance." When used as a measure of variability, the variance is the standard deviation squared (don't bother taking the square root).

Now let's see if we can't make some sense of all this jargon. Well, the mean is pretty straightforward; it's going to tell you what your average win or loss is over an extended series of sessions of play. You've got to know what this number is. There is no sense in trying to duck reality here—the size of your bankroll doesn't change when you lie about it, either to yourself or others. If you are playing Type L games for any length of time your bottom line is virtually certain to be a number less than zero, and it is worth knowing just how far below zero it is. If it is getting painfully low, perhaps it is time to shift to other games. If you are playing Type W games, whether your mean is above or below zero is a clear and compelling indicator of how well you're playing. If it's below zero over an extended series of sessions, this is, as we scientists like to say, data—data that suggest you are not playing the game as well as those you are playing against. If this is the case, don't despair. Read chapters 5, 6, 7, and 8.

The standard deviation (SD) can give you additional information about the nature of your play and provide insights into how to manage your bankroll. The SD provides a measure of how wild your session-to-session bottom line swings are. If your SD is small, you are playing a conservative, consistent game and are wagering fairly small stakes. If your SD is large, just the opposite is true. Players who have large SDs are likely to have "home run" days when they win large amounts of money. They are also likely to have days when they take a serious bath and go home broke—or, as they say, "tapped out."

You need to be aware that the formula for the standard deviation is accurate only when you are calculating variability when all the sessions are of the same length and your average bet size doesn't vary. Clearly, it would be wrong to include sessions when you played for ten minutes along with ones when you played for two hours. It would be equally misleading to include sessions when you bet a range of $1 to $5 along with ones when your wagers ranged from $10 to $20. The interested reader should see Mason Malmuth's *Gambling Theory and Other Topics,* where the use of maximum likelihood approximations to the standard deviation that take these factors into account are explained.

Randomness

Ah, here's a tricky concept! Strictly speaking, random events are events whose occurrences could not have been predicted at rates greater than chance. In most gambling situations the specific outcomes are, indeed, random. For example, let's take roulette. The number that little white ball will land on during any given spin of the wheel is random in the sense that knowing where it landed on all previous spins provides no information that will allow you to predict at rates greater than chance where it will land on the next spin. This does not mean that its ultimate location was not caused by particular events, for the infuriating little spheroid is quite clearly following the basic laws of physics. It simply means that its ultimate location on any given spin is not predictable. Virtually all casino games are constructed on the assumption that the outcomes of particular events are, indeed, quite random.

Unfortunately, the notion of a single "random event" actually doesn't make a heck of a lot of sense from a mathematical point of view. In order to determine true randomness one must observe a very large number of events and determine that no biases are apparent. Despite this distinctly abstract element, from a practical point of view we only need to think of randomness as the lack of a pattern, the lack of predictability at rates above chance.

It is important to understand that a casino's very livelihood is predicated on the randomness of its games. The last thing a casino wants is a roulette wheel or a pair of dice that is not random. People pay attention. In roulette, players often keep careful logs of where the ball landed on every spin and peruse the sequences looking for patterns and biases. You will see this especially in Europe, where roulette is a much more popular game than it is here in North America. If the wheel were not random the casino would soon be in financial trouble. There is an oft-told tale of the nineteenth-century British engineer William Jaggers, who, suspecting that the wheels at Monte Carlo were not carefully balanced, sent a group of assistants in to log the outcomes of several thousands of spins. After analyzing the data, Jaggers discovered a subtle but real bias in one wheel. He returned to Monte Carlo and, over a four-day period, is said to have won over one and a half million francs before the casino keyed in on what was happening and had the wheel corrected.

Nonrandomness means simply that there is a bias, a pattern to the events—and if you could discern that pattern you could predict which event would occur next with greater than chance probability. Modern casinos, however, are so confident in the randomness of their roulette wheels that many of them hand out paper and pencil and encourage their players to try to find patterns in the sequence of numbers. They know that there are, in fact, no such patterns, and they know that even if there were, the couple of dozen spins the typical player records is far too small a sample to find them. Nevertheless, the players who think they have discerned a pattern will often increase the amount of money they wager. Good for the casino, not so good for the player.

So, for those of you who, when getting clobbered while playing roulette or craps, have started feeling a bit paranoid and begun to think that the wheel or the dice are "fixed," have faith. They are not. You're just having a lousy run, which, as any good student of probabilities (or any experienced gambler) knows, is certain to happen. Trust me on this one, the casinos are much more paranoid about nonrandom wheels and loaded dice than you are. True randomness is the casino's best friend.

The Gambler's Fallacy

You have been shooting craps for a time and have just watched the dice come up 10 three times in a row. You are amazed—and deeply sorry that you have not been laying place or buy bets on 10. Question: What's the probability of a 10 on the next throw? Answer: Exactly the same as it always is, $3/36 = .083$. If you think that a 10 is less likely because it has come up three times in a row you have just committed one version of the gambler's fallacy.

Why is it a fallacy? Because the several events in question here are independent of each other: Whatever outcomes occurred previously have no bearing on what will occur next. Hence, to assume that they do have a bearing is fallacious. The same interpretation holds when viewed from the other side of the argument, looking for something *to* happen rather than *not to* happen. Suppose you have been tracking the outcomes of a roulette wheel for some time and you notice, with some surprise, that the last twelve spins have all resulted in black numbers. Question: Should you now shovel all of your available cash to red since it is "due"? Answer: Nope. The probability that the next spin will land in a red slot is just what it always was, $18/38 = .4737$. The notion that red is due is just another version of the gambler's fallacy.

I've talked to a lot of people—gamblers, students, and friends— about this issue, and they tell me all kinds of interesting things. Most of what they tell me shows that they have failed to grasp the issue. Some people who have a little (but, unfortunately, not enough) understanding of probability theory tell me they know that "in the long run things always even out." So, they reason, if red hasn't shown up in twelve spins it's got to show up pretty soon and pretty often, otherwise things won't "even out." Not a bad try here, folks, but, alas, you're missing one of the fundamental aspects of probability theory. "Things always even out" is not the right way to think about this situation. The reason is simple. Probabilistic analyses are based on *theoretical* distributions of outcomes. That is, in the long run (there's that phrase again!) one does indeed *expect* that the events that occur in the real world will conform to the theoretical distributions. But in reality they are under no obligation to do so—particularly in the short run.

However, it is important to appreciate the simple fact that, while we expect to see results that are close to typical, since they are the most likely to occur, these short-run outcomes can vary all over the joint. That is, the more one plays, the more likely it becomes that extremely unlikely outcomes will occur and the more likely it becomes that the long-term average will be just where is it supposed to be.

The key to understanding this lies in what is called the "law of large numbers." This principle says that, while it is true that things tend to even out in the long run, getting to the point where this tendency becomes overwhelmingly likely requires a *really* long run! Theoretically, it requires an *infinitely* long run—which, frankly, you don't have the time to wait around for. In short, when you get a large enough number of events, they will tend to conform to the probabilistic analyses. But because of the variability inherent in these situations, don't expect that in any relatively short run of events (and trust me, twelve spins of a roulette wheel is a really short run) the proportions will conform to theoretical expectations. In the real world that all us players live in, each and every individual event must be viewed in terms of the theoretical probabilities that characterize it. The events that have preceded it have no impact on it. To use the terminology we introduced earlier, the spins of a roulette wheel and the tosses of a pair of dice are independent events.

If this somewhat esoteric analysis either doesn't help or simply confuses you even more, let's try a more basic one. Let's ask a simple question: How in the name of heaven could events that occurred earlier have *any* role in determining what will happen next? Roulette wheels and dice don't have any memory. People have memories. Roulette wheels and dice are made of wood, metal, plastic, and other stuff. Wood doesn't have a memory. Steel can't recall what happened before. Plastic can't keep track of what the last number was. Whatever happened happened. Whatever will happen next will be governed by the same principles of chance that govern every single spin of the wheel and each roll of the dice. You can get twenty blacks in a row, and—trust me—the probability of a red on the next spin is exactly the same as it always was.

Let's take one more example. You are playing bridge. You pick up your hand and, to your astonishment, it contains thirteen spades. All spades, nothing but spades. My God, you say to yourself, what an incredible thing this is! A hand like this could only occur once in several million hands. You end up with a contract of seven spades, play the hand out, rejoice over making a grand slam, and deal out the next hand. Now you pick up an absolutely boring, ordinary hand. It has the 3♣, the 4♦, the K♥, the Q♠, etc., etc., etc. There is nothing remarkable about this hand, nothing to make you sit up and pay attention, nothing to write home about. But guess what, folks—*this hand is just as unlikely as the one with the thirteen spades!* That's right, every hand in bridge is just as unlikely as every other. Work it out. The probability of ending up with the A♠ in your hand is exactly the same as the probability of ending up with the 3♣. The chance of having the K♠ is precisely that of being dealt the 4♦. And so forth. It doesn't matter what the cards are; each is just as unlikely to be dealt as any other.

The deep issue here is not probabilities, it is psychology. Ten reds in a row at a roulette wheel really gets your attention. The hand with thirteen spades in it means something in the game of bridge; the other one with all those junk cards means nothing except that you're probably going to take a bath on it if you're playing for money. But probabilistically the likelihood of one is exactly the same as that of the other. So, once again, it is critical to understand probability theory if you are going to get involved in gambling. Don't get suckered into thinking that numbers or cards or slot machines are "due." The gambler's fallacy is a most seductive fallacy, but it is still a fallacy. If you're playing casino games the only thing it can do is entice you into making larger wagers than you normally would. If you're playing poker, handicapping the horses, or betting on basketball games, raising your basic bet size because you think you are "due" for a decent hand or a win or a "break" can be equally disastrous. Remember, the probabilities haven't changed, and they don't give a fig how much you've lost that day.

Being "On a Roll" and Having "Hot Hands"

A lot of gamblers put a lot of emphasis on streaks both inside and outside the casino. Crap shooters are particularly prone to this kind of thinking, and, to tell the truth, there really is nothing quite like a craps table when a shooter is hot and everybody is making money. Sports bettors often wager based on whether a key player on a team seems to have a "hot hand." The feeling here is so intense that even the players get involved. You often hear basketball coaches and other players say things like "Get Kenny the ball, he's got the hot hand." And, not surprisingly, many books on gambling recommend that players look for hot tables at craps, leave cold shoes in blackjack, bet on teams with a hot shooter or a quarterback who is on a roll. Question: Does this advice make sense?

Well, it might make some sense some of the time. What we need to do here is to separate out cases where the outcome of a gamble is determined by inanimate objects like dice and cards from those where it is determined by animate objects like shooting guards and quarter-backs. Let's look at the inanimate cases first because they are easiest to deal with.

When dealing with dice, cards, roulette wheels, slot machines, keno tickets, and the like, there is no such thing as being on a roll in any sense other than what one might expect to occur by chance alone. Our discussion of the gambler's fallacy made this abundantly clear. What happens when you are shooting dice and things suddenly start going so very, very right is that the run of passes assumes a psychological poignancy that is memorable. The table is hot, everyone is pressing for a spot at the rail, cheers and high fives accompany each roll, and it seems that the odds are being magically defied. But they are not. Long runs of passes in craps occur with just the frequency that they would be expected to given a probabilistic analysis of the game. And to be sure, long runs of craps and 7-outs also occur with just about their expected frequency. Every table has the potential to be hot, cold, and tepid just as often as every other table. Does it make sense to leave if you're losing and stay if you're winning? Well, sure, provided that you are still having fun, but don't make either decision based on a subjective assessment of whether the dice, the table, the shoe, the wheel, or anything else is hot or cold. Remember, these inanimate objects have no memory. What has happened in the past has no bearing on what will happen in the future.

When dealing with the human element things get a little trickier. For example, it appears possible that a shooting guard can "get hot" in the sense that he has just hit five shots in a row and that this feeling of being "on" has a psychological impact on him. His confidence in his abilities goes up and his teammates get behind him and start clearing out the middle for his drives, setting picks, and generally supporting his play on the court. Under these conditions he takes his game "to a higher level," as sports fans like to say. He has "hot hands." If you talk with professional players in virtually any sport from basketball to bowling they will tell you that the scenario I just sketched is the absolute truth. But is it?

This issue has become a hot topic in experimental psychology lately. The debate began a couple of years back when Amos Tversky, a highly respected experimental psychologist at Stanford University, looked at the hot hands phenomenon statistically. He kept careful records of all the shots taken by every player on a professional basketball team for an entire year. He found absolutely no evidence for the hot hands phenomenon, none at all. He discovered that an individual player's overall shot percentage was the best predictor of whether or not the player would hit his next shot no matter how many shots in a row the player had just made or missed. Were there "streaks"? Of course. A player who hits 50 percent of his shots is going to have fairly long runs of success—and equally long runs of failure—but these runs occurred with just the frequency that would be expected. According to Tversky, our animate subjects behaved no differently than a pair of dice! However, more recent work by other psychologists has suggested that streaks may be a bit longer and occur with greater frequency than Tversky initially thought. The debate goes on. (By the way, every sportsman or sports bettor with whom I have discussed this issue resolutely refuses to believe that Tversky could be right. Fascinating!)

Regression to the Mean

This is a rather abstract notion that has a simple underlying principle—it is also immensely important and will pop up again and again throughout this book. Unfortunately, most gamblers have a lot of trouble understanding it, and not understanding it can be damaging to the pocketbook. Regression to the mean is a generalization that states that future outcomes will tend to be closer to the mean, or average of all possible outcomes, than the outcomes that immediately preceded them. It is a principle that shows up everywhere, not just in gaming situations. In fact, it was first noticed in studies of genetics, where it was called the law of filial regression. Here's an example that might help you see the principle in operation. Suppose that you and your spouse are both a good bit taller than average. Analyses of the inheritance of physical stature show that, while it is quite likely that your offspring will be above average in height, they will, on average, be shorter than you and your spouse! That is, their heights will tend to "regress toward the mean" of the whole population.

When first discovered, this principle seemed kind of mysterious. How can this be? How can there be a mechanism that would control this kind of process? But, of course, there is no mechanism. Regression to the mean is a simple statistical principle based on a rather simple idea. Unusual events are unusual and hence are unlikely to be repeated. Being really tall is unlikely, so it stands to reason that your offspring will tend not to be quite as tall since that kind of height doesn't happen all that often.

Let's try a couple of examples from gambling situations to help us understand this principle. You walk into a casino and sit down to play blackjack. You can do no wrong. Every "hit" gives you a total of 20 or 21; A's (aces) and 10's seem glued to your spot. Even when you're stuck with a bad hand, all goes well: your 12's, 13's, 14's, 15's, and 16's are followed by dealer busts. An hour later you walk out several hundred dollars richer. Question: What can you expect to happen next time you play blackjack? Answer: Something less—not necessarily a loss comparable to your win, but an outcome that is closer to your average. You are most likely to show regression to the mean.

Where the principle of regression to the mean wreaks the most havoc is with racehorse handicappers, sports bettors, and sports betting services. We will look at this issue more closely in the chapters devoted to those topics, but let me simply relate an event here to make my point. A couple of years back the Philadelphia Eagles opened the NFL football season with two impressive victories. I mean, they were stunning. The team looked so good that people started conceding the Super Bowl to the Eagles. But a closer look at those two games revealed some interesting things. For one, opposing cornerbacks slipped at critical times, allowing for long gains. A couple of timely penalties kept drives alive that should have resulted in punts. The quarterback, Randall Cunningham, had been as sharp as anyone had ever seen him. The Eagle defense was gambling, and had made several brilliant plays that could have been disastrous if their timing had been a split second off. It was pretty clear that virtually everything had gone just right for the Eagles for two straight weeks. Question: What's the probability that everything would go just right next time? Answer: Damn small! Question: What does the principle of regression to the mean predict in such a situation? Answer: A performance much closer to the team's appropriate level.

What happened? Well, just as you might guess, based on their dominant wins two weeks in a row, the Eagles opened up a seven-point favorite over the Raiders, their seemingly outclassed opponents. At the racetrack on the Friday before that weekend's games, all of my buddies were talking about the Eagles. Johnny T., a lawyer (he really is a lawyer; he spends his mornings defending what he calls "the scum of the earth" and his afternoons at the track), asked me what I thought of the Eagles. I told him they were overrated and probably would get their butts handed to them on Sunday. He looked at me as if I'd I just landed from Mars and told me he had just put $500 on the "Iggles," as he calls them, and was already counting his money. "Dese Iggles," he told me, "are at least twenty points betta den de Raiders. It's a freakin' mortal lock." (Yeah, he really talks like that, and yeah, lawyers bet with bookies.)

I gave my friendly bookie a ring and put $300 on the Raiders—who proceeded to not only cover the spread but actually win "for fun," as they say. When I saw Johnny T. the next week he looked kind of chagrined. "You soitenly were right about them freakin' Iggles," he said. "How'd ya know?" I tried to explain the principle of regression to the mean, but he just looked confused and walked away. (Johnny T., by the way, is also a terrible horseplayer.) When sports bettors and handicappers talk about the issue involved in the principle of regression to the mean, they call it a "bounce." So the Eagles had bounced from previous levels of performance. The pros routinely look for these situations.

That's probably enough probability theory for the average gambler. There is much more here, and the best players not only know the odds of the wagers they make but also understand the subtle aspects of probabilistic analyses. (Interestingly, they typically do not know *consciously* about principles like the gambler's fallacy or regression to the mean, but have an *intuitive* grasp of how these principles operate in real life.) What we have covered here will be sufficient for us to get a deeper understanding of the various games—Type L and Type W. So let's get down to business.

(The answer to the problem given on page 22 is .0964.)

PART II

TYPE L GAMES
THOSE AT WHICH YOU EVENTUALLY LOSE

3

CASINO TABLE GAMES: ROULETTE, BACCARAT, AND CRAPS

*T*ype L games are games in which the house has the advantage, where the expected value of your wagers is some number below zero, and where, if you play long enough, you will eventually go broke. There is no way around this fact, and we've got to be realistic.

The next time you go into a modern casino, stop and take a long look around you. Notice the opulence—the carpeting, mirrors, chandeliers, furnishings—indeed, the very splendor of the place. Notice also that in most casinos drinks are provided free, rooms are offered at reduced rates or free of charge to regular players, and meals in gourmet restaurants and choice seats to headliner shows are given away as complimentary services (comped). It should take but a second's reflection to realize that those guys have got to have the upper hand here. No sensible business is going to offer you a free room and comp you to expensive gourmet meals and a show unless it is counting on your losing a good deal more than the value of those items.

In fact, the casinos are so sure of their ultimate gain that they will even comp you when you win. Recently, a friend of mine was playing in a casino he had never visited before. He got on a serious roll at the craps tables and, being a fairly high roller, won something in excess of $30,000 in one long and wondrous session. When he went to cash in his chips, to his surprise, the pit boss congratulated him heartily on his terrific play and comped him to a three-room suite, dinner, and a show for him and his wife. My friend should not have been surprised. The casino was giving him the royal treatment for the simplest of reasons. The casino owners wanted those thirty big ones back. They wanted my friend to continue to play in their house and not somewhere else.

How big is the casino's edge in Type L games? That depends on the game and the way it is played. It tops out with a high in the neighborhood of 40 percent of money wagered for some bets in keno and goes as low as about .4 to .5 percent for some plays in craps. The others fall in between. How effective is this edge? As of the middle 1990s, each and every player who walked into one of the casinos in Atlantic City added roughly $55 to the casino's gross. This figure also holds for the larger Strip casinos in Las Vegas, although it is less for the smaller downtown joints.

So, if all this is true and well-known, why in the blazes would anyone play these games? There are a couple of reasons. First, just because the expected value of a game is negative doesn't mean you will always lose. Many players leave winners for that day. In fact, this is one of the things that keeps casinos thriving. Since the games are highly fluctuating, typical players will have enough winning sessions to keep them coming back. Second, gambling is fun and exciting. There is something immensely attractive in the action, the flow of the game. There is a special kind of seductive tension that attends the turn of a card that makes (or breaks) your hand, or that accompanies a pair of bouncing dice when your money is riding on them.

The key is learning how to get that psychological kick and not get hurt in the long run. That's what the rest of this chapter is all about. If you play Type L games you must do so knowing what your expected loss is. You should migrate toward games (or ways of playing them) in which the house has the smallest statistical edge. That way you will be able to enjoy yourself with minimum financial risk. Always remember: The longer you play a Type L game the more certain it becomes that you will lose and the more certain it becomes that you will lose what you are mathematically expected to lose.

At this point you might be wondering about all those other books that claim to be able to make you a winner at Type L games. Some of my favorite titles are *Lottery and Keno Winning Strategies*, *The Basics of Winning Slots*, *Craps—Playing to Win*, and *Beating the Wheel*. No matter how well intentioned the authors may be, most of the advice offered in these books is worthless and claims to the contrary are simply false. You cannot beat these games in the long run. While there are professional blackjack players and poker players, there is no such thing as a professional craps player or a professional roulette player. There cannot be. Anyone who tells you that he or she is a professional craps player who makes a living at the tables is either lying or is a cheat whom the house has not yet caught. These games are to be played for the fun of it, not to make money.

Okay? Let's get around to analyzing the most popular Type L table games. We'll take them in reverse order of the value of the game to the player, which means we will start with the one in which the house has the most pronounced edge, the game of roulette.

ROULETTE

I am not very fond of this game, at least not as it is typically played here in North America. Of all the casino table games, it offers the player the very worst of it.

The Play of the Game

There are two roulette wheels in common use; one is known as the French wheel and the other as the American wheel. The critical difference between them is simple but meaningful. The French wheel has thirty-seven slots, thirty-six of them numbered from 1 to 36, half black and half red, and a single green 0. The American wheel has thirty-eight slots with a green 00 added and placed opposite the 0. Figure 3-1 shows both wheels along with the betting layout used in each. The French wheel provides a better game for the player than the American wheel because the payoffs for particular bets are the same on both wheels but the added 00 seriously degrades the expected value for the player of the American game. For basic bets on the French wheel the player has an expected value of −2.70 percent of money wagered. The American wheel is almost twice as bad as the French, with an expected value of −5.26 percent of money wagered. A few casinos in the United States have a French wheel. However, they typically also have a rather large minimum bet: $25 and up to as high as $100. So while they offer the player better odds than the standard American wheel, the player has to risk considerably more money on each spin. The house's intention is pretty obvious. It can safely double its edge if it can insure that you will more than double your typical bet. Remember, the house edge is calculated as a percent of money wagered.

The layouts shown in figure 3-1 can appear intimidating to the newcomer, but they are actually pretty straightforward. Generally speaking, European casinos use the French wheel, although some of them, particularly the ones in Monte Carlo, have adopted the American wheel. In Great Britain the French wheel is used, but the layout is from the American game. In Europe, the wheel is often set in the center of the table with two betting layouts on opposite sides to accommodate more players. In North America there is a single layout. In both wheels the numbers are arranged to maximize the mixing of high and low and red and black numbers.

The European wheel usually has three or even four croupiers. Often the head croupier will sit in a chair above the wheel and adjudicate any disputes that might arise between players or between a player and one of the croupiers. Croupiers sweep up losing bets with elaborate movements of a wooden rake and pay off winners with a flourish not usually seen in North American casinos. Winning bets are left on the layout for the player to either remove or leave standing for the next turn of the wheel. In most European casinos all players use regular casino chips, which can occasionally lead to disputes over whose chips are whose. (Serious gamblers, particularly poker players, never call chips "chips." The preferred term is "checks." However, this convention is not followed everywhere, and in this book I will use the two terms interchangeably.) When playing in Europe you are advised to pay close attention to your bets, and when

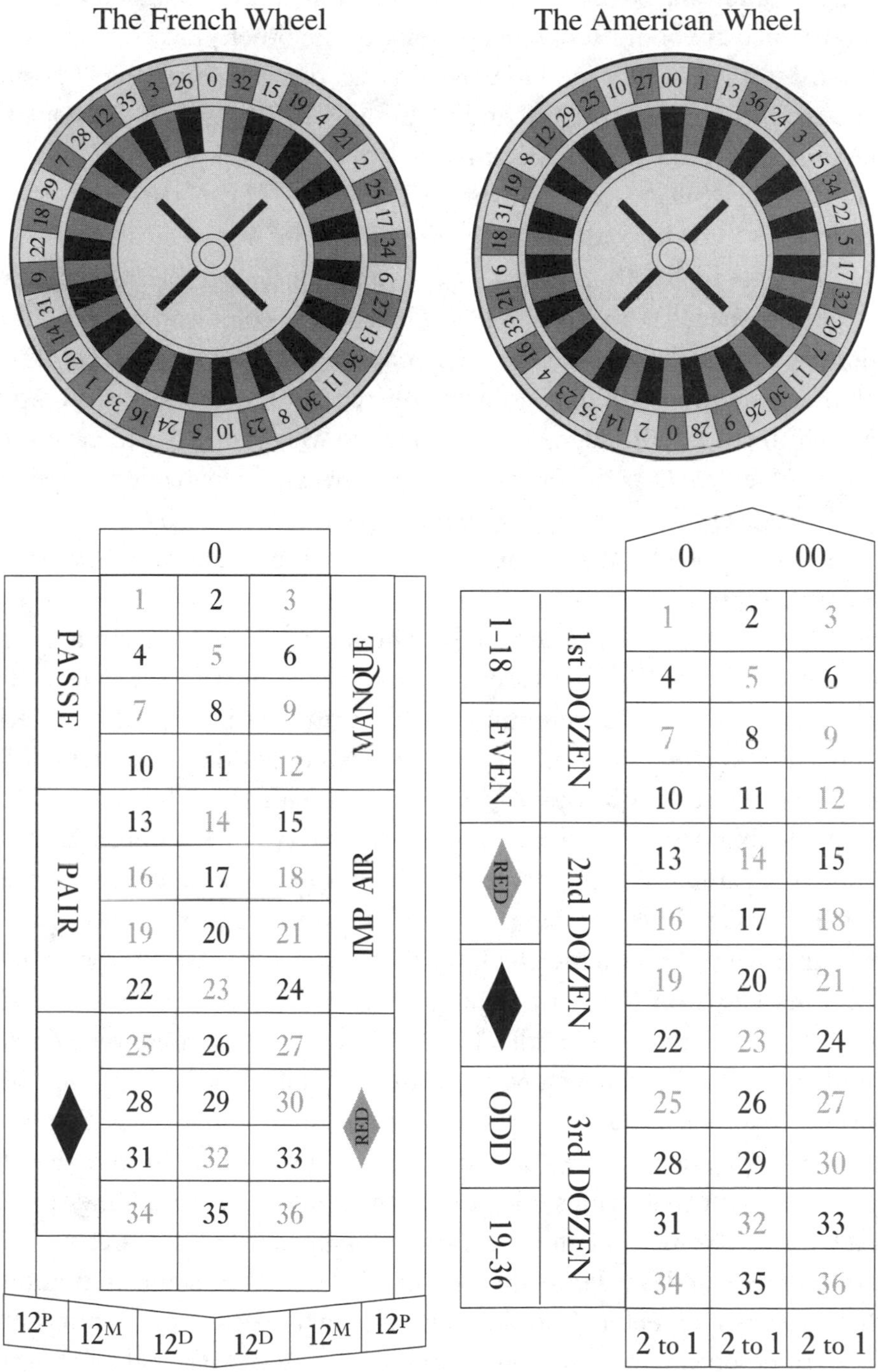

The French Wheel

The American Wheel

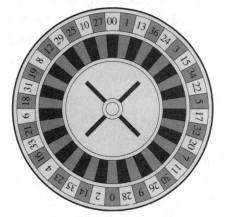

	0		
PASSE	1	2	3
	4	5	6
	7	8	9
	10	11	12
PAIR	13	14	15
	16	17	18
	19	20	21
	22	23	24
◆	25	26	27
	28	29	30
	31	32	33
	34	35	36

(right side labels: MANQUE, IMP AIR, ◆ RED)

| 12ᴾ | 12ᴹ | 12ᴰ | 12ᴰ | 12ᴹ | 12ᴾ |

		0	00	
1-18	**1st DOZEN**	1	2	3
		4	5	6
EVEN		7	8	9
		10	11	12
◆ RED	**2nd DOZEN**	13	14	15
		16	17	18
◆		19	20	21
		22	23	24
ODD	**3rd DOZEN**	25	26	27
		28	29	30
19-36		31	32	33
		34	35	36
		2 to 1	2 to 1	2 to 1

Figure 3-1 The French and American roulette wheels with the betting layouts.

you and other players have wagers on the same numbers, make sure you know which are yours and which belong to the other players.

In North America the table usually has one or two dealers. Losing bets are gathered up by hand and winning bets are paid off by stacking personalized chips for each individual player. After winning bets are paid, the original wagers remain on the table. The player may either retrieve them or leave them on for the next spin. When sitting down to play roulette in North America, you give the dealer either cash or regular casino checks. In return, you will be given color-coded chips that identify you and your wagers. You may be playing with green chips, another person with blue, another with red, and so forth. Each chip is usually worth $1, although you may arrange with the dealer to have your chips valued at $2 or $5 or whatever you wish. Color-coded chips are used to prevent disputes over who made what bet. They have value only at the roulette table. When you leave the table, make sure to have them converted into regular casino chips.

Play is the same in both games. The minimum and maximum bets are displayed, usually on a card that is mounted next to the wheel. If a table is marked as a $5 minimum wheel, it means that a total of at least $5 must be wagered by a player on a given spin. Minimum wagers of $1 may be made so long as the player makes at least five such bets.

Watching a busy roulette table—particularly in European casinos, where the game is extremely popular—is absolutely fascinating. As soon as the croupiers have finished paying off the winning bets from the previous spin, people all around the layout lean over the table and begin distributing chips on the felt as though they were farmers sowing seeds. Serious players reach out with a large stack of chips held between downward fingers and dribble chips all around the table, two on one number, three on another, a couple more as an *en carré* (four number) bet, a stack of five on the *premiere dozaine* (or first dozen). They hesitate, scan their bets, lean back with more chips and scatter them about, often adding to bets made earlier. Some land on their birthday, some on their children's birthdays, some on today's date, some on "magic" numbers, some on numbers they have won on before, some on numbers that haven't come up in some time, some on numbers that just came up, some . . . To make bets they cannot reach from their seats they will give the checks to the dealer and ask for particular wagers. After a moment or so the tuxedoed croupier

flicks the ivory ball (actually, it's plastic these days) in the direction opposite to the rotation of the slowly spinning wheel in a slot cut into the side
wall a few inches above the wheel itself. For many players this is the signal
to increase their action, and they scramble to get the last few bets down
before the call of "*Rien de vas plus*" ("No more bets") brings wagering to a
halt for that spin. As gravity does its inexorable thing a dozen or so pairs
of eyes watch anxiously as the ball bounces around on the various numbered slots, up onto the sloping wood center of the wheel itself, down onto
the numbers again, and finally rests in one. The croupier calls out the winning number, whether it is *pair* (even) or *impair* (odd), and whether it is
rouge (red) or *noire* (black). Pretty much the same thing happens in American casinos, only in English and without the flair.

Wagering

The layout of the table allows players to make a rather wide variety
of wagers. The full set of standard bets and the names by which they are
known in English and French are given in the following chart. Each letter corresponds to the chip position marked in figure 3-2, which gives
examples of how each of these bets is made on an American layout.

North American Term	European (French) Term	Payoff Odds	Chip Position
Single number	*En plein*	35–1	A
Two numbers (split)	*A cheval*	17–1	B
Three numbers (trio)	*Transversale pleine*	11–1	C
Four numbers (square)	*En carré*	8–1	D
Six numbers (line)	*Sixaine*	5–1	E
Dozen	*Douzaine*	2–1	F
Adjacent dozens	*Douzaine à cheval*	1–2	G
Column	*Colonne*	2–1	H
Adjacent columns	*Colonne à cheval*	1–2	I
Red or black	*Rouge* or *noire*	1–1	J
Even or odd	*Pair* or *impair*	1–1	K
Low (1–18) or high (19–36)	*Manque* or *passe*	1–1	L

All basic bets have the same expected value. As was noted above,
with the French wheel the player is at a disadvantage of 2.7 percent of

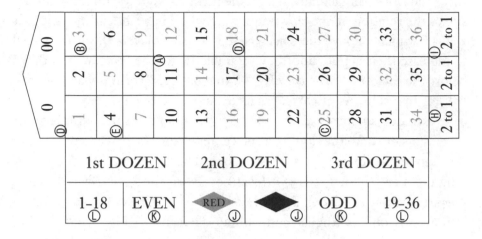

Figure 3-2 The American roulette layout showing various bets marked.

monies wagered. With the American wheel, by virtue of the 00, this disadvantage increases to 5.26 percent. There are two exceptions to this, one of which favors the house and one the players. The one favoring the house is found only on the American wheel. It is the five-number bet, involving 0, 00, 1, 2, and 3, which pays 6–1 (D in figure 3-2). This particular wager has a 7.89 percent edge for the house, and I wouldn't play it with your money and neither should you. The one favoring the players involves the even-money bets of red or black, even or odd, and low (1—18) or high (19–36). Should you have such a bet on the table in a European casino when the ball lands in the 0 you will lose only half of your wager; the other half remains *en prison* and becomes an additional wager for the next spin. Occasionally, a casino in North America will have a similar proposition but will call it "surrender." It has the effect of cutting the house edge on these wagers in half. Hence, these even-money bets have an expected value of only −1.35 percent on the French wheel and −2.63 percent on the American wheel. On the French wheel this house edge is at a manageable level. In North America the surrender rule, if you can find it, helps a bit, but it still leaves roulette a generally dreadful game for the player.

The above discussions cover most of the bets made at roulette, but there are a couple of additional special wagers. They are rarely made in North American casinos, although European players are fond of them.

These bets all have the same negative expected value as the standard bets; their main virtue is adding variety to the game.

Final (usually pronounced as the French finale)

This wager is made on the last or final digit of a set of numbers. The bet "final four" is a bet on the numbers 4, 14, 24, and 34, and costs four chips. Since it is often difficult to reach all the numbers from a single seat, to make such a wager give the dealer four chips and ask for the bet. When playing an American wheel, final 0 will cost you five chips, finals 1 through 6 four chips, and finals 7 through 9 only three chips. Each chip is treated like a single number bet and is paid off at 35 to 1.

Neighbors

It is popular in Europe to bet on a particular number and its "neighbors"—or, in French, *les voisins*. That is, a wager is placed on several numbers that occur next to each other on the wheel in the hope that if the ball lands in that area of the wheel any of several neighboring slots will produce a winner. If you look back at figure 3-1 you can see how the various numbers are distributed around the wheel and how particular bets can be made. For example, if you wish to bet on 11 and a group of six numbers surrounding it on the actual wheel, you simply hand seven chips to the dealer and ask for "eleven and neighbors." If you are playing a French wheel, your bets will be placed on 27, 13, 36, 11, 30, 8, and 23; on an American wheel your bets will be placed on 32, 20, 7, 11, 30, 26, and 9. Again, each chip is treated like a single number bet and is paid off at 35 to 1.

By the way, you can make this and similar bets in European casinos with full confidence that the croupier will place your bets accurately. However, few North American dealers know the layout of the wheel accurately enough to carry out your request and it isn't marked on the table layout. If fact, they are just as likely to look at you with bewilderment as anything else. If you want to make "neighbors" bets in North America, I recommend that you learn the layout of the wheel and place the bets yourself.

The Bottom Line

The bottom line on roulette is pretty clear, and the player is pretty much in the red. Of course, it depends on which wheel you are playing, but no matter how you cut it roulette is the very worst standard table game in the casino. The best bet for the player is to cut the basic casino edge in half by restricting wagers to even-money bets in establishments where the *en prison* or *surrender* rule is in effect. If you can find a game using the French wheel and if you restrict your bets to even-money propositions, then the game can be played at a "mere" expected loss of 1.35 percent of monies wagered. This brings the game down into the same realm as baccarat and the straight pass and come bets in craps. That's not bad, and when the game is played with moderation this is a reasonable edge to give up to have a good time.

The game itself has two very different faces to it. In Europe, especially at the tonier casinos, it has a distinct cachet. In North America it is an entirely different story. The European game is dressed with elegance, exuding a kind of grace, a *je ne sais quoi* that accompanies serious money, and a touch of snobbery—besides, it is carried out entirely in French. Americans generally don't cotton to games like this. Most of our gamblers stroll into a casino in jeans and sneakers or at best leisure suits, they don't anticipate and don't take kindly to being intimidated by some guy dressed like a penguin who insists on terminating betting by intoning "*rien de vas plus.*" Americans may be snobs, but we are a different kind of snob. My guess is that the only thing that would get a bunch of typical American casino rats to the roulette table would be if Frank Sinatra were playing at it.

Could roulette become a better game? Without a doubt. Two changes are needed. First, get rid of that ridiculous 00 and convert all tables to the French wheel, which is used everywhere else in the world. Second, dress the game up a bit. Make it a bit exotic. Not necessarily to the point of resembling the high-stakes wheel at Monte Carlo, but give it the kind of veneer that is found in baccarat. Add a dealer or two to each table. Instruct them in the nuances of the wheel so that a variety of exotic bets can be requested without receiving looks of incredulity. Make the players feel as though something special were happening; for example, bring the drinks in glasses instead of plastic and Styrofoam cups. It really shouldn't be difficult to do, and the increase in the rake for the house might actually make it worth all the effort.

Before I end this section let me tell you a little story. I've been criticizing roulette largely because it is such a poor bet for the average player. However, even the worst statistical play can occasionally yield surprising gains. In some measure, the possibility of the magical wind-fall, no matter how unlikely, is what seduces many a player. Is it possible to win at roulette even with the odds stacked as they are against you? Sure—at least in the short run. No matter what the odds may be, all kinds of wonderful things can happen, and there isn't a serious gambler alive who hasn't witnessed at least one magical mystery tour around the spinning wheel.

The one I was privileged to observe took place while I was playing at the tiny, but lovely, dark-paneled casino in the resort town of Seefeld in the Austrian Alps just north of Innsbruck. I was playing roulette for dis-tinctly modest stakes when a well-dressed gentleman who looked as if he had stepped right out of a James Bond movie came in. He was wearing a very expensive Italian designer gray suit and dark, silver-rimmed glasses that made it impossible to see his eyes. As he settled in at the table across from where I was playing I noticed that his right hand was false; it was shaped like a hand but had none of the natural movements of a normal hand. Moreover, it was encased in a very expensive-looking black leather glove. As he held this hand rigidly at his side he reached over the wheel with his left hand and placed a series of bets, a substantial one of about $100 (in Austrian schillings, of course) on *noire* (black), a somewhat smaller one of about $50 on *impair* (odd), and several *en plein* (single-number) bets, with the largest (roughly $20) on the number 17. He then stood up and went over to the bar to get a drink, asking the croupier to take care to mind his bets. The wheel spun and the small ivory ball dropped cleanly into 17. The croupier stacked up approximately $850 in chips in front of the gambler's seat. The *en plein* bet on 17 won about $700 at 35 to 1 and the *noire* and *impair* wagers were paid at even odds.

As the croupier prepared for the next spin, all of us standing around the table realized that the original winning bets were still on the table. Those bets can only be removed by the player, who in this case was still waiting for service at the bar. We watched in fascination as the next two spins produced two more 17's! When the gentleman finally returned with his drink, there was in the neighborhood of an additional $2,500 sitting in front of his seat. What are the chances of something like this happening? Pretty remote: 50,652 to 1 (on the French wheel—they would be an even higher 54,871 to 1 on an American wheel). Pretty unlikely, but not all that wildly improbable. My guess is that many well-seasoned croupiers have witnessed similar if not even more dramatic happenings. Oh, by the way, the one-handed player gave the croupiers who "managed" his money while he was away a thousand-schilling tip —about $60 in those days.

In case you're curious, the way to calculate the probability of hitting a given number three times in a row is straightforward. Recall from the previous chapter that, when calculating independent events, merely multiply the likelihood of each of the several events against each other. Since the chances of any single number's coming up are 1 out of 37 on the French wheel, simply multiply $1/37 \times 1/37 \times 1/37 = 1/50,653 = .000019$. For the American wheel it becomes $1/38 \times 1/38 \times 1/38 = 1/54,872 = .000018$.

With this little fantasy episode bouncing around in your brain, let's move on to another of the Type L games, baccarat.

BACCARAT

Baccarat—or, more properly, baccarat punto or punto banco—is one of a family of games that includes baccarat banque (also known as *baccara à deux tableaux*) and chemin de fer (also known as *baccara à un tableaux*). The element that distinguishes these games is who is permitted to play the role of the bank. In the United Kingdom and in North America, only the baccarat punto version, where the house plays the role of banker, is found. The other two versions, in which the players act as the bank, are found in some European casinos. When these other versions are played, the stakes rarely reach the levels typically found in North American casinos, since few people could afford the potential losses they might incur should players win large bets against another player's bank. For example, in a typical game of chemin de fer or baccarat banque, the player who is acting as banker puts up the equivalent of perhaps four or five hundred dollars against which other players may wager. Of three versions of the game, baccarat punto is the most common, so common that when the term "baccarat" is used it is typically assumed to be referring to this game. And so it is the one we will examine here.

Baccarat is thought to have been played in various European cities for over five hundred years. However, David Parlett's authoritative *A History of Card Games* claims that, myths aside, no reliable record of the game exists before the middle of the nineteenth century. The best guess seems to be that it was an Italian invention, a spin-off of the French game *vingt-et-un,* or "twenty-one"—or, of course, what we call blackjack. It is similar to *vingt-et-un* in that participants draw cards in an attempt to get as close as possible to a set number without exceeding it. It differs from it, however, in several ways. First, the total aimed at is 9 rather than 21. Second, if that total is exceeded the player does not automatically lose, as in blackjack. Rather, the total cycles around a base of 10 so that, for example, if an 8 is drawn to a 5 the total is treated as 3. Finally, and most important, when an additional card may be pulled is determined by a fixed set of rules rather than being left up to the player's judgment. The name of the game comes from the Italian *baccara,* or "zero," and refers to the fact that in the game all ten-valued cards count as zero.

Baccarat is an intriguing game. When we get around to specifying the rules of the game you will probably say, as I did the first time I saw them, "Huh?" I mean, this is nothing short of silly. The game is totally under the control of an arcane set of rules that determine who draws a card and when. It has no choice, no strategy, no subtlety. Indeed, as the English writer Barrie Hughes put it, "Most children's games are infinitely more complicated, and it is doubtful if Baccara played without stakes could hold the attention of any but the most backward child." But it is, dear reader, played for stakes!

If you walk into a modern casino, go watch (or, of course, if you wish, play) baccarat. The baccarat pit will generally be found off to the side. The area will be furnished more elegantly than the rest of the casino, the lighting is usually indirect and subtle, and the dealers will be either tuxedo-clad or wearing elegant but understated black. The whole scene is one of elegance. This is serious business, and it is often played for very serious money. Although some casinos have small-stakes games with minimum bets of as low as $5, the fascination the game holds is due to the tradition of playing it for sometimes staggering sums. It is not unusual to see ten or twelve players wagering between $500 and $5,000 (or even more) on each hand. It can be unnerving to watch, as I have on more than one occasion, a modestly dressed individual wagering on each hand enough money to pay off my mortgage.

But don't be intimidated by all this money. The game can be played for less, particularly during the day or in the early evening, when table minimums of $25 or less can be found. Just because the folks around you are betting $1,000 when you've got only $25 or $50 up makes no difference. The casino will treat you with the same graciousness as it does everyone else. Enjoy the experience. It's nice to get away from the madness of a busy casino, and it is a distinct pleasure to have your drinks served in a glass. And, as we shall see, baccarat actually offers the player a reasonable set of odds to play against.

In Las Vegas you will often see a baccarat table with one, two, or even three young, good-looking women playing, particularly early in the day. These women are "shills"; they work for the house and are playing only to attract other players to the table. Once they have succeeded in doing so they will quietly cash out their checks and leave. In Atlantic City you will often see empty baccarat tables and dealers all standing around and gossiping and looking bored. Shills are not permitted in New Jersey casinos.

The Play of the Game

Baccarat is played on a large table with a layout like the one shown in figure 3–3. There are places for from twelve to fifteen players, depending on the size of the table. Three dealers (or croupiers) run the game; one handles the cards and is also known as "the caller," the other two handle the wagers and the commission that is paid on winning "bank" bets. Where a player sits is irrelevant except that bets must be made in the area of the layout that corresponds to the player's seat.

The hand is played between "the players" and "the bank" to determine, after all the cards are drawn, who has a total closest to 9. Each participant may wager on either the players or the bank, depending on which he or she believes will win that hand. The wager is indicated by placing one's chips in the appropriate area on the layout. It is also possible to bet that the hand will be tied. A player wishing to make such a wager places the bet in the area marked "Ties."

Winning player and bank bets are paid off at even odds. On hands that result in a tie, tie wagers are paid off at 8 to 1 and a bank or player bet is treated as a "push"—that is, such bets neither win nor lose, and the money simply sits there for the next hand. In these cases, the bet can, of course, be reduced or raised or shifted as the player wishes.

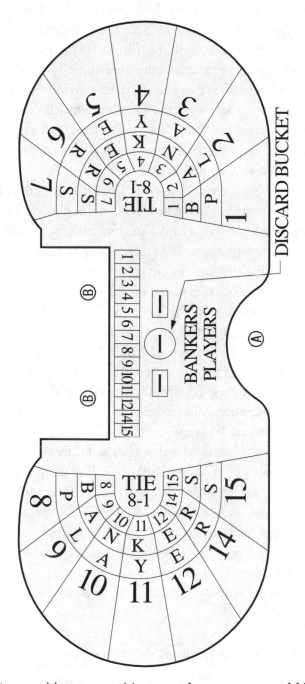

Figure 3-3 A typical baccarat table set up for a maximum of fifteen players. The dealer who acts as the caller stands at the spot marked A, the other two dealers who handle the payoffs and the commissions position themselves at the spots marked B.

Play begins with the dealers shuffling the eight decks that are used in the game. Some casinos use six decks, but this practice is declining, since it requires more frequent shuffling. All the cards are elaborately spread out on the layout and are shuffled initially by the dealers, who swirl all 416 of them about in a large, ever-moving "muck." The cards are then straightened and shuffled in more usual fashion. After one of the players cuts the cards they are rearranged, the cut card is placed about 20 percent up from the bottom, and all the cards are put into the dealing shoe. Players then make their bets.

Play begins with the player in Seat 1, who is designated to act as the bank and deal the cards. All cards are dealt facedown. The first card is for the players and is handed to the dealer, who, by tradition, gives it to the player with the largest player bet. In European casinos the caller uses a large, flat wooden paddle to deliver the card to the player; in North America the card is usually just handed over by sliding it across the table. The second card is for the bank and is kept by the shoe, the third is sent to the players, and the fourth is kept by the shoe, so that each hand has two cards. The player who acts for the players now typically goes through an elaborate ritual of squeezing the cards slowly (often agonizingly so) until their denominations can be determined. They are then handed to the caller, who announces their sum and places them face up on the spot marked "Players" on the layout. The player who is acting for the bank duplicates the ritual with the other two cards, which are then placed in the spot marked "Bankers." The total in each hand is the sum of the cards. Each card's value is its face value, except that 10's and face cards all count as 0 and aces count as 1. If the sum of the cards exceeds 9 it cycles back through 0.

Once the initial sums have been determined, the fixed rules of the game come into play. The players' cards are always played first according to the following rules (which are always posted at the table for anyone to consult):

Total of Player's First Two Cards	Action Taken
0, 1, 2, 3, 4, or 5	Draw a card
6 or 7	Stand
8 or 9	Stand—naturals

The totals of 8 and 9 are called "naturals" and no additional cards are drawn. Hands of 6, 7, 8, or 9 are strong hands, although they are treated differently. The bank hand may draw against a player 6 or 7 and thus beat or tie it, but the bank may not draw against a "natural" and must beat or tie it on the first two cards. The bank draws cards depending on the total of its own first two cards plus the value of any third card that the players' hand has drawn. To see how these conditions operate, let's look at the rules that determine the play of the bank hand.

Bank Hand	Draws When Giving*	Stands When Giving
0, 1, 2	Any card	
3	1–7, 9, or 10	8
4	2–7	1, 8–10
5	4–7	1–3, 8–10
6	6–7	1–5, 8–10
7	Stands	Stands
8, 9	Stands	Stands

* This term giving is used because no other term is accurate. The rules that determine whether the bank draws a card depend first on what the players total on the first two cards was and second on the denomination of the third players card (should that hand be required to draw it). So the notion is that the bank s play is determined by what the bank is giving up at that point in the game.

Notice that, except for the players' two-card totals of 6 to 9, the rules that determine whether or not the bank draws a card depend not on the players' total after the third card but on the value of that third card. This seems nothing short of silly. How did they come up with a set of rules like these? The answer, of course, is that they were carefully worked out so the bank would have a probabilistic edge over the players.

An interesting element to the game is that the player has no decisions to make. In fact, many baccarat players don't even know the rules. They merely sit there waiting for the dealer to inform them whether they have won or lost.

So if the rules are fixed and there is no choice, what's the attraction of the game? Well, one inducement is exactly that. Many players enjoy the slow, modulated pace of the game. They sit in comfortable chairs, turn or watch others turn cards, and win or lose without having to make critical decisions that could be nerve-racking given the sums wagered.

Another factor is the high stakes for which the game is often played. When you've got a couple thousand dollars riding on the turn of a card, it can give you a pretty good rush. A third element emerges from the rules and the manner in which they control play. For example, suppose you have bet on the players; they have drawn a hand in which the first two cards total 5, and the bank's total is 4. It would be just fine if you could leave well enough alone and take your win. Unfortunately, the rules say you must draw to a 5, and it is pretty clear that it is more likely that your hand will get worse by drawing than it will improve. That is, only an A, 2, 3, or 4 will help you, while a 5, 6, 7, 8, or 9 will lower your total. Any ten-valued card, of course, leaves you at 5. A total of 5, therefore, while not a bad hand, has one frustrating element: it's more likely that the draw will diminish rather than improve its value. Hence, drawing a card to a total of 5 can produce considerable agony for someone who has bet on the players in the scenario we set out. You can imagine the relief when a 3 or a 4 is pulled, and the cries of agony when a 5 is. Of course, even drawing the dreaded 5 still leaves the players with one slim out—the bank (which must also draw under these conditions) can draw a 6 and create a saving tie. Similar kinds of financial pain occur on the bank's final draw. All this is very much what people go though when watching the bouncing ball in roulette.

The Bottom Line

Baccarat has a pretty reasonable set of odds for the player, especially when compared with roulette. On player bets the house has a small edge of 1.36 percent, which is not bad, given what we just saw in our discussion of roulette. The unadjusted bank bets actually have a positive expected value for the player. To compensate for this and to restore its probabilistic edge, the house takes a 5 percent vigorish (called "commission") on winning bank bets. If you look back at the layout you will see that in front of the two dealers who handle the wagers is a set of small boxes numbered 1 through 15. These are for keeping track of the commissions that are owed by each player. After each winning bank bet, the dealer will put a marker that denotes how much is owed on that winning bet in the box that corresponds to the player's seat number. When you are ready to leave the table you must make good on these commissions. So don't lose your last dollar without first checking to see how much you owe. Even with this 5 percent vig, the bank wager has only a −1.17 percent expected value, making it an even better bet than the player bet. The tie, on the other hand, is a poor bet. With a house edge of 14.04 percent, it's among the worst wagers in the casino.

In case you're curious, here's how the odds of these various bets are calculated. First, let's look at the probability of obtaining a winning hand for the bank and for the players. We can ignore the probability of a tie, since a tie is a "push" for anyone playing as either bank or players. It is known that the bank wins 50.68 percent of all nontie hands and loses 49.32 percent of them. You're just going to have to believe me that these numbers are correct; the calculations are far too complex to be carried out here. However, knowing these figures, it's easy to calculate the expected value of a player bet. For simplicity let's pretend we're making 100 wagers of $1 each. On such a series of bets on players an average of 49.32 of these will be winners and 50.68 will be losers. So the player can be expected to lose a total of $50.68 and win a total of $49.32. Subtracting yields an expectation of −$1.36 for each $100 wagered, or a house edge of 1.36 percent.

Similarly for the bank bet there will be, on average, 50.68 winning bets and 49.32 losing bets, but, because of the vigorish, each winning bet yields only $.95. Hence the 50.68 winning bets can be expected to yield $.95 × 50.68 = $48.15, and the losing bets, as before, will cost $49.32. Subtracting yields an expectation of −$1.17 for each $100 wagered, or a house edge of 1.17 percent.

Ties have been calculated to occur on 9.55 percent of all hands. So the true odds on a tie are 9.47 to 1. To calculate this, simply divide 9.55 into 100, which yields 10.47 as the true payoff on the bet. Since you always get your initial bet back, the proper odds for the wager are 9.47 to 1. But the casino payoff on a tie bet is only 8 to 1, which means that rather than ending up with $10.47 you end up with only $9. This represents a loss of $1.47 out of $10.47, or a −14.04 percent expected value for the bet. I wouldn't make this bet with Monopoly money.

Clearly the standard bank and player bets in baccarat give the player a better game, statistically speaking, than roulette, although it is not quite as good for the player as craps played correctly. However, given the elegance of the surroundings and the leisurely pace of the game, it is not a bad game to play.

Mini-Baccarat

Mini-baccarat is played at a blackjack-size table with up to seven players, each sitting at a specific numbered position. The rules of the game are exactly the same as those in the full version of baccarat. However, the feeling of the game differs in that the tables are typically out on the casino floor itself, amid the noise and crowds rather than in the cloistered and elegant baccarat pit, and the game is handled by a single dealer who deals both the players and bank hands and handles all bets and commissions. The agonizing squeezing of the cards by the participants is not permitted here; indeed, the players do not touch the cards. Mini-baccarat is typically played for much lower stakes than the full version. Players who like the odds of baccarat but are either intimidated or simply put off by the showiness of the baccarat pit prefer to play the mini version.

Counting Cards in Baccarat

Since baccarat is played with a fixed number of cards and with fixed rules, the possibility suggested itself that, as in blackjack, particular combinations of cards might be advantageous to the players and/or the house. For example, if it could be discovered that a deck rich in one or another combination of cards favored the players or the bank, appropriate adjustments could be made in wagering to exploit these situations when they arose. As we shall see in chapter 5, this is exactly how card counters gained an edge over the house in blackjack.

However, none of these attempts yielded anything of value in baccarat. One analysis carried out by Griffin, Thorp, and Friedman identified particular situations—mainly involving 2's and 3's (which tend to favor the player) and 7's and 8's (which tend to favor the bank)—that provide the player with a minuscule edge. Unfortunately, the edge is so small and occurs so infrequently that it has no practical value. Hence, baccarat appears, from the house's point of view, to be safe from the kinds of betting strategies that reveal blackjack's vulnerability.

CRAPS

Craps is the fastest, most volatile, and loudest table game played in casinos. While more money may be lost and won in a shorter period of time in baccarat, owing to the enormous sums many players wager, no game can match craps for the proportion of one's bankroll that can be won or lost in routine play in remarkably short periods of time. Although it appears to have lost a bit of its popularity in the last couple of years, craps is still right up there with blackjack in terms of the number of people who play and the profits generated for the house.

The allure of craps comes from a number of features. First, it is fast; the dice are rolled every thirty seconds or so, and a large number of different bets can be made on each and every roll. Second, it offers the widest array of wagers with the greatest range of payoffs of any game in the casino, giving players with a quest for diversity all they could ask for. Third, by virtue of the speed and multiplicity of wagers, it offers the player the very best and the very worst of the basic casino table games. You can quickly win or lose a stunning proportion of your bankroll. A simple, basic $10 bettor, for example, can win or lose over $100 in about a minute and a half while making nothing but the most ordinary (and most recommended) of bets. Finally, the culture of craps gives the player something that no other casino game does: the opportunity for sensible, mature adults to scream, holler, whine, and cheer like pubescent teenagers. All in all, craps is a game for the masses.

When a craps game is in full swing, there may be twelve or fourteen players ringing the table with racks of chips in front of them and more in their hands, drinking, yelling, cursing, littering the table with white, red, green, and black checks, exhorting the dice along, and engaging in some of the most wonderful and bizarre rituals to be seen anywhere in the casino. No one is as superstitious as the inveterate craps player. If a shooter is on a hot roll and one of the dice should hop over the side wall onto the floor, groans of despair will be heard from players around the table, who are sure that whatever magic the dice had will be lost by contact with the carpet.

Craps players also develop oddly stereotyped ways of throwing the dice. I played one evening with a shooter who would not throw the dice until a "test roll" yielded one or another of his "magic" numbers. He would give the dice a short roll out of his hand in front of his position and look at the result. If he didn't like it he would do it again—and again. One time he did this fully six times until he was satisfied. Only then would he throw the dice down the table. This player would also smoke his cigar only while he held the dice. After his roll ended he put it out, and he only relit it after the dice traveled around the table back to him. Other players will preposition the dice by turning them over and over until the numbers they want show before throwing them. Someone like myself who picks up the dice and tosses them without looking is a rarity—and is often regarded with suspicion by other players.

The only thing that seems to explain these odd rituals and superstitions is that craps is the only Type L casino game in which the player actually *does* something that is relevant to the outcome. A crap shooter can actually think, "If only I had thrown the dice a little bit harder last time I wouldn't have thrown that 7" or "If I had only started with a 4 up on the second die instead of a 3 I'd still be holding the dice." In roulette the dealer puts the ball into play; in baccarat players draw the cards from the shoe but their order is fixed by the shuffle and cut of the decks. A baccarat player holding the shoe never thinks that he or she could have controlled the outcome of a hand; whatever card is next in the shoe is next in the shoe no matter how it gets pulled out. It is true that the slots are operated by the players but only in the sense that they "release" the wheels to spin; they do not actually control the spin itself.

For a novice, a craps table in full swing can be a bit intimidating. A table full of players cheering and cursing, tossing checks about the table, and yelling arcane things like "Press my hard 8" and "A deuce on the yo and five horn high 12" is enough to send someone back to the baccarat table, where they don't have to know the rules to play, or to the slots, where mindless lever pulling or button pressing is all that is required. On the other hand, once you learn what the game is all about and what all these people are doing, it becomes one of the most seductive of table games. Nowhere else do you have such an array of possible wagers. Nowhere else do you have the opportunity to make multiple bets on multiple outcomes on each and every play. Nowhere else can you change bets once made by raising or lowering the amount wagered or even remove a previously made bet. And nowhere else do you actually hold the objects of the gamble in your hot little hand and thus, in some sense, make the whole thing happen.

From the betting side, craps has bets that go from an expected value of –16.67 percent of money wagered to an expected value of −.61 percent (or even less in some casinos). The former wager will extract money from your pocket at a rate that is twenty-seven times the latter! One craps wager is the very worst that can be found at any of the standard casino table games, another is among the very best. Quite a range.

Craps has also attracted the attention of "systems" players, players who have worked out what they believe to be systems for betting (generally based on one or another form of bet progression) that increase the likelihood of large payoffs and highly profitable runs at the table. While betting systems can be used in any game, they are more commonly employed by craps players because the speed of the game gives a progressive systems player a chance for very large gains in shorter periods of time. The craps section of virtually every gambling book I have examined gives the player advice about some wagering system to use when rolling the dice. Alas, I will not recommend any such system. It is with regret that I inform my readers that all such systems fail. In chapter 11 we'll look more closely at the issue of wagering systems in Type L games. There we will examine several of the systems that have been proposed and the kinds of outcomes each yields. We will discover why betting systems are mathematically doomed to fail.

The Play of the Game

Craps is played on a large table like the one shown in figure 3-4. Note that there is some variation in these tables—in their size, in the layout itself, and in the odds offered on particular bets. As we go through the various wagers marked on the table, how to make them, and what the

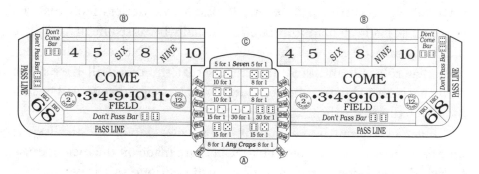

Figure 3-4 A typical craps table. The stickman or stickwoman stands at the position marked A, the dealers who handle the betting and payoffs at positions marked B, and the boxman or boxwoman who controls the game sits in position C.

payouts are for each, I'll note where differences may be found from casino to casino and what such differences mean for the player's bottom line. For now, let's just use the layout in figure 3-4 as representative of craps as it is played in North America.

Note that the layout contains two identical sections, one at each end of the table, and a single section in the middle. The middle area is for what are called the "proposition" bets, which are handled by the stick-man or stickwoman. The two identical areas are for the players at the ends of the table to make other wagers, some of which are placed directly by the players and some of which are handled by a dealer.

The table itself, unlike the tables for all other casino games, has a wall around it. The top of the wall contains cutouts in which players keep their chips; the inner surface of the wall is covered with an irregu-lar surface with cones of rubber or soft sponge jutting out from it. When the dice are thrown they must be tossed with sufficient force so that both of them hit the inside of the wall and bounce off. Moreover, the shooter must throw the dice from his or her own end of the table up against the far wall. The reasons for these regulations are simple. Dice "mechanics" can control the roll of dice with remarkable accuracy and greatly increase the likelihood of particular outcomes. For example, in what is called a "blanket roll," since it was first perfected by cheats who played in private games where the dice were thrown on a blanket, the shooter slides the dice so they don't tumble, thereby gaining control over the outcome of the roll. Throwing the dice with sufficient force to make them bounce off the irregular inner surface of the wall makes it virtually impossible to control the outcome. If one of the dealers feels that the shooter has made an inappropriate roll, usually because one or both dice did not bounce off the wall, he or she will call out "No roll," which ren-ders that roll null and void and means that the dice will have to be thrown again. A shooter who consistently makes such throws will be for-bidden to throw the dice.

The dice are put into action by the shooter. He or she throws the dice for everyone at the table. That is, bets are made on the dice no mat-ter who is throwing them. A shooter will continue to throw the dice (termed "holding the dice") until he or she rolls a 7—or "sevens out." At that point the dice pass to the next player clockwise around the table. When your turn comes you will be given a set of five or six dice from which you select two for use. You are under no obligation to throw the dice. Many craps players, in fact, do not like to throw the dice and simply pass their turn to the person on their left.

It all begins with a "come out" roll. If the shooter throws a 7 or 11 on this roll it is an immediate win for anyone betting the pass line and an immediate loss for anyone betting the don't pass line. If the shooter throws craps (2, 3, or 12) pass line bettors lose and don't pass bettors win. If any other number is thrown it becomes "the point." If the shooter throws this number again before throwing a 7, he or she "makes the point" and all pass line bettors win and don't pass bettors lose. If the shooter throws a 7 before the point ("sevens out") then all pass line bettors lose and don't pass bettors win.

There is no limit to how long a shooter may hold the dice. The shortest possible turn is two throws—establish a point on the first and seven out on the next. Establishing a point comes about when a 4, 5, 6, 8, 9, or 10 is thrown on the first roll, which is more likely to happen than anything else, accounting for fully 24 (or .667) of the possible outcomes. Once the point has been established (no matter what it is) the most likely of all possible outcomes on the second roll is, of course, the 7, which occurs on 1/6 (or .167) of all throws. The two-throw roll is the most common of all and will happen roughly 11 percent of the time (.667 $\times$ .167 = .11139). The dice can, however, be held for a long time; rolls lasting up to an hour and amounting to more than a hundred throws are not unknown. If you ever get lucky enough to be at a table where the shooter holds the dice for just ten minutes or more you will find it a most profitable experience—provided, of course, that you are betting with the shooter.

The game is run by a crew of four dealers and a boxman or boxwoman. Two dealers stand in the two spots marked "B" in figure 3-4. Each is responsible for the bets, collections, and payoffs made at his or her end of the table. A third dealer, usually called the stickman or stickwoman, stands in the position marked "A," in front of the area for the proposition bets. He or she is responsible for the dice, using a hooked stick to rake them in after each throw and push them back to the shooter for the next throw (dealers never touch the dice with their hands). The stickman or stickwoman also takes care of the proposition bets that are made by players and is responsible for keeping up a running patter on the game, calling for the shooter to throw, announcing when the dice are out, what the throw resulted in, when a point is made, and when the shooter sevens out. A good stickman or stickwoman can keep a game rolling along efficiently and encourage additional wagers from players with friendly but often persuasive chatter, rather like a barker in the old carnies. The boxman or boxwoman sits between the two dealers in the spot marked "C" in figure 3-4—right in front of all the chips. It is his or her responsibility to oversee the game. The job covers counting out cash and chips, keeping track of and verifying the often fast, furious, and confusing array of bets, collections, and payouts, and settling occasional arguments between players and dealers. For example, if a player disputes whether a particular bet was or was not on the table or whether a payout was made correctly, the boxman's or boxwoman's decision is final. While the dealers wear the casino's standard uniform, the boxman or woman, who is part of the casino's management staff, will typically wear a suit or other business clothing. The crew of four dealers usually works together every day; the boxman or boxwoman is not part of this fixed group. The crew of dealers rotates from position to position every twenty minutes or half hour so that three are always working and one is on break.

Before we get into the varied ways in which bets can be made in craps and the odds associated with each, let's take a quick look at the several outcomes that can occur when the dice are thrown and the probabilities associated with each.

Number	Combinations that Yield It	Number of Ways to Obtain It	Probability
2	1-1	1	.028
3	1-2, 2-1	2	.055
4	1-3, 2-2, 3-1	3	.083
5	1-4, 2-3, 3-2, 4-1	4	.111
6	1-5, 2-4, 3-3, 4-2, 5-1	5	.139
7	1-6, 2-5, 3-4, 4-3, 5-2, 6-1	6	.167
8	2-6, 3-5, 4-4, 5-3, 6-2	5	.139
9	3-6, 4-5, 5-4, 6-3	4	.111
10	4-6, 5-5, 6-4	3	.083
11	5-6, 6-5	2	.055
12	6-6	1	.028

The situation is pretty clear. A 7 is the only number that can be thrown no matter what number appears on one of the dice. Hence, 7 is the most likely outcome, accounting for fully six of the thirty-six possible outcomes (or nearly 17 percent of the tosses of a pair of six-sided dice). Herein lies the essence of craps. A 7 on what is known as the "come-out" roll of the dice makes a winner out of all pass line bettors and a loser out of all don't pass bettors. Conversely (and perversely), on all subsequent throws a 7 makes a loser out of these same pass line bettors and a winner out of the don't pass bettors. The 7 also has a direct impact on a host of the more exotic bets at the table. The whole game rises and falls on the appearance or nonappearance of the 7, the most likely of outcomes. If this language seems arcane, hang in there. It's second nature to a craps player and it will all be explained in the next couple of sections.

Ways to Bet in Craps

Craps can be intimidating to the uninitiated. When I first began playing I felt very much an outsider and more than a bit uncomfortable. Don't worry about it. If you follow the advice given in this section you'll be fine. Just belly up to the table and place your bets. If at any time you feel confused, simply ask one of the dealers or one of the floorpersons behind the table to help you out. They will be glad to be of assistance. A well-managed casino is always on the lookout for new players, and its floorpersons and pit bosses are encouraged to be cooperative.

Of all the various wagers that can be made at the table it is easiest to begin with the most basic of bets, those that involve the pass line and the don't pass line. These bets are made on the come-out roll, and virtually all players, no matter what other bets they may have a fondness for, will make one of these, usually the pass line bet. After these, we will look at the come and don't come bets, which are exact parallels of the pass and don't pass bets but are made on the rolls after a point has been established. Third, we will examine the most interesting bets in the game, the odds or free odds bets. These bets are the only bets that can be made at any of the Type L games where the player is even with the house, for they are paid off at true odds. Finally, we will look at the array of other wagers available to the player. Frankly, I would really prefer not to even mention this last category of wagers, let alone tell you how to make them. These include some of the worst bets that can be made in a casino.

Yet they are oddly popular, and if you watch any craps table in action you will see many players making one or more of these bets on virtually every roll. If you get nothing else out of this book, I hope you will become convinced never, ever, to make any of these bets.

Pass Line

The pass line bet is the basic bet in craps. It is made at the come-out roll, when a new shooter first throws the dice, or after a point has been made. To make a pass line bet simply lean over the table and place your wager in the area marked "pass line." Protocol calls for you to place your bet directly in front of you to make it clear whose bet is whose. With up to twelve or even fourteen people at a table, things can get hectic. As I noted earlier, if the shooter throws a 7 or an 11 on the come-out roll, you will win your bet. If the shooter throws a 2, 3, or 12 (singularly and collectively known as "craps"), you will lose your bet. If any other number (4, 5, 6, 8, 9, or 10) is thrown, that number becomes the point. If the shooter throws the point number again before throwing a 7, you will win your bet. If he or she throws a 7 before throwing the point you will lose. Winning pass line bets are paid off at even odds.

The odds favor the pass line bettor on the come-out roll. The probability of a 7 is .167 and the probability of an 11 is .055, giving you a .222 chance of an immediate win, while the probabilities of 2, 3, and 12 are .028, .055, and .028, respectively, giving only a collective .111 chance of a craps and an immediate loss. However, once a point has been established, the odds shift against you, since 7, which will now lose for you, is the most likely of all possible outcomes. Overall, the pass line bet has an expected value of -1.414 percent of money wagered. This is not a bad bet at all. It compares quite favorably with roulette's -5.26 percent and is only a tad worse than the expected value of baccarat's two basic bets.

By the way, on the come-out bet a disk or button is placed on the "don't pass bar 12" rectangle on the layout with its "off" side up. After a point is established the button is turned over so that "on" shows and it is moved to the line just above the point number (see figure 3-4). If a shooter makes his or her point, the button is turned to "off" and is moved back to the don't pass spot for the new come-out roll. A new player coming up to a table in full swing can tell exactly what is going on by looking at where the button is.

Don't Pass Line

Like the pass line bet, this bet is also made on the come-out roll. To make a don't pass line bet simply lean over the table and place your wager in the area marked "don't pass bar 12" (the "12" is usually represented by two dice, each showing a 6 on its face). Once again, make your bet in front of where you are standing. However, to make don't pass bets you need to be on the appropriate side of the table. If you look at the layout in figure 3-4 you will see that while the pass line wraps all the way around the layouts, the don't pass line is much shorter and doesn't wrap around. Don't pass bettors are much less common than pass bettors, and so the area for them to wager in is much smaller. Notice also that "bar 12" on the layout. Should a 12 come up, the bet is a "push" or standoff, with neither side winning or losing. Without this element, the don't pass bet would have a positive expectation. With it the edge is restored to the house.

Don't pass bets are won and lost in a virtual mirror image to the pass line bets, and, like them, are paid at even odds. That is, if any craps (other than 12) is thrown on the come-out roll, you win. If a 7 or 11 is thrown, you lose. After the point has been established, you win if a 7 is thrown before the point number but lose if the point number is thrown first. Your chances of winning on the come-out roll are, of course, rather poor. Only a 2 or a 3 will win for you, which gives you only a .083 shot, while your chances of losing are nearly triple that at .222. However, once the point has been established, the odds shift so that they are now in your favor, since 7 is the most likely number to be rolled. The extent to which you have an edge depends on what the point is. If it is 4 or 10, you have a 2-to-1 edge (since there are six ways to get a 7 but only three ways to get either a 4 or a 10). Similarly, a 5 or a 9 gives you a 3-to-2 edge and a 6 or an 8 gives you a 6-to-5 advantage. Overall, the don't pass line bet has an expected value of -1.403 percent, which is slightly (.011 percent) better than the pass line bet. For practical purposes, though, this difference is meaningless.

Come

A come bet is exactly the same thing as a pass bet, only it is made after a point has been established. If you wish to make a come bet, reach out in front of you and place your wager in the "come" area on the layout. Come bets are commonly made by pass line bettors who are look-ing for more action. They will place a pass line bet on the come-out roll and come bets on subsequent rolls. Come bets are paid off like pass line bets. If the shooter throws any craps you will lose. If 7 or an 11 is thrown you will win, although a 7 will, of course, cause you to lose any previous pass line bet you may have made. Once a point has been established, you are in the same situation as with a pass line bet: A 7 will lose; the point number will win.

Once you have placed, say, two come bets in addition to your original pass line bet, three different points can win for you. Here's how this happens. Suppose the come-out throw produced an 8, making that the point for the pass line. On the next throw you made a come bet and the dice came up 6. The 6 is now the point for this second bet. On the next throw you make another come bet and this time a 4 comes up. You now have three separate points. If the shooter throws a 4 or a 6 or an 8 you will win that bet. If the shooter throws a 7 you will, of course, lose all three bets. Perhaps you can now begin to see the attraction of craps and the wonderful things that can happen when a shooter is "throwing num-bers." If you cover the board with come bets and the shooter is throwing 4's, 9's, 8's, 6's, and so forth with abandon, you can win money on every single throw. That is when all the hollering and cheering is heard from a craps table. This is what craps players mean when they talk about "hot dice" or a shooter "on a roll." However, be careful. If the shooter throws a 7, you will lose all of these bets. This is why "Seven out" is such a ter-rible thing to hear in craps, for it can wipe out your entire board. In fact, it can be really painful if you make a pass line bet, three come bets, and a 7 shows up on the very next roll. You will lose all four of these bets with-out ever taking a penny off the table.

If there are six or seven players at one end of a table and each of them is making a series of come bets for different amounts of money, it can get pretty confusing and the board can get rather congested. How-ever, if you watch the table you will see that the checks you put out for your come bets are not left where you placed them but are moved by the dealer to the numbered square that marks the new point for that roll. The reason for this is simple. The button marks the point for all the pass line bettors on the come-out roll, but since any player can make a come bet on any subsequent roll there has to be a way to keep track of who has made what wagers. Moreover, the dealer will not just put your checks in the box at random; if you watch carefully you will note that the dealer has put your checks into a particular location within the numbered box. If you are standing in the very last position at the table, your checks will be placed in the upper corner of the box closest to your spot. The player standing next to you will have his or her chips placed in the middle of the top of the box next to yours, and so forth. This way the dealers know exactly who has made which come bets and who to pay off when a particular point is made. This also explains why dealers do not want you to change positions at the table, for it screws up the mnemonic device they use to keep track of who made what bets.

Each come line bet, since it is treated exactly like a pass line bet, has the same expected value of -1.414 percent of monies wagered.

Don't Come

Just as come bets are treated exactly like pass line bets, don't come bets are treated like don't pass bets. Don't pass bettors will typically make one or more don't come wagers after the point has been established, just as pass line bettors will make come bets. Don't come bets are paid off just as don't pass bets: a 2 or a 3 will produce a win, a 7 or an 11 a loss. Once a point has been established, don't come bets will be moved by the dealer to the small rectangle just above the point number. If the shooter throws a 7, all these bets are winners. If the shooter makes the point, these bets are losers. A don't come bettor can't get on an extended roll like a come bettor can, but if he or she has a number of bets up when the shooter sevens out, all of them become winners.

Don't come bets have the same expected value as don't pass bets: -1.403 percent.

Odds Bets

Odds or, as they are sometimes called, "behind the line" or "free odds"—bets are not marked anywhere on the standard craps table layout. They are, however, part of the standard game in all casinos and can be made in tandem with the bets already discussed. As was noted above, odds bets are unique in that they are paid off at the true odds. That is, the house has no edge on these bets. Their expected value is a pristine 0!

In order to place an odds bet you must first have on the table one of the four bets we have already discussed. The wagers differ slightly depending on whether you are betting pass and come or don't pass and don't come, so let's take them one at a time.

Taking the odds on pass and come bets: Odds bets are additional wagers that may be made on top of an original pass or come bet—you are, in essence, "pressing" (or increasing) your original bet. However, unlike the original pass or come bet, which is paid off at even odds, the free odds bet is paid off at the true odds and so your winnings will depend on what the point is. For example, suppose you have an original pass line bet of $5 and the point comes up 4. You now "take the odds" on the point by making an additional $5 bet. If a 4 comes up before a 7 you will win $5 on your original pass line bet and $10 on the odds bet (since there are twice as many ways to throw a 7 as a 4). Of course, if the shooter throws a 7, you will lose both bets.

The odds bets are paid off depending on the point. The true odds for each particular point are as follows:

Point	Odds
4 or 10	2 to 1
5 or 9	3 to 2
6 or 8	6 to 5

Because of these different payoffs you should make odds bets that allow the dealers to make easy payoffs. That is, a free odds bet on a point of 5 or 9 should be an even number and an odds bet on a point of 6 or 8 should be in multiples of $5. For a point of 4 or 10, it doesn't matter.

To take the odds on a pass line bet, reach down and place your wager behind your original pass line bet, just off the area marked "pass line." To take the odds on a come bet, put the chips on the table in the layout and tell the dealer that you wish to "take the odds" on whatever number was just rolled. It is easiest if you state the point number and the amount you are betting—to make a $10 odds bet on a point of 4, simply put down $10 in checks and say "Ten odds four." The dealer will take the chips and place them on top but slightly off-center of your come bet.

The size of the odds wager that you can make will depend on the rules of the casino. Every casino will permit a "single odds" bet; that is, one that matches the bet made on the pass or come. If your original bet was $5, your maximum odds bet is $5 (or $6 on 5 or 9). Some casinos (these days, most) will permit you to take "double odds." This means that you can wager up to twice your original bet. If you have a $5 pass line or come bet, you may make a $10 odds bet on top of it. Some casinos permit three- or five-times odds, and a few allow ten-times odds. One, the legendary Binion's Horseshoe in downtown Las Vegas, will, on occasions, offer its customers twenty-times odds.

The larger the odds bet the casino will allow, the smaller the house edge on the total bet becomes. The reason is simple. Since the odds bet is merely a way of pressing your original wager, its effect is to blunt the edge the house has on that original wager. Recall that the house has a 1.41 percent edge on the original pass and come bets. On the free odds bets, however, the house has no edge. Hence, on the combined bet the house has a slight edge on one part of it but no edge on the rest, and as a result, the house edge on the combined bets is lowered. The effect of the odds bets on the house edge on the total wager is as follows:

Odds Bet	House Edge (%)
None	1.41
Single odds	.85
Double odds	.61
Triple odds	.47
Five-times	.32
Ten-times	.18

No other Type L game gives the player anything like this. Five-times odds, which can be found at several casinos in Las Vegas and Atlantic City, cuts the house edge down to a minuscule one third of 1 percent of monies wagered, and ten-times odds cuts it to less than one fifth of 1 percent.

Finally, note that odds bets are off during a come-out roll. Suppose the shooter makes his or her point and your pass line bets get paid off. The disk is now turned to "off" and there is no point. But if you have been making come bets and taking the odds, you may have several wagers still on the table. Your come bets are on here but the odds bets are not. Thus, if the shooter throws a 7 on the come-out roll your come bets are losers but not your odds bets, and these will be returned to you.

Similarly, if the shooter throws a point number on which you have a bet, you will win your come bet but not the odds bet. It will simply be returned to you.

Laying the odds on don't pass and don't come bets: These bets are handled just like the odds bets on pass and come except that here, rather than taking the odds, you must lay the odds. Once the point has been established the don't pass/don't come bettors actually have the odds in their favor. So the true odds requires them to risk more for less gain. In a nutshell, the bet here is the mirror image of the one made by the pass line and come bettor. Hence the true odds are as follows:

Point	Odds
4 or 10	1 to 2
5 or 9	2 to 3
6 or 8	5 to 6

To lay the odds on a don't pass wager, place your bet behind your original wager. To lay the odds on a don't come wager, place your checks on the table and tell the dealer that you want to lay the odds. The dealer will move your don't come bet into the area just above the point number and stack your odds bet on top and slightly off-center of that bet. If the shooter sevens out you will win your bet and be paid off at even odds on the original wager and true odds on the odds bet. For example, suppose you have made an original don't pass bet of $5. When the point came up 4, you laid the odds with an additional $4 (or more, depending on the casino's rules). If the shooter now sevens out, you win your original bet at even odds and the odds bet at 1 to 2. Of course, if the shooter throws the point, you will lose both bets. Just as with the odds bets on pass and come, you may make several don't come bets and lay the odds on all.

Because the don't pass and don't come wagers have slightly better expected values than the pass and come wagers (-1.403 percent versus -1.414 percent), laying the odds on these bets has the tiny advantage of about one one-hundredth of 1 percent over the comparable pass and come bets.

Some Words of Caution

Most books (correctly) advise their readers to restrict their craps play to the bets we have just discussed and encourage them to take or lay maximum odds. The argument is basically sound. From the point of view of probability theory, these bets give the player the best odds. Indeed, these are the best odds to be found in any Type L game any-where in the casino. However, before you cash in Aunt Sadie's hand-me-down brooch and head for the nearest casino, remember that the house still has a statistical edge. Moreover, if you increase the size of your wagers markedly in order to take advantage of the high odds bets, you will increase your session-to-session variance and run the risk of taking a serious bath on any given day.

To get a feeling for the problem, it is important to understand just how much money a craps player can put on the table during a session of play. For example, even a moderate stakes player making nothing but pass and come bets and taking double odds will wager in the neighbor-hood of $1,000 over an hour or two at the table. If this seems like a high estimate, it isn't. The typical hour will see you making forty bets. If you start with a mere $5 base bet, you will put approximately $600 into play every hour. If you move up to taking five-times odds, you will be putting $1,200 in play an hour. This is serious money for the average punter, and a long run of cold dice can get very expensive.

So what should the average crap shooter do? What's the *real* best advice that can be given? Theoretically, what you should do is find a table with a minimum wager that is *below* your typical bet. That is, if you feel comfortable with a base bet of $10, look for a $5 table and take single odds. This way, your $10 is being bet against a house edge of −.85 per-cent rather than one of −1.41 percent. Similarly, if your base bet is $20, try to find a $5 table that will allow triple odds. Now your $20 is only up against a −.47 percent edge. The point is to stay within your established wagering range while improving your expected value.

Finally, let me end this section with a little story that helps to make my point about odds, probabilities, and cash on the table. At the famous Binion's Horseshoe, the ten-times odds recently attracted the attention of a serious high roller. As the story goes, the dice were unusually kind to this fellow, and over a period of about ten days he managed to take away $1.1 million. Did the casino suffer? Well, in one small sense it did, since Binion's lost over a million to the high roller. However, in another and much more real sense it profited wondrously. By the third day, word had got out that something really extraordinary was happening downtown at Binion's and every tinhorn in Vegas headed there to watch the action—and, of course, to be a part of history. Needless to say, all these sightseers proceeded to play and, not at all surprisingly, play at levels higher than normal. The wonder of watching this guy raking in thousands of dollars an hour, hour after hour, day after day, got the crowd into a kind of "gold rush fever" mentality. Everyone wanted to get rich quick. Well, only Binion's got rich. The high roller might have walked out with over a million, but Binion's took in four times that much from the hordes of hopefuls who bombed the tables with their chips. It isn't for nothing that Binion's is one of the more successful casinos in Las Vegas.

Right and Wrong Bettors

Players who bet the pass line, the come, and take the odds are known as "right" players, or players who bet "with the dice." The pass line is also known as the "front line," and when a shooter makes his or her point, the dealers will often call out "Pay the front line." Although, as we have seen, the don't pass and don't come line bets have a better (although insignificantly better) expected value for the player, they are much less popular. In fact, many craps players look with disdain at players who bet "against the dice," known as "wrong" bettors who bet the "back line." Although common sense and rational action indicate that the "wrong" bets are the right ones, for all my cajoling about making only optimal plays in the casino I must confess that I bet only pass and come lines and take the odds. True, I give up around one one-hundredth of a percentage point, but I do it for the sheer joy of being with the rest of the table when a shooter goes on a hot roll. These are moments unmatched in the casino. The dice are hot, the shooter is on a roll, and everybody is making money and letting everyone within earshot know about it—of course, the bedraggled wrong bettors are all alone, ignored and looking distinctly out of it. There is absolutely nothing fun about being a wrong bettor. You win only when all the right bettors (usually the rest of the table) lose. There is no cheering, no collective joy at winning, no camaraderie. It is almost as though you have to slink away with your winnings like some slumlord whose profits came at the expense of everyone else. I am a right bettor and proud of it. If I stay at a table for an hour, which is about my limit for a single session, and make a total of about $4,000 in bets, I am costing myself, on average, about seventy cents over what a wrong bettor would expect. I can handle it.

Other Wagers

Craps offers a large array of other bets. I suppose I'm under obligation to at least note and characterize these, though I really don't want to. With the possible exception of place bets on 6 and 8, which are only moderately bad bets, the others range from the merely awful to the breathtakingly bad. Some of these bets actually approach casino disaster areas—like the Big Six Wheel (which I will not discuss) and keno (which is dealt with in the next chapter).

Place Bets

There is a dreadful lack of understanding about place bets. A place bet, in a nutshell, is a side bet that a particular number will be rolled before a 7. All of the numbers that can become point numbers for a pass line player are open for a place bet. To make a place bet, simply give your checks to the dealer, who will place them in the appropriate position on the layout. Place bets are "off" on the come-out roll but operative on all other rolls of the dice.

One way to think about a place bet is that it is analogous to a come bet with the odds except that the player may make the bet on any number at any time. The price paid for this is that the payoff is at different odds—*odds that favor the house*. Players who like lots of action and who want to have several, if not all, of the numbers covered like to make place bets. In fact, as soon as the point has been established many players will make a place bet on every number other than the point, which they will have covered with a pass line bet and the odds. The casino obliges these bettors by allowing them to make all these bets, but it extracts a price. Unlike the odds bets, they are not paid off at the true odds. The following table shows each of the possible place bets, along with the true odds, the payoff odds, and the house edge on each.

Number Bet	True Odds	Payoff Odds	House Edge
4 or 10	2 to 1	9 to 5	6.67%
5 or 9	3 to 2	7 to 5	4.09%
6 or 8	6 to 5	7 to 6	1.52%

Notice that if you make these bets, you need to make them in denominations that can be paid easily. For example, place bets on 4, 5, 9, and 10 should be made in increments of $5, place bets on 6 and 8 in increments of $6.

What makes these bets attractive is their availability, since they can be made at any time other than the come-out roll, and their contribution to the player's desire for action. What makes them unattractive is their terrible odds when compared with the come bet with the odds.

Place bets are extremely popular. If you watch a typical craps table in action you will see more than half of the players making place bets. My feeling is that this popularity comes largely from simple ignorance of basic issues of probability theory. The main reason people make these bets rather than making a come bet and taking the odds is that, to quote one of my interviewees, "The number's got to come up twice to get paid on a come bet but only once on a place bet." This reasoning is at once both seductive and flawed. At first blush the argument seems to make sense—so much so that I have actually seen it put forward in books written by supposed experts on gambling. It's true that to collect on a pass bet your number has to be thrown twice, once to establish the point and a second time to win the bet. But the first throw doesn't mean anything. Some number *has* to come up. Whatever number it is doesn't matter, it just establishes the point. To argue, as several of the people I interviewed did, that a player could collect right away if he or she hit a place bet but not with a come bet completely misses the critical point. Players could collect on this first bet only if they *knew* what number was going to come up. But since they don't know, they are making the initial bet on a blind chance that the place bet they put on the table is going to get paid. In reality, the most likely thing to happen is that a 7 will be thrown, in which case all of the place bets are losers. Even if they do win, they are not being paid off at the true odds. The come bettor doesn't know *and doesn't care* what the point turns out to be. It is completely irrelevant. The come bettor knows that he or she is going to be able to take the odds on the initial wager and get paid off at the true odds on this bet no matter what the point is.

Put simply: The number really has to come up only once, not twice. Any number that can function as a point number that comes up is the first number, and if and when it is thrown later the come bettor has much better odds than the place bettor. The only real difference is this: The place bettor can make a bet on any number he or she wishes, whereas the come bettor can bet on a number only after it has been thrown. But that's okay. In the final analysis, who cares what number the point is? The come bettor who takes the odds certainly doesn't, for he or she is always going to give up only a small 1.414 percent edge to the house on the come bet and be even with the house on the odds bet. The place bettor is always going to be giving up between 1.52 percent and 6.67 percent of monies wagered. If this still seems mysterious, go back and read over the discussions of independent and dependent events in chapter 2. The two throws of the dice in this situation are independent events. Knowing the outcome on the first toss has no bearing on what will happen on the second.

However, if you must make place bets, restrict yourself to 6 and 8, where the house edge isn't so bad—being within .1 percent of that on the pass line bet. But trust me on this one, in the long run you are much better off being a little patient. Make come bets and take the odds on whatever number comes up.

One last issue here. Many players have told me that one of the reasons they make place bets is that it drives them nuts to see numbers come up that they don't have covered. These are players who typically hurl themselves into the game by making a pass bet and then immediately making place bets on every number other than the point. Such maniacal sorts should try this. Remember that while you are sitting at home in a comfortable chair reading this book, somewhere someone is throwing the dice and a 10 has just been rolled. Had you been there, you would be collecting big bucks. But you're not. You're at home reading this book. What difference does it make if you are standing at a table when a 10 is rolled or are home reading a book? None at all. Get used to this way of thinking. Practice by standing next to a craps table *without betting* and watch all those beautiful numbers being thrown. Who cares?

It doesn't make any difference in the long run. Each and every toss of the dice is one more independent event. That lovely 10 will still show up (or not) with the same expected probability when you do belly up to the table and put down your hard-earned cash.

Buy Bets

These bets are similar to place bets except for the manner in which they are made. Like place bets, they are paid off when the number "bought" is rolled before a 7. While place bets are paid off at set odds, buy bets are paid off at true odds—but the house charges a 5 percent vigorish on the wager. Since the smallest chip in play these days is $1, the minimum buy bet is $20, for which you must put up $21 (the $1 being the 5 percent vig). Hence, you are risking $21 to $20, which puts you at a 4.76 percent disadvantage. Only with the 4 and the 10 does a buy bet give you better odds than the comparable place bets.

To make a buy bet (which I hope you will never do), give your checks (in multiples of $21) to the dealer and tell him or her that you wish to "buy the 4" or "buy the 10." The wager will go in the same area as the place bets, but with a token on top that reads "buy."

Lay Bets

Lay bets are the wrong bettors' buy bets. That is, you are betting that a 7 will be rolled before the number you have wagered on. Like buy bets, they are paid off at true odds and the player must pay a 5 percent vigorish. However, here the vig is paid not on the wager but on the anticipated win. For example, if you wager against the 10, you put up $40 and pay a $1 vig, since if a 7 is rolled before a 10 you will be paid true odds of 1 to 2, which gives you a win of $20, 5 percent of which is $1.

Just as wrong bettors have a slight edge over right bettors on the pass and come wagers, so they give up less on the lay bets than right bettors do on buy bets. The house edge on lay bets is 4 percent on 6 and 8, 3.23 percent on 5 and 9, and 2.44 percent on 4 and 10. All these bets are far worse than betting don't pass/don't come and taking the odds.

Big 6 and Big 8 Bets

Luckily for the player, not all layouts have these bets. If playing at one that does, the best advice is to pretend you're playing at one that doesn't. These bets pay off if a 6 or 8 is rolled before a 7—exactly like a place bet on 6 or 8—except that they pay only at even odds. Place bets on 6 or 8 give the house a 1.52 percent edge. On the Big 6 and Big 8 bets, however, the house edge is 9.09 percent! Why anyone would make one of these bets is beyond me—especially when the place bets are there for folks with preternatural affection for 6's and 8's.

Field Bet

The field bet is one of what are called "one-roll" bets, where the player makes a wager that a particular outcome will occur on the very next roll. With field bets the wager is that one of the "field" numbers (2, 3, 4, 9, 10, 11, 12) will show up on the next throw of the dice. This bet runs from bad to worse depending on how it is paid off. In some casinos, the payoff is a straight 1 to 1, in which case the player is at an 11.11 percent disadvantage. Somewhat less devastating are casinos where the payoff is increased to 2 to 1 should a 2 or a 12 be rolled. Here the house edge is "only" 5.26 percent. This is a familiar number, yes? It's the same edge the house has in roulette with the American wheel. A tad better are casinos where either the 2 or the 12 (but not both) is paid off at 3 to 1. Here the house edge is reduced to 2.56 percent. Better, but still high.

Any 7

This is one of the many proposition (or "prop") bets that are marked on the layout in the center section in front of the stickman or stickwoman. Of all the bets at craps, this is the ultimate, the very worst. It's a one-roll bet that a 7 will appear on the next roll. It is paid off at 5 to 1 and has a house edge of a staggering 16.67 percent. 'Nuf said.

Any Craps

Another one-roll prop bet; it's a wager that craps (2, 3, or 12) will be thrown on the next roll. It is paid at 7 to 1 and the player is at a disadvantage of 11.11 percent.

Individual Number Bets

These are also one-roll prop bets that a particular number will come up on the next roll, and are marked on the center area of the layout. Bets on 2 and 12 are paid at 30 to 1, those on 3 and 11 at 15 to 1. The former have a house edge of 13.89 percent; the latter, 11.11 percent. Because "eleven" sounds like "seven," the latter bet is usually called the "yo." If you see a bettor toss a red check to the stickperson and yell out "Five on the yo," you know you have just seen someone make a really stupid bet.

These bets are rather popular. One reason is the potentially large instant payoff, which is always attractive to gamblers. However, it is my experience that the bet on the 11 is the most popular. I think people just like to yell out things like "A deuce on the yo."

Horn Bets

The standard horn bet combines wagers on 2, 3, 11, and 12 into a single wager. The bet is made in units of $4 since one fourth of the bet goes onto each of the four numbers. If one of them comes up, the payoff is made at the odds for that number and the other three bets are lost. A variation called the "horn high" bet takes five checks, and the extra wager goes on the 12.

Hardways

These are prop bets in which the gambler is betting that an even point number (a 4, 6, 8, or 10) will come up with the same denomination on each die (the "hard" way) before it either comes up the other ("easy") way or a 7 is thrown. For example, a hardways 4 bet is paid off if the dice come up $2-2$ before they come up either $3-1$ or $1-3$ or a 7 is thrown. Hardways 4 and 10 bets are paid off at 7 to 1 and the house has an 11.11 percent advantage. Hardways 6 and 8 bets are paid off at 9 to 1 and the house's edge is 9.09 percent. The different odds and payoffs here may, at first, seem strange. Shouldn't they all have the same odds since each hardways total can only be made in one way? It's true that they can only be made (won) in one way, but they can be lost in differing numbers of ways, and this is what causes the odds to change. For example, the hard 4 can be won one way $(2-2)$ but it can be lost in eight ways $(1-3, 3-1,$ or any of six ways to throw a 7). On the other hand a hard 6, which can only be won with $3-3$, can be lost ten ways $(1-5, 5-1, 2-4, 4-2,$ and six ways to throw 7). Hence, hardways 6 and 8 bets are less likely to be won than hardways 4 and 10 bets. But all of them are terrible bets that put the player at a severe disadvantage.

The Bottom Line

For all the apparent but utterly superficial complexity of craps, for all the hype surrounding the game, for all the in-group vernacular that accompanies the play, for all the stylized rituals, the superstitions, the flat-out weirdness of it all, craps can be a wonderful game for the player. It has, dead-on, the very best plays that can be found in any Type L game. In fact, if you just ignore all the nonsense that swirls around you as loser after loser tosses away money on prop bets, field bets, place bets, and all the rest, and narrow your focus on the pass, come, and odds bets, you will do just fine. In the midst of the cacophony of the game is a small, quiet spot. Find a low-minimum table, make the smallest possible pass line wagers, take one or two come bets and maximum odds on these. You will give up only about one half of 1 percent of money wagered. It is possible to play craps with all of the enthusiasm you can muster and stay about as close to even as is possible with a Type L game. Just stay the blazes away from all those other seductive but perilous bets that lay there in front of you on the green felt.

The following table summarizes the various bets available to the player in craps and the house advantage in each. It is, as they like to say in those ads in magazines, "for informational value only."

Wager	House Edge (% of money wagered)
Pass line	1.41
Pass line (or come) with single odds	.85
Pass line (or come) with double odds	.61
Pass line (or come) with triple odds	.47
Pass line (or come) with five-times odds	.32
Pass line (or come) with ten-times odds	.18
Don't pass (or don't come)	1.40
Don't pass (or don't come) with single odds	.84
Don't pass (or don't come) with double odds	.60
Don't pass (or don't come) with triple odds	.46
Don't pass (or don't come) with five-times odds	.31
Don't pass (or don't come) with ten-times odds	.17
Place bet on 4 or 10	6.67
Place bet on 5 or 9	4.09
Place bet on 6 or 8	1.52

Wager	House Edge (% of money wagered)
Buy bet on 4 or 10	6.67
Lay bet against 4 or 10	2.44
Lay bet against 5 or 9	3.23
Lay bet against 6 or 8	4.00
Field bet (all numbers paid at 1-1)	11.11
Field bet (2 and 12 paid at 2-1)	5.26
Field bet (2 or 12 paid at 3-1)	2.56
Big 6 or 8	9.09
Any 7	16.67
Any craps	11.11
Single numbers, 2 or 12	13.89
Single numbers, 3 or 11	11.11
Hardways 4 or 10	11.11
Hardways 6 or 8	9.09

Before we move on to more interesting games, a short story. There was this guy, a high roller who was shooting some serious craps at a very serious casino somewhere in Las Vegas. He was in one of those zones where he could do no wrong. All bets, from the banal to the exotic, won with magical grace. He tipped the dealers, he tipped his friends, and he tippled the rounds of scotch brought to him by well-tipped waitresses. His bankroll grew, his circle of supporters and hangers-on increased, and his bladder swelled. He turned, after a time in true desperation, to the boxman and asked if the game could be suspended while he sought relief. Alas, the reply was "no," the game must go on whether he was there or not. But, the man complained, if he were away from the game the rhythm would be disturbed, the gods of the cubes upset, the magic roll would surely end. They must stop the game for but a minute. No, the pit boss backed up the boxman. The game must go on. With surprising grace and no real warning for any of the people surrounding our hero, he quietly slipped his masculine member from his trousers and relieved himself on the floor under the craps table. "No way," he was heard to mutter, "am I going to break this roll."

Is this story true? Who knows? However, when I related it to a pit boss in Atlantic City he laughed and nodded knowingly. "You really haven't seen anything until you've seen what happens at the slots," he said. "We get these old ladies who simply will not leave a machine that has been paying off for them. They don't wear underwear to make it easier. You wouldn't believe how often we have to clean the carpets." Was this story true? Who knows?

4

SLOT MACHINES, KENO, AND LOTTERIES

*T*he games we will discuss in this chapter have distinctly poorer expected values for the player than those we looked at in the preceding chapter. However, they are immensely popular and are major revenue generators for private operators (in the case of slot machines and keno) and state treasuries (in the case of lotteries). As we shall see, their two main attractions are that they are easy to play, with virtually no decision making required, and that they hold out the possibility, however remote, of enormous wins.

Slots provide the casinos with the lion's share of their profits.

Indeed, in their wildest dreams, casino owners could not possibly have concocted anything to match a slot machine's raw capacity to generate profits. A slot machine takes up relatively little space; requires minimal maintenance and supervision; is in operation virtually twenty-four hours a day, 365 days a year; doesn't go on strike; works without Social Security payments or health benefits; and generates revenue for the house, depending on the machine, of between 1 percent and 16 percent of the cash dropped in the slot on each play. A single quarter slot in a high-traffic area in a major casino can produce in excess of $1,000 a week for the casino. It is no wonder that slots produce between 50 percent and 75 percent of the revenue of major casinos.

Although there is a bewildering variety of coin- and token-operated machines available these days, all of them have a common ancestor. They trace their lineage back to the original slot machine invented in the early 1890s by a Bavarian immigrant named Charles Fey, a machinist. Fey's machine established the design that is in use today: a set of three wheels with a variety of different symbols on them, with payoffs based on particular combinations of symbols. The wheels on these early machines were bedecked with hearts, spades, diamonds, and clubs, along with various other symbols, including horseshoes, stars, and Liberty Bells. The big payout occurred when three Liberty Bells showed up in a row. The machines quickly became known as "Liberty Bell slots," or simply "Bells."

Fey, who lived in San Francisco, installed his machines in numerous bars around the Bay Area, where they quickly became a palpable hit. The machines sat on top of the bar, where customers could easily play them. At first, the payoffs were free drinks, though cash soon became the medium of exchange. The machines accepted nickels (don't forget, in those days a nickel could buy a decent lunch) and paid out up to ten nickels if the right combination lined up in the window. Fey and the bar owners split the profits from each machine. Soon other manufacturers entered the scene with their own machines. Although all used the same basic format, the wheels were bedecked with a variety of different symbols, fruits being common (so common that in many places slots are still called "fruit machines").

Around the turn of the century, Herbert Stephen Mills widened the payout window so that the player could see not just the symbols on the payoff line but also those just below and above them. Today virtually all slots have this feature. One day I was walking through a casino in Atlantic City when I heard a strangled cry of agony and rushed over to see what had happened. A young woman was staring in disbelief at the window of the slot machine into which she had been pumping $1 coins. The row just above the payoff line displayed the symbols representing a progressive jackpot of over $22,000. On the payoff line itself were three unrelated symbols signifying absolutely nothing. The kind of delicious agony she felt would never have been possible if we had stayed with Fey's original design. Modern slot aficionados owe their deepest and most masochistic pleasures to the genius of Mr. H. S. Mills.

Actually, Mills was a genuine innovator and a clever man who understood the psychology of gambling. He also introduced the visible coin bin. Each coin that went into the machine could be seen behind a glass window. The gambler who played one of his machines was not merely playing for a theoretical payout; the nickels to be won were actually in plain sight. Mills also increased the size of the wheels in each machine so that each had twenty symbols, making certain combinations particularly unlikely. (If there is but one of a given symbol on each wheel, the chances that all three will line up are exactly 1 in 8,000; remember that in situations with independent events we multiply the likelihood of each of the several events to find the probability of the joint occurrence: $1/20 \times 1/20 \times 1/20 = 1/8,000$.) With this new design Mills introduced the concept of the big payoff, the jackpot. There is little doubt that, psychologically speaking, the jackpot is the single most important factor in the stunning popularity of the slot machine.

Indeed, all three of the games we will discuss in this chapter share this feature. For relatively little initial outlay the player can win life-affirming sums of money. Of course, the games also share a second, equally important feature: the odds against winning one of the jackpots are staggering. Oh, yes, they also share yet a third feature—the house edge in almost all of them is devastating to the player.

The jackpot fantasy keeps these folks going. They can feel it coming. They gravitate toward the progressive machines like moths to a flame.

The search is always on for the machine that is "due," the machine that "owes" them. Casinos know this; their press releases show winners holding oversized checks for $10,000, $50,000, and the granddaddy of them all (as of this writing, anyway), $8,545,506.82, won by a guy in Atlantic City in 1994 who wandered over to the slots because they wouldn't let him smoke his cigar at the blackjack table!

But there's more to these games than just the off shot at a big win. Slots, keno, and lotteries share another important element. They are easy to play. Except for the video poker machines, which I will discuss below, there are virtually no choices involved and no decisions to be made. Let's examine briefly the standard slot machine and its various spin-offs, including the video poker machines, where the player actually does get to make decisions that can make a difference. After that we'll take a fast glance at keno, a game unrivaled in the casino for giving the player the very worst of it. Finally we'll take a glimpse at the standard state-run lottery.

SLOT MACHINES AND THEIR BRETHREN

The Basic Slot

Modern slot machines are sophisticated, electronically controlled devices based on Mills's early design. Many of them now use a button to set the wheels spinning instead of the traditional handle; many also have electronic counters that keep track of how much players have bet and how much they have won. Others are completely electronically controlled and have even sacrificed the wheels for computer-generated symbols that scroll by on a video screen.

Slot machines come in a variety of forms and have diverse symbols on the wheels and numerous different payout systems, but all basically operate on a single principle: The payouts for lining up particular symbols are smaller than the true odds that those events will actually occur (except, of course, for the monstrous payouts that can occur on progressive jackpot machines). Some have a single payout line and pay out only on the sequence arrayed on that line. Others have up to five payout lines (three horizontal and two diagonal) and will pay out on sequences on all. Most variations involve the manner of betting and the payouts. The early machines were all single play; that is, one coin was inserted and there was only one payout. These have been replaced by more complex machines, such as:

Multiple-Coin Machines

Modern machines will accept two, three, and in many cases five coins for a single spin of the wheels. In some machines, each additional coin adds a payout line. However, on most multiple-coin machines, each successive coin increases the payout on a single line. The basic payouts go up at the rate you would expect. For example, on a three-coin machine the second coin doubles the payout, so that, for example, 3 cherries now pays out 40 coins rather than 20 and the third coin makes the payout 60. However, the third coin on these machines also brings the jackpot into play. For example, a multiple-coin machine might have a top payout line of 2,000 coins if one coin is played, 4,000 coins if a second coin is played, but 10,000 coins if the third is played.

This jackpot payout is significant in modern slot play. It has two important elements to it; one favors the player, one the house. First, it makes playing all three coins clearly the proper play (statistically speaking, anyway), since the jackpot makes the expected value of the third coin much greater than that for the first two. This element works to the advantage of the player, since the higher expected value of the third coin dilutes the house edge on the first two coins. However, it increases the base bet. This element works to the advantage of the house, since, as we have been noting ad nauseam, the bottom line is dictated by the percent of money wagered. If the house can get you to triple your base bet, its revenues will increase accordingly. The jackpot line will cut into the house edge somewhat, but it is easily made up for by the increase in the base wager.

Many casinos have banks of machines, all of which are connected to a central board that displays the payoff for hitting the jackpot. These machines are always multiple-coin machines, but the jackpot, instead of having a set worth, increases with each play. If no one has hit the jackpot for a long time it can grow to gargantuan size. However, it's important to understand just how screamingly unlikely it is that you will hit a jackpot. It's also worth noting that the house's edge is a tad larger with these progressive machines than it is with regular machines. The additional rake goes into the jackpot. There are two types of progressive machines currently sitting on the floors of casinos. We need to look at them separately to understand the odds facing the players.

Regular progressive machines: These are machines where each wheel stops at a symbol if the ratchet system clicks in for that symbol. For example, if you have a slot with four wheels and twenty-five locations on each, only one of which represents the symbol for jackpot, the chances of hitting the jackpot are $(1/25)^4 = 1/390,625$. When playing a machine with 390,625 possible combinations, to have just a 50 percent chance of hitting you would have to play 270,761 times. Suppose you are a maniacally dedicated slots player and make an average of four plays a minute for eight hours each day with a five-day workweek. It will still take you about six and a half months to make this many plays. Moreover, if we are talking about a $1 machine that takes three coins, which is typical for these large jackpots, you will be putting $812,286 into the machine during this six and a half months. And you are still giving yourself only an even shot to win. You could make millions of plays and still not hit the jackpot.

Actually, a potentially profitable scenario does present itself. Given the kind of machine we have been discussing, a dedicated group of players could come close to guaranteeing themselves a sizable profit—and such teams of "professional" slot players do exist. What they do is find a really huge jackpot, one that is way over the true odds of hitting it, and arrive with enough players to lock up every machine connected to that jackpot and enough money to keep going until one of them hits it. However, just in case you're now thinking about rounding up all of your buddies for a coup at the local slot jackpot, read on.

Computer-controlled progressive machines: The above approach works only with the older machines, where you can calculate the probability of hitting the jackpot by knowing the number of symbols on each wheel. Increasingly, modern slot machines are computer controlled and much more sophisticated. A machine with 30 symbols on each wheel may actually have up to 256 individual "spots" on each wheel that determine where it will stop, and only one of these may be keyed to the symbol for the jackpot. You may think that the odds of hitting the jackpot on a three-wheeler with 30 symbols is $30^3 = 27,000$, but it actually may be as high as $256^3 = 16,777,216$. It is no longer a simple matter to determine when a jackpot has grown to the point where it becomes a positive expectation play for the player.

By the way, if you do hit a jackpot *do not leave the machine*. Jackpots are usually paid by check, not by coins. When a jackpot is hit, bells will go off and lights will flash. Stay where you are until a casino employee comes over, verifies the jackpot, and arranges for payment. If you are playing at a machine where part of the payout is in coin and the rest is by check, don't walk away after the coins have finished dropping. There are scam artists just waiting to jump in front of your machine and claim the rest of your payoff.

Double-or-nothing machines: Some slots have a side wheel that can be engaged after a win. Suppose that 3 cherries show up with a win of 20 coins. The player may now attempt to either double the win or lose it all by playing the double-or-nothing wheel. This wheel has only two symbols on it, one for doubling and one for losing. These doubling wheels are honest even bets, with half the locations being doublers and half being losers. They do not change the house edge on the machine, but they do add a bit of spice to the game.

Nudge machines: Some slots have the added feature of a light that will come on occasionally, indicating that on that play you have the option of nudging a wheel forward or backward one location. When this happens, it occasionally is possible to turn a losing arrangement into a winner. Don't get too excited. The house edge on these machines is generally the same as for the regular slots.

The Bottom Line

The bottom line on slots is nothing short of dismal, except for the highest of high-rolling players. Depending on the machine, slots will return to the players between 85 percent and 98 percent on each play. The larger takeouts are, not surprisingly, from the lower-denomination machines, the smaller from the higher. The following table shows the slot payout averaged across all the slots in Atlantic City during a typical month. The figures are more or less reflective of the industry nationwide, although Las Vegas machines, particularly those in downtown casinos, tend to be a bit "looser" and pay better.

Cost per Play ($)	Average Payout (% of money wagered)
.05	84.8
.25	89.8
.50	90.9
1.00	91.9
5.00	94.5
25.00	94.7
100.00	96.1

Since the high-stakes machines are played less frequently and with larger denominations, the casino takes a smaller percentage from them than from the low-stakes machines, which are played much more frequently. This way, the casino balances the profit from all of its machines while managing to satisfy the desires of various levels of slot players. However, the slots are a regressive operation, and in terms of percentage of money wagered, the low-stakes player is at a serious disadvantage.

Actually, it is even worse than it looks. Casinos almost engage in false advertising when they publicize the payouts of their machines. For example, the $1 machines in the above table will be presented as something like "returning virtually 92 percent." Well, in a sense they do—in the same sense that a baccarat table could be advertised as "returning virtually 98.5 percent." Just as with any other gambling venture, players keep reinvesting their winnings, and the house edge slowly nibbles away at their bankrolls. With the slots holding an average edge of approximately 10 percent of money wagered, the casinos have a devastating advantage. And here's an interesting tidbit: While it was easy for me to determine what the casinos like to call the "average payout," I found it difficult to determine just what the typical drop for the average slot was. I won't reveal my sources here, so you'll have to take it on faith, but it turns out that in the Atlantic City casinos the average percent held runs in the neighborhood of 50 percent! It probably runs a tad less than that in Nevada, but even if it is around 35 percent or 40 percent it is devastating to the player. Compare this figure with the 25 percent PC in roulette, which is, as we saw in chapter 3, the worst of the table games. No wonder the slots are the bread and butter of casinos.

Is there a strategy to playing the slots? Nope. Sorry about that, but there just isn't. My recommendation is that you play for fun. Play at a level you can afford. Take your wins when they happen and enjoy them. When you lose, don't increase your level of play in an attempt to recoup losses. On multiple-coin machines, the jackpot won't come into play unless you play what they call "maximum coin." From a mathematical point of view, that is the proper play since it yields the highest expected value. However, it means that you are increasing your basic bet size, so beware.

Consider moving down to a cheaper machine and playing maximum coin. For example, if you routinely play the $1 machine one coin at a time, you move down to a quarter machine and play maximum coin. This will bring the jackpot possibility into play and cost you less on each play. But, of course, dropping to a quarter machine means that the house's edge will go up and the size of the jackpot will go down.

Unfortunately, aside from a squadron of players' commandeering every machine in a bank of older machines, the game is strictly "advantage house," and seriously so. Of course, there are books on gambling written by supposed experts that will provide you with what they think is good advice that will "make you a winner at the slots." And what is this magical piece of advice? Find the machine that is "due" for a payout. Alas, this is that sorry old chestnut again: the gambler's fallacy. One book, described on its cover as "one of the best all-around books on beating the casino," gave the following advice: Go up to the clerk who is making change for a bank of slots. After getting change, give her (why he assumed it would always be a woman I don't know) a couple of bucks as a tip and strike up a conversation. Once you have gained her interest and confidence ask her which of the slots has not paid off a jackpot in some time and therefore is clearly "due." Then play this machine.

Now, if this nonsense worked, why would a change clerk tell some stranger which slot to play? Because of a lousy $2 tip? If I had this kind of information and it were reliable, I'd have a friend come to play these "due" machines. We'd clean up! Anyway, unlike a lot of really bad advice you can get from books written by "experts," this one won't cost you anything except for the tip. But it won't gain you anything, either. Machines are not "due" for anything. They have no memory. A slot machine doesn't know whether it paid out on the last play or hasn't paid out in three years. Each spin of the wheels is an independent event and has no bearing on future spins. The probability of hitting a jackpot is exactly the same on every spin no matter what has happened before.

A little story. I was walking across a casino floor one day on my way to the poker room when I passed a grinning gentleman at a $5 slot machine who was in the process of being paid for a $5,000 jackpot. I gave him a thumbs-up of congratulations and went to the poker room, only to find no seat available. I left my name and headed back out through the casino to get a newspaper, and there was the same guy at the same machine. I stopped to watch, and on the very first spin after being paid off he hit the same $5,000 jackpot. "Due" machines, indeed!

Another piece of useless advice to slot players is to follow hunches. Another book I recently was reading suggested that these hunches were based on a "sixth sense" that could tell when a machine was primed for a jackpot. There is no validity in these hunches. There is no "sixth sense" (or seventh or eighth, either) that can provide you with any useful information about the profitability of one slot machine over another. However, facts notwithstanding, these vague hunches, these feelings of "There stands the machine of my dreams," are quite real. The feelings are real, that is, not their prognostications, and these feelings can be quite compelling to the player. Chapter 10 is devoted to the issues of intuition, hunches, ESP, fortune-telling, and the like. We'll do our debunking there.

Video Poker

The advent of computers made it possible to use the basic slot machine format for a variety of gambling games. The one that has caught on to a rather remarkable degree in the past couple of years is video poker. The game is like a slot in that coins are inserted and buttons are pressed. But instead of spinning wheels, the machine electronically deals out a hand of five-card draw poker. The player holds those cards he or she wishes to keep by pressing the appropriate buttons marked "hold" on the machine and the other cards are replaced. The machine pays out depending on the final hand. The size of the payouts follows the strength of the hands in standard poker fashion: one pair, two pair, three of a kind, straight, flush, full house, four of a kind, straight flush, royal flush.

These machines have become popular for a couple of pretty good reasons. First, they tap into the long-standing affection North Americans have for poker without all the trappings and competition of a poker room. Second, they are close enough to the standard slot that they catch a kind of "crossover" crowd, the slot players who are getting bored with the no-brainer routine of the wheel-based machines. Third, and most important, when played properly some of the machines have an expected value damn close to zero—indeed, with perfect play a few variations have the ability to produce a return of over 100 percent. No matter which machine you play, compared with the standard slot, the video poker machine takes your money very slowly even when played in an untutored manner.

In fact, with the right machine, the proper strategy, and a progressive jackpot, it is actually possible to play video poker as a Type W game. But since these circumstances don't pop up every day or in every casino, for the majority of players the game is still one with a negative expectation. In this section we'll look at three basic video poker games and explore the conditions under which video poker can be treated as either a Type L or a Type W game.

There are quite a few variations on the basic video poker machine, most of them involving wild cards. Some have deuces wild, some introduce a joker (or two) that acts as a wild card, some require jacks or better for minimum payout, some tens or better, some pay double on hands based on a particular suit, and so on. In a 1995 article in *Card Player Magazine*, forty-two different variations of video poker were noted, and there are surely more by now. No matter, the payouts of these machines have been adjusted to compensate for the relative ease of getting particular hands. For example, on a Deuces Wild machine a royal flush with wild cards pays out less than a straight flush on a Jacks or Better machine.

When video poker machines were first put on casino floors in the 1970s, there was relatively little interest in them. Then, in 1981, gambling authority David Sklansky presented an analysis that made it clear that, under the proper circumstances, some of these machines could actually be beaten. It wasn't long before the proper calculations were carried out to allow optimal strategies of play for each type of machine. In the sections that follow, the recommended plays are the ones for which the expected value is highest.

There are currently several excellent books on the market that describe the optimum strategies in full detail, much more detail than I will go into here. If you wish to get serious about video poker, I will recommend a couple of these books. But before I get into the details, there are a couple of things you need to appreciate about these games.

Poker Strategy

Although these games are all based on poker, skills developed by playing the regular card game don't always work. Video poker has to be played with its own brand of logic—and the particular logic used must be adjusted depending on the machine being played. Remember, there are no opponents. It's just you against the machine. Subtlety and subterfuge are of no value; there's no one to bluff. But do read chapter 6 thoroughly for a deeper understanding of the basic game of poker.

The Payout Schedule

If you look at the front of each video poker machine you will see a list of the payouts it makes for each particular hand. Note that the payouts are given using the "*x for y*" form, not the "*x to y*" form. A flush might be listed as paying "6 for 1," meaning that you will get back six coins for each one played, not seven.

Full-Pay and Partial-Pay Machines

Not all video poker machines pay out at the same rate, even for the same hands. There are full-pay machines and partial-pay machines. For example, a Jacks or Better machine that pays 9 for 1 for a full house and 6 for 1 for a flush is a full-pay machine and is also known as a "9/6 machine." An 8/5 machine, which pays only 8 for 1 and 5 for 1 for these two hands, is a partial-pay machine. Not all casinos have full-pay machines, and those that do often have them intermixed with partial-pay machines. If you are going to play video poker with any regularity, you should definitely play only full-pay machines.

The Progressive Jackpot

Just like regular slots, many video poker machines are connected to a progressive jackpot. Like the ordinary slot, when the jackpot grows sufficiently large, the machines actually have a positive expectation for the player. A video poker jackpot can grow sufficiently large so that the scenario of a squadron of players locking up all the machines connected to a particular jackpot not only makes sense but is practiced by professionals.

Moreover, from a purely mathematical point of view, the video poker jackpot is much more likely to be hit than a slot machine jackpot, and unlike the newer computer-controlled slots, where you cannot determine the true odds of hitting the jackpot, here you can calculate exactly how large the jackpot needs to be for the player to gain the statistical upper hand.

The Three Most Used Machines

The following paragraphs present an overview of the basic principles for playing the three most popular machines: Jacks or Better, Deuces Wild, and Joker Wild.

Jacks or Better: A full-pay 9/6 Jacks or Better machine has the following payout schedule:

Hand	Payoff
One pair (jacks or better)	1 for 1
Two pair	2 for 1
Three of a kind	3 for 1
Straight	4 for 1
Flush	6 for 1
Full house	9 for 1
Four of a kind	25 for 1
Straight flush	50 for 1
Royal flush	800 for 1

A partial-pay 8/5 machine will look much the same, only the flush will pay off at 5 for 1 and the full house at 8 for 1. These payouts are per coin played. If you play five coins, then each payout is multiplied by five.

The key to playing Jacks or Better is to focus on the hands with the highest expectation, which translates into aiming for straight flushes and the royal flush. Also remember, in this game there is no payout on low pairs. Let's take a baker's dozen examples to get a feel for these principles.

1. Suppose you are dealt 5♦, 10♦, J♦, Q♦, K♦. You already have a flush, which is a winner. Do you hold all cards? Absolutely not. The flush payout has low expected value compared with the royal flush, which is what you are after. Hold all but the 5♦ and hope for the A♦. Sure, the odds are 47 to 1 against you, but the payout is much greater than the odds.

2. You have 4♣, 8♠, K♦, 3♦, J♥. Here you have no real shot at a royal flush, so you look for maximum value in a lower hand. Hold the K and J, which gives you a decent chance for a high pair and an outside shot at a straight.

3. You hold 4♣, A♠, K♦, 3♦, J♥. Notice that this is the same hand as above but with the A♠ instead of the 8♠. However, the proper play remains the same: hold the K and J. That's right, toss the A. Holding it actually reduces the chances of catching the straight, and so lowers the expected value of the hand. If you don't believe this, try working it out. Hint: With the A, the only cards that help are Q's and 10's.

4. You are dealt 7♣, K♥, Q♦, 7♦, J♥. Since there is no sense in holding a high kicker, you hold the 7's and draw three cards, hoping for three of a kind, a full house, or, of course, four 7's, which will pay handsomely.

5. You are dealt 9♣, A♥, K♥, 9♦, Q♥. Here you have three to a royal and a pair of 9's. Hold the three high hearts, chuck the 9's, and go for the big payoff. Sure, it's a lot less likely than getting three 9's, but the payout makes it the right play. Three to the royal has a higher expected value than a low pair.

6. Suppose you have 2♥, 2♦, J♦, Q♦, K♦. The flush would be nice, so would catching a third deuce. However, the proper play here is to hold the three to the royal. Here's why. In addition to having a long shot at making the royal flush, you can make many other hands that have decent payouts—such as a flush, trips, two pair, etc.—when you draw two cards here. It is the combination of all these possibilities that makes drawing two cards correct, not just the fact that the royal pays off big.

7. You hold 4♥, 4♦, 9♦, 10♦, J♦. Go for the flush. Unlike the previous two examples, this time there is no reasonable shot at the royal, and the expected value of this play is better than holding the 4's.

8. You hold 4♥, 4♦, 5♦, 6♥, 7♦. This hand is very similar to the one in example 7, but here you have a draw to a straight where before it was to a flush. This time you hold the small pair. One-card pulls for a straight are less likely than for a flush (there are but eight cards to make the straight and nine to make the flush), and straights pay less than flushes.

9. You are dealt J♥, J♦, 5♦, 6♥, 7♦. Hold on to the high pair. You already have a winner, and the hand can still improve to trips, a full house, or even four of a kind.

10. You have 4♦, 5♣, 6♠, 8♥, 9♣. Don't hold any cards. The inside straight is unlikely (only four cards will make it), and your expectation is higher if you draw five cards.

11. You have 4♦, 5♣, 6♠, 8♥, K♣. This is just like the previous hand but now you have a high card. Hold on to it and draw four.

12. You are dealt 4♦, 8♦, 10♦, 2♥, 3♠. Like example 10, draw five new cards. The chances of catching the two-card flush are just too remote. By the way, such worthless hands still have a return of some thirty-three cents on the dollar.

13. You are dealt 4♦, 8♦, 10♦, 2♥, A♠. Like example 12, hold the A.

These examples present the guts, as it were, of Jacks or Better. I hope you appreciate how the basic principles operate. You are always looking for the highest expected value for any particular play, and your focus is on the major payouts for straight and royal flushes.

Deuces Wild: Here we will see the same general principles apply, but with subtle adjustments made necessary by the wild cards.

A full-pay Deuces Wild machine has the following payout schedule:

Hand	Payoff
Three of a kind	1 for 1
Straight	2 for 1
Flush	2 for 1
Full house	3 for 1
Four of a kind	5 for 1
Straight flush	9 for 1
Five of a kind	15 for 1
Royal flush (using a deuce)	25 for 1
Four deuces	200 for 1
Royal flush (natural)	800 for 1

Just looking at this table makes one thing apparent. Deuces Wild is a much more volatile game than Jacks or Better. That is, there are *lots* of hands that are worth little or nothing and a couple with huge payouts. The estimate is that the expert Jacks or Better player replaces all five cards on some 3 percent of the hands; with Deuces Wild it is more like 20 percent. Also note that hands that had serious payouts in Jacks or Better, like a straight flush, have a distinctly middling payoff here. Hands that actually have different probabilities of occurring, such as straights and flushes, have the same (small) payout. However, the hands with reasonable payouts, like five of a kind and the deuce royal, occur with surprising frequency. The key is to play for the outcome with the highest expected value, which, in many cases, means maximizing your chances for the big payoffs.

Let's work from examples.

1. You have K♣, K♥, 7♠, 7♥, 3♦. Keep one of the pairs and draw three cards. Yup, that's right; toss away the other pair and draw. Two pair is worthless, and drawing only one card seriously reduces the expected value of the hand.

2. You are dealt 3♦, 8♦, 9♦, 10♦, J♦. Hold all but the 3♦ and draw one to the straight flush. The expected value here is higher than holding on to the flush, which is worth a measly 2 for 1.

3. You have 7♣, 8♦, 9♦, 10♦, J♦. Same as example 2. Give up your made straight. Hold all but the 7♣ and go for the straight flush.

4. You are dealt 3♦, 8♦, 9♦, 10♦, Q♦ or 3♦, 7♦, 9♦, 10♦, Q♦. Hold all five cards. In each case there is a gap (or two) in the straight flush that gives the made flush the highest expected value.

5. You hold 2♣, 8♦, 9♦, J♦, A♦. Here the wild card fills in the gap so, as in example 2, you should hold all but the A♦ and go for the straight flush.

6. You are dealt 2♠, 9♠, 10♠, J♠, Q♠. Here you have a made straight flush and a draw for a deuce royal flush. The deuce royal doesn't pay enough. Hold all cards and take the payout.

7. You hold 9♠, 10♠, J♠, Q♠, K♠. This is just like example 6, only the deuce is replaced by the K♠. Here you go for the royal, since the chance of catching the natural royal markedly increases the expected value of the hand.

8. You hold 2♣, 2♠, 2♦, J♣, 7♥. Toss the J♣ and 7♥ and look at two new cards. Even though the J♣ theoretically is a card that can be used in a royal flush, you are better off with two new cards. Similar logic holds in hands that have two deuces and three uninteresting cards.

9. You are dealt 2♣, 8♥, 9♦, 10♣, J♦. Not much is likely to happen here, so you might as well hold all five cards and cash in your straight.

10. You hold 3♦, 8♥, 9♥, J♥, A♦. Boy, are you going to see a lot of hands like this. Chuck all five and hope for the best. As in Jacks or Better, hands full of "rags" are still worth an average return of roughly 33 percent of your investment.

In recent years, Deuces Wild has become a very popular version of video poker. The reason is simple: It has the highest payout, and when played properly, it is virtually an even game. However, as was noted above, it is a volatile game with extremely high variance. Anticipate many losing sessions punctuated by rare days where you will win a great deal. We'll have more to say about the impact of high variance on your bankroll and your psyche in chapter 11.

Joker Wild: There are several different Joker Wild machines on the floors of various casinos. Some pay only on hands of two pair or better, some pay on a single pair (provided that the pair is aces), some pay if the pair is either aces or kings, some pay a particularly large bonus for a natural royal but reduce the payouts on joker royals, and so forth. Each of the variations has a different expected value. Here I will focus on the version in which a pair of aces and a pair of kings pays the same as two pair. This particular version, when played on a full-pay machine (and provided proper strategy is used), actually gives the player a small statistical advantage.

A full-pay Joker Wild machine has the following payout schedule:

Hand	Payoff
One pair (aces or kings)	1 for 1
Two pair	1 for 1
Three of a kind	2 for 1
Straight	3 for 1
Flush	5 for 1
Full house	7 for 1
Four of a kind	20 for 1
Straight flush	50 for 1
Joker royal	100 for 1
Five of a kind	200 for 1
Royal flush (natural)	800 for 1

First off, notice that the full-pay machine pays 20 for 1 for four of a kind. Play only this machine. Do not play one that has a similar payout schedule but scrimps on the four of a kind by paying only 15 for 1. Second, appreciate that while this machine can be played profitably, it is somewhat more complex than the other two and tricky situations pop up more often. I'll try to cover them in the examples that follow.

1. You hold Jok, J♥, J♣, Q♣, 2♣. Hold the three of a kind and draw two. Three of a kind has higher expectation than a four flush.

2. You hold Jok, J♥, J♣, Q♣, K♣. This is similar to the first example, but this time you have a shot at the royal. Now you hold everything but the J♥ and draw for the joker royal.

3. You have Jok, 6♥, 7♣, 8♣, 9♣. Here you have a made straight, but also four to a straight flush. The proper play is to hold all but the 6♥. The straight flush draw has higher expectation than the made straight.

4. You are dealt Jok, 6♥, 7♣, 8♣, 10♣. This hand is very similar to the one in example 3, but now there is a gap in the possible straight flush. Nevertheless, the proper play is the same. Hold everything but the off-suit 6.

5. You hold Jok, 6♥, 7♣, 8♣, J♣. This hand is just like example 4, but now there is a double gap. Nevertheless, the straight flush draw is again proper. In hands like those in the previous three examples, you must remember that in addition to catching a hand with a serious payout, you still have a shot at refilling your straight or flush. This is the reasoning behind the recommended play.

6. You have the joker but do *not* have any of the following: three to a straight flush, a four flush, a four straight (open-ended), an ace, or a king. You should hold the joker and draw four new cards. Some 10 percent of all joker hands will be of this variety. Surprisingly, these hands still have positive expectation. Any hand with a joker has positive expectation, no matter what the other cards are.

7. You are dealt 10♦, 10♥, 9♣, 8♥, 7♦. Hold the pair. Playing your hand this way produces the highest expectation.

8. You hold 10♦, 10♥, J♥, 3♥, 7♥. This is similar to the preceding example, but now you have a four flush. Hold the four suited cards and draw for the flush. Flushes are worth more than straights.

9. You have A♦, A♣, K♥, Q♥, J♥. Even though you already have a winner with the high pair, you should hold the three to the straight flush and draw two cards.

10. You are dealt Jok, 9♦, 8♣, 7♠, 2♠. The best play is to hold all but the 2♠ and draw for the straight.

11. You hold Jok, 9♦, 8♣, 6♥, 2♥. While similar to the preceding hand, your straight draw here contains a gap that significantly reduces the value of the hand. Hold only the joker and take four new cards.

12. You hold Jok, 9♦, 8♣, 6♠, A♠. Similar to example 11, but here you have a winner with the pair of A's. Hold these.

13. You are dealt K♥, Q♥, 10♥, 7♥, 3♦. You have a four flush and three to a royal flush. Hold the three to the royal. Like so many of the earlier hands we looked at, the shot at the royal produces a higher expectation than going for the flush. Remember, part of your expectation here includes making other hands that pay out, such as straights, flushes, or even a pair of K's, which will get your money back.

14. You hold K♥, Q♥, 10♥, 7♥, 3♥. This case is just like example 13, but now you have a made flush. Hold all cards. The made flush is better than the long shot at the royal.

A couple of themes can be sensed here. First, there is a clear emphasis on forming straight flushes. On a full-pay Joker Wild machine, the payoff for the straight flush is the same as on Jacks or Better, where there are no wild cards. Second, the joker is the critical card—so much so that something like 10 or 12 percent of all joker hands are best played by drawing four new cards to the joker. Third, it is fairly obvious that Joker Wild is a more complex game than either of the other two and requires much more careful thought. However, it is statistically as good a game for the player as Deuces Wild and much less volatile. It is the game I recommend.

Some Final Advice

First, it is important to recognize that everything we have said so far about these machines may be totally out of sync with what individual readers may find themselves up against. The analyses presented are keyed to the full-pay machines that are distributed around Las Vegas and some Atlantic City casinos. Such generosity is not always to be found. For example, there are Jacks or Better machines lurking in many casinos in Atlantic City and on riverboats and reservations that have payout schedules that are even worse than those for the Las Vegas partial-pay 8/5 machines. These miserly devices are a player's nightmare, paying out at 6/5. Even worse are Deuces Wild machines that pay a mere 12 for 1 on five of a kind and a pathetic 8 for 1 on a straight flush. Even expert play on such machines leaves you at a disadvantage in the neighborhood of from 5 to 8 percent! Fascinatingly, you can often find a full-pay machine sitting within a backflip of one of the tightfisted critters. If you are going to play video poker, avoid the bankroll beaters and play only the full-pay machines.

Second, don't forget machines that are connected to progressive jackpots. While they will have a reduction in the normal payout, under the right circumstances the jackpot will make up, statistically speaking, for this. For example, we referred earlier to a full-pay Jacks or Better machine as a 9/6. A full-pay machine that is connected to a progressive jackpot will pay at only 8/5. This adjustment reduces the expected value of the machine on "regular" hands by about 2 percent. Therefore, before you play a progressive jackpot machine, you need to determine whether the jackpot has grown to the point where it is large enough to overcome this reduction. According to an analysis worked out by Lenny Frome, here's the rule of thumb to use: The jackpot needs to be some 2.2 times the regular payout in order for the machine to be played with a positive expectation. Of course, the higher it grows the better the game becomes. A machine that has a normal royal flush payout of 800 for 1 needs to have the following jackpots in order to compensate for the reduced payout:

Nickel machine	$ 420
Quarter machine	$2,100
Dollar machine	$8,400

Hence, if you focus your attention on those machines that have sufficiently large progressive jackpots, all of these games become, mirabile dictu, player advantage. But, as always, there is a caveat. While it is clear that these numbers represent a statistical reality, getting this edge is dependent on learning the full set of principles that define perfect play and on catching the occasional royal flush. On average, royal flushes show up (depending on the game) only once in some 40,000 hands. If you plan to get serious about video poker, with its storied volatility, you are going to need to have a bankroll sufficient to keep you going long enough to hit your share of royals. So, while it is possible to play at a level that makes these Type W games, the player must be prepared financially and psychologically for many more losing sessions than winning sessions. Gambling expert Stanford Wong maintains that someone who plans to play video poker seriously and for profit needs to have a bankroll of $10,000 if playing a quarter machine. A dollar player needs a bankroll of at least $40,000.

Interestingly, despite the fact that the game can be played for profit, my informants inside various casinos tell me that the house drop on video poker machines runs between 2 percent and 6 percent. This suggests that most folks are either playing the wrong machines or are playing the right ones poorly and for longer than they would a regular slot. The information provided in this book should help the typical player considerably—and lower the casino's edge to the neighborhood of 1 percent or less of money wagered.

If you plan to get serious about video poker, I suggest you consult Lenny Frome's new book *Winning Strategy for Video Poker,* which goes into these games and dozens of others as well. It presents perfect strategy for all the pay machines. For the well-bankrolled potential pro, Stanford Wong's *Professional Video Poker* is pretty much what it claims to be: a handbook for those who want to play the game seriously.

Finally, while we have covered the three most popular machines available today, I cannot recommend that you bounce from machine to machine. I suggest that you pick one and learn to play it properly. After that you can stretch out to a second and, if you crave variety, learn a third. There are over forty different varieties available these days, but unless you understand the nuances of each particular variation you are likely going to be giving up an edge. Never give up an edge!

KENO

The modern version of keno is apparently derived from an Oriental game developed over two thousand years ago in China by an aristocrat named Heung Leung as a way of raising money for the army. This should be a pretty good hint about who has the edge in this game. Armies are very expensive. In the original version there were 120 different Chinese characters from which the player tried to select a subset of which would be drawn. Today the principle remains the same—though the total has been reduced to eighty and numbers are used rather than characters. The player selects a subset of the total set and hopes that some of his or her selections come in.

I really don't want anything I say here to be construed as encouraging anyone to play this game. I wouldn't play it with Monopoly money, and I hope you never will. In terms of expected value, *it is the very worst game for the player to be found anywhere in the casino.* You would have to leave the casino and head for the state-run lotteries to find a worse play. The house edge in keno is between 25 and 40 percent. Question: Why in the name of heaven or hell would anyone play this game? Answer: The same reason people buy lottery tickets—it's easy, relaxing, and there is always the possibility of the big payoff. For a lousy $2 you can win $250,000. Keno is also a slow game. That is, the time between games can be a couple of minutes, so you don't make many wagers per unit of time. While the expected value of the gain is compellingly negative, most keno players don't lose all that much, simply because they don't bet all that much.

Keno is played with a card containing the numbers 1 to 80. The player marks some number of them and presents the card to the keno ticket writer. Twenty numbers are then pulled at random, and the player is paid depending on the number of numbers selected and the number that actually came up in the magic twenty. The following is the basic bet in the game.

Straight Tickets

The player selects from one to fifteen numbers (or twenty in some casinos) by marking them on the keno ticket. Payoffs depend on how many numbers have been selected and how many of those are hit. Figure 4-1 shows a keno straight-bet ticket with nine numbers selected. The following table gives the payoffs for a straight ticket using nine numbers, depending on how many the player has caught. Bet sizes of $1, $2, and $5 are shown. In some casinos, smaller or larger wagers are permitted and appropriate payoff rates will always be posted.

Catch	$1	$2	$5
5	4	8	20
6	44	88	220
7	300	600	1,500
8	4,000	8,000	20,000
9	24,000	Jackpot	Jackpot

The jackpot is based on the same principle as the progressive jackpot in the slots. That is, it increases by a small amount with each ticket purchased and builds until someone hits it. However, the progressive jack-

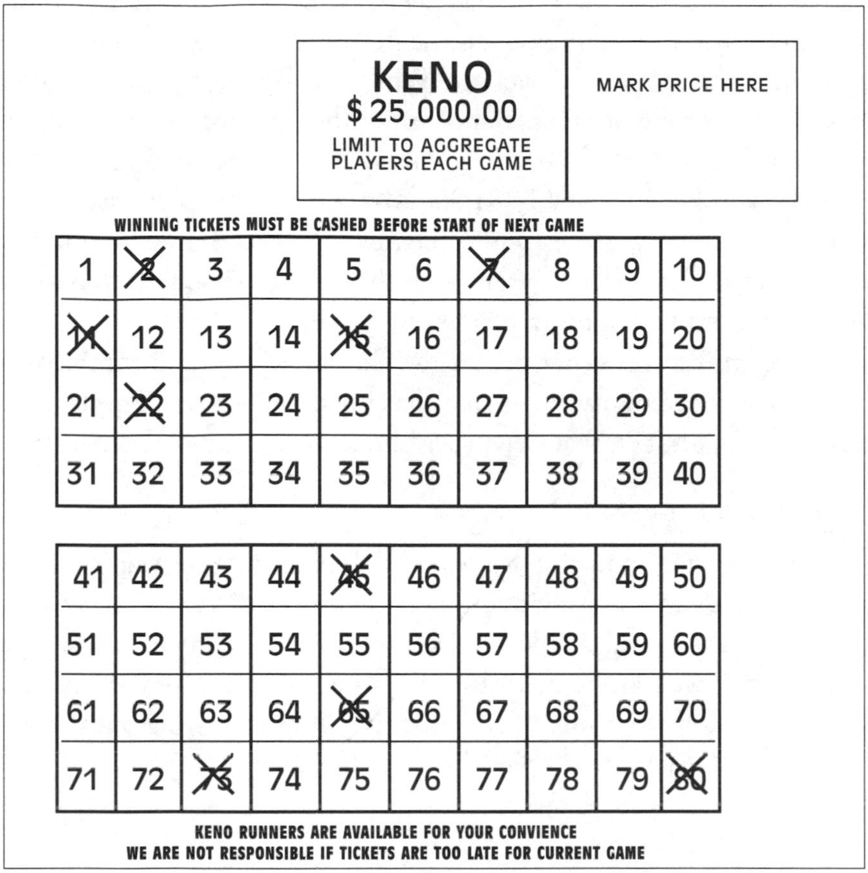

Figure 4-1 A keno ticket with nine numbers marked.

pots in keno have a ceiling, usually $250,000. Unlike the slots, where the odds are long but not impossibly so, hitting the jackpot in keno is so bizarrely improbable that, without the cap, it could very well reach tens of millions of dollars. Not all keno games have this progressive jackpot. Note that each individual game will have a ceiling of $250,000, so if two people hit the jackpot in the same game they will have to share the prize. I wouldn't worry about this happening too often. The jackpot gets hit about every couple of months.

In most casinos the keno payouts are set up so that the first time the progressive jackpot shows up is when the player hits nine out of nine while wagering $2 (and typically the jackpot cannot be hit unless a minimum of $2 is bet). This bet was recommended in a recently published book on casino gambling on the grounds that it gives you the best shot at hitting a progressive jackpot. While this is true, the probability of picking exactly nine numbers out of nine when pulling twenty numbers from eighty is .0000007. In other words, your chances of getting nine out of nine in keno is over 1,381,000 to 1. Of course, there are smaller payouts for hitting eight, seven, or six, or five of the nine numbers, so that the house edge for the wager is in the neighborhood of 40 percent, but the bet is still crushingly against the player.

There are various other bets, known as split, way, and combination tickets. If you really want to make these bets, which are simply variations on a straight bet, feel free to ask about them at any keno parlor.

The Bottom Line

From the standpoint of the expected value of the wager, keno is clearly not a good game for the player. However, it is a relaxing game that is typically played in a leisurely manner and for small stakes. Keno players don't lose a lot because they don't bet a lot, and they always have that jackpot, however unlikely it is that they'll hit it, sitting out there on the horizon. Rather like people who play the lottery.

LOTTERIES

Lotteries have an interesting history. They were introduced during the sixteenth century, in a form that is really closer to a raffle, by Italian merchants who discovered that, in addition to raising cash, lotteries could be used to attract customers and dispose of unsold goods. The first government lottery was established in 1539 in France by Francis I to raise revenues to cover his uncontrolled spending. Since that time lotteries have been a generally accepted means for governments to raise cash. Elizabeth I used them regularly, and the first American lottery was established in 1612 by the Virginia Company. In Colonial America and in the postrevolutionary United States, lotteries became a standard way of raising money for public works and the military. In 1890, after a number of scandals involving lotteries that failed to raise sufficient funds to pay off winners, Congress banned the United States Post Office from being used for any purposes related to lotteries. The largest lottery at the time, the Louisiana Lottery, was so heavily played that fully half the mail processed by the New Orleans post office was for the lottery.

Congress's ban, which was upheld by the Supreme Court in a squeaker 5 to 4 decision, effectively killed off lotteries. In fact, individual states went into an antilottery mode, and by 1930, forty-three states had banned them. It wasn't until 1963 that New Hampshire broke ranks and authorized a lottery to support local educational programs. Suddenly lotteries were viewed again as they had been four hundred years earlier, as a way to raise money without increasing taxes. Today, state-run lotteries are an integral element in the panoply of devices governments use to raise revenue—although, ironically, they are illegal in Nevada.

As games of chance, there really isn't much to say about state lotteries. It should be pretty clear to the reader that any game run for the express purpose of raising money is unlikely to give the player much of a shot. The odds are even worse than in keno. Most state lotteries return to players less than half of the money taken in, which makes for the worst expected value of any legal wager in the land. However, there is a distinction between "big" payoff games and "small" payoff games.

The "Big" Games

These games typically ask the player to select, say, six numbers from fifty. They are usually run once or twice a week, and the winning numbers are drawn on locally televised shows so that the players can tell immediately whether or not they've won. The major drawback to these lotteries is that the odds against hitting are astronomical, in the millions to one. Their attraction is that large wins are possible. With carryovers from previous drawings for which there were no winners, payoffs can and have run into the tens of millions of dollars—and herein lies the seductive power of lotteries. Despite the odds, it is almost impossible not to be drawn into the rags-to-riches fever that can spread through a state. It's like that feeling that keno imbues you with: What's a buck or two when I could have millions? These feelings, combined with the insurmountable odds against the player, have so fascinated various scholars that they have dubbed this phenomenon the "lottery fallacy."

However, remember that when such astronomical sums are paid out there are some serious strings attached. For one, as of this writing, in most states the payout typically takes place over twenty years. If you win a $5 million lottery prize, which is way above average, you get only $250,000 each year. The state holds the rest "for you"—although the state (are we surprised?) keeps the interest that the money earns. Second, since the payout takes place over an extended period of time and the payout is fixed in terms of the number of dollars involved, the buying power of the money will be eroded by inflation. If we assume a very low inflation rate of 3 percent per year, a quarter million will be worth only in the neighborhood of $130,000 in twenty years. More realistic inflation rates will erode the value of each year's payout even further. Third, you must pay federal, state, and local taxes on the income which, should you live where I do in New York City, can amount to over 40 percent of your net. It is possible—you may be the amazingly lucky person who hits the lottery with the only winning ticket, but don't think for a second that this is going to let you live like Donald Trump.

The "Small" Games

These minilotteries involve picking a three-digit number out of all (1,000) possible numbers or a four-digit number out of all (10,000) combinations. There are also myriad other games involving picking different combinations of numbers from different pools of numbers. And there are "instant" lottery games where you scratch off the film occluding the numbers of boxes on a ticket, and if you hit a winning combination you are paid immediately by the ticket seller, and so on. All of these games have much smaller payouts than the major lotteries and, of course, they have correspondingly better odds of being hit. However, they share with the big games the devastating house (state) edge, which typically runs around 50 percent.

The Bottom Line

Terrible! I have seen several books that claim to provide the lottery player with strategies for winning. For the most part, the advice they give is total nonsense, like listening to your hidden psychic powers or using your horoscope. However, here's one piece of advice that makes some sense (although it has only marginal value in the long run). Avoid common numbers. Avoid playing numbers like 3, 7, 11, and the like; avoid numbers such as the day's date (e.g., if it's April 22 don't play 4 or 22); avoid playing the set of numbers that lie just underneath each other on the ticket or along a diagonal. The reason is that if you were to hit using these numbers, you would likely have to share your bounty with others. Instead, pick numbers larger than thirty-one (that way you won't use anybody's birthday) or use the numbers that won the previous lottery. Practically no one bets yesterday's winning numbers since nobody expects the same numbers to come up two days in a row. All these outcomes are wildly unlikely, but as I've been hammering home in this book, they are exactly as unlikely as every other combination of six numbers.

Since writing this section, I discovered a little volume by William Ziemba titled *Dr. Z's 6/49 Lotto Guidebook*, which gives similar advice. Ziemba is, like me, a "research scientist," and so, of course, everything he writes is surely correct.

PART III

TYPE W GAMES

—THOSE IT'S POSSIBLE TO WIN

5

BLACKJACK

*T*he various games of chance we've discussed to this point are all basically closed-end enterprises. All the table games in chapter 3 can be beaten once in a while, but our analyses showed that these are games to be enjoyed for the moment while trying to keep your long-term losses at manageable levels. The games we looked at in chapter 4 have the interesting wrinkle that it's possible, in a remote kind of way, to win huge amounts of money. But unless you're playing some forms of video poker, the odds are stacked against you to such an extent that it doesn't make much sense to try to do this in a serious way. In this chapter, we will examine the first game where a shrewd, knowledgeable player can actually turn a profit: blackjack.

The element that distinguishes blackjack and other Type W games from Type L games is that these games are not ruled by incontrovertible odds that are fixed independent of the play of the participants. These are games of skill. The only element of skill in Type L games is the ability to identify the least unfavorable propositions and stick with them while maintaining control over both your emotions and your bankroll. Everyone who plays Type L games for any length of time is going to end up losing, and the longer he or she plays the more likely it becomes that he or she will lose exactly what a probabilistic analysis dictates. In Type W games, on the other hand, winners and losers sort themselves out on the basis of their understanding of each game and how they play it.

This chapter is written with several audiences in mind. First, I want the material to be accessible to a reader who is new to blackjack, so each section will begin with an overview of the basics. Second, I will be presenting some heuristics (rules of thumb) to provide the semiserious player with a deeper understanding of how to maximize his or her bottom line. But most of all, this chapter is for the "average player." In my years of play, I've known an awful lot of "average players," some of whom are enthusiastic and frequent visitors to the green cloth. Surprisingly, many of them, though they know the basic rules of blackjack and play it regularly, play it rather poorly. They do very "human" kinds of things that ultimately hurt them; most often they fail to follow basic strategy: the set of fundamental decision-making rules that will minimize their losses. The casinos show an average percentage held (PC) of roughly 14 percent for the game, which means that the typical player is leaving behind some $14 out of every $100 brought to the table. Let's see what we can do about this.

Some Things to Think About

Before we get into this game in a serious way, there are a couple of caveats that need to be laid out. First, even though what I'm giving you is basically good advice, it will not magically turn a novice into a skilled player. Blackjack isn't like the Type L games, where you could improve your bottom line by following relatively simple wagering strategies.

Becoming a good blackjack player requires, in addition to a basic understanding of the game, putting in dozens, if not hundreds, of hours of practice. Becoming an expert requires thousands of hours. It's like that old joke about the tourist in New York City who asks a guy on a street corner how to get to Carnegie Hall. The answer, of course, is "Practice, man, practice."

Second, even after you have learned the game and practiced it thoroughly, you must still learn to deal with its financial and psychological aspects. Just because an expert player has a small statistical edge over the casino does not automatically mean he or she can start filling out deposit slips. A little story to make my point.

A year or so ago I was playing in my favorite casino in Atlantic City. The house rules are reasonably favorable and the shoe was nicely positive—by the way, if some of the terms here seem foreign, hang in there, all will be explained. I had a $75 bet on the table when I was dealt 8, 8 with the dealer showing a 6. Blackjack was made for moments like this! I put up another $75 and split the 8's. On the first 8 I was dealt a 3. No question in my mind, up went another $75, for a double down. I pulled a 9 for a total of 20. On the second 8 I drew another 8! Up went another $75 and I resplit. On the first 8 I pulled a 2 and, no hesitation at all, doubled down again. I was dealt a 10 and now had two 20's. On the third 8 I pulled a "mere" ace for 19. I now had $375 on the table. The dealer turned over a 10. A deep sigh—there were precious few cards left in the deck that could hurt me. An A, 2, 6, 7, 8, 9, or any of the four 10-valued cards would make me a winner of $375; a 3 would make me a winner of $300. Only a 4 or a 5 could hurt me—with a 5 wiping me out completely. But the deck was rich with 10's and only two more had shown themselves. The odds favored a serious win on the part of yours truly by a significant statistical margin, in excess of 90 percent. The dealer proceeded to turn over a 5! I went to take a walk on the boardwalk, to listen to the plaintive cries of the omnipresent seagulls.

A LITTLE HISTORY

Blackjack came from the French game *vingt-et-un*, or "twenty-one," although there has been much tinkering with the details of the game in recent decades. When it first became a casino staple, it was assumed that it was rather like baccarat, where the house, by virtue of the rules determining play, had a statistical edge. This apparent advantage was borne out by the casinos' consistently high PCs and by the standard assessment of the game, which focused on the crucial element. Since the player had to act first and all busts (hands totaling over twenty-one) were losers no matter what the dealer later drew, the house seemed to have an incontrovertible edge.

Indeed, until 1956, when a paper by Baldwin, Cantey, Maisel, and McDermott was published in the *Journal of the American Statistical Association*, this conventional wisdom seemed to hold true. Baldwin and his colleagues worked out—painstakingly, since they lacked access to a high-speed computer—a set of recommendations for the play of the game that were surprisingly close to today's basic strategy. The following year, Baldwin et al. published a manual that provided the general public with their system of play, but it attracted little interest. However, Edward O. Thorp, a scientist at MIT, saw the Baldwin paper and understood its implications.

Thorp recognized that there were two elements to the game that had previously gone unexamined. First, the composition of the deck changed with each card dealt. Second, some combinations of the remaining cards favored the house and others favored the players. In 1962, Thorp published his now famous book, *Beat the Dealer*, which contained a simple yet profound message. Unlike dice, roulette wheels, and slot machines, decks of cards have "memory." Each hand dealt at blackjack is dependent on the makeup of the deck at that time; the currently dealt hand is hostage to those previously dealt. In craps, each throw is independent of the outcomes of all previous throws. Toss three 7's in a row and the likelihood of a 7 remains exactly the same. However, when dealing from a deck of cards, the situation is very different. Deal three 7's from a single deck and the probability of a 7 on the next card is dramatically lessened, since only a single 7 remains. By paying attention to the cards already played, one can home in on the outcomes most likely to occur on future hands.

Having computational power at hand that Baldwin and his coworkers lacked, Thorp carried out what is known as a "Monte Carlo" simulation of the game (yes, the mathematicians who developed this kind of analysis named the procedure after the famed gambling resort). A computer was programmed to play out tens of millions of hands of blackjack. It was then used to analyze the outcomes and determine which circumstances tended to produce wins for the player and which tended to produce losses. Thorp confirmed that 10's and A's remaining in the deck were good for the player, while 5's and 6's remaining in the deck were bad for the player. He refined and sharpened the Baldwin et al. basic strategy and worked out the circumstances under which particular combinations of cards remaining in the deck gave the player an advantage over the house. He also presented the first two-card counting systems, Thorp's five-count and Thorp's ten-count. The latter, which is more powerful, was based on determining the ratio between 10's and non-10's remaining in the deck.

Up to this point, the house had been winning steadily, not due to any inherent advantage, but because no one had worked out the conditions under which the players had the upper hand. Card counting was born from irrefutable logic: Keep track of the cards; make small bets when the deck favors the house and large bets when it favors the players.

Thorp's analysis was later improved upon by the work of many others, notably Julian Braun, Lawrence Revere, Peter Griffin, Stanford Wong, Ken Uston, Arnold Snyder, and Lance Humble. Today the game is understood at a rather deep level, and sophisticated systems exist that give the knowledgeable player a distinct edge over the house. However, you can't jump in and expect to play at this level. First, you need to understand some things about the ways in which the game is approached.

Four Classes of Play

Class 1: Ordinary, Untutored Play

This is the kind of action that virtually everyone gave before Thorp, and, alas, many people still play this way today. They try to beat the dealer by guessing and by hoping for the right cards. Depending on the pattern of decisions made by the player and the house rules, the Class 1 player has an expected value of somewhere in the neighborhood of -2 percent of money wagered.

Class 2: Basic Strategy Play

Decisions here are made based on the Monte Carlo analyses, which have determined the optimal play for every circumstance that can occur in blackjack. These decisions are made without taking the makeup of the deck into consideration. Depending on the casino's rules, the basic strategy player has an expected value that runs from about even to roughly –.6 percent. Basic strategy can be easily learned and adds from 1.5 to 2 percent to the player's expected outcome. It also gives the player a better shot than any of the Type L table games no matter what the house rules are.

Class 3: Basic Strategy Combined with a Simple Card Count and Adjustments in Bet Size

A simple card count provides the player with information about the composition of the deck that is used to make adjustments in bet size. Minimum bets are made with unfavorable counts; maximum bets with favorable counts. Class 3 play can be learned with some practice. It enables one to play close to even with the house under unfavorable rules and enjoy a statistical edge in the neighborhood of +.1 percent to +.4 percent with the more favorable rules. With a few additional minor modifications in play and betting, the edge can be pushed up another .2 percent.

Class 4: Card Counting with Adjustments in Both Betting and Play

The key to play at this level is that both bet size and play are adjusted with shifts in the composition of the deck. This level of play, which requires considerable training and study in addition to hours upon hours of practice, can give the player an edge in the neighborhood of 1 percent (depending on the house rules). This may not seem like a lot, but it is not far from the edge the casinos enjoy in baccarat and in the basic pass line bet in craps.

In this chapter I am going to concentrate on Classes 2 and 3. My first goal is get every reader to at least learn basic strategy so that he or she can play at or close to even with the house. My second goal is to get more interested players to learn a relatively simple count that will bring them even with the house or give them a slight but meaningful edge. I'll give some hints about how the highest levels work, but won't go into great detail. These systems become exceedingly complex and require full mastery of the lower levels before they can be attempted.

THE PLAY OF THE GAME

The Layout

Blackjack is played at a table with a single dealer and from one to seven players. The layout gives a few basic rules, such as the payoff for a blackjack (3 to 2); for insurance (2 to 1); and whether the dealer hits on soft seventeen. There will usually be a small sign to one side of the dealer that gives the table stakes and any special rules, such as whether surrender is allowed. You must ask to discover the other unposted rules and regulations. You will need to know, for example, whether doubling down after splitting is allowed, whether a player may double down on any two cards, whether pairs may be split a second time, and whether aces may be resplit. Such rules determine whether the basic game is favorable or unfavorable.

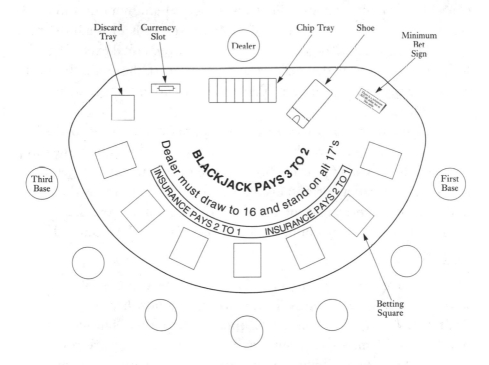

Figure 5-1 A typical blackjack table.

The Basic Game

The game itself is simple. You, the player, attempt to accumulate cards with a numerical total closer to (but not in excess of) twenty-one than those accumulated by the dealer. If you do so, you win. If the dealer's total is closer to twenty-one than yours, you lose. Winning hands are paid off at even odds. If you and the dealer both arrive at the same total, the hand is a "push," or standoff, and nobody wins. All bets must be made before any cards are dealt, and no bet may be changed once the first card has been dealt.

Each player is initially dealt two cards; they may be face-down or face-up, depending on the rules of the casino. The dealer gets two cards, one face-up and one face-down. The value of the cards is given by their face value except that the ace (A) counts as either 1 or 11 and the 10, jack (J), queen (Q), and king (K) all count as 10 (and will be referred to as "10").

The combination of an A and any 10 on the first two cards is a black-jack and is an automatic winner (unless both dealer and player have it, then it is a push). A player blackjack is paid at 3 to 2. When the house has a blackjack the player merely loses his or her bet and not one and a half times that bet. Any combination of cards that exceeds 21 is a bust and a loser. The player always goes first, so if the player's total exceeds 21 the hand is lost—even if the dealer also busts later. If the dealer busts, all remaining players are winners. The dealer has no options; play is fixed by the rules.

After the first two cards are dealt, the player must decide whether or not to take additional cards based on two pieces of information: the cards held and the dealer's upcard. This is where the game starts to get inter-esting. A wide variety of options offer themselves, and unless the player understands the principles of the game there are numerous ways to go wrong. Let's review the options first; correct play will be discussed later.

Standing

The player elects to stay, or "stand," with the current total and not to draw any additional cards. If you are in a game where the cards are dealt face-down, slip your cards under your chips. The dealer will understand the message. If you are in a face-up game, wave your hand back and forth in a wiping motion just above your cards, which is the signal for "I'll stay with these." All casinos insist on some form of hand signal; verbal statements are not accepted. Casinos can get rather noisy, and it is easy for a dealer to mishear a player. Also, the cameras hidden in the casino's ceilings can be used to resolve disputes only if hand signals are used, since they do not have an audio component.

Hitting

The player elects to draw an additional card or cards. If you are in a face-down game, draw your cards toward you with a quick scratching motion against the felt once or twice. In a face-up game, make a similar motion with your fingertips or, preferably, point to your cards with your index finger.

Splitting

If your first two cards are of the same value, you may split them and play each as a separate hand. To indicate a desire to split your cards, place an additional wager equivalent to the original one to the side of it. If you are playing in a face-down game, you must expose your cards. After splitting a pair, various other options become available. You can re-split if a third like-valued card appears. Or you can double down on the split hands should an appropriate card be drawn. For example, if you have split 8's and catch a 3 on the first 8, you may now double down on this total of 11. Both resplitting and doubling down after a split are to the player's advantage.

Doubling Down

The player may double the size of the original bet and elect to draw only one additional card. The typical doubling situation is where you have a hand that stands a chance of becoming a *very* good hand with one additional card; for example, your first two cards total 10 or 11. To indicate a double down bet, slide a second wager to the side of the original bet. This wager may be as much as but no more than your original bet. If you are playing in a face-down game, you must expose your cards. Virtually all casinos permit doubling on 11 and 10; most on 11, 10, and 9, and many will allow it on any two cards. The latter rule is the most advantageous to the player.

Insurance

When the dealer shows an A, players are given the option of taking insurance against the dealer's having blackjack. Calling this "insurance" is a bit misleading. Actually, it is nothing other than a side bet that is paid, as is noted on the layout in figure 5-1, at 2 to 1. If you wish to take insurance (which, by the way, is not recommended except under particular conditions that only an expert card counter can detect), place a bet equal to half your original bet in the semicircle running just in front of your betting spot. If the dealer has blackjack, you will lose your original bet but win the insurance wager and break even on the hand. If the dealer does not have blackjack, you will lose the insurance bet and the hand will be played out normally.

Surrender

If your hand looks particularly unpromising against the dealer's exposed card, you have the option of surrendering half of your bet and retiring from the hand. For example, should you have 9, 7 against a dealer 10 your chances of winning the hand are slim—indeed, less than .5— and it would be to your advantage to give up half your bet. There are two forms of surrender: "late" (also called "conventional") and "early." In the late form, the player may surrender after the first two cards provided that the dealer does not have blackjack. In early surrender, the player may surrender after the first two cards even when the dealer is later revealed to have blackjack. Both forms of surrender are to the player's advantage, with early surrender being most beneficial. Not all casinos permit late surrender, and those that do don't necessarily post it at the tables. Except for the occasional promotion, no casino offers early surrender any longer.

Surrendering, by the way, is the only play at the table that requires a verbal response; there is no hand signal. If you wish to surrender your hand, just say "Surrender." The dealer will remove half your bet and return the other half.

Those are the basics of the game. If you're a novice don't stop reading now; without the information in the next two sections you won't be playing a Type W game, you'll be playing a Type L game. Nobody should venture within a stone's throw of a blackjack table without mastering basic strategy.

Basic Strategy

Since the essential features of basic strategy were developed, a number of refinements have given us the current optimal set of principles for standing, hitting, doubling, splitting, and surrendering. These, along with the other more sophisticated forms of Class 3 and Class 4 play, were worked out by using Monte Carlo techniques based on the analysis of literally billions of hands. If I tell you that you should hit a total of 16 against a dealer's 7, there is no specific mathematical proof behind this recommendation. It emerged from an analysis of the several million times this situation emerged in the Monte Carlo analyses of the game. Hitting a 16 against a 7 loses less often than standing pat. Sure, following this advice produces a bust on a lot of these hands, but analysis shows, utterly compellingly, that if you don't hit this hand you are more likely to get beat by a higher total—like 17.

When possible, I will give a logical analysis of particular aspects of basic strategy, but there are going to be situations where the reader is just going to have to accept the outcomes of the Monte Carlo analyses. The following description of basic strategy is based on the multideck game found in several Atlantic City and Las Vegas Strip casinos, where the dealer stands on a soft seventeen, pairs may be resplit once, doubling down is permitted after a split, and the player may double down on any two cards. Other games require some minor adjustments that I'll note where appropriate. However, just as was stated in our discussions of video poker, never give up an edge. My strong recommendation is that you play in casinos where the more favorable rules are in effect.

Hitting and Standing with "Hard" Hands

A hard hand is a hand without an ace where the player's total is given by the face values of the cards. The rules for hitting and standing with these hands are straightforward. If the dealer shows 2 or 3, hit until you reach a total of 13; do *not* hit any total of 13 or above. If the dealer shows 4, 5, or 6, hit until you reach a total of 12; do *not* hit any total of 12 or above. If the dealer shows 7, 8, 9, 10, or A, hit until you reach a total of 17; do *not* hit any total of 17 or above. In summary:

Dealer Shows	Hit Until You Have
2 or 3	13
4, 5, or 6	12
7, 8, 9, 10, or A	17

There is actually a simple logic to these principles.

- If the dealer shows a 7 or above, then the most likely two-card total is 17 or above (with a 10 or an A in the hole), so you are going to have to take a card on any total under 17 or likely lose.

- When the dealer shows a card less than 7, the two-card total will likely be less than 17 (it can be exactly 17 with a 6 and an A) and the dealer will be forced to take another card. Since there are more 10's in the deck than any other denomination, the dealer will have a fairly high probability of busting and you will win.

- If you were to take a card with a total between 12 and 16 you would be likely to bust. In situations like this the proper play is to let the dealer pull. If the high card shows up and there is a high card in the hole, you will win.

- Hit a total of 12 against a dealer 2 or 3. I've seen books that tell you to stand in these situations. They are wrong. You must take a card.

- Hit a 16 against a dealer's 7. Many untutored players have trouble believing that this is the proper play, but it is. Countless computer runs have proved it again and again. From the player's point of view a total of 16 is no better than a total of 12; you can win with such totals only when the dealer breaks. Besides, there are still five cards that can help out a 16 (A, 2, 3, 4, and 5).

Hitting and Standing with "Soft" Hands

A soft hand is a hand with an A which can be counted as either 1 or 11. For example, A, 2 is a soft hand, as is A, 2, 7. But A, 5, 6 is not, since counting the A as 11 would be a bust. The principle for soft hands is simple. If the dealer shows 2 through 8, hit a soft hand until reaching at least a soft 18. When the dealer shows a 9, 10, or A, hit until you reach a soft 19. If a soft hand "hardens" (you catch cards that prevent your using the A as 11), then revert to the rules for hard hands. In summary:

Dealer Shows	Hit Until You Have
2 through 8	Soft 18
9, 10, or A	Soft 19

Comments:

- You take a card whenever you have A, 6 (except for possible doubling down, which we'll cover below) and you hit an A, 7 against 9, 10, or A. It's true that in hands like these you will occasionally find yourself "going backwards," as when you hit A, 7 against a 9 and catch a 6, giving you a hard 14, which is a distinctly weaker hand than you just had. However, it is still the proper play, as shown by extensive Monte Carlo simulations.

- It may come as a surprise to inexperienced players, but 18 is not a strong hand when facing a dealer 9, 10, or A.

Splitting Pairs

The principles are straightforward.

Split	If Dealer Shows
A, A	Any card
10, 10	Never
9, 9	2–9 except 7
8, 8	Any card
7, 7	2–7
6, 6	2–6
5, 5	Never
4, 4	5–6
3, 3	2–7
2, 2	2–7

Comments:

- Always split A's. The totals of 2 or 12 are nowhere near as strong as hitting a pair of 11's, which is what you are doing when you split them. However, you will receive only a single card on each, and resplitting is typically not allowed (there's a limit to a good thing).

- Never split 10's. All you would be doing is screwing up a good hand.

- Never split 5's. They should either be played straight or doubled down, depending on the dealer's upcard (as is described in the next section).

- Whether to split 4's or not is a close call. You should split them against 5 or 6 in multideck games, but only when the casino permits doubling down after a split, which increases their value a bit. In single-deck or double-deck games, they should just be played straight, but it won't make much of a difference to the casual player.

- Split 9's against 2 through 9, except when the dealer shows a 7. The reason for this wrinkle is simple: You have 18 against the dealer's most probable hand of 17 and, just as with 10's, you don't want to screw around with a likely winning hand.

- How 8's are handled depends on the casino rules. They should always be split when facing 2 through 9; the problem comes when you are against a dealer's 10 or A. Where early surrender is allowed, just give up half your bet when facing 10 or A and get ready for the next hand. Unfortunately, early surrender has virtually disappeared, so the basic strategy player should always split them. Just how valuable a pair of 8's is depends on whether the casino permits doubling down after a split. When it does, then splitting 8's becomes a much stronger play.

- Split 6's and 7's whenever the dealer shows a card equal to or lower than your pair. If the dealer shows a higher card, treat the hand like a simple hard total of either 12 or 14 and follow the rules given above.

- 2's and 3's are much stronger cards than most untutored players realize, and should be split against any dealer card up to a 7.

- The value of splitting most pairs is increased in casinos that permit doubling down after the split.

Doubling Down

The rules, in table form:

Double Down	If Dealer Shows
11	2–10
10	2–9
9	3–6
A, 7 and A, 6	3–6
A, 5 and A, 4	4–6
A, 3 and A, 2	5–6

Comments:

- The first three situations are called "hard" doubling. Virtually everyone knows about them and virtually every casino permits them (though a few won't allow doubling down on a total of nine).

- The others are called "soft" doubling, and many untutored players are not aware of them. They are not as advantageous to the player as hard doubling hands, but they should not be discounted.

- When casino rules permit it, all proper double down bets should also be made after splitting pairs.

- Splitting pairs and doubling down are critical parts of the basic strategy game. Situations where these opportunities present themselves either favor the player or reduce the house's expectation. They permit you to increase the amount of money you have on the table in a situation where you have the probabilistic upper hand. This is the principle that should drive the game for the player: Have more money on the table when the situation favors you and less when it favors the dealer.

Insurance

Never take insurance! Some people, including well-meaning pit bosses and self-styled experts, will tell you that you should always insure your own blackjack on the grounds that you "cannot lose." The argument goes like this. Suppose you have made a $10 bet. If the dealer has blackjack, your hand becomes a push but you win the insurance bet and end up winning $10. If the dealer does not have blackjack, you lose the insurance wager (−$5) but win the hand (+$15) and end up winning $10. While it is certainly true that you will always win an amount equivalent to your base bet in this situation, in the long run the bet is a bad one. The insurance bet is a side bet and it has absolutely nothing to do with your having blackjack or any other hand.

Let's examine the situation carefully. Assume you are playing alone with the dealer, using a six-deck shoe and making a $5 insurance bet on a base bet of $10. A six-deck shoe contains 96 10's and 216 non-10's. After you and the dealer have been dealt your cards, you have blackjack and the dealer shows an A, so there are 95 10's and 214 non-10's left. There are then 95 ways for the dealer to have a 10 in the hole, and if you take insurance, you will win $10 on each of these occasions for an income of $950. However, there are 214 ways for the dealer to have a non-10 in the hole, and on these occasions you will lose $5 each, for a loss of $1,070. The bottom line here is pretty painful. Out of a total of 309 possible $5 bets (a total of $1,545 wagered) you have an expected loss of $120, an expected value of −7.8 percent of money wagered, which is a very bad bet indeed. As a basic strategy player, if you take insurance you are undercutting yourself in a serious way.

However, this analysis holds only for the basic strategy player, who does not count cards. That is, the rule is based on the assumption that the non-10-to-10 ratio is 214 to 95, or a bit greater than 2 to 1. If you are counting cards, you will be aware of those times when the deck is sufficiently rich in 10's that the ratio shifts to the point where it is less than 2 to 1. Here it becomes advantageous to take insurance.

Surrender

These days, unless someone is hosting a promotional event, you're just not going to find a casino that has anything other than conventional surrender (and even this isn't all that common). Early surrender, when used properly, is worth +.62 percent of monies wagered to the player, and casinos have dropped it like a hot potato. The best you're likely to find these days is conventional surrender, the table of basic strategy rules for which follows:

If Dealer Shows	Surrender if Holding
A, 10, or 9	16 (but not 8, 8)
10	15

Should you be fortunate enough to find a casino that allows early surrender, use the following principles:

If Dealer Shows	Early Surrender if Holding
A	All hard 5–7 and 12–17
10	All hard 14–16
9	10, 6 and 9, 7

Comments:

- Throw away a 17 when facing an A; similarly, toss 7, 7 and 8, 8 when facing a 10. However, split 8's against a 9.
- The surrender option should be restricted to those situations where the player's likelihood of winning the hand is less than .5. Admittedly, there are few things in this game more annoying than giving up half your bet to a dealer 10 and then watching a 6 appear from the hole—but trust me here, these are the proper plays to make.

The Bottom Line on Basic Strategy

Proper use of basic strategy puts a player within a statistical stone's throw of the house, with the bottom line depending on the individual casino's rules—which can vary considerably. The following table provides the impact on the player's bottom line of each of a number of adjustments in the rules. The optimum game, where all the positive factors are operative, is rather like a unicorn, beautiful but fictitious. But you will be able to find casinos that use variati‹ favorable game; one where you can get pretty house.

The figures given below are relative to a base gle deck and by the following rules: dealer stands bling is permitted on any two first cards but is no no resplitting of pairs is permitted, and there is playing flawless basic strategy under these conditions is essentially even with the house—although, as I mentioned above, you aren't likely to find such a game anymore.

Variation of Casino Rules	Impact on Player (% of money wagered)
Early surrender*	+.62
Conventional surrender (one or two decks)	+.02
Conventional surrender (four or more decks)	+.07
Doubling on three or more cards*	+.20
Drawing more than one card on split A's*	+.14
Doubling on split pairs	+.10
Resplitting of A's	+.03
Resplitting of pairs	+.05
No doubling on 11*	−.89
No doubling on 10*	−.56
No doubling on 9	−.14
No doubling on soft hands	−.14
Two decks	−.38
Four decks	−.51
Six or more decks	−.60
Dealer hits soft 17	−.20

*Rarely found these days.

With this table, a good basic strategy player can estimate the expected value of any game. For example, my favorite Atlantic City casino uses six-deck and eight-deck shoes (−.60) but allows late surrender (+.07), of pairs (+.05), and doubling down after splitting a pair Playing basic strategy here yields a game at which the player is ing up an edge of about −.38 percent. Back in the early days of Atlantic City, when early surrender was allowed, the basic strategy player at this casino was actually playing a game with positive expectation. Alas, casino managers can also count.

When people see figures like these they often wonder why increasing the number of decks works against the player—after all, doesn't each deck have the same makeup? The reason is that using multiple decks diminishes the likelihood of high-quality hands like blackjack, nineteen and twenty, while increasing the likelihood of "stiff" (terrible) hands. Presenting this analysis would take more space than I want to devote to it here, but the reader can try working it out. If you do, you'll notice, for example, that the proportion of hands that yield blackjack is lessened with increases in the number of decks in use.

Casinos aren't generally concerned about basic strategy players, since, for the most part, they still have a statistical edge over these players. As a result, they will typically permit players to use a "crib sheet" giving the basic principles of play in a tightly compressed form— although using one might reduce your comps. You can pick one of these up anywhere gambling material is sold—including some casinos' newsstands. I'd give you one here, but I don't want you to fall into using one as a crutch. You must eventually become "fluent" in basic strategy in order to be able to move on to Class 3 play, which is where blackjack becomes a Type W game.

The Simple Count, or How to Become a Class 3 Player

Untutored blackjack players, when they hear about card counters, often get an image of people who keep track of each and every card that has been played. Some of my racetrack cronies—who, when they play blackjack, play it very badly—look at me in confusion and say things like, "Jeez, man, I can sorta understand doin' it with one deck but I just don't see how anyone can keep track of six or eight decks." But counters aren't keeping track of the actual cards, they are keeping a running count of particular *ratios* of cards. The principle involved is the same whether you are counting with an eight-deck shoe or a single, hand-held deck. The multiple-deck shoe does produce difficulties in that you must keep the count going for longer and are therefore more likely to lose track or make an error, but the principle is the same no matter how many cards are involved.

This misunderstanding about what is involved in card counting was reinforced by the movie *Rain Man*, in which Dustin Hoffman played a young autistic man with savant abilities who was able to carry out rather extraordinary feats of memory and calculation. The Hoffman character and his brother make a killing playing blackjack in Las Vegas, with Hoffman keeping perfect track of every card and making only the optimum plays. The episode is fictitious, and nothing in the psychological literature on human memory, ordinary and extraordinary, suggests that such a feat is possible.

Card counters do not—indeed, *could* not—keep track of every card. Nor is there a need to do so. Card counting is really keeping track of the ratio between the cards that benefit the player and those cards that benefit the house. Cards like 5's and 6's benefit the house because the dealer is forced to draw on all hands below seventeen. These medium-value cards turn stiffs into winners. High cards, like 10's, benefit the player in several ways. First, they turn dealer stiffs into busts. Second, they are used to make blackjacks—and while they make them for both dealer and player, the player gets paid 3 to 2 on a blackjack but loses only a base bet to a dealer blackjack. Third, they turn doubling hands into likely winners; catching a 10 on a total of 10 or 11 creates a very strong 20 or 21. Aces also function as valuable cards for the player in several situations. They are used to make blackjacks, for which the payoffs favor the player; when paired, they provide the player with a splitting opportunity with positive value; and they can be used to create soft doubling opportunities.

Keeping track of the makeup of the cards remaining in the deck is the essence of counting. In this section I will present a counting system based on tracking 2's, 3's, 4's, 5's, 6's, on one hand, and 10's and A's on the other. First, it is important to understand how knowing something about the constitution of the deck can be to your advantage. This comes down to two fairly straightforward strategies: bet adjustment and play adjustment.

Bet Adjustment

The size of the base bet is adjusted to reflect the count: Small bets are made when the makeup of the deck favors the house; large bets are made when it favors the players. Proper bet adjustment turns a basic strategy player into a Class 3 player, for it provides him or her with a small but real statistical edge over the house.

Play Adjustment

Decisions for hitting, standing, taking insurance, and so on are modified to reflect the count. Play adjustment is more complex than bet adjustment; indeed, mastering this element of the game takes a Class 3 player to Class 4 by permitting the exploitation of certain critical situations. For example, when the deck is 10-rich, a Class 4 player will often stand with stiffs rather than risk busting, double down more often, and split pairs more liberally, especially when the dealer shows potential busting hands. On the other hand, a 10-poor deck invites hitting stiffs more often and being more conservative with doubling and splitting. Even rules that are iron-clad in basic strategy play can be violated with impunity when the circumstances are right, including doing some seemingly odd things like doubling on A, 9 or even splitting 10's when encountering a seriously 10-rich deck. However, these rule adjustment strategies are really beyond the scope of this book, which focuses on Class 3 play.

A Simplified Version of Wong's High-Low Count

Of the many counting systems that have been put forward, the one that best combines ease of learning and use with power is the High-Low count expounded by Stanford Wong in his book *Professional Blackjack*. The system is based on maintaining a running balance between low cards, which benefit the house (specifically 2, 3, 4, 5, and 6), and high cards, which favor the players (specifically A and the 10-valued cards). The variation presented is one that a player who has already mastered basic strategy can learn in a couple dozen hours of practice, although learning to adjust playing strategy will take a lot longer. This counting system, with attendant bet progression and some relatively minor adjustments in play, can provide players with an edge of about .8 percent over where they would be with basic strategy alone.

The count: At this level we need to differentiate between two counts, the running count and the true count. Card counting begins by establishing the running count and then making adjustments to produce the true count. For reasons that will become obvious, decisions are made on the basis of the true count.

The running count: After the cards have been shuffled and before any cards have been dealt, you should start your count at 0. For each 2, 3, 4, 5, and 6 that is dealt add 1; for each A and 10 subtract 1. The system has a distinct advantage in that there are the same number of cards with values 2 through 6 as there are A's and 10-valued cards. Hence, a neutral deck is at zero; any time a deck is positive it favors the player (unless the rules are poor); any time it is negative it favors the house. This procedure will produce an estimate of the degree to which the remaining cards favor one or the other party in this little drama known as blackjack. If you are playing in a single-deck game, the running count is a true count.

The true count: While the running count provides important information about the makeup of the remaining deck, this information is unfortunately limited in multiple-deck games. The problem is that it fails to take into consideration the number of cards left to be dealt. Clearly, a count of +5 is a lot less significant if only a single deck has been dealt from a six-deck shoe than if three or four decks' worth of cards are out. The ratio of favorable to nonfavorable cards in the second case (which is really what counts here) is much greater than in the first. Since betting strategies call for larger bets with positive counts and smaller ones with negative counts, if a player overestimates the value of a positive count early in a shoe it can be costly. Accordingly, proper play calls for the player to keep a "true count," which is arrived at by dividing the running count by the number of decks left in the shoe. For example, the +5 running count noted above yields a true count of +1 with five decks left in the shoe but a true count of +5 with only one deck left.

The operation of converting a running count into the true count can be a bit tricky at first. The easiest way to carry it out is to look at the discard pile and estimate how many decks of cards have been played, subtract this estimate from the number in the original shoe, and then divide. A general rule of thumb is that any time you have a true count greater than 1/2 you have an edge. Any time you have an edge you should increase the size of your bet. By exactly how much, however, is not a simple decision. Let's look at this issue.

Betting: Various betting progression schemes have been suggested and argued for. I'll discuss two of the more sensible, the count-matching rule and the Kelly criterion. My preference is the count-matching rule for its simplicity of use, although the Kelly criterion is more efficient.

Count-matching: The bet is determined by the true count. If playing a single-deck game with good rules, start by wagering two units with a neutral deck where the count is zero. If the true count becomes negative, drop your bet to one unit; if it becomes positive, increase your bet so that it matches the count. That is, if the true count is +1, add one unit to your bet. If you are starting with one unit = $5, your base bet is $10 and your bet with a +1 count will be $15. If the count is +2, add two units (bet $20). If playing a shoe game, reduce the bet level by one. That is, where you would be betting two units in a single-deck game, bet one unit and, so forth. Since the true count rarely exceeds +5, you will seldom bet more than seven units. However, because of splitting and doubling, you may find yourself from time to time with twenty-one units or more of bets. Remember, risk attends the use of these counting systems. In order to take advantage of the statistical edge you enjoy you must not be what we call in psychology "risk aversive."

The Kelly criterion: Named for the mathematician J. L. Kelly, this wagering strategy is mathematically optimal in that it maximizes return for minimal risk. It is more complex and harder to implement than the count-matching strategy, but no other system can exceed it in betting efficiency.

The Kelly criterion dictates that you should wager the percent of your bankroll that corresponds to the probabilistic advantage you have on that hand. Hence, if you start with $1,000, and on a particular hand, owing to the constitution of the deck, you have a +1 percent edge, you should wager $10; if your edge is +2.5 percent you should bet $25. If the house has the edge, you should bet the table minimum. In order to use the Kelly criterion, you must know fairly precisely what your edge is at each point in the game. The player's momentary edge depends on three factors:

1. The player's expectation using basic strategy under particular casino rules (let's call this BS).
2. The true count (TC).
3. The gain the player accrues from each increment in the true count.

It has been calculated that each $+1$ in the true count using the High–Low system adds approximately .5 percent to the player's edge. So the formula for calculating the player's advantage (PA) is:

$$PA = BS + (.5 \times TC).$$

With this formula, it is possible to work out tables that give optimal bet size for each individual PA. For example, suppose you are playing the standard multideck game found in Atlantic City and the Las Vegas Strip casinos. As we noted earlier, in this game the BS equals $-.38$ percent. Hence, the player's advantage (PA) for each of the more commonly confronted true counts (TC) will be as given in the following table along with the bet progression for two sample bankrolls:

True Count	Player Advantage	Bet Progression with $1,000 Bank	Bet Progression with $2,000 Bank
+1	.12 percent	table minimum	table minimum
+2	.62 percent	$ 6	$12
+3	1.12 percent	11	22
+4	1.62 percent	16	32
+5	2.12 percent	21	42
+6	2.62 percent	26	52

For casinos using different base rules, consult the table on page 135 that lists the impact on the game of the many rule variations. Once you know the BS for the casino in which you are playing, you can calculate your own PAs and corresponding optimum bet sizes.

Implementation of the Kelly criterion may appear formidable to the untutored player. However, once you have figured out what the expected value of basic strategy is in any given casino and you have chosen the bankroll you feel comfortable working with, the rest is easy. The Kelly criterion is a conservative progression, but it maximizes gains while minimizing risk. In other words, it guards against the gambler's ruin.

Play: For Class 3 play, stay with basic strategy. However, the player who has begun to get a feel for the game and can keep an accurate true count without making errors can make one simple adjustment that will add to his or her edge: Take insurance whenever the (true) count is +2 or higher in a single-deck game and +3 or higher in a multiple-deck game.

Learning a Counting System

Much of the preceding probably sounds intimidating to the beginning player. That's okay, it should. Blackjack is a complex game, and getting an edge on it isn't easy. Nevertheless, it's certainly within the realm of possibility for the average bloke to move from being a losing player to one who is, at worst, even with the house and at best enjoys a small but statistically significant edge over it.

Counting cards can actually be fun, adding an intellectual element to a game that can at times become unhappily mechanical. Playing basic strategy leaves little or no latitude for the player, since any shift away from the recommended lines of play reduces the player's expected value. With counting, the player gets a deeper understanding of the game. The easiest way to learn is to start out by carrying a deck of cards around with you. Whenever you have a couple of free moments, run through the deck, subtracting 1 each time an A or 10 is dealt and adding 1 for each 2, 3, 4, 5, or 6. When you reach the end of the deck you should be at zero. Keep practicing this routine until you can pull it off rapidly and smoothly with virtually no errors. Then, start pulling cards off two at a time and practice adding and subtracting based on each two-card combination. Combinations such as 2, 4 are "plus two"; J, Q is "minus two"; 3, 10 is "zero"; 9, A is "minus one"; and so on. Again, the deck should come out at zero.

The advantage of doing this is that you will learn to deal with the cards, not as single entities but in groups, which is the easiest way to deal with them when they are dealt at the table. Once you have learned to assign values to cards in combinations, you will find it surprisingly easy to maintain a running count in the hot action of the casino. But don't underestimate the amount of practice needed to become proficient. And don't try to be a counter until you have mastered the process. Counting derives its prime advantage from increased bet size in favorable situations, and increasing bet size carries risks.

The Bottom Line

The bottom line in blackjack is a slithering thing. Before Thorp, from the players' point of view, it seemed to be a game with negative expectation. Today it is mathematically clear that it can be played with positive expectation. However, it isn't easy to determine the degree to which blackjack can actually be played as a Type W game by the average punter operating in the real world of a casino. We need to look at a couple of important issues.

The Gambler's Ruin

The proper assessment of the play at any game where the odds can be specified requires an analysis of the gambler's ruin—or, as it's sometimes called, the "element of ruin." For a gambler, ruin can mean only one thing: He or she is out of money and cannot play further. In a game like blackjack, the astute player has a small but authentic edge over the house. But having a statistical edge does not guarantee winning; it merely makes winning more probable than losing. It is still possible to fall into ruin and be unable to play any longer. The reason that this is such a poignant issue here is that the expert player *knows* that he or she has the probabilistic upper hand and that the longer the game goes on the more likely turning a profit becomes. Alas, if one is out of cash the game cannot go on; hence, the gambler's ruin!

Probably the easiest way to understand the gambler's ruin problem is to view it in terms of how large a bankroll the player needs to have, given the statistical edge enjoyed over the house, the size of the average bet, and the probability of ruin that the player is financially and psychologically willing to live with. This analysis makes sense only when talking about games with a positive expectation. If the house has the edge, no bankroll is big enough. The table that follows presents the issue using a 5 percent risk factor (for each level of play and size of bankroll there is a 5 percent chance that you will lose your entire bankroll before getting into the black). That is, it tells you just how large your bankroll has to be to give yourself a 95 percent chance of coming out a winner, given that you know the edge with which you play the game. This table is based on an analysis presented in Mason Malmuth's *Gambling Theory and Other Topics*, which the interested reader can consult for more detail and an explanation of how these figures are calculated.

Player's Win Rate (%)	Average Bet Size ($)						
	2	5	10	15	25	50	100
0.1	1,627	4,068	8,136	12,204	20,304	40,680	81,360
0.3	542	1,356	2,712	4,068	6,780	13,560	27,120
0.5	325	814	1,627	2,441	4,068	8,136	16,272
0.8	203	509	1,017	1,526	2,543	5,085	10,170
1.0	163	407	814	1,220	2,034	4,068	8,136

These figures should make the typical blackjack player sit up and take notice. If you have gotten to the point where you are playing the game with a small positive expectation, like .01 percent or .03 percent, and are making modest bets averaging only $5 or $10, you are still looking at the possibility of taking a serious bath. If you have become a true expert and play with an edge of .08 to 1.0 percent, your risk factor is dramatically reduced. But players who are this expert typically use much higher average bet sizes, and so they too put themselves at considerable risk. The expert whose average bet is $100 still needs a bankroll of $8,000 to $10,000 to protect against a 5 percent element of ruin.

These figures also assume that the expert blackjack player can sit at a table and play an optimal game without receiving "heat" from the pit bosses or, worse, being barred from playing. As a result of these factors, real-life fluctuations are actually much more severe than these figures show and the gambler's ruin is more likely. The key point here is variability, which, as will become increasingly apparent here and in succeeding chapters, is one of the most important statistics when attempting to calculate a player's (mis)fortunes.

How the Game Has Changed

Soon after *Beat the Dealer* appeared, nontrivial numbers of card counters descended upon Las Vegas. The casinos initially viewed it all with studied amusement. They had been raking in serious dollars from the tables for years and were secure in their assessment that the game could not be beaten. However, it quickly became apparent that something was amiss. Particular individuals were winning much more money more frequently than before. The casinos introduced a variety of what we can simply call "player unfriendly" rules. Not surprisingly, the impact of these adjustments in the basic game was a serious decline in the table drop for the most obvious of reasons: The average bloke, who hadn't a clue about counting but sure as hell didn't like the new game, simply stopped playing.

The casinos restored the basic game but made various adjustments, like the early shuffle, in an attempt to blunt the counter's edge. Dealers were instructed to shuffle up whenever a player made a significant increase in his or her wager. The thinking was that such a bet increase was a signal that a card counter knew the deck now favored the players. Card counters simply started making dramatic increases in their base bets when the deck was negative—thereby inducing dealers to shuffle up decks that actually favored the house.

Rather than continue this peculiar game of chicken, the casinos shifted to the multiple-deck shoe, with an unfavorable (for the players) cut card. The cut card is a colored plastic card that is inserted partway into the deck. Hands are now dealt up to the cut card and then all the decks in the shoe are shuffled. One significant factor in the original game that gave the counter the edge was "deep penetration": The more deeply into the deck the dealer went, the more efficient the count became. By introducing the six- and eight-deck shoe with shallow cut cards, the counter had much less reliable information about the makeup of the remaining decks.

However, there is a fascinating wrinkle to the use of the shallow cut card. It means more frequent shuffling. During a shuffle no one is playing; if no one is playing, the casino isn't making money. It is not a simple matter to determine whether the casino loses more money to a counter who gains an additional edge with a deep cut card than it loses during the frequent shuffles necessitated by a shallow cut card. But casino paranoia tends to run high, and so the shallow cut card is becoming the industry standard.

In addition to the multiple-deck shoe, some casinos no longer permit mid-shoe entry. That is, no player can enter the game once the first hand has been dealt. This procedure neutralizes one of the most lucrative gambits of the late, great Kenny Uston, whose teams made stunning amounts of money by having an expert counter make modest wagers at a table until the deck became highly favorable. The counter would then signal the "big player," who would stagger over, often pretending to be drunk, and make huge bets. As soon as the deck shifted back to neutral or became negative, the big player would pick up his or her profits and leave. Banning mid-shoe entry also eliminates the device of a player's deciding to sit out a couple of hands. I routinely do this when the deck shifts, particularly if I have just lost several hands in a row. I'll look pained and frustrated and tell the dealer in my most disgusted voice, "Just leave me out for a couple of hands till I get back my composure." I jump back in when the deck drifts back to positive.

But banning mid-shoe entry is no panacea for the casino. It produces a problem similar to that of frequent shuffling. Does the casino save more money by cutting into the card counter's routine than it loses by denying "regular" players the opportunity to sit down at the table any time they wish? I suspect the casinos are losing out on this one.

Casinos have also made modifications to the play of the game that are designed not so much to neutralize counters but to counteract various forms of player cheating. For example, it is becoming increasingly rare to find a face-down game. Most casinos have adopted the version of the game where the player's cards are dealt face-up and the player is not permitted to touch them. This adjustment has virtually eliminated the impact of card daubers, crimpers, and folders, and has made card swapping impossible. However, the face-up game provides a Class 4 card counter with a tiny additional advantage. Since a counter gets to see the cards of all the other players at the table, a more accurate count can be made.

With these adjustments in the play of the basic game, the life of the card counter has become increasingly difficult. Many casinos no longer bar people suspected of being counters. They just lean on them a bit by using ever poorer cut cards, which makes favorable decks less likely. Their plan is to encourage the counter to move to another casino. Some Atlantic City casinos, unable to legally bar suspected card counters, have adopted what may turn out to be the ultimate solution. They forbid the player to bet more than his or her basic wager. The casinos claim that the regulation that allows table limits to be adjusted for an individual player also permits them to limit the bet size of an individual player. As of this writing there have been no legal challenges. If a casino suspects that someone who starts betting with a quarter check is a counter, it will limit bets to $25, thereby removing the primary weapon in the counter's arsenal. In a sadistic kind of way this maneuver is the ultimate slap in the card counter's face. It's worse than being barred, since the only thing left to do is to play the game like everybody else! So, the question is: Can the game still be beaten? I mean, what really is the bottom line here?

The *Real* Bottom Line

Clearly, it isn't easy to determine the degree to which modern blackjack can be played as a Type W game. Let's look at the game's bottom line from the perspective of both the typical recreational player, who plays every now and again, and of the serious player, the potential or actual professional.

The Recreational Player

Everything we know about blackjack points to one conclusion: The sensible player who masters basic strategy, implements the rudiments of Wong's High-Low count, and makes appropriate bet adjustments will be playing either even with or slightly ahead of the house. This, in and of itself, is cause for rejoicing, particularly when compared with the bottom line analyses for the games in the previous two chapters. What more could the recreational gambler ask for? If you visit your favorite casino on a semiregular basis and make modest bets in the $10-to-$30 range, you will find yourself being reasonably well comped—and for fairly obvious reasons. The typical $10 player making sixty bets an hour will be putting something in the neighborhood of $600 into play each hour. Since the untutored player is playing at a disadvantage in the neighborhood of 2 percent, the house figures on a profit of some $12 an hour. Over ten hours, the average "green-check" ($25) player will be putting $15,000 into play, of which the casino anticipates a profit of $300. The comps will go up accordingly. If the house views you as a typical player, it will lay serious perks on you. By mastering only the simplest lessons given here, you can play virtually even with the house in matters financial, and walk out legitimately ahead in matters psychological.

This goal should be the one the recreational player aims for. Learn to play even with the house, but play at a high enough level so that you will enjoy the comps that come with putting serious money on the table.

The Potential Pro

Can you take the next step and actually play blackjack for profit? Could you become a professional? My assessment: It's possible but not all that likely. Make no bones about it, learning a counting system to get to Class 4 takes time and effort—and this is but half the battle, for you still need to deal with the financial and psychological factors involved in playing for high stakes in a game fraught with risk. You will have to decide for yourself whether the gain is worth the effort. The world is full of authors of blackjack books who will tell you on every other page how wonderful their systems are and how much money you can make using them. It is also full of people who have tried to use such systems and gone broke or given up—or both.

Some people make their living playing blackjack, but there are fewer today than there were just a couple of years ago. Adjustments to the basic game have blunted the counter's edge and removed many of the most profitable gimmicks. Some wildly optimistic authors will present mathematical projections of Class 4 counting systems that indicate that an expert player can gain an edge of up to 2 or 3 percent. Were this true there would be many more professionals playing the game than there are. Given the vagaries of life, memory lapses, errors of calculation, anxieties, noise, other annoying and intrusive players, hovering pit bosses, six- and eight-deck shoes with poor cut cards, early shuffles, unfavorable house rules, and the need to build cover on your act, it seems wildly unlikely that such edges can be achieved in the short run, let alone maintained.

Contemporary experts such as Mason Malmuth put the expert Class 4 counter's edge even lower, at around 1 percent. I concur.

6

POKER

*T*his is the chapter my heart is in, for I do love to play poker. I'm a pretty good middle-stakes poker player, although my style is best called intuitive. I have a good feel for the game, for situations, and for my opponents. However, my approach to the game could never be called mechanical, and as I began writing this chapter I realized I had a problem. You simply cannot teach other people how to play poker by telling them that all they need to do is play a lot and watch their intuitive skills develop. It may work, but it's very expensive. My struggle to make my intuitive, implicit knowledge explicit was aided by Mason Malmuth, and this chapter was ultimately crafted through long and extensive interactions with him.

Of all the games covered in this book, poker represents the purest form of gambling. It's player against player on an even field, and the edge goes to the one who is more skilled. In the long run, the smiles of lady luck are equally distributed among all of the participants in the game. If you do not understand this most basic of principles in its fundamental, naked truth you are not going to get very far playing poker. If you think that luck is the main element in this game, go back and play the slots.

In a modest-stakes hold 'em game a couple of months back, I sat next to the poker player from hell. This guy bitched and moaned loudly about almost every hand he was dealt for about two hours, regularly hurling his cards into the muck (the discards) with curses and complaints. Despite an admittedly awful run of cards, he continued to play aggressively, pressing, raising, reraising, and trying to force hands that were better quietly folded. He lost something like $700. During the same period, a quiet and composed player sitting across the table matched him hand for hand for lousy cards. But this player tightened down, played conservatively, and took advantage of the few opportunities that presented themselves. When he left (largely, I suspect, because he was sick of sitting across from the first guy), he was up a shade over $100. In this chapter, I hope to teach you how to play like this second gentleman.

We're going to approach poker from the point of view of the semibeginner. I'll assume that you, the reader, are an intelligent individual who knows something about the game and has at least played penny ante by the kitchen sink. But the game we'll be discussing is played in an organized setting such as a casino or a poker room; it is a moderate-stakes game in the $5/10 to $10/20 range. (In a $5/10 game the smallest bet or raise that can be made is $5 and the largest is $10.) The basic principles presented are applicable to lower-stakes games in the $1/3 and $3/6 range, as well as to higher-stakes games such as $15/30 and $20/40, but adjustments need to be made when moving up or down from the basic mid-stakes games. For readers ready to move on past the levels presented here, I recommend additional readings.

An awful lot of poker players are losers. In the typical game in a poker room the house's vigorish (or vig) comes from what is called the "rake" (a percentage of each pot that the house extracts) or a time charge (a fee that each player pays per unit of time played). The overall game, thus, has a negative expectation—in the sense that the players put more money on the table than they take off it. Were every player of equal skill, they would all, in the long run, lose a certain proportion of their bankrolls to the vig. But many people play these games for profit— a small number even play as professionals and take their primary income from poker. That money is being donated by the losers, whom serious Las Vegas poker players call "the tourists."

This chapter is for the low-to-moderate-stakes player who has been losing and thinks it's because he or she has lousy luck. Most players lose because of ignorance and their failure to appreciate the need for study, hard work, and practice. A game as complex as poker cannot be mastered by reading a book, so take to heart my comments in the chapter on blackjack concerning practice. Becoming an expert in poker is a lot like becoming a good cook. Sure, you have to read cookbooks and review recipes, but you've also got to get into the kitchen and stir the sauce.

IN THE BEGINNING

Poker appears to have emerged as a distinct game in the New Orleans area of the old Louisiana Purchase back in the early 1800s. By the 1820s, the game was played using a twenty-card deck with four each of A, K, Q, J, and 10. There were no suits, and hands were ranked by one pair, two pair, triplet, fulls (what we call today a full house), and four of a kind. The name itself is most likely a corruption of *poque*, the French term for this early game. The fifty-two-card deck with four suits and thirteen denominations first appeared in the 1850s and gradually became the standard during the middle and late decades of the nineteenth century. The modern deck, in addition to providing a much more varied game, allowed more than four people to play at a time. By the 1870s, the basic probabilities had been worked out, the standard ranking of hands had been developed, and poker was established in essentially its present form. Interestingly, there were several false starts in ordering hands that resulted in embarrassing errors, including, for a time, ranking straights above flushes.

THE BASICS

As a refresher for those who haven't played in some time, here's a quick rundown on the ranking of hands from the strongest to the weakest:

- *Five of a kind*. Five cards of the same value. Such hands can occur only in games that use wild cards; for example, Jok, Q♥, Q♦, Q♣, Q♠ in a game where the joker is used as a wild card.

- *Straight flush*. Five cards in a row, all of the same suit; for example, 10♦, 9♦, 8♦, 7♦, 6♦. When the five cards are the ten through the A, it is a *royal flush*.

- *Four of a kind* (also called *quads*). Four cards of the same value. If there is more than one set of quads in a hand, the higher ranking wins.

- *Full house* (also called, especially on the East Coast, a *boat*). Three cards of the same value plus two cards of another value; for example, K♦, K♣, K♥, 2♦, 2♠. If there is more than one full house in a hand, the player with the highest set of three equal-valued cards wins.

- *Flush*. Five cards of the same suit; for example, A♦, 10♦, 7♦, 6♦, 2♦. If there is more than one flush in the same hand, the one with the highest card wins. That is, A♥, 6♥, 4♥, 3♥, 2♥ beats K♣, Q♣, J♣, 10♣, 8♣.

- *Straight*. Five cards in a row; for example, 7♦, 6♣, 5♦, 4♥, 3♠. If there is more than one straight in a hand, the one with the higher-valued cards wins.

- *Three of a kind* (also called *trips* or *a set*). Three cards of the same value; for example, J♦, J♥, J♠, 9♣, 4♥. If two players have three of a kind, the hand with the higher-valued set wins.

- *Two pair*. For example, K♦, K♥, 7♠, 7♦, Q♥. If two players have two pair, the one with the highest pair wins. If both players have the same top pair, the one with the highest lower pair wins. If both have the same two pair, the one with the highest other card (called the "kicker") wins.

- *One pair*. For example, A♦, A♠, Q♣, 10♥, 5♣. If two players have one pair, the highest pair wins. If they have the same pair, the one with the highest kicker wins.

- *High card*. The highest card in any player's hand.

Note that this ranking holds only for standard poker, where the high hand wins. There is also a version called lowball (or "loball"), where the lowest hand wins. Here the best hand is 5, 4, 3, 2, A; the next best hand is 6, 4, 3, 2, A; the third best hand is 6, 5, 3, 2, A, and so forth. The 5, 4, 3, 2, A hand is also known as the "wheel" or the "bike."

Some Basic Money Issues

The Stakes

The stakes at a poker game are specified at the outset. In a casino or poker parlor, each table will be marked for the stakes played there.

Limit games: In limit games, the lowest and highest bets permitted will be posted. For example, in a $1/5 (also written $1–$5) game the lowest (or small) bet is $1 and the highest (or big) bet is $5. Occasionally a game will be posted as $1/5/10, which means the minimum bet on the river (the last card) is $10, or $1/4/8/8, which means the last two bets have a maximum of $8. The vast majority of games played in modern casinos and poker parlors are limit games, though the limits vary tremendously—from $1/3 up to $500/1,000 and even higher.

Pot limit games: In pot limit games, any wager is permissible up to the amount of money already in the pot. Pot limit games can run from modest to high-stakes games, depending on how much money each player puts on the table and how large the initial blinds, or antes, are. If each player puts up $100, the game will be a modest one; if each player brings $10,000 to the table, the game will be anything but. Pot limit games are usually played for high stakes.

No limit games: In no limit games, the only limit on bet size is the amount of money a player has on the table. No limit games run from modest stakes to the very highest of high stakes games, depending on the amount of money each player brings to the game and the size of the blinds or ante. I recommend that the beginning player stay out of pot limit and no limit games. One mistake against a good player can cost you all your money.

Nuances of Betting

The capped pot: Most games place a limit of three (occasionally four) raises on any one round of betting. After the final raise, the pot is capped and remaining players can only call. This rule keeps the weak player from losing all of his or her money too quickly. It also limits the impact of two players in a partnership from squeezing a third player unfairly. In most games, if only two players remain in a hand, there is no limit on the number of raises that can be made and the two can rock back and forth until one calls or runs out of money.

Check raising: Virtually all organized games permit the check raise. If no one has bet, a player may check (that is, not bet) but then later raise a bet made by another player. Many private games do not allow check raises, but they are an integral part of organized games in casinos and poker rooms. Check raises make perfect sense since they help lessen the disadvantage a player is under when he or she must make the first bet. They also make the game more exciting.

Being all in: In all games, no matter what the stakes, one principle always holds: No player may bring money into the game once a hand has been dealt. A player's wagers (and, of course, liability) for that hand are limited to what he or she has on the table either in cash or chips before the hand is dealt. The old tales about people going out to a bank to borrow money on the strength of a hand are things of the past (and primarily of fiction). When a player has put his or her last dollar into a pot—is "all in"—and there is still more betting, a side pot is formed. The player who is all in is competing only for the main pot; the players who had sufficient funds to cover the additional bets compete for the side pot.

While this rule helps protect a player from serious loss, it can also hurt, since a player with a good hand may win substantially less than he or she might have because of an inability to call or raise the later bets. To keep this from happening, a good rule of thumb is to have between ten and twenty big bets on the table before the hand is dealt. In a $5/10 game you should have between $100 and $200 up; in a $10/20 game, between $200 and $400. There are few things more frustrating than sitting there with "the nuts" (the unbeatable hand) and not being able to get maximum value from it because of a lack of cash on the table. Just how much money you want on the table will also depend on how tight or loose the game is. In a tight game, where most players are conservative and do not raise often, ten to fifteen times the big bet is probably enough. In a loose game, where raises and reraises are common, you will want fifteen to twenty times the big bet on the table.

Freeze out: In some games, and most tournaments, a player may continue to play until he or she has run out of money (is frozen out) and must drop from the game. In freeze-out games, everybody buys in for the same amount and play continues until one player has all the money or, commonly, the last couple of players remaining strike a deal to split the take.

The ante: Some, but not all, games have an ante, which is a token amount of money that all players put up before any cards are dealt. The ante functions to sweeten the pot so that even before any bets are made there is something to be contested for. The ante is more than just a lure; it also changes a good player's strategy. In a game without an ante, a player can develop a kind of bunker mentality and play like the proverbial rock (a tight, conservative player), who plays only opening cards that are reasonably strong, since weak hands can be thrown away without incurring any financial penalty. On the other hand, when there *is* an ante, this strategy doesn't work as well. The antes will gnaw away at your bankroll, and you have to start playing hands that are a little weaker than you might like. Antes loosen up a game. The size of the ante typically runs from 10 to 25 percent of the small bet.

Blind bets: Hold 'em and lowball draw poker games use what are called "blind bets" or simply "blinds." The first player or two to the left of the dealer is obligated to place wagers before the cards are dealt. In hold 'em, where there are typically two blinds, they are called the "small blind" and the "big blind." The small blind is usually in the neighborhood of half the small bet, and the big blind is equivalent to the small bet. In a $5/10 game the small blind is usually $2 and the big blind $5; in a $10/20 game they are typically $5 and $10. The players who have put up the blinds retain the option to fold, call, or raise when their turns come.

The bring-in bet: Since in casinos and poker parlors the games are dealt by professional dealers, there needs to be a procedure so that position (an important element of all games) is evenly distributed. In most stud games, where there is an upcard, the first (or bring-in) bet is made by the player with the lowest card showing. If this bet is raised, the player has the option to fold, call, or reraise. In games where there is no upcard, the first player to act is determined by the location of the theoretical dealer as marked by "the dealer's button," which moves clockwise from player to player after each hand. At the outset, the player(s) immediately to the left of the button have, in a sense, already opened the hand by putting up the blinds. Hence, the first real option goes to the player to the left of the big blind. After the first round of betting, the blinds act first and the dealer last.

A historical tidbit for you: Harry S Truman was a topflight poker player as well as a superb politician. His famous remark, "The buck stops here," did not refer to money, as most people think. It was based on the dealer's button, also known as the "buck." Truman was referring to the obligations of being the designated dealer for a hand—or, in his case, the designated president after the death of Franklin D. Roosevelt.

The vigorish: The vig is the cost to play a game and a significant aspect of the finances of a player. The cost is greatest, proportionally speaking, in low-limit games and becomes less of a factor as the stakes go up. When a rake is used, it is typically 10 percent of the pot up to some limit, such as $40 (maximum vig of $4). When time charges are used, they usually are in the neighborhood of $5 or $6 per half hour for $10/20 and $15/30 games.

THE MOST COMMON GAMES

In private poker games, all manner of madness reigns. Players are forever coming up with loony games with wild cards galore ("seven-stud night baseball," where 3's and 9's are wild, 6's draw an extra card) or common cards in lunatic designs ("fiery cross," with nine common cards arrayed in a cross from which a player may use up to four provided that they are in a row). But in organized settings, only about six or seven games are played with any regularity; the two most common are hold 'em and seven-stud. Others played with some frequency are Omaha eight or better, seven-stud lowball (or "razz"), and various draw games such as straight high, jacks or better, and lowball.

In this chapter I will focus on hold 'em and seven-stud. They are, overwhelmingly, the two most popular games these days, with hold 'em being the most frequently played, particularly in the western states. The reference section at the end of the book lists additional reading for players interested in other games.

Hold 'Em

This game is also known as Texas hold 'em, since legend has it that it was first played in quasilegal games in Texas in the middle 1950s and 1960s. Its progenitor was likely the game of spit (or spit in the ocean), which was the first to use a common card. On the surface, hold 'em is about as simple a poker game as you could imagine. However, lurking below this veneer of simplicity is a complex subtlety that has made it immensely popular. The final tournament of the World Series of Poker, played every year at Binion's Horseshoe, is the $10,000 buy-in, where they play hold 'em and nothing but hold 'em. The attraction of the game derives from the fact that a player has precious little information about his or her opponents' cards since there are no upcards and no draw. Hence, the game maximizes strategy and psychology, the true poker skills.

The Deal

The game is played at a large table seating up to ten players. Each player receives two cards face-down; these cards are referred to as "pocket" or "hole" cards. The player sitting just to the left of the big blind is the first to act on this round. This player may fold, call the blind bet, or raise it. Each player in turn has similar options up to and including the blinds. After a round of betting based on these cards alone, three cards are dealt face-up in the middle of the table. These cards are collectively called the "flop" and are common cards used by all players. A second round of betting ensues; on this and all subsequent rounds the small blind (assuming he or she is still in) is first to act. This round is followed by a fourth common card, called "fourth street" or the "turn." A third round of betting now takes place, followed by a fifth common card, known as "fifth street" or the "river" (hence, to play a hand to the end is known as going to the river). Between each element in the deal, a card is buried unseen; these cards are known as "burn" cards. Burns play no part in the game; they are merely a ritual. The practice originated as a way of reducing cheating.

Some examples and some analysis: A player's hand is composed of the best combination of five cards using any combination of his or her pocket cards along with the common cards. Let's look at a couple of hands to see how this works.

In our first example there are four players who stay to the river. Player 1 holds K♦, 7♦; Player 2 has Q♥, J♦; Player 3 has 10♣, 10♠; Player 4 holds 7♥, 7♣. The flop comes down K♣,10♦, 2♦, fourth street is the 2♥, and the river brings the A♦. Player 1 makes a flush by combining his two original diamonds plus the 10♦, 2♦ on the flop, and the A♦ on the river. This hand beats Player 2, who has a straight (Q♥, J♦ preflop, the K♣, 10♦ on the flop, and the A♦ on the river), but it loses out to Player 3's full house (two 10's preflop, a 10 on the flop, and the pair of deuces). Player 4 is out of this hand with a pair of 7's that never improved.

Let's try another one—only this time let's look at the kinds of thought processes of one of the participants in the game. If you're new to the game, this may feel a bit complex and overly detailed, but stay with me here. Good poker players go through this kind of analysis on virtually every hand.

In this example there are three players. Player 1 holds A♥, 7♥; Player 2 holds K♦, K♣; Player 3 has 9♣, 9♠. The flop comes down A♣, 9♥, 7♦, fourth street produces the K♥, the river brings the 2♥. Player 1 wins the hand with a flush; Player 2 has the second strongest hand with a set of K's; Player 3 is only third best with a set of 9's.

These are the bare facts. But the game is much more than seeing who is dealt the best cards. Let's look at this hand as it develops based on who bet, how much, and when; what cards each player holds relative to what he or she suspects opponents are holding; what cards show up on the board as the hand progresses; and what impact all of this has on the betting.

For the sake of this analysis I'll present it from the point of view of Player 1; let's call her Jean. (This hand, by the way, is a real one and was played in a $15/30 game just a couple of months ago at the Taj Mahal in Atlantic City. Unfortunately, I was Player 2.) Notice that Jean won this hand on the river. Until then, she actually had the weakest hand in that her two pair was getting beat by the trips in each of her opponents' hands. So, did Jean do the right thing by staying all the way to the river? Was this a good call? I don't mean "good" in the sense that Jean won the hand. The real issue here is whether it was a good percentage play, a good poker play. One of the agonizing aspects of hold 'em is that players can always see what would have happened had they stayed in the pot. But knowing that you would have won had you stayed does not mean staying would have been a good play.

Jean's staying in after the flop certainly makes sense since she has aces up with a three-flush, which is a pretty strong hand. Fourth street is a little more problematical since her opponents are both still playing and could easily have improved. They aren't just hanging around because they like the company. They can both be read for an ace in the hole with a likely suited high kicker, a decent-size pair, or even possible trips. However, the fact that the king is a heart is important since now Jean has both two pair and a four flush. If she catches her flush and no pairs show up she has the nuts. If the river brings an ace she could lose only to someone holding an ace and a king, although a seven on the river could actually leave her with the third best full house.

On fourth street, Jean should be calculating the odds on these possible outcomes and determining a course of action. As any good hold 'em player can tell you, the likelihood of catching the flush on the river in this situation is $9/46 = .196$ (there are forty-six cards whose identity is unknown and nine of them are hearts), so Jean will assume that she has roughly a 1 in 5 chance of drawing her flush. In addition, either of the other two aces will give her a very strong full house.

But she's also got to be thinking about how she could get hurt. There are three 2's, three K's, three 9's, and two 7's that could show up, and any one of these cards can hurt her. She doesn't know that both of her opponents have pocket pairs that match cards on the board, although she's got to suspect that at least one of them does and must take this factor into consideration. Hence, there is a maximum of eleven cards that can hurt her. She must consider the possibility that she is facing at least one set somewhere, and she shouldn't really feel comfortable if anything other than one of her eleven cards shows up on the river. Although two pair will win many pots in hold 'em, it may not be good enough here.

Hence, Jean should be thinking two kinds of thoughts. First, she should guess that she is a favorite to win the pot since aces up is a very good hand and she has quite a few "outs" in her flush and full house draws. Second, she should look at how much money is already in the pot, estimate how much more she will have to invest on the bets and possible raises on fourth street, approximate how many more bets she can get out of her opponents on the river if she catches her hand, and determine a course of action. Once the 2♥ shows up on the river, she knows she has the nuts.

This analysis, as any good hold 'em player will tell you, was still a bit simplistic, having left out several important factors: where Jean was sitting at the table relative to the other players; the playing history of Players 2 and 3; how the betting went preflop; and how the betting went on fourth street. So, let's look at these factors. Suppose Jean was the first to act preflop and merely called the big blind. If no one raises, she is quite content to take a look at the flop for a single bet since her hand has potential. If there is a raise she should call. If there is a reraise she should fold—her hand may have potential, but it is not worth two more bets. For whatever it's worth, Jean called from a late position; I, as Player 2, raised on the button; Player 3 was sitting on the big blind and called; and Jean (properly) called.

After the flop comes down, Jean has got to be feeling a bit better with aces up and a three flush. The ace is an important card, since a likely read on Player 2 is that he has a medium to high pair. Having the second pair also makes Jean strong, since another likely read on Player 2 is ace with a high, possibly suited, kicker. However, Jean needs to see how the other players react to the flop. If Player 3 checks from the blind, she should bet out. If Player 2 raises, she should call. After fourth street, her hand has improved significantly since there is now a roughly one in four chance for the nut flush. At this point she should call any and all bets and raises and may even consider raising herself.

For a reader who has never played hold 'em, that analysis probably felt a bit overwhelming—although there are still some elements of the hand left out. However, I hope that by looking fairly deeply into a single hand, we managed to get a feel for the game of hold 'em and a sense of the kinds of analyses that good players carry out as a matter of course.

By the way, both examples I've used here were won by pretty good hands: a full house in one and a flush in the other. Don't for a second think it takes hands like this to win in hold 'em. The typical winning hand in hold 'em is closer to a pair of queens.

Seven-Stud

The game shares some features with hold 'em in that there are seven cards from which the best five are chosen to form a hand and that some of these cards are known to all players while others are known to only one. In my opinion, seven-stud is harder to learn to play at a medium level of skill than hold 'em. This is because there are fewer clear principles to be invoked in seven-stud; much more of the play of the game is based on careful "if-then" kinds of analyses.

The Deal

The game is played at a table with eight seats; with more than eight players, the risk of running out of cards becomes too great. If there aren't enough cards for all players to receive their own on the river, a common card will be used. This situation rarely occurs in medium- and high-stakes games, but it happens with regularity in low-limit games, where many players stay to the bitter end.

Initially, each player receives three cards, two face-down and one face-up, and a round of betting ensues. The player with the lowest upcard is obligated to "bring it in" for at least the table minimum, although a raise is permitted. The bring-in bet is typically less than or equal to the small bet: in a $1/5 game it usually is $1; in a $5/10 game it may be $1 or $2; and in a $10/20 game, $2 or $3. Each player has the option in turn of folding, calling, or raising. If the bet is raised, when it comes back to the player who acted first, he or she has the option to fold, call, or reraise.

After this round of betting, another upcard, called "fourth street," is dealt to each player, and there is another round of betting. On fourth and all subsequent streets, the hand with the highest board (upcards) acts first. The seventh card (the river) is dealt face-down. Between each round, a card is buried unseen, or "burnt."

Seven-stud invites a good deal of action. Like hold 'em, it's a game of position in which betting and playing strategy, particularly in the early rounds, are sensitive to the position of each player at the table. We will look at the issue of position play in more detail later.

Some examples and some analysis: Let's take some examples and see how things work. I will use [ ] to mark hole cards that are known only to the player.

In the first hand we have four players who stay to the river. Player 1 has [10♦, 9♦], 9♣, 10♥, 2♠, 2♥, [A♣]; Player 2 has [A♥, J♦], J♣, 4♥, 8♠, 3♦, [J♥]; Player 3 has [6♦, 6♣], 6♠, A♦, K♣, 7♥, [5♣]; and Player 4 [K♦, Q♦], 7♦, 4♦, 7♠, 10♣, [2♣]. The hand is won by Player 2 with a set of J's. Each of the other players was either strong or reasonably strong early on or had reasonably good drawing hands (hands that have straight or flush potential). Player 3 started with rolled-up 6's (trips on the first three cards), which is a very strong start—although, alas, it never improved. This player is in a most interesting situation. While he might feel he can take control of the hand, he must always be wary of Player 4. Anytime an opponent pairs his door card (first upcard) he must be respected; an early pair is often enough to keep a player in the game, and pairing the door card could signal trips. Player 1 actually has a rather weak hand in that 10's up is nothing to write home about, especially in a multiway pot (one with more than two players). However, except for Player 2's J, no one is showing a scare card (a high card like an A or K that could be paired with a hole card), and so, except for Player 4's paired door card, his 10's up don't look all that bad. Player 4 is holding a four flush on fourth street and, since he sees only one other diamond, feels that he has a pretty good shot at a flush. Indeed, on fourth street his chances of making the flush are in the neighborhood of .6. Unfortunately, like our rolled-up Player 3, he never improves.

Should all these players have stayed to the river? Well, we really can't answer that question without knowing a good deal more about this hand, such as who bet and when, who raised and when, where was each player sitting relative to each other player, and what each player knew about the style of play of the other players. On the face of it, though, it doesn't look like anyone committed any egregious errors.

One more example: Again, this is from a real game I was in, but this time I won—on a fluke. The bring-in bet is from the 4♦. All intervening players fold to me, and I'm sitting next to last. I call with [A♣, 2♣], Q♥. The last player is showing K♠, and he raises. The 4♦ folds; I call. (I do not recommend calling a raise with hands like this. I called only because I know this player is a maniac who often attempts to "force" hands with a high door card and nothing else.) Fourth street brings me the A♦ and my opponent the 6♣. I am high and bet. He raises, so it looks like he might be legit this time. I put him on a pair of K's, possibly two pair. I call. On fifth street I am dealt a blank (a useless card, denoted by "*x*") and he, too, gets no apparent help from the 7♥. I'm still high and check. He bets; I call. Sixth street doesn't appear to help anyone. I am now showing Q♥, A♦, *x*, *x* and looking at K♠, 6♣, 7♥, *x*. On the river, I am dealt [2♥], giving me two pair. I check; he bets, I call, and we showdown our hands. My two pair wins, but he turns up pocket A's. I had the worst of it all the way (his K outkicks my Q) till the deuce rescued me.

There is an important lesson in this hand that every poker player must learn. You try to put your opponent on a hand given the cards showing, his or her manner of playing and betting, and then you act on the basis of that assessment—adjusting, of course, as the hand progresses.

That's about as quick a look at these two most popular poker games as it makes sense to give. We'll come back to each of them for a longer examination later.

HEURISTICS FOR POKER PLAYERS

A heuristic is a rule of thumb, a guiding principle that makes solving a problem easier or provides an avenue for dealing effectively with a complex situation. Basic play in poker is grounded in a number of heuristics that usually apply no matter what the specific game is. However, I concentrate on principles and provide examples that apply most clearly to hold 'em and seven-stud.

Odds: Proper, Pot, and Implied

How do you determine, in any given situation, whether you are getting proper odds for your play? Several elements are relevant: the amount of money you are going to have to invest; how much money is already in the pot when you have to make a decision; your estimate of any additional money you can extract from your opponents if you win the pot; and the chances of winning the pot. Many players use the term "pot odds" as a cover term, but as David Sklansky has pointed out, the manner in which they use it fails to take into consideration a subtle but important distinction between money currently in the pot and money that might show up later in the hand. To prevent confusion, I will use "proper odds" as the generic term, with the understanding that there are two components: pot odds and implied odds.

In order to have pot odds in a given situation, there must be enough money currently in the pot to cover the investment you will have to make, adjusted for the probability of making your hand. For example, if you are drawing for a gut straight on the river in hold 'em, you have about a 1-in-11 shot of getting your card. If you assume that you won't be able to extract any more bets out of your opponents if you catch your hand, there has to be at least eleven times the amount of your bet in the pot to make calling on the turn the proper play. Implied odds refers to your estimate of anticipated additional money coming from your opponents through further action relative to the investment you are called on to make. You may not have pot odds at the time you make your play, but it will still be the proper play if you determine that you have implied odds. Suppose that in the above case there is only nine times your bet in the pot on fourth street, but you are sure that you will get two callers if you catch your hand. You have implied odds for your play. If you didn't think you could get those two additional bets, the call on fourth street would not be a good move.

Appreciating the concept of proper odds is a critical part of poker. This topic will pop up in several places as we go along.

Position Play

Position play is an extremely important aspect of poker and should be an integral part of your game. The general rule is simple: The earlier in a betting round you must act, the stronger you need to be. Most players who first sit down to a game of poker do not adjust their betting and play based on where they are sitting on each hand. This is a big mistake. Just how strong you should be when in an early seat and just how weak you can be and still limp in from a late seat are complex issues that are determined by factors such as: How many people are already in the pot? Have there been raises and reraises? How much money is in the pot? What is the initial strength of your hand? What kind of potential does your hand have? How well do your opponents who are already in the pot play? Just how such factors operate, generally speaking, is covered by the following guidelines:

- If you must act early, you should be quite strong or have a hand with potential for strength. This is especially true in hold 'em, where, if you are first to act, as many as nine players remain, any one of whom could raise or reraise. Obviously, hands like big pairs (A's, K's, or Q's) and big suited connectors (A♥, K♥, or K♠, Q♠) are strong in both games, but there are lots of other combinations that have potential strength. Be wary of seven-stud hands like [2♥, K♣] Q♣ and hold 'em hands like A♠, 6♦, which are not as strong as you may think. You will eventually acquire a sense of what a strong starting hand in hold 'em and seven-stud looks like.

- If you are sitting late, you can limp in with considerably weaker hands, especially in hold 'em. Good hands for limping in are drawing hands that have straight and flush potential or medium and small pairs where catching a set can prove profitable. These hands can also be played from an earlier position if you expect a lot of players. However, in seven-stud you should not automatically be calling from a late position if you have a small pair, the pot is multiway, and it is raised. In a situation like this, you are a distinct underdog.

- No matter where you are sitting, if you think you might still face additional raises you should be stronger than if you can draw a card or see the flop by simply calling a single bet. However, there are exceptions. If, for example, you hold something like a small or medium pair in hold 'em and there are many players in the pot, you don't really care if it is raised or not. If you catch trips, fine; if not, just fold when someone bets.

- If you are sitting late and have a drawing hand, you are in a reasonable spot. This is especially true if there is a raise and several players in front of you have called it. You, however, do not generally want to raise in early rounds with drawing hands since you do not want to drive people out. Drawing hands are maximally efficient in multiway pots, since you need proper odds for your call.

- If you are sitting late with a medium pair, your hand may have more value than you suspect. If you can call a single bet and see the flop, do so. If you flop a set, you're in good shape; if you don't, you get out. If the pot is raised before it gets to you, just fold—unless it is a multiway pot, in which case you should call as in the third item above.

- With a strong hand, particularly a high pair, you should raise no matter what position you are in. Big pairs play better against a limited number of opponents, and you want to trim the field as quickly as possible. Do not "slow play" big pairs.

These principles of position play are based on simple logic. If you call in an early position, you may be raised and even reraised by players who act after you. You need to be strong, otherwise you will have to fold and will have just thrown away a bet. It can get even worse. Once you've made that first call, you can start feeling committed to your hand and get suckered in by saying to yourself, "Well, I'm in for one bet already, might as well go for one or two more and see what happens." Down this road looms disaster. You are already weak, and everything we learned about probabilities in earlier chapters should be screaming out that even if you do improve, the most likely thing to happen to the second-best hand is that it ends up second best. Folding weak hands in an early position is the safest, and in the long run most profitable, strategy. In later positions, when there are fewer hands behind you that can hurt you, either with good cards or with additional raises, it is reasonable to call with weaker hands.

Let's look at an example or two and see what lines of thinking you should be following. Suppose you are on the button in hold 'em and have 65 suited (a 6 and a 5 of the same suit, such as 6♣, 5♣). The first two players folded, and everybody after that called the big blind. It is proper to call with this hand. If one of the blinds raises after you it is still proper to call. However, if there is only one player in before you, calling would be wrong. You have a drawing hand. You are not strong now, but you could become very strong. In such a situation, you want as many people as possible in the hand since you need to have proper odds for your flush or straight. If there is only one other player in the hand, you will not be getting value for your hand should you make it. If you are in an early position, do not play this hand.

Here's an example from Sklansky's *The Theory of Poker*: Suppose you are sitting in second position in hold 'em with A♦, 10♦ and the flop comes down A♣, Q♣, 9♠. On the face of it you have a strong hand, but suppose the player in front of you bets and there are several players yet to act behind you. Your position puts you in a tricky spot, particularly if the pot was raised preflop. The problem is that the first player is likely very strong to be betting in a situation like this, and worse, the possibility of raises from later hands who might be holding hands like AK or AQ suited or even a set makes it pretty clear that you are getting negative implied odds in this situation. The players yet to act may very well be holding flush or straight draws, further compromising your situation. So, despite sitting there with what looks like a rather strong hand, you are best advised to toss your aces into the muck.

Position play is an important element in terms of reading your opponents. Since the general principles outlined here are known and practiced by many players, you can often read your opponents' play in terms of where they are sitting. Early raises are generally signs of strength, since the player feels comfortable enough with his or her hand to handle possible reraises. Late raises are often book bets (ones that follow advice given in books like this one) and do not necessarily signal as much strength. Indeed, these raises may be attempts to steal the ante and the blind.

Ante and Blind Stealing

A surprising amount of money can be swiped by well-timed bets and raises that serve to steal the antes, the blinds, or even a couple of first-round bets. Ante stealing, however, is tricky, since the attempt is liable to be called or even reraised. You should try to steal when you have a hand with some strength, so that you can play if called and still have a chance. But it should be a hand that, were it to be called, would likely not be best.

Even if called, an attempted ante steal can also serve to set up a hand for a pressed bluff, where you begin your bluff early and press it throughout the hand. Suppose in seven-stud you are sitting next to last, are showing K♠ (which happens to be the highest card on board), and no one called the bring-in bet. Raise almost no matter what you have as pocket cards. Now suppose you get called by the player behind you and the bring-in. This may turn out to be okay since it's entirely possible your next card is something like the 7♠. If you are still high, bet once more. Should fifth street bring you another spade, you may still have nothing, but you are looking very scary—especially given your earlier raise. And you don't need to catch suited cards; another K should win you the hand outright, as might another overcard such as an A or even a Q. Moreover, your opponents who haven't shown any obvious strength are likely playing drawing hands, and if they fail to improve they will probably concede the pot to you. An attempted ante steal can frequently gain you an even larger pot without your ever having to show your cards.

Playing Big Pairs versus Drawing Hands

I hinted at these situations earlier, but let's make things explicit here. Bet big pairs early and hard, raise, and even reraise. You want to reduce the number of players in the hand. Big pairs play best against a small field because your implied odds drop as the number of opponents goes up. While big pairs like aces or kings are certainly good starting hands in hold 'em or seven-stud, they are not as profitable in multiway pots as they are with a small number of opponents.

On the other hand, drawing hands play best against many opponents since you will be getting good implied odds. This argument is based on the simple observation that you are going to fail to make your hand a lot more often than you are going to make it. Hence, you want to have as many players as possible hanging around and putting money into the pot for those times when you do catch your cards. Moreover, you want to be able to play as cheaply as possible while your hand is developing (or failing to develop), and you want to step up the betting only when the odds shift in your favor.

Bluffing and Semibluffing

Bluffing is both a wonderfully simple and a wonderfully complex element of poker. In a nutshell, bluffing is representing a hand as something other than what it is—giving the impression you are strong when you are somewhat or very much weaker. A bluff is a bet that you prefer not be called.

A semibluff is a bit different. The term was coined by David Sklansky, who used it to refer to a bet or raise that is made with a somewhat stronger hand. What distinguishes a semibluff from a real bluff is that you semibluff with a hand when you want your opponents to fold but you still have a reasonable chance of improving to the best hand if they don't.

Here are some rules of thumb:

- Your bluffs should be based on their expected value. If you are considering running a bluff against a single opponent, you should try to first estimate how likely it is that he or she will fold, and second, how much money is in the pot. If you judge that there is only a one-third shot the bluff will persuade your opponent to fold, you need to have at least twice as much money in the pot as the bluff will cost you, otherwise you are not getting proper pot odds. Counting the size of the pot is the easy part. Don't forget, the bigger the pot, the more reluctant your opponent is going to be to fold. Bluffing gets tougher as the pot gets larger.

- Bluff a strong player, not a weak one. One of the hallmarks of strong players is the ability to throw away good hands when they believe they are beaten. When you have the appropriate position or scare cards showing and you are thinking of running a bluff, you must take into account the level of your opponents. Weak, passive players, particularly those who do not understand the principles of position play or who fail to judge the importance of a scare card, should not be the targets of your bluffs because they are going to call you with hands they should fold. When your opponents are passive players, wait until you are strong and then hit them, since they are prone to making inappropriate calls anyway. The only time you should try a bluff against such a player is if it appears he or she doesn't have anything either, but you think that his or her hand is still better than yours.

- Try to evaluate the entire situation at the table as a way of tailoring your bluffs. Here's a standard ploy that works surprisingly often. You're playing hold 'em and no one shows any preflop enthusiasm. The flop comes down K♥, 8♣, 3♦. A bet will often win the pot, especially if you are up against a small number of opponents. But be careful: Don't try this if the flop shows suited or connected cards. You could be walking into a strong hand.

Let's take another example. You're playing seven-stud; no one raised the bring-in bet, and signs of weakness abound. You catch a scare card like a suited A or K on fourth street. A bet here can often have the same effect as above. Again, do not try this if your opponents show suited or connected cards.

- You shouldn't generally try to bluff more than one or, occasionally, two players. You can sometimes get away with forcing several players out (particularly in hold 'em, when a pair flops or when there was no bet on the previous round), but it isn't recommended; the likelihood of getting called is just too high. On the other hand, semibluffing more than one player is often worth trying, because the play is made when your hand has clear possibilities of improving.

- From time to time take advantage of the pressed bluff; a bluff that you start early in a hand and continue to press as though you held a strong hand from the outset. Such opportunities occur most often in seven-stud, where, for example, you show a scare card on third street and catch one or more cards that make you look strong. Press bluffing is not recommended against more than one or two opponents.

- Adjust your bluffing to take into account the nature of the game in which you are playing. In particular, tight and loose games need to be approached differently. You should rarely bluff in loose games.

Playing Against a Bluff or a Semibluff

Knowing how and when to bluff or semibluff is only half the story. You also have to know how to deal with such plays when you suspect they are being made by your opponents. If you think your opponent is on a bluff and you have a strong hand, set the trap with a simple call. The interesting situation is when you have a dreadful hand yourself, one that could win only if your opponent is indeed bluffing. The standard procedure is the reverse of that given above: Call a suspected bluff when you anticipate a positive expected value for the play. Suppose you've estimated that there is about a 10 percent chance your opponent is running a bluff. You should call the bet if the money you figure to win is more than nine times what you would need to pay to make the call. As your estimate of the likelihood your opponent is bluffing goes up, the amount of money needed for the call goes down. As before, the easy part is counting the money in the pot.

Playing in Loose Games versus Tight Games

A loose game is one where people are playing many hands. A tight game is one where players look for strong hands before calling and go to the river only with hands that have a high likelihood of winning the pot. Loose games are the best games to make money in, especially if you are a controlled and sensible player who knows probabilities and pays attention to whether or not you are getting proper odds for your plays. When you catch your hand in a loose game, you will typically get maximum value from it because you're not going to have any trouble getting callers. In loose games, you should bluff less (if at all), semibluff occasionally (but pick your spots), and play more on the conservative side. In tight games, you should bluff more often, semibluff frequently, and raise (not call) with weaker hands than you normally would. In tight games you do *not* want to play weak hands if someone is already in the pot.

Keep in mind that there are variations within loose and tight games. A game can be loose but active and aggressive, with players raising and reraising on virtually every hand. You need to be very careful in this kind of game, especially in early position, since you are almost certain to be facing raises. Or a game can be loose but passive, in that there are several players who don't always bet their hands but tend to call when others raise. These are, for good players, the very best games. You typically will be able to get maximum value for your winning hands but won't be under pressure all the time.

Tight games don't show this kind of variability, but they do differ in the degree of skill displayed around the table. Tight players tend to be either blindly conservative, timorous players who fail to understand the value of many of their hands, or strong players who know their probabilities but tend toward a conservative approach to the game. The former kind of player can be beat by bluffing, semibluffing, and frequent ante and blind stealing. The latter is the kind of player I am recommending you become. Such players cannot be easily beat. If the table is full of them, move.

Know Your Opponents

A lot of poker strategy is built around your ability to read your opponents, to put them "on a hand" and act accordingly. Proper reading of an opponent is not easy; it takes experience and practice. However, a couple of basic principles can keep you in the game while you hone your psychological skills. The main thing you want to do is try to place each of your opponents along the following dimensions.

Weak to Strong

How strong do you judge each of the players sitting at your table to be? Within an hour or so, a sufficient number of circumstances will have emerged so that you have a sense of who knows how to play the game. You should then begin to adjust your play accordingly. Follow the heuristics given above for dealing with different situations. Be aware of the fact that a good opponent will be making the same assessment of the other players, including you. Strong players spot each other quickly and pay greater attention to each other's play than to that of the lesser players at the table.

Loose to Tight

Loose players call more often, play weaker hands, and pay to see more cards than tight players. Try to get a sense of the other players in terms of how likely they are to play particular kinds of hands in particular positions. This kind of understanding becomes critical when you must go against an opponent heads up. For example, you are playing seven-stud and your opponent, whom you read as a tight player, calls in early position with a weak door card like a 4. You should initially put him on something like [A, K] or [K, Q suited] or even a pair of 4's with a high kicker. You probably shouldn't read him for a high pair, since he didn't raise. Whether you stick with this read or adjust it will depend on what happens on subsequent streets and how the money flows.

On the other hand, loose players are much tougher to read with a weak door card like a 4. They could have a small pair, or something like [7, 6] and be willing to draw a card or two to see if the straight starts to shape up. If the tight player pairs a weak door card, the chance of trips is not as great as it would be with the loose player.

Maniac to Rock

Maniacs are scary players. They bet aggressively, raising and reraising on hand after hand. Maniacs tend to lose in the long run because they overplay hands, play too many hands, and typically do not have the subtlety needed to become really strong poker players. They can, however, wreak havoc on a table. If you let them control you, they can take your money away quickly. The best way to deal with maniacs is to tighten up your game, become more conservative than usual, and wait for the right opportunity to emerge. You need to be patient and willing to absorb the initial losses you will incur from stolen antes, blinds, and first bets. Maniacs are notable for having huge variances in their day-to-day fortunes. When they are catching cards, they can win gobs of money; when they are not, they can lose at stunning rates. At the beginning of this chapter I mentioned sitting next to "the poker player from hell." He was a maniac.

Be careful to distinguish between the true maniac and the solid but aggressive player. Many extremely good players are quite aggressive and will raise with any hand they feel has either an immediate edge or an excellent chance of gaining an edge. These folks are not maniacs, anything but. Do not treat them like maniacs or they will eat you alive. The main distinguishing feature is the number of hands played. Maniacs play too many hands.

Rocks, on the other hand, are boring players. They sit at the table, impassive and conservative, looking for the nuts on every hand. They have often read books that lay out the theoretical value of each starting hand in hold 'em or the probability of winning with any given third street hand in seven-stud. They won't call a first bet without what they think is a substantial edge. A table full of rocks is about as much fun as a convention of teetotaling accountants. But they can be beat: They tend to undervalue their own hands, mistakenly tossing away potential winning opportunities; and they are vulnerable to steals and bluffs.

Watch out that you don't mistake a strong but conservative player for a rock. Strong conservative players are merely a bit more risk-aversive than average, but they know probabilities, use position play, and can spot situations with positive expected value. If you try to muscle a good conservative player by treating him or her like a rock, you will find yourself in uncomfortable and expensive traps.

Tells (Others' and Yours)

Tells are players' mannerisms that signal information about their cards or their intentions. Tells can occasionally be so obvious that the average player can spot them. For example, some players like to talk about a hand they don't have. They may be showing 7♦, 9♣, 8♥ in seven-stud and say something like "Three connectors and you guys aren't convinced yet?" as they toss in their checks on fifth street. If you are dealing with an unsophisticated player, it is pretty safe to read such a ploy as a tell of a bluff. Other players develop odd habits like putting a chip or two on top of easily remembered pocket cards like a large pair but not on top of more ordinary hands, which they need to keep consulting as the hand progresses.

If you manage to pick up a tell, good for you. Use the information wisely. But it is more important to become aware of *your own* actions, facial expressions, movements, and verbal tendencies to make sure you are not giving critical information to other players. Let me reiterate my buzz line for this book: Know thyself. When you are at the table, try to step back from yourself and get a sense of what you look like, what kind of image you are projecting, how you act and react to particular situations. Do you hunker over your shoulders when bluffing? Do you tend to lean forward when pressing a strong hand? Does your demeanor shift when you catch a miracle card on the river? Do you act the same when you're rolled-up as you do when you've just been dealt all rags (worthless cards)?

It is not easy to do this. I had been playing poker for only a short time when I realized that I had developed that stupid tell in seven-stud where I would remark on the strength of my board when bluffing. But rather than dropping this verbal gesture (I am by nature a talker at the table), I counteracted its downside by occasionally commenting on the strength of my board when I had a made hand. Now it's no longer a tell.

For the reader who is becoming expert enough so that the issue of tells has become important, I recommend *Mike Caro's Book of Tells*. If you read this book, don't take seriously Caro's estimates of how much money reading each tell is worth. A friend of mine calculated that, according to what Caro says in this book, if you learned all of the tells and could use them, you would be winning an average of something like twenty big bets every hour on tells alone! This, of course, is silly.

Raising or Folding versus Calling

Calling is often the worst option for a player, though it is the most common. It frequently feels appropriate since it is cheaper than raising and, unlike folding, still leaves you with a shot at the pot. But the proper option in many situations should be limited to folding or raising, with calling being the least effective and least profitable in the long run. The principles are straightforward.

- If you have a strong hand and your good poker judgment tells you that you have the advantage over most of your opponents, you should raise rather than call.

- If you start out with weak cards and are in doubt about their value in the hand, you want to get out before you have wasted a bet. Calling in such a situation could make matters far worse, since if you were to improve slightly you could be induced to toss in an additional bet and then find yourself chasing a hand in which you are not getting implied odds all the way to the river.

- If you have a decent hand but strongly suspect you are beaten and have little chance for improvement, fold. Get out as soon as possible. Calling in such situations is almost always a bad move. It is what Sklansky and Malmuth call "a compounding error." Not only does it cost you a bet now, it is likely to cost you several more should a teaser show up on the next card. Here's a classic example. In seven-stud, you have [Q♣, 10♦], 10♥ and (mistakenly) call the first bet and a raise from the A♥ in an early position. On fourth street, you catch 8♦ but the A♥ catches K♦ and bets. You are virtually certain you are facing a higher pair, since your opponent shows two overcards. But the three straight beckons, and you let yourself get suckered into calling. On fifth street, you catch a blank, but since you're in for so much already, lo and behold, you find yourself calling another bet. This kind of thing happens to weak players all the time, and good players feast off it. This hand should have been folded on third street when the A raised.

- If it is early in a seven-stud hand and you have what you are pretty sure is the top pair against one or two opponents, do not call. Raise like a citizen of Chicago, early and often. If you can force your opponents into folding, you take the pot. Calling (or worse, checking) gives your opponents either a cheap or a free card. Of course, once the hand has progressed you may need to adjust your play. If an opponent is drawing to something like a four flush you won't be able to force him or her out. Slow down, call, and see what develops.

- Frequent (appropriate) raising is one of the keys to taking control of an opponent. But be careful. While raising is often a better strategy than calling, your raises should be appropriate. How often you raise and how aggressively you play should be determined by factors like your position at the table, the nature of the game, and the skill of your opponents.

Throwing Good Money After Bad

You're going to make mistakes and toss in a bet or two that your hand and/or position really didn't rate. Many players, once they realize they have committed such an error, tend to reason "I'm in this deep already, might as well go to the river." What can I say? If you're not getting proper odds, do not do this! There is, of course, more to this advice. Most weak players don't know whether they are throwing in "good" or "bad" money. Suppose you have pocket 7's in hold 'em, and call in late position. The flop comes down with three overcards. There is now a bet and a raise in front of you. How do we evaluate this situation? Well, the preflop call was okay, a pair of 7's isn't a bad hand in late position, but any postflop bets would be a mistake. The first call wasn't "bad," it was reasonable. It only began to look "bad" after about the worst flop that you could imagine. A flop with three overcards plus a bet and a raise virtually guarantees that you are most likely third best, and there is essentially no hope for you in this hand. And don't even think about a set of 7's, since you'll never get pot odds for the draw.

Here's another one, the kind of bonehead play we've all pulled at one time or another. You're playing seven-stud and you think you have [9♦, K♦], 9♠, which isn't a terrible hand. So you call a raise by the Q♦ from late position. After you are dealt 6♥ on fourth street, you check your hole cards and discover that the 9♦ has been transmogrified into the 8♦. This officially makes that first call a bad bet. Fold. Don't even think about those diamonds.

Your Kicker

Most players neglect to take their kicker into account when two opponents have hands of similar strength. This problem is not as important in seven-stud as it is in hold 'em, where it plagues unsophisticated players who tend to focus on their highest card and neglect the impact of their kicker. Put simply, AK unsuited is stronger than AQ unsuited, which in turn is stronger than AJ unsuited, and so forth. If you are hold-ing A7 off suit and the flop comes down A, 4, 2 you should not feel all that secure with your pair of A's. My intuitive estimate is that, in hold 'em, on average about two to three times in every hour or so of play a hand will be decided on the basis of the kicker. This rarely occurs in seven-stud. If you don't think that winning or losing one or two decent-size pots an evening is a critical element in the game of poker, then per-haps you should head back to the roulette table.

When to Chase

One of the many factors that differentiate weak from strong players is the propensity to chase (pay to draw additional cards in the hope of making a strong hand). Weak players tend to chase with hands that appear to have potential, such as three straights, three flushes, and two small pair. Weak players also tend to chase with hands where they have a decent pair but a weak kicker or weak overcards—although in these sit-uations they often don't realize they are chasing, since they fail to appre-ciate the importance of kickers and overcards.

Strong players will chase, but only when the conditions are right, such as:

- The potential the hand affords makes it a sensible play. An example: In seven-stud you have [A♥, Q♣], K♣, 7♣, 3♣ and you are looking at 7♦, Q♦, Q♥. So far you are beaten, but your hand has tremendous potential while your opponent has but a small number of outs to improve to a very strong hand, like a full house. You've got two overcards, a four flush, and even a long shot at a straight. If your overcards and your suit are both live (not many of them are out) you have a strong drawing hand and should definitively "chase."

- The size of the pot makes it a reasonable play. An example: In hold 'em, you've got suited connectors like 8♥, 7♥ in the pocket, there is a raise and five callers, and suddenly the pot is quite large. The flop comes K♦, 6♥, 4♦. You are pretty sure you are facing a pair of K's, probably with a good kicker; indeed, you may even be facing a set. However, it is proper to call a bet to look at fourth street. A 5 fills your straight outright, a 9 gives you an open-ended draw on the river, and any heart gives you a shot at a flush. This is a hand to "chase" with— at least till fourth street.

I put "chase" in quotes in the two examples above because strong players would not regard these two plays as chasing. They tend to use the term derogatorily to designate a poor play made when proper odds are not being offered. They would view the two plays above as well-judged draws. Generally, seven-stud invites more sensible chasing than hold 'em. Lots of situations emerge in seven-stud, as we will see when we look more closely at the game, that give a player implied odds for a chase. Such situations are less frequent in hold 'em.

Playing in Low-Stakes Games

In poker, there are three primary elements of the game: the cards, the betting, and your opponents. They interact in subtle ways depending on the stakes. A complaint you will hear over and over again among decent, modest stakes players is that they can't seem to beat the $1/5 and $3/6 games. They routinely get killed whenever they step down to them. One reason is that they are not adjusting properly to a game that is looser than they are used to. In lower-stakes games, the cards are nearly everything. Most players don't attend to subtle psychological ploys, and few of them appreciate well-judged raises designed to thin out the field. As noted player Chuck Thompson puts it, you need to play low-level games with a "drawing mentality," while you are best served in higher-stakes games by a "pair mentality."

One good way to judge how important the cards are in a particular game is to get a sense of the proportion of hands that go to a showdown. If your poker-playing experiences are anything like mine, most hands in $1/5 games have a showdown. But the proportion drops systematically as the stakes go up, so that in $15/30 games a large number of hands, perhaps even a majority, are won without a showdown. Since the cards are randomly distributed without prejudice for the cash on the table, clearly the betting and the psychology of the game increase in importance as the stakes go up.

Logic and Psychologic

An awful lot of what we've been discussing has involved a delicate balance between clean probabilistic and logical analyses and the psychological elements that temper them. In order to play this game and have the remotest chance of winning you must understand its probabilistic aspects and be able to calculate proper odds. You must appreciate the role of logic. Every interesting hand (and, of course, not all hands are interesting) plays itself out as a series of "if-then" judgments. If my opponent has X and I have Y, then I should play my hand one way; but if he or she has X and I have Z, then other action is called for. It is essential that you learn to understand these situations when they emerge and make the appropriate logical analyses. Finally, a strong player must learn how to view his or her opponents as people who think, feel, react, hope, wonder, guess, and pray.

In his wonderful book *Big Deal*, Anthony Holden tells the tale about how the late, great Jack "Treetop" Straus psychologically maneuvered a losing hand into a winner. Straus, a one-time college basketball star, had achieved a certain deserved fame as an excellent high-stakes poker player, having won the annual tournament at Binion's Horseshoe in 1982. Straus found himself drawn into a hold 'em hand with 72 off suit, which, as every hold 'em player knows, is the very pits, the worst of all possible starts. However, the flop brought 7, 3, 3, so that Straus was sitting with what might just be the top two pair. He bet $1,000 and got a $5,000 raise tossed back at him, which suggested that his opponent had a decent-size pocket pair (in fact, he had jacks). The proper play is to fold, but Straus had been on a rush and didn't even consider it. However, the only thing that could save him was a 7 or a bluff. He decided on the latter, and called in preparation for the turn, which produced a deuce. This card gave Straus three pairs, which didn't help his hand at all but gave him the card he needed to pull off his now-legendary ploy.

He went all in, shoving every last check he had into the pot. The psychological message was clear: "I've got a pocket pair of 2's or 7's or one of them with a 3." It didn't matter which, of course, since any of these hands gave him a full house and the pot unless the river brought his opponent a miracle card. Then Straus pulled his con. He pushed his pocket cards toward his opponent and told him, "For a little bitty green check [a measly $25, when they were playing for thousands] I'll let you look at one of these." The other guy tossed over a quarter check and pointed to the leftmost card, which turned out to be a deuce. The message was clear: Straus had two deuces, otherwise he wouldn't have given the guy the option to pick either card. After all, Straus would never have paid to see the flop with 72, would he? The guy folded and Straus took the pot.

Fascinating, yes? Well, yes and no. The problem is that Straus's opponent lost this hand because he didn't balance probabilities with logic and psychology. What he should have been thinking is, "Why in the name of heaven would a predator like Jack 'Treetop' Straus let me off the hook? If he's giving me the option to pick either of two cards, there are only so many things he could have and they all involve deuces, treys, and 7's. If he's full or has quads I'm in serious trouble. But we're playing no-limit poker, folks, and there is no way someone like Straus is going to give me a chance to fold my two pair for nothing but a lousy green check. If he's got only 7's up he is much the worst at this point, and his only real [probabilistically speaking] chance is to get me out of the pot. Hence, he really did call with 72 and must be running a con. Screw this. I call!" Now, *that's* fascinating.

The Leather Ass

Poker is a game of patience, and a good poker player needs to develop a leather ass. Poker professional Roy West once said: "Poker is hours of boredom interspersed with moments of terror." I would add "and exhilaration." You cannot force a poker game to cooperate any more than you can force someone to love you. When the interminable run of rags goes on longer than you believed it ever could, just pull back. Relax, watch the other players at the table. Scrutinize their faces, their mannerisms, their betting patterns. Use the dead time for gain, learn things about them that you will be able to use later. Just make sure you don't chase hands or decide to play with weak cards because you are tired of tossing everything away. Keep reminding yourself, you didn't come here just to play cards, you came to win some money while playing cards.

This is a hard lesson to learn, especially when the run of unfilled flushes and stillborn hands is starting to get expensive, but it is essential. You cannot become a strong poker player if you play in situations where you have the worst of it. Just sit there and feel the calluses forming on your butt. You'll need them for the next time this happens.

When a Player Gets "Your" Card

In seven-stud, don't get upset if an opponent gets "your" card. It can be really annoying when you have a pair of jacks and watch the player to your left get a jack. But don't be upset. In many cases, this may actually improve your chances. While it's true that the likelihood of catching your set is diminished, it's also true that your opponent just got shortchanged, since he or she was just dealt a card that is unlikely to be of any help. Hence, you are now playing against an opponent who is effectively working with only six cards, and if your hand were already best it is now more likely you will end up that way. Exposed cards cut both ways, and you must evaluate the total impact they have on the hand as it develops.

The Importance of "a Bet"

Saving or winning a mathematical fraction of a bet amounts to much more than the average player realizes. Much of the advice in this chapter involves subtle plays and decisions that don't look big. An unsophisticated player would hardly recognize them as having any importance at all. But they do! These decisions gently shift the game from one with negative expectation to one with positive expectation. When you put money into a pot you should do so only when your action is an investment with long-term positive expectation. Even the best players average something like only one big bet per hour profit. Pay attention to the little things; it is amazing how quickly they'll add up.

Computer Simulations

There are a number of computer simulations of various poker games that profess to give the player advice about the relative strengths of starting hands. Some are for sale by themselves, some are presented in books on poker. There is information of interest in these analyses, but be careful before using them in a serious way at the table. Most of them are based on Monte Carlo analyses, which assume that your opponents start with random cards and that all players stay until the end of the hand. But these games just aren't played this way. From a third to a half of all hands in middle- and high-stakes games are won without a showdown; another third to a half or so are won in a heads-up situation. Hands in which many players stay to the river are not all that common. While these simulations are useful in helping a player identify strong initial hands, they should not be used slavishly.

Heuristical Overview

We've covered a good bit of material so far, and the beginner may feel a bit confused. At one point I emphasized the need to play aggressively, suggesting that raising is a better strategy than calling. A couple of paragraphs later I focused on the need to play tighter and more conservatively in order to save bets. At another point I counseled ante stealing and then recommended against playing hands where you didn't think you had the best of it at the early stages.

What's going on here is that poker is a very complex game. In a typical game, a good player must play somewhat conservatively, yet raise and fold more often than call; but adjustments in this strategy are called for if the game is loose. It's just as right that you go for the occasional ante or blinds steal as that you should generally approach the initial round of play with a keen conservative eye. The trick is to know when to raise and when to fold, when to attempt to steal antes, when to attack and when to slow-play a hand and let an opponent build a pot for you, when to bluff and when to call a suspected bluff, when to bet with weak cards and when to toss a made flush into the muck. Different circumstances call for different actions. If you feel confused, continue with the rest of this chapter, then go back and read it all over again. Then play some hold 'em or seven-stud for a couple dozen hours, try to use the advice you recall, and go back and read the chapter again. Then play some more poker. Then pick up some of the other books I've recommended. Then . . . Listen, do you want to get to Carnegie Hall or not?

A DEEPER LOOK AT HOLD 'EM

Preflop Hands, or, What's in Your Pocket?

The most important decision you will make in a hold 'em hand is whether or not to pay to see the flop. On the surface this question seems trivial; you toss in a couple of bucks and you get to look at three cards. In hold 'em, any hand can turn into a monster; start with 72 off suit and you can flop 7's full or even quads. What more could anyone want? The problem is that this attitude is a prescription for financial ruin. How you play your first two cards is critically dependent on their value, your position at the table, and the betting pattern that has occurred.

So, let's first get a sense of the value of the various playable starting hands. There's no simple mathematical algorithm that can rank the starting hands. While it is clear that starting with a pair of A's is stronger than starting with a pair of K's, it is not so clear that something like 88 is better than A♦, 6♦. There are several published rankings of the value of starting hands in hold 'em, and the proponents of each argue over which is best. The one I present here is the one published in Sklansky's and Malmuth's excellent book *Hold 'em for Advanced Players*. I believe it has the highest *playing* efficiency. For example, 88 is ranked above A♦, 6♦ because with a medium pair, if you flop a set you are in good shape, and if you don't and overcards show up, you just get out. But with A♦, 6♦, while you will also occasionally flop a strong hand, when you don't you will frequently find yourself seduced into several additional bets before your hand displays its weakness. Medium pairs have higher expected value than hands like A♦, 6♦. They *play* better.

Sklansky and Malmuth distinguish eight categories of playable initial hands. They are reproduced here (within each class, the hands are ranked by strength). Suited cards are denoted by *s*; *x* stands for any low card.

—Group 1: AA, KK, QQ, JJ, AK*s*

—Group 2: 1010, AQ*s*, AJ*s*, KQ*s*, AK

—Group 3: 99, J10*s*, QJ*s*, KJ*s*, A10*s*, AQ

—Group 4: 109*s*, KQ, 88, Q10*s*, 98*s*, J9*s*, AJ, K10*s*

—Group 5: 77, 87*s*, Q9*s*, 108*s*, KJ, QJ, J10, 76*s*, 97*s*, A*x*s, 65*s*

—Group 6: 66, A10, 55, 86*s*, K10, Q10, 54*s*, K9*s*, J8*s*

—Group 7: 44, J9, 43*s*, 75*s*, 109, 33, 98, 64*s*, 22, K*x*s, 107*s*, Q8*s*

—Group 8: 87, 53*s*, A9, Q9, 76, 42*s*, 32*s*, 96*s*, 85*s*, J8, J7*s*, 65, 54, 74*s*, K9, 108.

In tabular form, the patterns become more obvious and easier to remember (first for pairs, then for nonpairs):

Pocket Cards	Group
AA, KK, QQ, JJ,	1
1010	2
99	3
88	4
77	5
66, 55	6
44, 33, 22	7

Pocket Cards	Group If Suited	Group If Not Suited
AK	1	2
AQ	2	3
AJ	2	4
A10	3	6
A9	5	8
A*x*	5	—
KQ	2	4
KJ	3	5
K10	4	6
K9	6	8
K*x*	7	—
QJ	3	5
Q10	4	6
Q9	5	8
Q*x*	7	—
J10	3	5
J9	4	7
J8	6	8
J7	8	—
109	4	7
108	5	8

Pocket Cards	Group If Suited	Group If Not Suited
107	7	—
98	4	7
97	5	—
96	8	—
87	5	8
86	6	—
85	8	—
76	5	8
75	7	—
74	8	—
65	5	8
64	7	—
54	6	8
53	8	—
43	7	—
42	8	—
32	8	—

If we scan this table a number of intriguing aspects of hold 'em appear.

- It is pretty clear that high pairs are strong hands. You've already got good cards; the others are going to have to draw theirs. However, the value of a high pair is diminished when there are many other players in the hand.
- All pairs, no matter how small, have some value. First, a pair gives you a shot at a set. Second, a pair appearing on the board gives you two pair. Note, however, that if your pocket pair is low, two pair is not necessarily a strong hand. The probabilities that these outcomes will actually take place are given at the end of this section.
- Big connectors are strong, especially when they are suited. Connectors give you a chance at straights, and when they are suited, at flushes. The

strength of suited connectors is seen by the fact that hands like 98s are ranked in Group 4, and even 32s is in occasionally playable Group 8. Hands of superficial similarity actually have rather different strengths. For example, A10s is a Group 3 hand, but A9s is in Group 5 because of the loss of the straight possibilities—and the obvious fact that 9 is a smaller card than 10.

- Spaced connectors lose value compared with connectors. KQ is in Group 4 but K9 is in Group 8. Similarly, QJ is in Group 5 but Q9 is in Group 8 and Q8 is "off the board." These rankings reflect the impact of two factors. The first is the lessening of the chance of drawing a straight with spaced connectors; KQ has much more straight flexibility than K9, which requires three perfect cards. The second is the impact of pairing either card. If you pair either the K or Q when holding KQ, you have a high pair with a high kicker. However, if you hold K9 you lose a lot of flexibility. If the board shows a K, you have a high pair but only a modest kicker; if the board shows a 9, you have but a middling pair.

- The role of the kicker is evidenced by the rapid drop off of hands with an A or a K as the other card gets smaller. AK is ranked in Class 1 but Ax and Kx are unranked. If an A flops, the one in your hand derives a good deal of its value from your second card. On the other hand, when these cards are suited the flush possibility raises their value significantly.

This table represents an approach to the game that is regarded by some as conservative. Of the 2,652 possible pocket hands only 566, or a tad over 21 percent, are listed. Does this mean that you will never play an unranked hand? Not at all; other factors will often dictate action on your part, as we shall see.

Preflop Play: Position Is Critical

Knowing the relative value of hands is just the beginning. Their value depends largely on where you are sitting and the betting that has occurred before you are called upon to act. Recall that in hold 'em, the button determines the dealer, and the blinds sit just to its left. The person to the left of the big blind must act first preflop; the blinds act first on all subsequent rounds. The typical table has ten players. The first three positions to the left of the blinds can be regarded as early positions, the next three as middle positions, the next two as late positions. The blinds, since they have already committed money to the pot, need to be looked at separately.

Early Position Play

Here you need to be strongest in order to play, because there are so many people who have yet to act that the chances are high one or more of them will be strong and will raise and even reraise. Some principles:

- If you are the first to act or there has been a call to your right, don't call with anything less than a Group 4 hand.

- Adjust the first principle depending on the type of game you are in. If the game is loose and passive, you can call in this situation with hands as low as those near the bottom of Group 5. If the game is tight, you may want to limit your calling to hands in Groups 1, 2, and 3.

- If there is a raise to your right, you should limit your calling to Group 1 and 2 hands in tight games and Group 1 to 3 hands in loose games. Raises in early position tend to come from players with strong hands, so you need to be that much stronger to stay in. Calling raises in loose games with hands like AJ can get very expensive. In situations like this, you should be more conservative than when you need to call only one bet. Once you have called the first bet, you are pretty much committed to calling the raise (or raises) that follow it. The pot is now so large that it is proper to play.

- If you are holding strong cards, such as those in Groups 1 and 2, you should often raise even in early position. This play is especially recommended with high pairs. Remember, high pairs play best against few opponents, so you want to cut the field down as much as possible. Nothing accomplishes this like a preflop raise from an early position—unless, of course, the game is very loose, in which case you will likely get callers. This ploy is important, and if you are holding AA or KK you should even reraise if there is a raise to your right.

- Occasionally you want to play suited connectors, even those as weak as those in Groups 3, 4, or even 5 or 6. Such plays keep you from getting typecast. Besides hands like 76s, 65s, or even 54s go way up in value should the flop come down with no high cards.

- Your early position play should be a bit more routine and conservative than middle or late position play because the sooner you must act, the more jeopardy you are in. You don't want to call with a hand that can't stand a raise. Group 6 and 7 hands are examples, which is why they should be called only in passive games where raises are unlikely—although if you do get raised you should probably call. You also want to avoid calling with stronger hands that can stand a single raise but really aren't strong enough for a reraise. For example, a Group 3 hand like QJs can be called with but should be folded if the betting goes to three bets.

Other difficult situations are Group 4 hands like 10♥, 9♥. When holding something like this, if the pot gets reraised you should fold. The predicament you're likely to find yourself in is that flops with overcards can really hurt. If you flop something like A♦, Q♣, 4♠, your expectation on the hand is extremely poor.

- Remember, you will be in an early position for some 30 percent of the hands. Just batten down the hatches and play clean, conservative poker.

Middle Position Play

With fewer opponents to your left, you can loosen up a bit in terms of the level of playable hands. Although, as above, the action before you and the nature of the game are adjustment factors that need to be fit into the equation.

- The basic rule of thumb here is that hands down to Group 5 are almost always playable, and even weaker hands can occasionally be played if you are in a loose, passive game. If you hold strong cards, such as the hands in Groups 1 through 4, a raise is almost certainly called for—particularly if you are holding a pair or two high cards, since these hands play best against few opponents. If there is a raise in front of you, a reraise is often called for when you're holding a Group 1 or 2 hand, especially a high pair, AKs or even AK. Depending on the nature of the game, you might consider a reraise with slightly weaker hands, such as 1010. Against an early position raise, you would usually throw away a hand like 99 or 88 unless the game is loose and you expect a lot of callers. However, adjust your play if you hold suited and connected hands, since drawing hands tend to offer maximum value against multiple opponents and raises and reraises will drive out players you would rather have in the pot.

- Hands that can be problematic in middle position play are pairs like JJ or 1010 and suited connectors like QJs or J10s when the hand has been raised or reraised. If there is a raise, you should usually reraise with the pairs but throw away the suited connectors. If there is a reraise making it three bets to you, toss away the pairs as well. Although these hands look like they have potential, in situations like those outlined here you won't be getting proper odds.

Late Position Play

The principles governing late position play are a bit more complex than those for early and middle positions because the range of options open to you is greater. Since you will be last or next to last to act on all subsequent rounds, you will know how your opponents have bet before you act. You will have a tactical edge (stronger than many players realize) for the rest of the hand. Here are some rules of thumb for late position play.

- Call with much weaker hands than you would in an earlier position. Hands up to Group 7 are worth a call if you are on the button, and up to Group 6 hands are playable if you're next to last.

- If you hold a hand that you would normally call with in an earlier position, you can often raise with it here. I'm not saying that you should always do this; like everything else in poker, you need to pick your spots. Pay attention to who has called before you. If they are from early seats, a raise is riskier than if they are from middle positions. Group 4 hands like Q10s, 98s, and J9s can often be played this way, as can even weaker hands such Q10 or A9. Such a play can gain you several advantages. Since your hand has some potential, you have a legit shot at a decent win with a favorable flop. Even if the flop is uneventful, it may give you control over the hand so that everyone will check to you after the flop, and a bet can sometimes win you the pot outright.

- If there is a raise in front of you, you need to tighten up a good deal. If several players have already called, you should upgrade drawing hands with suited connectors, since the multiway pot works to your advantage. If you are holding Group 1 or 2 cards you should frequently reraise— although not with AJs or KQs. As above, your decision on a reraise should be determined in part by where the raise came from and your assessment of the kind of player who made it. Early raises, generally speaking, hint at stronger hands than those from a middle position, but loose players may raise with less.

- If the opportunity presents itself, try to "buy the button." That is, make a tactical raise that may drive out the player(s) on your left, in which case you would be the last to act on subsequent rounds.

- If you are on the button you can call with weaker hands, including unranked suited hands such as Q7s or Q6s. Be careful, though; calling with hands like J8 and K9 can be very expensive. Resist the temptation to call with any two suited cards like 83s. The value of these hands exists primarily in your fantasy life.

- If everyone in front of you has folded, you should almost always raise the blinds with any ranked hand. In these latter situations, you should almost never call. Either raise or fold. The raise may win you the blinds or allow you to take control of the hand. Remember, you will act last on subsequent rounds.

- Finally, remember that when you make some of these "formulaic" plays like raising on the button, you provide a lot of information to the rest of the table. Take what they know about you into account in the postflop play of the hand.

Blind Play

Preflop blind play can be tricky. On the one hand, you have the advantage of seeing how everyone else has acted by the time it gets to you. However, this information must be tempered by the fact that you will be first to act on all subsequent rounds, which puts you at a tactical disadvantage. Also, don't forget that sitting on the big blind can occasionally provide you with unanticipated windfalls if no one raises and you flop miracle cards. We have all won hands on the big blind that we never would have thought of playing in any other position.

- If you are the small blind, you can follow generally the same advice given for late position play.

- If the only players to call before you are in late positions, you should play somewhat more aggressively. Late position players who do not raise are often limping in with weak hands.

- With Group 1 hands, especially high pairs, you should raise. But with other reasonably strong hands—like AK, AQ, or KQ—calling is often the better strategy, especially if the pot has been raised and called from an early position. Being on the blind, you are in the worst position and are probably going to need to hit the flop to win.

- If it is a multiway, unraised pot, play small suited connectors in the small blind more often than you would in early positions.

- You should play a bit more conservatively from the small blind than from the big, for three reasons. First, you may be hit with a raise from the big blind; second, you will have to act first on subsequent rounds; third, it costs more to play. However, if there have been no raises, weak hands can and should be played.

These principles will hold you in good stead in preflop play. However, as you become more experienced with hold 'em, you will have to learn to modify your early patterns of play, especially if you move up to higher-stakes games. If you are too mechanical, good players will pick up on your patterns of play and take advantage of you. You must appreciate that these general principles have become something like basic strategy in blackjack. They have been worked out through experience and logic and are known and used by most good hold 'em players these days. How you read your opponents is going to be based in part on whether or not they too are using these standard strategies. If they are not, then you must make adjustments. You should also adjust your style to match the kind of game you are in. Play more aggressively in loose, passive games and more conservatively in tight games. In fact, in games where preflop raises are rare (usually the lower-stakes games) you can call with weak hands even in early position.

Postflop Play

New issues emerge after the flop, so many that we no longer have the luxury of being able to outline a set of basic principles. Things from here on out are too complex for that sort of thing. I've seen books that break down postflop play into the three separate bets that are made and outline specific strategies for each. While there is merit to this kind of deep analysis, it is a bit too refined for the level of play we're aiming at. There are some basic aspects of postflop play that do pertain throughout the rest of the hand, through, and we will concentrate on these.

The Impact of the Flop

The flop needs to be viewed not only on the basis of the cards that appear but in terms of preflop betting. When several players have called and/or raised from early positions, a flop like A♦, Q♥, J♣ is dangerous —especially if you were playing a medium pair or medium suited-connected cards. In fact, in such a situation you should absolutely fold at the first sign of a bet, since you are most certainly facing high pairs or straight draws with overcards and you have no real out on the hand—at least none that will give you proper odds.

Similarly, suppose the flop is Q♦, Q♥, J♣ and you are holding 1010. Toss your pair in the muck, for you are certainly beaten by a higher pair or a set or both.

On the other hand, a flop of 9♦, 6♣, 4♠ is much less threatening, since it is unlikely to have helped your opponents. Should you be holding something like 9♦, 8♦, you are in reasonably good shape with top pair. Generally, rag-filled flops won't help players in early positions, but they often help those in later positions.

The "Free Card"

Many books misrepresent this ploy. The standard analysis is that if you make a tactical raise after the flop, you can occasionally get a free card on fourth street. The most typical situation is when you are sitting in late position and raise, thereby inducing your opponents to "check to the raiser" on the turn. Of course, as Sklansky and Malmuth point out, it's not a free card at all, since you already paid for it with the raise on the flop. Nevertheless, it can be an effective move since it gives you a measure of control over the hand. If the turn wasn't helpful, you can check and look at the river without having to worry as much about extra bets. In this case your raise really does save something, since it took place with a small bet, while your free card was obtained on the turn, where all bets are big bets. On the other hand, if the turn was helpful you can bet and gain an additional bet.

Handling an opponent who (apparently) has tried for a free card: If you think an opponent has just tried this ploy and you have a legit hand such as top pair or a solid draw, you should bet to prevent your opponent from gaining the free card. This is one of those situations where your course of action should be to either bet or check with the intention of folding if bet into.

Slow Playing

Most books on poker recommend against slow playing a strong hand to induce others to stay in the pot. By and large, that's pretty good advice. The problem with slow playing is that it allows weak drawing hands to hang around cheaply and increases the chances that one of them will beat you. In the vast majority of cases, when you've got the best hand simply bet and/or raise and take the pot whenever they decide to give it to you. The only real exception is when you are best but the board looks like one where someone just might end up with the second-best hand and stay with you if you check. For example, you are holding something like 99 and flop 9♦, 7♠, 2♥. There is little chance for straights or flushes, but an opponent may be holding an overcard (or two), and should one of them appear on the turn, it just might get you two or three additional bets.

Check Raising

Here you check your hand with the intention of raising should an opponent bet. Hands that invite the use of this strategy are strong hands, like those that call for slow playing, although the tactic can be used successfully with strong drawing hands in multiway pots. Here's an example of the latter. You hold K♦, J♦ and the flop is J♠, 8♦, 4♥. You have top pair with an overcard and a three flush. If a diamond appears on the turn, check with the intention of raising. If they give you the pot, that's fine; if you get called, you still have a strong hand with lots of potential.

Fourth Street

Play on the turn can be complex. Use the advice outlined above, but there are a couple of fourth street plays that a good player needs to learn. For example: You are sitting in early position, there was no betting on the flop, suggesting weakness everywhere, and the turn produced a blank (that is, it was not an overcard, a third suited card, or a third card to a straight). Bet with virtually anything. This bluff, in moderate-stakes games, is one of the safest plays in the game and has very high expected value. It works because it is wildly improbable that any of your opponents has top pair, or they would have bet on the flop. You look like someone who was hoping for a check raise but didn't get it.

Here's another useful play that Sklansky and Malmuth suggest. Bet strong flop hands and then try for the check raise on the turn. This strategy works because it balances your semibluffs and makes you hard to read. Remember, an awful lot of playable flop hands fade away on the turn. If you routinely check all such hands, then your observant opponents will soon recognize that a check from you on the turn gives them free rein to jump all over you. Conversely, if you routinely bet all those flop hands that did improve, these same astute opponents are going to fold mediocre hands that they might otherwise call with. If you frequently check raise on the turn, you keep your opponents off balance. This ploy also fits in with the concept of the "free card," discussed above. Once you have become known as someone who will often check raise, your opponents will be less likely to bet after you have checked to them and you may get the occasional (really) free card when you need it and are out of position. Moreover, your *unobservant* opponents will still bet into you, and when you do have a strong hand you can get extra bets from them.

The River

Play on the river can be tricky. Your decisions need to be carefully balanced between your assessment of the likelihood that you are best or that you are beat measured against the size of the pot and your knowledge of your opponents. Here's a couple of basic principles of river play:

- If you are pretty sure you are best, then bet. You hold pocket jacks and the top card on the board is a 10 with no flush or straight possibilities. Just bet.

- When the issue isn't so clear, be careful. If you are called on the river, you generally are no longer the favorite. If you think you are best, but it looks like the river card might have improved your opponent's hand, then check. For example, you have two pair, your opponent has been calling your bets all along, and a third suited card shows up on the river. Betting could be a mistake. If your opponent bets, whether to call or fold will depend a lot on how well you know this individual.

- If you are pretty sure you are best but you think your opponent may think otherwise, check with the intention of raising. This kind of situation pops up when you have a small set, for example, but a high card like a king or ace lands on the river, which likely gives your opponent a high pair.

- Fold when all indicators point to the fact that you are beaten. Here's a classic case. An opponent raises when the flop produces two suited cards, checks on the turn when a card of another suit shows up, and bets on the river when a third suited card lands. If it's a multiway pot and you can't beat a flush, get out.

- The river presents bluffing possibilities. These generally appear when your opponents have been showing little enthusiasm for the hand and just the right card lands on the river. Here's one I witnessed recently. There was a raise preflop from the player on the button, and three players called. The flop came down 7♦, 6♣, 2♣. There were three checks to the button, who bet. All three players called. The turn was the J♦. Again, everyone checked to the button, who bet. The player on the small blind, who had been getting hammered all evening and was down several hundred dollars, tossed in his checks with a disgusted "Why the hell do I keep getting sucked into hands like this?" The other two players called. The river produced the 10♥. The small blind muttered, barely audibly, "Hmm, that's why," and tossed in a bet. The first two players folded quickly; the guy on the button, who was a strong player, pondered the situation for a time and finally tossed his hand away. While taking in the pot, the winner's cards caught on a chip and everybody got to see 4♦, 5♦. It is tough to push three players out of a pot this big, but this time it worked. The keys were: (1) position, since the player on the small blind took the initiative after calling all previous bets; (2) the fact that the flush draws failed to materialize; (3) the possible straight that the 10 on the river produced; and (4) the fact that no one showed much enthusiasm for his or her hand except the player on the button, who was probably playing over-cards. It was also the only way the small blind could possibly win the pot. A word of caution, though. While this play worked, the situation needed to be, like Baby Bear's porridge, just right.

Probabilities and Proper Odds

It is important to understand that a good bit of postflop play must be based on whether you can get proper odds for your play. You can't begin to calculate proper odds unless you know the probabilities of the outcomes you are looking for, like these:

Hand	Probability
Flopping a pair of your top pocket card	.165
Flopping a pair of either of your two pocket cards	.330
Flopping a set of your top pocket card	.008
Flopping a set of either of your two pocket cards	.016
Flopping a set when holding a pair	.115
Flopping a flush	.008
Completing a set on the hand when holding a pair	.184
Completing a four flush with one card to go	.196
Completing a four flush with two cards to go	.350
Completing a backdoor flush (last two cards of your suit)	.042
Completing an open straight with one card to go	.174
Completing an open straight with two cards to go	.315
Completing a gut straight with one card to go	.087
Completing a gut straight with two cards to go	.165
Completing a full house with two pair with one card to go	.087
Completing a full house with two pair with two cards to go	.165
Completing a full house with trips with one card to go	.218
Completing a full house with trips with two cards to go	.334

What we've covered so far will give the modest stakes player a solid foundation. But I'd like to give a couple of additional pieces of advice that will add to your edge.

When to Be Afraid (and When Not to Be)

You are holding A♣, 7♣ and the flop is something like Q♣, Q♥, J♣ or J♣, J♥, 10♣. Be afraid. Sure, you've got a shot at the top flush, but a full house is not unlikely—especially if there were raises preflop. On the other hand, you are holding the same two cards, but the flop comes down 8♣, 8♥, 3♣. It is unlikely that anyone would have called two or more bets with 83, so someone filling up on you is unlikely. This set of circumstances has produced some interesting exchanges in the poker literature. The standard advice, as put forward by Doyle Brunson in his book *Super System*, was to always fold a hand like A♣, 7♣ when a pair flops. Only recently has this changed after Sklansky and Malmuth pointed out why flops made up of medium to small pairs with nonconnectors are not that dangerous.

Connectors and Two Pair

Since many players will pay to see the flop with connectors, you can use this information to assess the likelihood that you are facing two pair, postflop. For example, if the flop is 9, 8, 4 you are more likely to be facing two pair than if it is 9, 7, 4, since 98 is a much more likely pair of pocket cards for an opponent to be holding than 97 or 94.

The Pocket Ace

Many players overvalue a pocket ace. Their thought is that if they flop an ace, they have top pair. But there is always the possibility of another ace being out there. I've asked a lot of inveterate hold 'em players how likely they think this is. Their answers typically run from about 20 to 50 percent. But the strong players usually get it right: When you are playing at a full table, the likelihood of there being at least one other ace in one of the other nine hands is .747. That's right, on three quarters of all hands in which you hold an ace someone else was dealt one too. So much of the value of a pocket ace comes from its kicker. Moreover, consider the effect of pairing the other card. If you hold AQ and the flop is Q, 10, 7, you have top pair, top kicker, and need not worry too much about overcards. But if you hold A10 or A7, you are much more vulnerable.

Pocket Pairs: What Do You Do with Them?

With big pairs like AA and KK play is pretty straightforward: Bet them with enthusiasm to try to trim the field. With less powerful pairs like QQ, JJ, 1010, and 99, matters get more complex. Suppose you have pocket J's, you raised in middle position, and were called by several players. The flop is K, 8, 7, and you are bet into. It is awfully likely that you are facing K's; fold like a Japanese fan. However, if no one bets, you should, since there is a good chance you have the best hand.

Where to Sit

All sorts of nonsense has been written about choosing your seat at a table and choosing the table that you want to play at. The reason much of it is nonsense is that you typically have no choice. You arrive at the poker room, put your name on the waiting list for your game of choice, and take the first seat that opens up. You can, if you wish, leave your name on the list so that you can switch tables, should you spot one full of tourists, but these situations are not all that frequent.

Once you're at the table there are a couple of things to think about. It is an advantage to be on the right side of a strong player, who will respect your raises. Similarly, it is to your advantage to be on the right of a rock or a weak, tight player, who is easily intimidated. Both kinds of players play few hands. But you definitely don't want to be sitting on the left of a wild, loose player. If a seat opens up that you feel might give you a small advantage, take it. Poker room protocol says that a player already at the table who wishes to move has the right to the seat, the newcomer then takes the vacated one.

The Flop that (Probably) Helped No One

Flops like K♦, 4♣, 2♥ are pretty uninspiring. Depending on how the preflop play went, this is frequently a situation in which you can steal the pot with a bet. However, watch out for late position players or the blinds, who may have limped in with less and now may be holding pairs or straight draws.

Don't Get Too Cute

Hold 'em players who have learned a bit about the game often get caught up in delicate psychological ploys. It can be an ego boost to pull off a well-timed bluff based on nothing other than position and a hint of weakness from your opponent, but it would be a mistake to try to play the game this way all the time. The optimum approach to hold 'em emphasizes conservative, aggressive play. Play your cards cleanly, judge your hands accurately, press the advantage when you have it, and bluff enough to keep the rest of the table honest.

A DEEPER LOOK AT SEVEN-STUD

Mathematically speaking, seven-stud is a more complex game than hold 'em. Since four of the cards dealt are face-up and as many as eight players may be in a hand, the number of alternative hypotheses a player entertains about possible hands quickly becomes very large. Analyzing them becomes cognitively cumbersome. It is for this reason that I feel (although admittedly I don't really have any hard data for this, it's just a feeling) it may be easier to make money at seven-stud than at hold 'em. I think there are many more bad and many fewer expert seven-stud players in the mid-level games than in hold 'em. So a solid, conservative game might very well have higher positive expectation.

The inherent complexity of the game means that many decisions in seven-stud are based more on a vague kind of subjective sense or "feel" for a particular hand than on well-developed, articulated strategies. Seven-stud is a game in which experience counts for a lot. Expert players learn to trust their intuitions about how particular hands have developed based on betting patterns and exposed cards.

By virtue of the way in which the game is played—the first player to act on each round is determined by the value of the upcards—position play becomes a more delicate element of the game than in hold 'em. Position play is important in seven-stud, especially in the first betting round, but it must be approached from a conditionalized perspective. That is, you can't think about what you will do *when* you are first to act on the next round; you must learn to think about what you will likely do *if* you are first to act on the next round.

Appropriate chasing is more common in seven-stud than in hold 'em. There will be many hands that are worth going to the river with, particularly those that have high pairs and live overcards along with straight or flush possibilities. When we look at some of these situations, appreciate that when you win with these hands, in most cases it will be precisely because you caught a second pair, or paired a high card. What gives a good drawing hand its value here is not just the draw for a straight or flush but the number of outs the hand has.

Finally, a note on betting procedure. Most casinos and poker rooms use an ante. Its size will vary depending on the stakes. In a $5/10 game, the ante will typically be fifty cents or $1. The bring-in bet will be something like $1 or $2, although raises of up to $5 are permitted. Fourth street bets are still small bets, although if a pair is showing anywhere on the board, $10 bets are permitted. All subsequent bets must be made in increments of $10. In a $10/20 game, these bets are generally doubled. Some lower-stakes games (such as $1/5) are "spread games," which means that you can bet anywhere from $1 to $5 at any time. Occasionally you will see a game listed as $1/5/10, $5/10/15, or $10/20/30. The last number represents the minimum bet on the river, which adds an interesting element to the game. It gives a player with a scary-looking board better bluffing opportunities; however, it also rewards the bad player who is always trying to draw out on the river.

Third Street Play

The decision you make on third street is the most important one in seven-stud. Psychologically speaking, the situation in seven-stud is different from preflop play in hold 'em, since you know not only your hole cards but everyone's door card. There is more explicit information available on which to act. But it is critical that you make well-judged decisions at this point in the game. In seven-stud more money is lost because of poor third street decisions than anything else.

There are several reasons for this. First, the temptation to call with a weak hand that would be better off thrown away is great, particularly if it looks like you can get in for a half bet. Second, it is easy to get sucked into a seven-stud hand, because you watch the (apparent) helpers and blanks fall on each of your opponents' hands and keep thinking that the next street will provide the card(s) to give you the upper hand. If you have a tendency to chase inappropriately, seven-stud can be a risky game. Third, unlike hold 'em, where you get to see three upcards after a single round of betting, in seven-stud, getting to see three upcards involves two rounds of betting. Fourth, since the player who must act first on every round after third street changes depending on the upcards, strategies based on position play are less useful here. You must pay more attention to the cards and your opponents' betting patterns and manner of play.

Nevertheless, a number of basic principles can be applied to third street play. Let's take a look at them:

The Ante Steal

The equivalent play to stealing the blinds in hold 'em is stealing the antes in seven-stud. The same basic principles hold. You should attempt this when you estimate you have about a 30 to 40 percent shot at a successful steal. You should also have a decent hand, one that can withstand a call and still have at least a semireasonable chance at winning. Don't try it with rags unless you're in a weak, tight game. The two factors that play the most significant roles in attempted filches are position and a scary door card—with the latter being most important. Here's the classic ante steal: You are last to act, are showing A♣, and no one called the bring-in bet. Raise. Even if you are called, one more scare card on third or fourth street and the pot should be yours. This ploy can also work in an early position, and it can work with a lesser door card if none of your opponents is showing one higher.

Question: What do you do if your steal attempt is reraised right back at you? That depends. Suppose your attempt was made from the last position with a hand like [8♣, 9♥], Q♦ and the bring-in bettor reraises. It helps to have a sense of how your opponent plays. Unless you have a reasonably good sense that he or she is running a bluff, you probably want to fold. However, if there is a good chance that you have three overcards, you want to call. On the other hand, suppose you have [6♦, 6♥], A♦ and the bring-in reraises. Here you have a hidden pair, an overcard, and a two flush. Calling is best—unless, of course, your cards are duplicated on the board. You need to make your decisions based on your cards, how live they are, the potential they have, your knowledge of your opponent, his or her likelihood of bluffing, and the looseness of the game.

What do you do if you suspect someone else is attempting an ante steal? Again, it depends, but basically you should use the above advice in reverse. If you hold several overcards or a modest to high pair, you might want to reraise. Or you might simply call and then try playing aggressively on fourth street—unless, of course, your opponent catches a scary card. If you are weak, just fold. Remember, someone on a steal is not the same as someone on a bluff; ante steals are plays made with less than wonderful cards, but they usually are not made with rags.

Attempted steals have their highest expectation in tight games, but be less prone to try to steal when your cards are duplicated. If your hole cards are on the board, your chances of improving are reduced. If your door card is duplicated, you are more likely to be reraised by observant players.

What do you do if you're last and no one has called the bring-in bet? Sklansky and Malmuth recommend that you attempt a steal 80 to 85 percent of the time against typical players, and a bit less often against strong players. For medium- and low-level games, this number can be even higher. Fold only when you have total rags. If you are in a late position and have the highest cards showing, you should virtually always attempt the steal.

Position Play and the Key Question: How Live Are You?

On third street, position should be a significant factor in determining your play, but it is not as important as it is in preflop play in hold 'em. The impact of one's position in seven-stud is mitigated somewhat by each player's door card. The principles, however, are pretty much the same. You need to be strongest in an early position (the two after the bring-in), less so in middle positions (the next three), and you can limp in with much less in a late position (the last two).

Unfortunately, there is no clean ranking of hands that can key a player into the kinds of hands that are playable in each position. The reason is simple: all those door cards. In hold 'em, all you know are your pocket cards, and these can be ranked relatively easily. In seven-stud, the value of your initial three cards is dependent on what else is showing. While it is certainly true that [A♣, A♥], 9♠ is a good start, it loses a lot of value if you look out and see the other two A's and a 9 sitting in opponents' hands. Similarly, a start like [J♥, 8♥], 3♥ is pretty strong if no other hearts are showing but near worthless if four opponents are showing hearts. How strong you are is given not just by your cards but also by: (1) your position relative to the bring-in; (2) how your cards compare with your opponents' door cards; (3) what the betting action is so far (if a K raises and an A reraises, throw the [J♥, 8♥], 3♥ away); and (4) how live both your and your opponents' cards are.

The last of these is the most important, since without live cards your chances of improving are compromised. However, the same holds for your opponents. It's tough to overstate the importance of being live in seven-stud. This is most important on third street but holds throughout the hand.

Scare Cards

A scare card is any upcard that poses a potential threat. While scare cards can be used as the basis for an ante steal, they can also be used to establish a strong bluff, particularly when played against one or two (but not more) drawing hands.

Overcards

Overcards and their lack are important elements of early play. If you have something like [A♠, J♦], 5♥ and a raise by a K is called by a Q, you should almost certainly fold, especially if one or more of your A's is already out. On the other hand, if you are holding [K♦, Q♥], 10♦ and an 8 or a 10 raises, you should definitely call or even reraise, especially if the raise was from a late position and your cards are live.

Big Pairs

As in hold 'em, big pairs play best against few opponents, preferably only one. However, unlike hold 'em, where you should virtually always press a high pair, in seven-stud you may want to make adjustments based on your opponents' upcards, how live your cards are, and the way the betting has gone. In early position you should always raise with aces and virtually always with kings—provided, of course, that your cards are still alive. With smaller pairs like jacks, tens, and nines you must consider other factors. If you are looking at an A who has raised and a K (or even a Q) who has called, your pair is best tossed into the muck. Getting sucked into a hand when you are holding second- or third-best pair is absolutely to be avoided.

A good bit of your strategy with high pairs will depend on whether or not one of the paired cards is your door card. For example, if you have [A♣, A♥], 6♣ and raise, you look very different to the rest of the table than if you have [A♣, 6♣], A♥ and raise. In the former case, you might be read as representing anything from a hidden high pair to a small pair with a high kicker, a three flush, a three straight, or even rolled-up 6's. In the latter case, you look like a pair of A's. How your opponents react to you will differ dramatically.

Modest and Small Pairs

In early position, especially when you are facing overcards, you need to be careful. This is the first situation we've looked at in seven-stud where other factors, such as your kicker and whether or not you have a two flush or two straight, come into play. Suppose you've got [7♠, A♣], 7♣ and there are a K and a Q yet to act. A call here would be okay since you've got an overcard kicker and a two flush. But if your kicker is a J or you don't have a two flush, a call is problematical. If you think you can get a look at fourth street for a small bet, you might want to call—provided you understand that if you fail to improve you should fold at the first sign of a bet. Medium and small pairs present the most difficult and potentially expensive third street situations in seven-stud.

Being Rolled Up

The odds are 424 to 1 against being dealt a set on the first three cards, but when it does happen you want to take advantage of it. Lots of "experts" will tell you to slow play a rolled-up hand. This is bad advice; there's just no point in it. Just act like someone with a high pair in the hole and raise. The only exceptions might be if you're holding aces or kings in early position where a raise might drive everyone out—you don't want to "steal" the antes when you are rolled up.

Three Flushes and Three Straights

These are often strong starting hands, although their true value depends on how high and how live your cards are. In general, if three or more of your cards are already out you should not call—unless, of course, your hand has other value.

Some flush examples: You hold [K♥, Q♥], 7♥; a 4 brings it in, a J raises, and there are three other hearts out but no K's or Q's. This hand is not only playable, it is a good one. Your flush chances are diminished, but you have two live and connected overcards. However, if you hold [J♥, 8♥], 4♥ in a similar situation, things don't look so hot. Not only are your hearts reduced in value, it appears that two of your J's are sitting elsewhere, as is one of your 4's. Fold. In this case you must be careful not to overvalue your hand, even if your hearts were more live than in the example given here. When you win hands like these three flushes you frequently win them with overpairs and two pairs, not with flushes. It's simple probabilities: Flushes aren't all that frequent even when you start with three suited cards. When you have no overcards and suspect you are looking at a high pair, you should be cautious. If you pay to look at fourth street and do not get any sort of improvement, get out.

Some examples with three straights: You have [K♠, Q♦], J♠; a 10 raises, and there are two other callers, neither of whom is showing a J, a Q, or a K. Call. While it's true that your straight chances are looking pretty dim against a likely pair of tens, you still have three live overcards, two of them suited. On the other hand, you have [9♠, 8♣], 7♥ in the same situation. As above, those apparent 10's cut down on your straight chances, but the problem this time is that you don't have any overcards to give you a reasonable out on the hand. You should not call the raise from the 10's. However, if the pot is not raised, a call is okay. This hand is very vulnerable and should not be played past fourth street without immediate improvement, like catching a 6 or (preferably) a 10.

Three straights gain in value when two of the cards are of the same suit, and three flushes gain in value when two of the cards are connectors. Both situations increase in value when the cards are high. For example, [K♦, Q♦], 10♦ is a strong hand with all kinds of potential, including big pairs. By the way, three flushes and three straights are excellent hands for attempting an ante steal.

Weak Hands

The modest-stakes player is best off treating weak and semiweak hands as basically unplayable. While it is true that many less-than-wonderful hands, given proper position and the right kind of game, have potential for profit, it is not easy to extract it. When deciding whether or not to take a flier with a weak hand, the factor that should weigh heaviest is how live your cards are. It's simple probabilities: If no one is holding your cards, you have a shot; if your cards are sprinkled about the board, you don't. If you look at your first three cards and don't see one of the situations outlined up to here and someone throws a full bet at you, you should just quietly retire and get ready for the next hand.

Fourth Street Play

The Notion of Commitment

On fourth street the concept of commitment first comes into play in a serious way. It is an interesting notion—indeed, a double-edged one. When you are strong and likely have top hand, it is to your advantage to get weaker opponents committed to their hands so they are willing to toss in several bets to chase, when, if they knew what you had, they would fold. Here's an example. You've got [A♠,10♥], 10♠, A♣ and you're facing [x, x], K♠, 7♠ to your left and [x, x], 8♠, 7♥ to the left of that. The first of your opponents is a decent player, the second an inveterate chaser. You called the bring-in from an early position and the K raised. The 8 and you were the only callers. In all likelihood, the K is either paired or chasing a flush (or both), and your other opponent is likely on a straight draw or perhaps overvaluing a pair of 8's. A good play here is the check raise. If you bet out you are, in effect, announcing A's. Since it is likely the K will bet and the 8 will call, you will probably get them both for two bets and get them committed to their hands.

But you want to take care not to let yourself get committed to hands where you would appear to have to worst of it. Here's an example from Sklansky, Malmuth, and Zee that makes this point nicely. You have [J♦, 9♥], J♣, 4♠ and are looking at [x, x], Q♣, A♥, who bets. Fold. Even if your kickers were better you should still fold. This is the kind of hand you do not want to let yourself get committed to. In this kind of situation, you really only want to play hands that can improve to better than aces-up.

Betting Strong Hands

By fourth street, it is possible to have a strong hand such as aces-up or kings-up, a set, or a live four flush or four straight. Many experts recommend slow playing these hands to induce other players to stay with you. I don't think this is very good advice. It's more sensible to continue to look at the overall situation and make well-judged, sensible plays. If you've got aces-up and you look like this—[x, x], 10♥, A♥— you can be read in any number of ways by your opponents, depending on how third street was played, the other upcards, and the like. This hand should be bet and raised with. It is not terrible to force everyone out at this point since you've already gotten several bets out of your opponents. Remember, they could always draw out on you. Moreover, if your opponents have committed themselves to their hands, they may chase you anyway.

The Paired Door Card

When you pair your door card on fourth street you have two basic choices: a small bet or a big one. Your decision should be based on whether you think you are best and whether you want callers. Say you have [6♠, 7♥], 8♣ and then pair your 8, and there are no scary cards on the board. You've got the straight draw as an out, but would be quite happy to take the pot right here. Make a full bet. However, if there are overcards on the board, betting the minimum is probably best. If you're looking at a high pair you're going to get called no matter what bet you make. Don't risk the extra money.

Or suppose you started strong with [A♣, A♥], 7♣ and now catch 7♠. Unless someone is rolled up, you are easily the best. Whether to go for a small or a full bet should be determined by your opponents' upcards and how the betting went on third street. If you think you will get callers with a full bet, make it. If you think a full bet will chase them out, make a small bet. Don't check (unless you are sure you can get a called check raise in). All that will do is give your opponents a free card and a chance to draw out on you.

The Pressed Bluff

Fourth street is the best point to establish a pressed bluff. This play works best in seven-stud since you have your upcards to help you represent a hand. A pressed bluff is a semibluff that you keep pressing hard all the way to the river. It is best set up on third street with a scare card that you raised with, and it is most effective when a second scare card appears here or on fifth street. For example, you have [3♦, 3♥], A♣, K♣. You raised on third street and got called by a player who looks like he is playing a drawing hand. Bet again on fourth street and continue betting on every street. If your opponent catches, you lose, but the odds typically favor you against only one opponent. If you catch another club or an open pair, he or she might fold, but that's okay too. Pressed bluffs work best against drawing hands where your opponent is not getting proper odds and will fold on the river if he or she fails to catch.

When Checked To

Often the high card will simply check showing no (apparent) strength. If you have any kind of hand at all or one or two scare cards up, you should bet. In fact, this is one of those times when you want to try to take control over the hand, become the aggressor, and try to drive everyone out. Unless you've got a monster that you want to slow play, you will already have gotten one or two bets out of your opponents. That's fine; take the money. Even if you don't push everyone out, you will most likely be able to trim the field and thereby increase your chances of a small win. A hand that fits into this situation is one like this: You have [J♦, 8♦], 7♦, J♠ and both [x, x], A♥, 2♠ and [x, x], K♣, 4♥ check to you, suggesting that you have top pair.

Another reason for betting here is that you don't want to give up a free card. This one would be a *real* free card, and it could give your opponents a chance to draw out on you.

When You Don't Improve

Simple probabilities will tell you that most of the time you won't improve on fourth street. Evaluate your hand by its strength, how live your cards are, how you read your opponents, and how the betting has gone. Hands with medium to high pairs are often worth playing, depending on your kicker; flush and straight draws that catch blanks might be folded, but again it depends on how live you are and whether you have overcards. Fourth street is the last small bet. If you don't improve with the next card, each bet will cost you twice as much. Don't let yourself get seduced into playing with a marginal hand that has little chance of improving enough to win the pot.

Fifth Street Play

This is where the game starts getting expensive, since all bets from here on out are big ones.

More on Commitment

Commitment becomes even more critical here since you start getting seriously attached to your hand when you start tossing in big bets. Such attachment can get expensive if it pulls you along to the river. Fifth street is a chaser's road to ruin, and you should approach it with as much caution as third street.

Big Pairs

Basically, they should be treated as they were on the earlier streets. Even nearer the end, you still need to reduce the field as much as possible with such hands. The more people playing, the greater jeopardy you are in. It is not at all unreasonable to raise with a big pair even if you suspect you may not be best. Say you have a pair of K's or Q's with one of them showing, and you are facing two opponents, one of whom, you think, may already have two small pair. A raise here probably won't get rid of the two pair, but it just might induce the third player to fold, which improves your position.

Don't Give the Free Card

If you've got any kind of hand at all, from a medium pair on up, and no one is showing much enthusiasm, you don't want to give a (real) free card. Since it has been fairly cheap up till now it's likely that you've still got chasers with drawing hands hanging around. But if you look out and see an opponent with a scary board, a check would be okay. If your opponent has a good hand you'll get raised, and even if he doesn't, the money will likely go into the pot anyway.

Flush and Straight Draws

Start counting the pot and making estimates of how many additional bets you can get from your opponents should you fill your hand. Whether you should press your hand or lay back will be determined by how live your cards are and whether you have other outs. If you are sitting with [J♠, 9♠], 6♠, 4♦, 2♠ and five other spades have already been seen, you really don't want to get too involved. On the other hand, something like [A♠, Q♠], 6♠, Q♦, 2♠ is much better, since you have a high pair and an overcard. If your cards are live, you should stick around even with all those spades out.

Generally, four flushes and four straights on fifth street are hands worth chasing with. If you have other outs such as overcards or a pair, so much the better. In such situations, you are almost always getting proper odds for the play.

The Check Raise

This is a useful device and its impact is especially strong here. An effective fifth street check raise is set up on fourth street. Let's take a classic case. On fourth street, you are holding a hand of modest strength like [J♥, A♦], 9♦, J♠. You bet but were raised by a Q. On fifth street you catch a scary K♠ but check. If the Q bets—and this is expected—you might consider raising. Lots of things could happen if you do. Your opponent could have been bluffing and simply fold. This would be fine. In all likelihood you'll get a call, but you will likely have earned yourself a free card on sixth street. So long as you have an overcard and your other cards are still live, your chances are pretty good. You must check out the pot, though; since you are still the underdog, you don't want to go for too much more money without getting 3 or 4 to 1 for future investments.

Getting Proper Odds

Proper odds is always an element in seven-stud, but it isn't until fifth and sixth street that it becomes really important. The situation is basically the same as in hold 'em. You are looking for value; you are trying to put yourself in a situation where you have a positive expected gain for your play. The formula is the same. Count the money already in the pot, estimate how much more you think you can extract from your opponents if you make your hand, and determine the rough probability of doing so. Unlike hold 'em, where we could outline the precise probabilities of particular outcomes, estimating odds in seven-stud is fraught with the vagaries of human memory. The problem is simple to state but not to solve. Estimating the likelihood of completing, for example, a 6 to 9 open straight is dependent on recalling how many 5's and 10's showed on the first three rounds. If you can't remember this you can't accurately calculate the pot odds.

The best players attempt to keep track of each open card that appears and use this information to make well-judged bets on later streets. However, everything that psychologists know about human memory points to the inescapable conclusion that carrying out such a task hand after hand for hour after hour is extremely difficult and subject to error. One huge problem is what is known as proactive interference, where events that occurred in the more remote past interfere with your ability to recall events that occurred more recently. For example, the cards played on earlier hands start getting mixed up in your mind with the cards on this hand. You aren't sure whether the guy to your left folded a ten two betting rounds ago or two hands ago.

There is no simple solution. Try to pay attention to each card as it is dealt and log it in your memory. Note each card as it shows and "interpret" it according to whether it is relevant or irrelevant to your hand. For example, suppose you started with three hearts. Hearts in this hand are very relevant to you, so you must track the suit of every exposed card in order to be able to calculate your proper odds.

Of course, this strategy is still a bit simpleminded. To be really good at seven-stud you also need to be tracking cards that are relevant for your opponents, since part of your decision making will be dependent on a sense of how likely or unlikely it is that they will make their hands. This is one of the things that makes seven-stud a fascinating game to play but extremely difficult to play well.

Sixth Street Play

The thing to appreciate about sixth street is that it is harder to get rid of an opponent than it was on earlier streets. Once your opponents have committed themselves psychologically and financially to the hand to this extent, it is unlikely you can push them out with a bet or a raise. If you are pretty sure you are best, then you ought to be able to pick up bets from your opponents here. Don't hold back. Of course, if you have gone this far yourself you should also continue with the hand against a bet even if you suspect that you are beat—with all the usual caveats about live cards, possible outs, best guesses about the river, and so on.

The River

The situation is pretty much like it was in hold 'em. Hence:

- If you are quite sure you are best, then bet.
- If you are pretty sure you are best, but think your opponent may think otherwise, check with the intention of raising.
- Fold if bet into when all indicators point to the fact that you are beaten. But be careful: Lots of players will routinely bet with a busted drawing hand in this situation if they think you will fold with the better but still weak hand—after all, this is the only shot they have at the pot. It is usually worth one last bet to prevent this from happening. Indeed, you

should probably call with a lot of hands that you think are beaten. Even if you lose the majority of these, the expected value of the call is still likely positive since you are balancing a single bet against a large pot. Just about the single worst mistake you can make is to fold the winning hand on the river with a large pot.

- Many players who fail to fill a drawing hand will toss it away with just the hint of a bet from an opponent. There will be times when you can steal a pot—even when you failed to fill a hand and were left with nothing but rags—by simply tossing in a single bet. If you think you are in one of these situations, do not check, for your pair of threes may just lose to a pair of fours that will fold if you bet. Notice that the concept of the pressed bluff is relevant here. If you were working a pressed bluff with a hand that looked like a flush or a straight but never improved and you are playing against another drawing hand, you must continue your bluff on the river.

- Since the pot is often large, you should be cautious in making a cold bluff on the river. Many players will (properly) call with weak hands simply because the pot is large.

As we did for hold 'em, let's end this section with some advice that will give you a bit of an edge in certain circumstances.

Loose versus Tight Games

The loose passive game is best. Such games can be even more advantageous for a strong player than in hold 'em, for what marks a loose game in seven-stud is the presence of a couple of inveterate chasers at the table. The signature of a loser at seven-stud is the inappropriate chase. I have never ceased to marvel at how much money people will toss into a pot in the faint hope that a hand like [9♣, 10♥], 7♣, 5♥, J♥ will turn into something that has even a prayer of winning—or of getting proper odds on the rare occasion when it does. They look for the miracle 8 to show up or pray for two hearts to make their backdoor flush. So long as these kinds of folks sit down to play this game, you should be sitting at the same table.

Tight games are another matter altogether. You can make money in tight games by stealing antes, bluffing, and semibluffing, but you must be wary of the shrewd conservative player—the one who is not so much tight as solid.

Bluff and semibluff less (if at all) in loose games and more in tight ones. You don't need to in loose games since you'll get paid off for your good hands. In tight games, be wary of calls from opponents who look weak. Be seriously concerned if one of your raises gets reraised. Good all-purpose advice is to play against the grain of the game. If everyone is tossing checks around with abandon, be more conservative and bide your time. If everyone is squeezing their quarters so tightly you can hear the eagles squawk, loosen up and force the play more.

Feeling Confused?

Because seven-stud is such a complex game, you will frequently hit an awful spot where you don't know whether you should call or fold. Here's a really good piece of advice: Fold! That sense of confusion should be taken as a clear sign that you don't have a grip on this particular situation. You might occasionally toss away a winner, but in the long run you will save a good piece of cash by not playing in situations you don't understand. The game is tough enough when you think you know what is going on.

The Bottom Line

Hold 'em is a game that is amenable to probabilistic analysis by virtue of the way the cards are dealt. On the other hand, seven-stud is a game that is highly resistant to sharp quantitative assessment because it keeps shifting as each new round of cards is dealt and the probabilities of particular hands change. There aren't as many clean, straightforward strategies that can be recommended because everything in the game is conditionalized. Each game must be approached on its own terms.

In analyzing these games, we've covered a lot of ground, and it is perfectly reasonable for the novice to wonder, "Do top players really think this stuff through in such a calculated manner on every hand?" Yes and no. Yes, expert players will often go through a careful, rational analysis of a hand, particularly if the pot is large, the play complex, and their opponents skilled. But on the other hand, they have no need to do so. After you have played these games for a long time and come to understand the situations that emerge over and over again, the proper line of play almost comes as second nature. But for the player just learning one of these games, a good deal of energy needs to be spent on analysis of individual hands and specific situations. With experience, this will become easier and more routine. It will also become a lot more fun. As you become more proficient at the game, you will be struck by how badly some of your opponents play. And you will also—let's be honest here—become aware of just how badly you yourself were playing before.

7

HANDICAPPING THE THOROUGHBRED RACEHORSE

*T*his was the most difficult chapter of all for me to write for the simple reason that I know more about handicapping horses than about any of the other topics. I've spent more of the rich and fertile years of my life playing the horses than anything else (except, of course, for marrying, raising kids, picking up a couple of degrees, writing a couple of books, and stuff like that).

Playing the horses is a lot like poker, where conditionalized probabilistic assessment is the key to the game, but there is a major difference. In poker you are playing directly against known and sometimes painfully obvious opponents. With the horses you are playing against a large number of unknown opponents who have registered their beliefs about the upcoming race by the most poignant of gestures: They have wagered their hard-earned cash. By virtue of the pari-mutuel system, in which the odds are determined by the actual betting, your goal is to be better than everyone else by a margin sufficient to cover the vigorish, the track takeout.

In New York, where I do the lion's share of my handicapping, the vig is now 15 percent on win, place, and show bets; 20 percent on exactas (or perfectas) and quinellas; and 25 percent on the so-called exotic bets, including the pick-three, the pick-six, and the triple (or trifecta). (An exacta is picking the first- and second-place finishers in exactly that order; the quinella also requires picking the first- and second-place finishers, but in either order. The triple involves picking the first three finishers in the exact order. In the daily double, the player must pick the winners of two successive races; in the pick-three the winners of three successive races, and in the pick-six, six consecutive races.) This is pretty much in line with other racetracks around North America and is one hell of a rake compared with the other games we've looked at so far. In addition to the basic vigorish, the total rake also includes what is known as "breakage." Simply, payoffs are rounded down, so that a horse that "should" pay, say, $7.39 will pay only $7.30 or even $7.20 depending on the formula in use. Breakage doesn't amount to much percentage-wise when the payoffs are large, but it is a substantial factor when they are small. For example, with a winning favorite that should pay $2.39 for a $2 bet but pays only $2.20, the track is taking nearly half your profit off the top!

The key to beating the vig is easy enough to state: Find the overlay and avoid the underlay. (In the horseplayer's lingo, an overlay is a horse or combination of horses that is going off at higher odds than you think it should, and an underlay is the opposite.) For example, you as an expert handicapper have estimated Beetlebaum to be roughly a 2-to-1 shot in the third at Santa Anita—meaning that you estimate he would win this race roughly one third of the time that it was run under these conditions. However, to your amazement and delight you look at the odds board and discover that he is going off at 4 to 1. That is, the public believes he would win this race under these conditions only one time in five. Assuming your handicapping is correct, Beetlebaum is a clear overlay, and a win bet on him has a palpable positive expectation. On the other hand, you could look at the board and see that old Beetle is going off at a mere 6 to 5. Again, if you are correct in your assessment of his chances to win this race, a bet on him would be a terrible proposition with a serious minus expectation. So, in essence, beating the horses is really beating the other handicappers. As we will note in several places in this chapter, it is the pari-mutuel system, wherein the payoffs are set by the distribution of money wagered, that is the heart and soul of the game. By the way, the pari-mutuel system of wagering was first developed in France, and the term means "between us."

Question: Is it possible to be better than the betting public by a sufficient amount to overcome the rather stunning vig? Answer: Yup, but it ain't easy. Question: Are there really people who manage to pull this off over an extended period of time? Answer: Yup, but not many of them. Accordingly, in the sections to follow I will present to you a sound foundation for handicapping the thoroughbred racehorse, a foundation that should enable you to stay even with the house and maybe win a couple of bucks.

But most of all, what I hope you will do is have a damn good time, for there really is nothing quite as exhilarating as a day at the track. If you don't think this is true, just check out your own emotions when two horses are pounding down the stretch, heads bobbing first one in front then the other as they near the finish line, muscles tense, veins marked sharply on their powerful flanks, jockeys whipping and cajoling, over a hundred years of breeding and training techniques driving these magnificent animals to give their all for one last surge before the wire. You will experience joy and elation, despair and frustration, wonder and confusion. No one is neutral at a time like this. As I have said, I love poker, and blackjack does fascinate, but no hand of cards will ever bring tears to my eyes as Secretariat did back in 1973, when he pounded down the stretch at Belmont to win the third and final leg of the Triple Crown in the still unbelievable time of 2:24.

That gets the sentimental stuff out of the way. Now, let's get down to the nitty-gritty. How can we go about handicapping the horses so that we can view it as a Type W game? How can we overcome that huge vig?

First off, the huge takeout is not as insurmountable as it may seem at first blush. The reason is that there are many "hunch" and "numbers" players out there, people who bet on birthdays, addresses, days of the week, the name of the horse, and stuff like that. After you have read over this chapter you will be able to look at a typical race and immediately be able to eliminate a couple of horses that have absolutely no chance at all. Yet these horses will have money bet on them. They will also be getting played in exactas and trifectas. The money bet on them is there for the taking. If you look at how much *really stupid* money is bet on every race you will quickly come to realize that it is possible to beat the vig.

Let's start out by taking a look at the manner in which a horse's past performances are presented in *The Daily Racing Form*. Since this book is being written for a geographically broad audience, I will use the *DRF* as the primary guide to handicapping. However, many tracks (such as those in New York) have begun to publish programs that include virtually all the information contained in the *DRF*. If your track has such a program, feel free to use it, although you may have to make a few adjustments in the advice provided here since the format will likely differ.

The Daily Racing Form

Basic handicapping begins with the primary source of data, a record of a horse's recent performances. Figure 7-1 gives a sample of how the *DRF* presents such data. There is a lot of information here; some of it is absolutely essential to handicapping, some of it less so. Some of it is found in each individual horse's chart, some of it requires careful comparisons among the various entrants. As we go along I will refer back to this figure and identify the primary factors that need to be taken into consideration. I will outline for you some two dozen or so heuristics (rules of thumb) for successful handicapping. Once you have mastered these, you should be able to treat racetrack handicapping as pretty much an even game.

Before we begin, appreciate that while there is a lot of information in figure 7-1, there is also a lot missing. For example, there is precious little information about exactly how the horse ran each of its races; the "Comment line" really doesn't give sufficient detail. Was the horse caught in traffic? Was there a speed duel in front? Was the race won by a

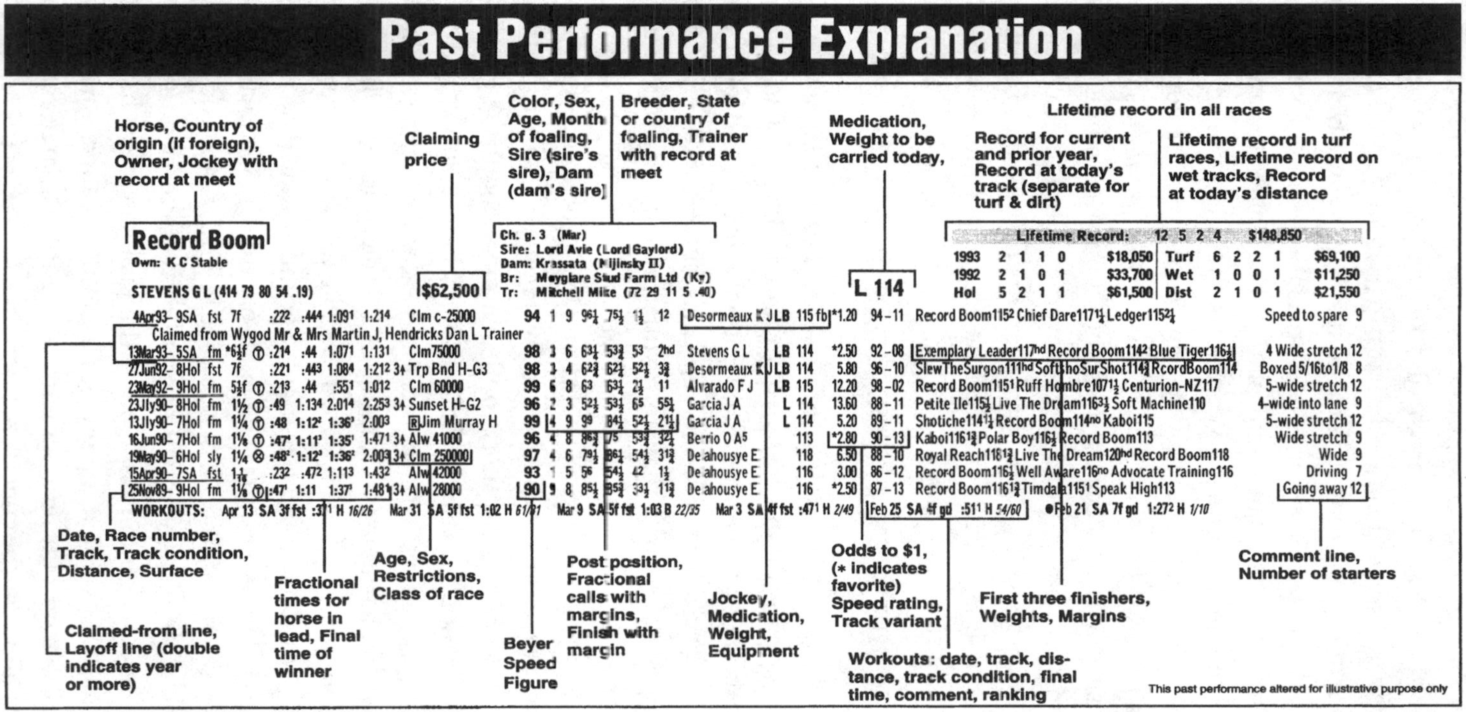

Figure 7-1   An example of a horse's past performances as presented in the *Daily Racing Form*. This is not a record of a real horse but a reproduction of the prototypical chart published daily in the *DRF*.

plodder who got an uncontested lead in a paceless race? There is also nothing about the track bias on the day of the race. Was speed holding that day or were the dead closers (what my friend Harry likes to call the "one-run varmints") winning? Was the inside post an advantage or disadvantage? Was a horse wearing any special equipment such as mud caulks (or stickers)? An aluminum pad? A bar shoe? Was an aluminum pad or bar shoe just taken off? Was the race around one or two turns? What is the horse's best lifetime Beyer Speed Figure? Its best Beyer in a sprint? In a route? What happened to the horse's opponents in races run since the last one in the charts? Did they improve coming out of the race? Or did they show no special improvement? In the discussions that follow I will introduce these and other factors that need to be taken into account. Remember, it will not always be easy to get this information.

HEURISTICS FOR HORSEPLAYERS

What follows is going to look pretty complicated to a novice. That's okay; handicapping the horses is complicated. The best handicappers are serious about what they do. They not only understand all of the factors we will discuss here, but they do their homework. We're going to cover the topics in an order that approximates their importance in handicapping, starting with the most important.

While it is possible to pick up your *DRF* when you walk into the track and proceed to handicap race by race, you will find that this becomes increasingly difficult as you learn more about the game. I recommend that you purchase the *DRF* the day before and spend an hour or two (or more) going over the next day's card. Coming to the track equipped with a basic understanding of the day's races will give you a number of advantages. First, you will be able to spend more time charting the odds board looking for overlays. Second, you will be in a position to handicap daily doubles, pick-3's, pick-6's and the like, which require selecting horses from more than one race. Third, since you will have a sense of the entire card you will have a better understanding of which races to bet and which to pass. One of the problems with handicapping race by race is that you end up investing money in a marginal early race when a really good betting opportunity exists in a later race that you didn't know about at the time.

Also, as we go through these rules of thumb it will be important to appreciate that, as happened in the previous chapter, some are going to appear to contradict others. For example, in the discussion of speed figures I am going to recommend that you toss out horses with what appear to be noncompetitive speed figures, and then later I will point out a couple of situations when you should ignore or at least downplay the predictive value of such figures. That's the way it is; handicapping is based on multiconditional principles. Stay with me; it'll all make sense.

Speed Figures

Speed figures are a most important tool. They are objective measures of just how fast a horse ran each of its races. The ones presented in the *DRF* ("Beyer Speed Figure" in figure 7-1) are calculated according to a procedure developed by Andrew Beyer, racing writer for the *Washington Post* and author of several important books on the sport. For those of you new to the game and unfamiliar with some of its storied characters, Mr. Beyer is just that. He has been a significant factor in the revolution in handicapping that has taken place over the past two decades, and is a man who, in his own words, "would rather win one buck gambling than earn two in honest labor." How can you not love a guy like this?

Beyer Speed Figures, or "Beyers," are only the stepping-off spot for handicapping a race. They do not provide anything like a magic number that will lead you to the winner. A speed figure is merely an estimate of how fast the horse ran a particular race. It is based on the actual time adjusted for the speed of the racing surface. Beyers, by virtue of the manner in which they are calculated, make it possible to compare horses across tracks and distances. A horse that ran an 80 at Suffolk Downs can be legitimately compared with a horse that threw a 78 at Saratoga. Speed figures are a nice place to start your handicapping.

Before I go on here, let me take a short aside to discuss another, basically outmoded, speed figure that is still used by many handicappers. If you look at figure 7-1 you will see a pair of numbers ("Speed rating, Track variant") that also can be used, after a fashion, to calculate a speed figure. The first of these two numbers is the horse's time for that race adjusted against the fastest time run at that track at that distance in the past three years. If the horse tied this time, its speed rating is 100. One point is added or subtracted for each fifth of a second below or above that time, so that a rating of 85 means that a horse ran three seconds slower than the par time. (The *DRF* used to use the track record for this calculation, which is even worse. For example, a horse that ran a mile and a half in 2:27 at Belmont, which is *sensational* time, would have earned a figure of only 85 because it would have been calculated against Secretariat's 2:24.) The second number is the track variant, which is the average of the winning times of each race at that distance that particular day subtracted from that same par time but using zero as the base. Thus, if the average winning time was two seconds slower than the par, the variant would be ten. Adding these two numbers yields a speed figure.

Makes sense, right? Well, not really. It's pretty easy to show why this speed figure is flawed. Take a very ordinary horse from a small track like Finger Lakes or Boise who's feeling really frisky, gets loose on the lead, and blows the field away. It might produce a speed rating and variant like 104-06, which adds up to 110. On the other hand, at Belmont or Santa Anita on that very same day, a graded stakes winner could have a similarly good day in a stakes race yet produce a speed rating and variant like only 96-04, or 100. If you honestly believe that a cheap claimer from the hinterlands could beat a stakes winner from a major track, come with me, I have this here bridge just down the road a piece that I can let you have for a song.

Clearly there are problems here. First, the speed figure is rated against the competition at that track and not on some idealized, projected norm. If lousy horses run there, the actual times used as the norm will be slow. Second, the variant is based on the actual races run that day and not on projected times based on the past history of the horses running. A day where the card is filled with cheap maiden claimers will have a slower variant than a day when several major allowance and stakes races were run. Third, the figures treat sprints and routes the same, with a fifth of a second equivalent to a length whether the race was five furlongs (5f) or $1\frac{5}{8}$ miles, which is preposterous. Horses run a lot faster in sprints than in routes, just like human runners.

A good question is why the *DRF* still calculates and publishes these figures. The only answer I can come up with is that some of the old-timers still like to use them. My clear recommendation is that they be ignored. Use the Beyers. Now, how should you use the Beyers?

- You should begin handicapping a race by scanning all the horses and checking to see which ones have posted the most recent top figures. The point is not so much to identify the horses worthy of an outlay of your cash but to eliminate the ones that have virtually no chance. Suppose you have a situation where five of nine horses in a six-furlong race have been throwing Beyers between the low 80s and the low 90s and none of the other four has a recent Beyer over 70. Since this latter group of horses is some four to eight lengths slower than the others, you can probably begin narrowing the list of legitimate horses down to the top five.

- However, don't just summarily toss out all the others. Look first for previous speed figures that indicate that the horse has some "back class" that suggests that recent performances may not be telling the whole story. Even good horses will have periods where they are "off their feed," only to recover their earlier form later.

- Next, look carefully at the comment line to see if a horse's poor figures might have been the result of some untoward events that imply that the horse may be better than the Beyers suggest. Getting stuck in the gate, being forced wide, encountering traffic, or the like suggests that the horse might be better than the raw figures indicate.

- Take a look at the pattern of speed figures. Are they on the upswing or the downswing? Is the horse improving or going into a bit of funk? Horses that show steady, gradual improvement are worthy of a deeper look; those that seem to be on a downslide might be eliminated from consideration. Watch out for subtleties in patterns. Be wary of horses that show a dramatic improvement (something like a jump of fifteen or twenty points) in their most recent race, for they may be due for a bounce—a significant drop in performance following an excellent race or two.

- Use the Beyers to eliminate horses that look like they are being overbet because the public has misread the horse's ability. Likely candidates are horses that have a penchant for a particular running style that appeals to particular handicappers but whose Beyers are clearly a cut below the rest of the field. For example, there is a clear (and quite understandable) preference for speed horses—horses with early speed—who are likely to break well and lead during the early phases of a race. However, many handicappers get suckered into a horse's front running style and fail to appreciate that its success was with weaker horses or in races where it got an uncontested lead. Such horses are often underlays, and you can profit significantly by tossing them if those favorable circumstances are not present in the race at hand. Similar lines of analysis exist for strong closers, particularly those who have profited from a race or two with blistering early fractions that set the race up for them but whose Beyers suggest that they cannot run with the field they are matched with the day you're there.

• Generally, treat the Beyer speed figures as a way of getting a good first approximation on the likely candidates for the race. Then begin looking at the other factors of importance, all the time matching each factor along with the Beyers.

By the way, there is an interesting background to how the *DRF* came to use the Beyer Speed Figures. A couple of years back, the Maxwell publishing empire started up a competitor to the *DRF* called *The Racing Times*. Its editor-in-chief was Steven Crist, who left his position as racing writer for the *New York Times* to take the post at the fledgling paper. Crist introduced a number of innovations in the presentation of information important to the handicapper. Among these was providing more detail on breeding, including the sire's stud fee and the dam's sire; a fuller and more informative comment line; fractional and final times in hundredths of a second instead of fifths; and the first set of useful speed figures—the Beyers. Alas, after Maxwell took his infamous swan dive off his yacht the publication also went under. Only later did the *DRF*, goaded by the success of the *Times*, finally begin presenting the Beyer speed figures.

It is worth noting that there are other sources of speed figures than those in the *DRF*. Some track programs publish their own, although typically they are not as carefully calculated as the Beyers. Various figures are produced by independent sources, the most commonly used of which are the ones produced by Len Ragozin, and the Thoro-Graph figures calculated by Jerry Brown, a one-time colleague of Ragozin. Collectively, these are referred to as "the sheets." These are very accurate, but they are expensive (between $25 and $35 for a single day's races at one track), and they require considerable study if you are going to understand the arcane notational systems they use. Before the general availability of the Beyers, the sheets users had a significant edge, since without the sheets handicappers were stuck with the flawed variant-based figures. The sheets continue to provide important information in that they take into account such factors as wind, the path the horse ran in, and any trouble encountered. They also display the data in ways that enable easy analysis of the pattern of races that a horse has run. I don't know that they add that much to what a good handicapper with solid background knowledge can extract from the *DRF*, but there are serious horseplayers who swear by them.

Pace

Pace refers to the fractional times in a race. For example, were the first two quarters run especially fast or slow? Fast early times set the race up for closers; slow early fractions allow the horse on the lead to control a race. A race that is complementary with a horse's running style can dramatically improve its time and vice versa. You should use pace in two ways: first, to get a sense of how the current race will likely shape up; and second, to evaluate a horse's previous races. Let's take these one at a time.

How Will the Race Shape Up?

In order to handicap a race you must get some mental picture of how you think it will develop. Who will likely take the lead? Will that horse be challenged in a speed duel, or is it likely to take an uncontested lead and be able to control the race? If there is no "true" speed in the race, which horse is likely to be the default speed and how much staying power does it have? These are very important questions, and without a sense of how the race is likely to unfold you can't really handicap it. Here's a couple of basic principles.

- The closest thing to a "sure thing" in racing is a race with only one legit speed horse. When a horse gets an easy lead and is able to control the pace of the race by setting slow fractions, it can usually wire the field uncontested.

- If there are two or more speed horses, there is a chance they will "cook" each other and set the race up for stalking, off-the-pace horses, and the closers. In races with several legitimate speed horses, look closely at the stalkers and the closers.

- It is not always easy to determine which horses are the speed and which are likely to lay back. It's not enough that a horse has taken the lead in one or two earlier races. If those races were "paceless," the horse may have become the "default speed." The best way to spot the true speed is to look at the fractions from earlier races (see the "Fractional times for horse in lead" in figure 7-1). However, it takes practice to learn to read speed. The best way to approach this issue is to spend some time looking over the fractional times for a variety of races at different distances from different tracks run under different conditions and compare them with each other. When doing so, be sure to keep sprints and route races separate*; twenty-three seconds flat for the first quarter is nothing to write home about in a six-furlong race but is pretty fast for $1\frac{1}{8}$ mile. Also make sure you correct for the class of the race. The single element that distinguishes poor horses from the great ones is how far they can run fast. Mediocre horses will typically tire after running fractions like "21⁴" (standard notation for twenty-one and four fifths of a second) for the first quarter and "44¹" for the first half mile. Great ones will not. In Secretariat's Kentucky Derby, he ran each quarter of a mile faster than the one before it.

- Don't make the common mistake of upgrading a closer in a race with little or no speed. Many handicappers think that with little upfront speed their dead closer won't be as far back and will be in a better position to win. Alas, this rarely happens. One-run varmints tend to be one-dimensional horses, and without the fast early pace they are usually in trouble from the start. Although there are topflight stakes horses who run from off the pace and have a terrific closing kick, for the most part, the dead closer tends to win not so much because it runs down the front-runners as because the front-runners tire and come back to it. If the early pace is slow, the front-runners won't tire.

- Generally speaking, pace is determined within the first couple of furlongs of a race, although the longer the race, the more attention you need to pay to later fractions. When you are trying to set up a mental picture of how you believe the race will develop, you should focus on the fractions for the first two quarters each of the horses has run in its most recent outings. Note that if a race was over $1\frac{1}{8}$ miles, the *DRF* will not provide the time for the first quarter. This omission on the part of the *DRF* drives me crazy. There is important information in that first fraction in route races.

- Some statistics: According to the calculations of William Quirin, who looked at the charts from several thousand races, the horse who was in front at the first call won 26 percent of the time, the horse in second won 16 percent, the horse in third 13 percent, and on downward. The first three horses at the first call accounted for over half the winners. Early speed is the name of the game these days.

---

* Races up to a mile are generally regarded as sprints; the most commonly run distances here are 5f, 5¹2f, 6f, 6¹2f, 7f, and 1 mile (or 8f). Races longer than a mile are considered routes. The most frequently run ranges from 1 mile and 70 yards up to 1⁵8 miles, although longer races are occasionally run. Distance as a separate factor is discussed below.

- Finally, pace in races run on grass is different from pace on dirt. Generally speaking, grass races show slower early fractions and more rapid closing fractions. More on this when we look at turf racing.

Using Pace to Evaluate Earlier Races

Frequently a horse will run an especially poor or good race largely because of the pace. When judging a horse, it is important to make adjustments in your assessment that take this factor into account. Some rules of thumb:

- A horse that runs uncontested on the lead is going to produce its best speed figures. Don't get seduced by one or more superb-looking races if the horse was loose on the lead and the early fractions were slow. Such horses are often overbet the the next time out, and you can find good betting opportunities by tossing such a horse if it looks like it is likely to get serious early pressure this time.

- The opposite angle also works. You can often upgrade an off-the-pace horse who was victimized by plodding fractions in an earlier race if the contest you're handicapping has a lot of early speed in it.

- If a horse was caught in a speed duel last time out but still managed to pull away to win, it is likely that you have a serious contender.

- When judging the pace of previous races and trying to project the race at hand, take care to take distance into account. We'll look more closely at this factor later, but it is important to understand that a horse that has run as a stalker in sprints may likely be the true speed in a route.

These principles will give a moderately dedicated handicapper a decent foundation on which to evaluate pace from earlier races. Judging pace in this manner is a kind of art based on making well-judged decisions using figures supplied in the *DRF*. However, it should be appreciated that there are dedicated pace handicappers who are nothing short of quantitative fanatics. They use elaborate formulas for breaking a race into segments and generating pace figures for early, middle, and closing fractions. Howard Sartin first developed these procedures, and Tom Brohamer has continued to develop and extend them in novel ways in his book *Modern Pace Handicapping*.

Trip

Like pace, trip is used both to assess previous performances and to help you form a sense of how the day's race will unfold. Here's how to use trip information:

Picturing the Race

What kind of trip do you think the horses you are looking at closely are likely to have? Will they be on or near the lead? Are they likely to get stuck in traffic? What sorts of problems might they encounter and why? Assessing the kind of trip a horse will likely have is dependent on such factors as speed, pace, post position, any possible track bias, the number of horses in the race, the distance of the race, and whether the race is around one turn or two.

To get some sense of how these factors interact, let's consider a couple of possible scenarios. Suppose it's a six-furlong sprint around one turn and the track has an inside speed bias. Here, a speed horse starting from an outside post position with other speed horses inside of it will likely be forced to run in the middle or outside portion of the track, will lose ground, and hence will be at a disadvantage. On the other hand, if the outside horse is the only speed, the post might not be too much of a handicap. The outside horse might be able to take an easy early lead and drop down to the rail.

Note that the distance from the starting gate to the first turn will be important. Suppose the race is $1\frac{1}{16}$ mile around two turns, with less than a furlong from the gate to the first turn. A speed horse starting from an outside post will have to run particularly hard during the first part of the race in order to keep from being pushed wide around the turn. This exertion can seriously compromise the horse's stamina, and if such a horse is challenged late in the race, it may just fold up. On the other hand, a speed horse breaking from the inside can just hug the rail, save ground, and enjoy a perfect trip.

Similar scenarios shape up for horses that run off the pace or who close from far back, but the picture is in reverse. Here the inside post is a disadvantage because everyone will come over on the horse and it is likely to get shuffled to the rear of the field and caught up in traffic. This problem is especially acute in a sprint, where there is less ground and less time for the horse to work its way out of trouble. On the other hand, the late runner breaking from an outside post can simply drop down to the rail and save ground until later in the race, when it makes its move.

The track bias is also an element in predicting a horse's trip. Horses that run from well off the pace usually must go around horses on the far turn. On those occasions where the track is showing a clear inside bias, such horses will be at a disadvantage relative to speed horses who run on the lead. On the other hand, when the rail is "dead" the horse that closes on the outside will get the better trip. You can see how such factors would play out during each of the stages of a race—just use your imagination.

Note also that all of these factors need to be adjusted by how many horses are in the race. As a general rule, the more horses, the more likely it is that off-the-pace horses and dead closers will have difficult trips. Front-runners are always less likely to get in trouble, even in crowded fields.

Using Trip Notes

One of the faults of the *DRF* is that it doesn't give adequate information in the comment line. When the line says "wide," it drives a handicapper nuts. How wide is wide? Two wide? Eight wide? When the line says "checked early," what exactly does that mean? That the horse pulled up briefly on the backstretch or checked right out of the race? Serious handicappers keep notes of each race and use them to provide a deeper understanding of how good or poor a horse's performance in a race actually was. In fact, in a perverse kind of way, the *DRF*'s failure to provide this information gives the serious horseplayer who keeps trip notes an extra edge. Here are some examples of the kinds of things to make note of.

- A horse that was severely compromised by being either caught up in traffic or bothered by another horse. A classic case here is the horse that was pushed very wide going into a turn and lost considerable ground.

- A horse that was stuck in a spot that worked against the bias. For example, a closer who was stuck on a dead rail and couldn't get free, or a speed horse who was bothered at the start of a sprint and found itself five lengths back before recovering its action.

- A horse that made a strong closing rush but whose path was blocked by another horse.

Horses that encountered these kinds of troubles are usually better than the line in the *DRF* looks and should be given serious consideration next time out. If you weren't at the track you can still get some of this trip information by using the *DRF*'s result charts or by utilizing the video rerun booth offered by most tracks.

FOURTH RACE — 1¹⁄₁₆ MILES. (1.40³) CLAIMING. Purse $17,000. 3-year-olds and upward. Weights; 3-year-olds, 118 lbs.

Meadowlands — Older, 122 lbs. Non-winners of three races at a mile or over since September 20, allowed 3 lbs. Two such races, 5 lbs. One such race, 7 lbs. Claiming price $25,000, for each $2,500 to $20,000, allowed 2 lbs. (Races where entered for $18,000 or less not considered.)(ORIGINALLY SCHEDULED FOR TURF.)

NOVEMBER 1, 1995

Value of Race: $17,000 Winner $10,200; second $3,400; third $2,040; fourth $850; fifth $170; sixth $170; seventh $170. Mutuel Pool $68,691.00 Exacta Pool $64,787.00 Trifecta Pool $48,578.00

Last Raced	Horse	M/Eqt. A.Wt	PP	St	¼	½	¾	Str	Fin	Jockey	Cl'g Pr	Odds $1
10Oct95 9Med⁷	Risk Your Wealth	Lb	4 115	5	6	6¼	6⁵	4⁴	3⁶	1¹¹⁄₂	Lopez C C	25000	2.40
11Oct95 7Med⁷	Barbada	Lf	5 114	3	4	4²	3¹⁄₂	3⁵	2¹⁄₂	2¹⁄₂	Colton R E	22500	1.80
13Oct95 7Pen⁴	Max Clearance	L	5 115	2	3	1¹⁄₂	1¹⁄₂	1¹⁄₂	1hd	3¹³¹⁄₂	McCarthy M J	25000	3.70
19Oct95 7Med²	Shoo In Action	Lb	4 115	1	1	3²	2²¹⁄₂	2¹⁄₂	4⁴	42¹⁄₂	Mino O A	25000	3.80
25Oct95 4Med¹⁰	Round My Door	L	6 113	6	7	7	7	7	5²	54¹⁄₂	Marquez C H Jr	20000	45.50
18Oct95 4Med⁷	Dancing Jason	Lb	7 113	7	5	5⁵	5¹	6³	6⁴	66³⁄₄	Diaz L F	20000	13.70
10Oct95 9Del⁹	Isobars	L	5 115	4	2	2¼	4⁶	5³	7	7	Homeister R B Jr	25000	15.20

OFF AT 8:40 Start Good. Won driving. Time, :23², :46³, 1:11¹, 1:37¹, 1:43⁴ Track sloppy.

$2 Mutuel Prices:

9–RISK YOUR WEALTH	6.80	3.00	2.60
4–BARBADA		3.00	2.40
2–MAX CLEARANCE			3.00

$2 EXACTA 9–4 PAID $23.40 $2 TRIFECTA 9–4–2 PAID $62.80

B. g, by Turkoman–Finalmente, by Danzig. Trainer Sciametta Anthony Jr. Bred by Gallo & Crowell (Ky).

RISK YOUR WEALTH launched his bid wide through the far turn, came five wide into the lane and closed determinedly to gain the lead midstretch and move clear. BARBADA rallied between rivals into the lane and held for the place. MAX CLEARANCE made the pace and weakened along the rail. SHOO IN ACTION tired from his early efforts. ROUND MY DOOR raced with mud caulks.

Owners— 1, Giacopelli Rich; 2, Broome Edwin T; 3, Labe Paul E; 4, Berkheimer Nancy & Jack; 5, Vena Joseph J; 6, Lembo Menotti; 7, Bennett Juanita

Trainers— 1, Sciametta Anthony Jr; 2, Broome Edwin T; 3, Lake Scott A; 4, Bouchard Leslye G; 5, Brennan Brian; 6, Berrios Manuel; 7, Bennett Juanita

Overweight: Barbada (1), Round My Door (2), Dancing Jason (2).

Scratched— Domperignon (21Sep95 4BEL⁶), Raise Your Blade (4Oct95 9DEL¹), Last Charge (20Oct95 2MED⁶), Palace Line (9Sep95 4MED⁴), Narrow River (4Oct95 9DEL⁵), Monacle (30Sep95 10DEL⁶), Undue Influence (22Oct95 8LRL⁷), My Brother Gary (13Oct95 5MED⁴), Amy's Harold (11Oct95 7MED⁴), Prize Writer (25Oct95 7MED⁹), Uno Dot Dash (18Oct95 10RKM²)

Figure 7-2 Chart of the fourth race at the Meadowlands, November 1, 1995.

Result charts: The *DRF* publishes charts of every race run, which can be useful in helping you figure out how to use information about pace, trip, and bias. Let's take a look at a chart or two to get a sense of what is involved here. In figures 7-2 and 7-3 are result charts for two races from the same day at the Meadowlands. In figure 7-2 you can see what happens when a speed duel develops. Max Clearance first hooked up with the longshot Isobars. He put Isobars away easily but then got collared by Shoo in Action. It was just too much, and he faded to third. The race was won by Risk Your Wealth, a closer who was a full 10½ lengths back after the first quarter. How would you use this information? Well, if in Max Clearance's next start it looks like he could be the lone speed breaking from an inside post, I would take him very seriously.

In figure 7-3 you can see what happens when a horse gets loose on the lead. Here Primordial gets token resistance from Cope with Peace for the first quarter. He easily puts him away, takes an uncontested lead, and

SIXTH RACE
Meadowlands
NOVEMBER 1, 1995

1¹⁄₁₆ MILES. (1.40³) CLAIMING. Purse $8,500. 3–year–olds and upward. Weights: 3–year–olds, 118 lbs. Older, 122 lbs. Non–winners of three races at a mile or over since September 20, allowed 3 lbs. Two such races, 5 lbs. One such race, 7 lbs. Claiming price $8,000; for each $500 to $7,000, allowed 2 lbs. (Races where entered for $6,500 or less not considered).

Value of Race: $8,500 Winner $5,100; second $1,700; third $1,020; fourth $510; fifth $85; sixth $85. Mutuel Pool $79,136.00 Exacta Pool $116,621.00

Last Raced	Horse	M/Eqt. A.Wt	PP	St	¼	½	¾	Str	Fin	Jockey	Cl'g Pr	Odds $1
24Oct95 2Med⁷	Primordial	Lbf 5 115	2	1	1¹	1½	1²	1⁴	15½	McCarthy M J	8000	2.00
24Oct95 2Med³	Eyes Ofa Bandit	Lb 5 115	3	4	3ʰᵈ	4¹	3²	2²	2⁴½	Vega A	8000	9.70
21Oct95 6Med³	Uncle Julius	Lbf 5 115	1	6	5½	5¹½	4³	3²½	3²³	Turner T G	8000	13.30
10Oct95 6Med⁸	Cope With Peace	Lbf 7 115	6	3	2¹	2²½	2ʰᵈ	4³	4¹½	Velez J A Jr	8000	1.60
21Oct95 6Med⁴	Bend The Buck	Lbf 9 115	4	2	4¹	3ʰᵈ	5⁴½	5⁵	5²¹	Santagata N	8000	4.30
24Oct95 2Med⁶	Moosethegoose	Lb 4 117	5	5	6	6	6	6	6	Bravo J	8000	5.40

OFF AT 9:28 Start Good. Won driving. Time, :24, :47³, 1:11⁴, 1:37, 1:43³ Track sloppy.

$2 Mutuel Prices:

2–PRIMORDIAL	6.00	3.80	3.60
3–EYES OFA BANDIT		6.60	3.80
1–UNCLE JULIUS			4.20

$2 EXACTA 2–3 PAID $51.40

B. h, by Risen Star–Mazatleca*Mex, by Ramahorn. Trainer Rojas Osvaldo. Bred by Axmar Stables (Ky).

PRIMORDIAL went right to the front, made all the pace while racing well off the rail, then was being geared down in deep stretch. EYES OFA BANDIT was clear for the place while no threat to the winner. UNCLE JULIUS finished evenly. COPE WITH PEACE tired in the drive. BEND THE BUCK could not keep pace. MOOSETHEGOOSE was outrun.

Owners— 1, Camuti Thomas E & Sisko John F; 2, Arraras Jose E; 3, Wizard Stables; 4, Buckley John F Jr; 5, Scanlon Robert N; 6, Precision Stable

Trainers—1, Rojas Osvaldo; 2, Cartagena Julio R; 3, Ciardullo Richard Jr; 4, Carey Charles A; 5, Scanlon Robert N; 6, Orseno Joseph

Eyes Ofa Bandit was claimed by McClain Larry V; trainer, Kunes Karen M.

Scratched— J. And P.'s Fire (30Sep95 6MED2).

Figure 7-3 Chart of the sixth race at the Meadowlands, November 1, 1995.

romps home, increasing his margin at each call. Notice how slow the fractions are. Primordial was in a stroll in the park. Next time out he is going to look good in the *DRF*, but if there is other honest speed in the race he should be downgraded.

Rerun Videos: Finally, most racetracks have a video rerun booth where you can ask to see any race run during that meet. By comparing the liner notes with the more detailed information given in the charts and your own evaluation of the race after you've seen the video, you can get a much better sense of just how good or bad a particular horse's previous races were.

Class

Thoroughbred horses range from superstars that are worth millions to cheap claimers that can be picked up for a song. There will be a range of talent stabled at every track, and the track will card races of varying levels for horses of varying talent. Here's a quick rundown of the major categories:

Maiden Races

Maidens are horses that have yet to win a race. Races restricted to maidens are either maiden special weight, meaning that the horses run under a specified weight, or maiden claiming, where the horses run for a specified claiming price. Maiden special weight races have better horses than maiden claimers. Once a horse has broken its maiden, it must race against winners.

Claiming Races

In a claiming race, any horse can be bought by any registered owner. If the horse's claiming tag is $10,000, you enter a claiming slip with the track secretary prior to the start of the race. When the race is over, you shell out the ten grand and the horse is yours. If anything happens to the horse, you are stuck with it. If the horse pulls up lame, you are the proud owner of a lame horse. Any money the horse wins in the race goes to the previous owner. The very best horses, especially those who have potential in the breeding shed, are never run in claiming races, and topflight horses rarely are, and then only with very high claiming tags.

Claiming races run the gamut from those for bottom-of-the-barrel claimers, who are one misstep from the glue factory, to rather classy races with claiming tags in the $75,000 to $100,000 range. You can tell what kind of a race the horse last ran in by looking at the claiming price and the conditions set for the race. For example, a race may be listed as *N2L*, meaning "for nonwinners of two races lifetime," or *N2Y,* meaning "for nonwinners of two races in the past year." Obviously, a race listed as *Clm 16500N2L* has much poorer horses than one without the *N2L* restriction.

Allowance Races

Since a horse cannot be claimed out of an allowance race, owners and trainers who do not wish to risk losing a horse will restrict it to such races. Allowance races are typically rated by the size of the purse: *Alw 36000* is a much classier race than *Alw 12000*. Allowances races are also rated by condition. For example, *Alw 15000N1x* means the purse is $15,000 and the race is restricted to horses who are nonwinners of more than one race other than maiden, claiming, or starter. In such a race, you may have some horses who have just broken their maiden and other horses who have won quite a few races in the claiming ranks.

Stakes Races

Stakes races are run for higher purses and usually with better horses. They are often named, like Calder Derby 150k or Royal Vale 35k. Generally, the higher the purse the higher the class of horse running. In standard notation, k stands for "kilo," so 35k is $35,000.

Graded Stakes Races

These are races for the very best horses. There are three grades. A notation like "Gallant FoxH-G3" indicates that the Gallant Fox Handicap is considered a grade 3 race, which is the lowest of the graded categories. European tracks use a similar system, but instead of grades they use Groups. The abbreviation is still G, so a group 1 race in France will still be listed as G1. Graded stakes races run in Canada are marked with C.

Races for Statebreds

Many states, in an effort to encourage breeding within their borders, will offer races restricted to statebred horses. Even though these races may have fairly substantial purses, they are typically a cut or two below open races run for similar purses.

How to Use Class

Class is an important element of handicapping. Here are some principles to guide you:

- Pay attention to whether a horse is dropping in class or going up. An example of a horse going up in class that should be taken seriously is one that won a 15k claiming race, was moved up to a 20k and won again, and is now running for 25k—especially if the horse's speed figures have been going up as well. An example of a notable class drop is a horse who ran reasonably well in one or two 36k allowance races and is now being dropped into a claiming race with a 25k tag. You've probably got a trainer who is looking for a purse and is willing to lose the horse for 25k if need be.

- But here's a pattern that should make you suspicious. A horse was claimed for 22k in a race where he finished a weak third; in his next two races, running with a 30k tag, he finished a pathetic eighth and ninth. He's running today for 15k. It's possible that the horse's connections are looking to grab a purse, but it's more likely that the trainer realizes that the horse was a bad claim and has hung a For Sale sign on his neck.

- Watch out for illusory class drops. A horse might run for a 25k tag and win, and two weeks later be entered in a 15k claiming race. At first blush, you might think this is a big class drop. It may or may not be. You need to look closely at the conditions of each race. Many tracks have taken to holding races with decent purses for horses who have been struggling all their lives. If the 25k race had been marked *N2L* (for nonwinners of two races lifetime) and the 15k race has no such restrictions, there is likely no drop in class at all. In fact, the horse may now be racing in better company.

- Generally speaking, class is a pretty solid indicator of a horse's ability. A horse that has performed well consistently in 40k allowance races is typically not going to have much trouble with a field of 40k claimers. A reasonable rule of thumb is to halve the level of the claiming race to match it in class with an allowance race. That is, a 40k claiming race is of approximately the same class as a 20k allowance race, and a horse that has been running with an 80k tag is about as classy as one that has been in 40k allowance races—provided, of course, that the other conditions in the races are comparable.

- Look for "back class"; that is, a horse that has run well in the past in classy races but hasn't looked all that good lately. Horses often wake up and return to form, and they often do so at long odds since the public has given up on them. If you spot a horse with back class, look for other factors that may clue you in to his condition, such as workouts, jockey shifts, recent races where he may have run better than the line in the *DRF* looks because of a troubled trip, trainer change, or other factor. One good way to spot back class is to look at how much money the horse has won and calculate its per-race average. A horse that has run well with better horses in the past will have a higher per race average, indicating ability that may be ready to resurface.

Breeding

There are no secrets here. The only thing that works in using breeding is study and more study. And although a horse's recent lineage is given in the *DRF*, you will have to learn about what these bloodlines represent yourself. Breeding as a factor in handicapping is most important when the horse is young, especially when making its first couple of starts; begins to mature as a three-year old; shifts from one condition to another, such as when stretching out to a route race after running in sprints; shifts surfaces, going from dirt to grass or vice versa; and encounters an off track, particularly a muddy or sloppy one.

Particular tendencies and potentials have been bred into the thoroughbred horse, and these manifest themselves under different conditions. The sire is regarded as a more important factor in handicapping than the mare. This is no mere sexist bias; it simply reflects the fact that stallions sire many foals every year while broodmares bear no more than one a year. Hence, more data are available on the sires to help us determine which ones are good and which are not. And it takes time to figure this out. Alydar was beaten by Affirmed in all three of the Triple Crown races but turned out to be the champion of the breeding sheds. Before his unfortunate death, Alydar had turned into a world-class stallion, while Affirmed's offspring have been, as many breeders suspected they might be, quite ordinary. However, it took a couple of years of comparing the successes of their respective offspring before these trends became apparent.

There are many excellent books on breeding. Buy one and study it. From time to time, the *DRF* will publish a list of sires whose offspring have run well either on the grass or on an off track. These lists are far from exhaustive, but they are decent starts. Next time you see one, cut it out and keep it in your wallet. Talk to people around the track. Ask questions of the more experienced horseplayers. If you can find out the horse's sire's stud fee, you can get an angle on breeding. If the horse was sold, the same thing holds for its price as a yearling. You will eventually build up the necessary background knowledge to know, for example, that when a horse sired by Roberto makes its first start on the turf you needn't worry about whether it is likely to handle the surface. Roberto horses tend to have green blood.

By the way, a lot of horseplayers make the mistake of continuing to make breeding a handicapping factor after a horse has run a bunch of races. Once the horse has shown what it can and cannot do, it really doesn't matter anymore who its papa was. If a Roberto horse has failed miserably in a dozen races on the grass, it would be foolhardy to think that somehow it is suddenly going to turn into a turf champion.

Spotting and Eliminating the False Favorite

The "false favorite" is the horse that is the betting favorite but, in the judgment of a skilled handicapper, is being seriously overbet and doesn't deserve the support it is getting. Along with finding the lone speed in a race, tossing the false favorite presents the skilled handicapper with one of the best betting situations in horse racing. Favorites win only about 30 percent of the time. This figure has held for decades, on dirt and grass, in sprints and routes, with older horses and younger, at the big tracks and in the boondocks. Since the favorite typically goes off at less than 2 to 1 odds, betting or keying the favorite is, in the long run, a bad bet. But there is more to this story. Whenever you can eliminate the overbet favorite, virtually by definition, other horses in the race become overlays. However, eliminating the inappropriate favorite isn't simple. You can't just toss all favorites because some of them deserve the short price. Situations like the following ones produce false favorites.

- The favorite is a speed horse that is likely to be pushed hard by one or two lesser horses, especially when the cheaper speed breaks from a post inside the favorite. While the favorite can often run the cheap speed down, it takes a lot out of the horse and sets the race up for a stalker or a strong closer. This is especially true when the track bias favors the off-the-pace horses.

- The favorite is a front-runner stuck in an outside post where there is a relatively short run to the first turn. Again, the favorite may be able to get good position, but it will take something out of the horse and make it less likely that it will have anything left at the end.

- The favorite is a closer breaking from an inside post. Under these conditions, the horse is going to get stuck behind a wall of other horses and is likely to encounter traffic that will compromise its chances.

- The favorite won its last race with a big Beyer but was loose on the lead and today is facing one or more horses with good early speed.

- The favorite has thrown one or two Beyers considerably above its norm. Such a horse may be ready for a bounce.

The Trainer

The trainer can be an important element in handicapping. However, this is a factor that can come into play only after you have gained experience and have gotten to know the trainers. The big names—like Lukas, McGaughey, Mott, Jerkins, Frankel, and the like—are known virtually everywhere. They typically will not put a horse out unless they believe it has a shot, although some of them (like Lukas) have a reputation for overrating some of their horses. Can you use the trainer's identity in a manner that gives you an edge? Here are a couple of situations where you can.

- Be wary of horses that are underlays because the public has become infatuated with their trainer. Racing fans can become so enthralled with a trainer that they shower money on any horse he or she puts on the track. Some of these horses are worthy favorites, most are not; you need to handicap closely to determine what is going on.

- Look closely at the hot trainer who seems to be performing miracles with cheap claimers. This genre was epitomized some years ago by Oscar Barrera, who, for a time, seemed to have the Midas touch. He could take a cheap claimer who hadn't run a lick recently, pick it up for 12k, and bring it back to win a race for 40k claimers the next week and a 40k allowance race two weeks after that. The speculation was that either Oscar had made a deal with old Mephistopheles or he had found an undetectable performance-enhancing drug. The consensus was the latter. Since then other trainers have had periods when they seemed to be able to perform miracles. Whether or not these guys were using illegal substances is beside the point. When one of these trainers is running a horse he has just claimed, you better pay attention. If the price seems right, bet the horse; if it is too short (and you wouldn't believe how the public can pound down one of these), just pass the race.

- As you get to know and understand the game, you will become aware of the particular specialties and angles of particular trainers. Some seem to have a magic touch with young horses, and a disproportionate number of their first-timers will win. Some have developed techniques that work particularly well with grass horses, others work wonders with sprinters, and so on. Some of these trainers have nationwide networks, and their horses run across the country; others are local trainers and handle horses in a particular geographical area only. Over time you will learn how to take advantage of individual trainers' tendencies. When you are first getting started, don't be afraid to ask some of the regulars; they usually have developed a pretty good sense of who trains how and when.

- Watch out for the "it's just a business" trainer. These trainers are often also owners, and they approach racing as just another way to make a buck. They have a tendency to run horses often and in races where they appear to be overmatched. They frequently don't put a horse out to win but rather to pick up a piece of the purse, enough to cover the expenses of the race and produce a little extra change. Oddly, their horses are often underlays. Because they have so many horses and run them so frequently, they tend to be known as reasonable trainers—and they typically are. However, the public's attention is often not in keeping with the overall performance of their horses. When these trainers have one of these horses in a race you can often get a solid price elsewhere.

The Jockey

The jockey, or jock, can be a significant factor in any race. But this cuts both ways. Since most handicappers appreciate the importance of the jock, the horse's odds will dip when a good rider is named. If a trainer has been using less than wonderful jocks or apprentices for a couple of races and then switches to a top rider, pay attention. It's usually a sign that the trainer feels the horse is in shape and doesn't want its chances jeopardized by a poorly judged ride. The same reasoning pertains to first-timers. A top rider suggests that the trainer has high hopes for the horse; a jock you never heard of before suggests the reverse. Also, upgrade a horse when a top jock stays even after the horse has had one or two poor races. Since the top riders usually have their pick of the horses in a race, the decision to stay with a horse is a positive sign.

But don't get too carried away with the supposed positive impact of a top rider. Be more concerned that an inexperienced and unskilled rider will screw up than that a top jock will pull off a miracle. In the long run it is more profitable to downgrade a horse when an unskilled jock is up than to upgrade one because a skilled rider has been named. The reason is simple: It is easy to give a bad ride, and so a horse can have its chances seriously compromised by a clueless jockey. But even the best rider cannot carry a horse across the finish line. Handicap the horse first.

Track Bias

For the most part, track surfaces are pretty honest and it doesn't matter all that much whether a horse is running on the rail or away from it. However, if a bias develops it is foolhardy to ignore it. When there is a detectable bias, you should use it in much the same way you use pace. It should enter into your calculations about how the race will shape up, and you should be adjusting each horse's earlier races based on information you may have about whether the horse ran with or against the bias.

It is not always easy to determine a track's bias. Some tracks have notorious biases: At Hawthorne, in Illinois, the rail is a nightmare; at Aqueduct's inner track the rail is usually the place to be. However, most tracks are not that consistent. Just because the first race was won by a horse that went six-wide around the turn and stayed in the middle of the track all the way down the stretch doesn't necessarily mean a thing. The horse could have simply been much the best and won even against the bias.

Even if you do detect one, a bias can change on you. Just after a heavy rain, there is often a distinct speed bias; the water on the surface tends to carry the front-runners home. However, after a couple of races the water seeps down and makes the surface gooey and heavy. The track can quickly go from one that is speed-favoring to one that is tiring and gives an advantage to the off-the-pace horse.

Racing on grass presents similar problems. Generally speaking, the turf favors off-the-pace horses and closers. However, the hard turf that develops when it hasn't rained in some time can become a speed horse's heaven.

The tightness of the turns can also create a bias. At Pimlico, in Maryland, where the turns are quite tight, speed horses have a clear advantage. On the other hand, at Belmont, where the turns are wide and sweeping, closers have the edge since they lose little ground when going wide around other horses. Then there are tracks like Suffolk, where every day brings a new and unpredictable bias. One day everybody can be winning while hugging the rail. The very next day the rail can be dead as a doornail, and to have any kind of a chance you need to be at least in the five path.

Handicappers who use the track bias to their advantage are those who bet at that track regularly and pay attention to past results. Some experts will argue that you should not place a bet at a new track until you begin to get some sense of the bias. While this recommendation makes sense (although it requires more patience and more of an ability to resist temptation than most of us have), I don't put much stock in it for the simple reason that watching nine or eleven races really doesn't provide sufficient data to reveal any reliable trends. This is particularly true when the races are run under different conditions, on different surfaces, at different distances, and with widely different classes of horses.

My recommendation is to pay attention to the track bias when you are fairly confident that you know what it is. When you don't, and this will be the majority of the time, just don't worry about it.

Track Conditions

Track conditions are important, particularly when they are "off"; that is, when the track is listed as anything other than "fast." Here are a couple of rules of thumb for dealing with various track conditions.

- Pay attention to breeding when the track is off. There are sires who have a reputation for producing offspring who excel on wet tracks.

- If you look back at figure 7-1, you will see that the *DRF* lists, in the upper-right corner, a record of the horse's races on wet tracks. This is important information. Some horses improve markedly on off tracks, others just can't handle them at all. However, the *DRF*'s data have an odd element in that they count a "wet-fast" track as "wet" but not one listed as "good." I personally think this is wrong and misleading. A track listed as "good" typically has as much or even more water on it than one labeled "wet-fast." Hence, in addition to looking at the horse's record on wet tracks, go back over its previous races to see how it has run on good tracks.

- With really wet tracks, those listed as "muddy" or "sloppy," also look at the horse's running style. Wet tracks tend to favor front-runners, and speed horses should be upgraded under these conditions. However, watch out for changes in the bias. As the track gets ground up by the horses and the tractors that smooth the surface between races, it sometimes will get very heavy and tiring, making speed horses lose some of their edge. Incidentally, when dealing with an off track, pay attention to who is wearing mud caulks. They typically improve a horse's ability to get ahold of the track.

- When the track is rock hard—when you get the "California asphalt" that tracks in the West and Southwest sometimes turn into—you will also tend to have a speed-favoring surface. Make appropriate adjustments.

Running on "the Weeds"

The majority of races in North America are run on the dirt. Accordingly, most of the discussions in this chapter are more relevant for the dirt than for "the weeds" (turf). So a couple of heuristics for handicapping grass races are in order here.

- Breeding is important. No one really seems to know what physical features of a horse make for a good grass runner, although there are various theories about the size and shape of the hooves. However, I've never seen anything to convince me that a trainer could predict how good a turf horse he or she had just by looking at hooves. Nevertheless, genes do tell a tale. Pay attention the first time a horse runs on the grass.

- In an odd sort of way, turf horses are classier than dirt horses. Don't misunderstand me, the world's greatest horses run on the dirt. It's not at the top that this class factor shows up, but nearer to the bottom: There's no real bottom-of-the-barrel grass racing like there is in dirt racing. For example, in New York there are claiming races on the dirt with tags as low as 10k; on the grass the lowest is 30k. Hence, horses switching from grass to dirt are often taking a class drop that is not always apparent from the description of the race.

- In a race to be run on the dirt, watch for horses that have just run a race or two on the grass with moderate success. There is a grass-to-dirt angle that is quite real. Races on the grass seem to give a horse new life that is often displayed next time out on the dirt.

- Early speed, generally speaking, is less important on the grass than on the dirt, and a higher proportion of grass races are won from off the pace. This is not to say that you shouldn't still respect the lone speed. Even on the turf, a horse that is on an uncontested lead can still wire the field. Look closely at horses that have shown strong finishing kicks, particularly those with a history of making up a lot of ground in the deep stretch.

Distance

Races are run over a considerable range of distances. Let's break them down into just the two primary categories, sprints and routes. In what follows, remember that there are eight furlongs in a mile.

Sprints up to One Mile

The shorter distances tend to be used primarily for young horses. Most two-year-olds run their first races at 5f or occasionally 4½f, 4f, or even 3f. After that they stretch out to longer distances. Mature horses run at 6f and up. Some handicappers like to treat a one-mile race as a route rather than a sprint. Their arguments revolve around the needs for tactical speed and position at 1m that are not so clear at the shorter distances. Of more importance is not whether you treat a 1m race as a sprint or a route but whether the race is around two turns or one. Going around two turns is what requires more tactical speed, and other factors like the post position and the distance from the gate to the first turn become important. If a race is around two turns, it should be treated more like a route than a sprint.

There are several things you need to be aware of about sprints. First, when the babies (two-year-olds) are running in their first couple of races, they simply go as fast as they can for as long as they can. You should look for sheer, raw, up-front speed and breeding that suggests the ability to carry it. With older horses, tactics start becoming important.

One of the keys to deciphering the classic six-furlong sprint is determining who the true speed horses are and whether they can be expected to carry the race or give it up to the stalkers. While there have been one-run varmints who succeed in sprints, they are rare and they usually need to have an honest pace up-front to be competitive. Most 6f and 6½f sprints are won either on the lead or by the just-off-the-pace stalkers. With the longer sprints, tactics become more important. In a 7f race, for example, you need to judge whether a horse can carry its speed that extra furlong, and if you suspect it can't, you look for the off-the-pace horses and the dead closers.

Routes Longer than One Mile

Mapping out how you suspect a route race will be run involves most of the elements we have already discussed. Here are a few more things to note.

- Don't be concerned about a horse that has shown some success in sprints stretching out for the first time. The classic situation here is a three-year-old who has run a couple of 6f races, won one and looked pretty good in a modest allowance race, and is now entered in a 1¹⁄₁₆-mile race, going around two turns for the first time. You will hear lots of talk about whether the horse can "carry his speed" for the route, whether it can negotiate two turns, and the like. Sure, these are considerations, but horses that have shown early foot at 6f and run decently when stepped up in class after breaking their maiden will often run quite well in their first route. And the reticence of many handicappers to back such horses means that they are often overlays. Take advantage. The best time to catch such a horse is when it also appears to be the true speed.

- Don't discount the importance of speed. Again, some handicappers worry unnecessarily about a speed horse's being able to last the distance. The true speed horse is a better bet in a route than in a sprint. There are usually more horses with early speed in sprints than in routes, and so speed duels are more likely in the shorter races. If a speed horse can control the pace in a route, no matter how long the race is, it has a better shot at a win than in a sprint, where controlling the race often means being forced to run fairly fast during the early part of the race. Also pay attention to the jock in situations like this. A good jockey is often said to "have a clock in his head" and can judge the pace with startling accuracy. Apprentice jockeys often can't and fail to reserve a horse's strength by pushing too hard during the early phases of a race.

- When trying to work out who is the true speed in a route, you will need to look closely at the fractional times (see figure 7-1). In many routes, there will be horses like those just described, sprinters stretching out. These horses may not have been on the lead or even near it in the sprints, but they may turn out to be the true speed in a route. A horse that was in third place two and a half lengths back after a quarter run in twenty-two and a fifth seconds in a 6f race is likely to show pretty good early foot in a 1⅛-mile race. When compared with other, experienced routers in the race who typically run their first quarters in something like twenty-three and four fifths and twenty-four seconds, the sprinter stretching out is almost certain to be on the lead and perhaps able to control the entire race.

Reading the Board

There is information on the tote board that can be of value; in fact, some handicappers regard money movement on the board to be one of the more important factors in handicapping. They call themselves "charters." They place themselves in front of the monitors, record the probable payoffs for all possible exacta combinations, and chart the movement of the odds from minute to minute to see where the money is going.

The argument behind reading the board is predicated on the existence of "inside information." That is, there are assumed to be folks who are in the know about a race. Perhaps the owner and trainer or their friends are placing wagers on horses they believe to have an edge. Or an owner or trainer is spreading the word that a horse is ready to go. If you hang around a track long enough, you will get in the pipeline, so to speak, and find yourself getting tips from all over the place. Since many people believe that this kind of information is reliable, they bet on those horses and the odds go down. The handicappers who carefully chart the movement of the board will be able to discern horses that are "getting money." To appreciate how powerful this rumor mill can be, you only have to be there for a race for two-year-olds when a first-timer with modest breeding and good, but not outstanding, works gets pounded down to 4 to 5.

If this kind of information is reliable, charting the board is a good way to handicap. If it's not, it's just another way to go broke. In my experience, such information is mostly mixed. I know some people who know some people who will very occasionally give me what I regard as a legit tip. It is often (but far, far from always) a good one. I also know many other people who routinely tell me that "they" (I have never figured out who "they" are) are betting such and such a horse. These tips are nothing but random noise—although if they're spread widely enough, they will have an impact on the tote board.

How should you handle this situation? Trust yourself. If you see movement in the prices and it fits with your handicapping, it probably means that a bunch of other players are seeing the same things you are. If you see sudden and inexplicable odds shifts (like those weird, short-priced first-timers), do one of two things. Either look elsewhere (if your handicapping is right and the tipsters are wrong, there will be real value with other horses), or simply pass the race. The latter is recommended if you also happen to like the tipped horse, since it is now at so short a price that it's not worth a bet.

Workouts

Workouts, or works, are primarily important when a horse is making its first start and when it is returning from a layoff. When a horse is in training, the works are mainly to keep it in trim and are less significant. A couple of pointers:

First-Timers

You want to look at the timing pattern of the workouts as well as the actual times. Times are a good indication of a horse's raw ability, but the pattern of workouts can give a hint as to how ready the horse is and how much attention the trainer has been paying. I like a horse that has worked regularly, with approximately the same number of days between each workout and between the last workout and the race. It takes planning and forethought to develop such a pattern, and it suggests that the trainer is attending to the horse and trying to bring it into the race in good form. Of course, if the times are all dreadfully slow, look elsewhere.

Pay attention to whether the works were out of a gate. A gate workout will be noted by a small "g" in the workout line (see figure 7-1). With first-timers, if a horse has a workout coming out of a gate that is faster than one at the same distance without a gate, it will probably have good early speed.

Time and/or Manner of Running

When judging the times of workouts, look to the manner in which the horse ran as well as the raw time. In figure 7-1, just after the time of each workout, there is either an "H" or a "B." The former means "handily" and the latter "breezing." In a handily work the horse was pushed more than in a breezing work, hence the time should be a bit better. Also look at the italicized comparison figure printed there. For example, "*16/26*" means that the horse had the day's sixteenth fastest workout out of twenty-six at that distance. Not so hot.

Track Conditions

Sometimes you can get a sense of a horse's ability to run on a wet track from its workouts. If a horse who has never raced on an off track shows one or two terrific works on wet tracks, take it seriously when it steps onto a muddy track for the first time.

Horses Who Have Been Away

When evaluating whether a horse that has been away for a time is ready to return, look more to the pattern of works than to their times. If the trainer is serious about getting the horse back on the track, there should be a fairly clean pattern of workouts. Otherwise, be suspicious of horses that have been away for a couple of months and are coming back with only one or two workouts. I virtually always throw such horses out.

Distance

Some handicappers pay attention to the distances of each of the workouts. Some argue that a horse needs a fast three-furlong blowout as a tightener right before a race; others maintain that a leisurely breezing five furlongs is just right. My guess is that it depends a lot on the horse, the trainer's overall philosophy, and the kind of race the horse is entered in. Frankly, I have given up on this angle. There may be something here, but if there is, it is too elusive and too insignificant for me to worry about.

Equipment Changes

Trainers will add and remove pieces of equipment such as blinkers, shadow rolls, leg wraps, and various special horseshoes, including caulks, blockers, aluminum pads, and bar shoes. They are of varying importance in handicapping. Some pointers:

Blinkers

Blinkers will usually give a horse more early speed. Some horses get spooked in the gate and get off slowly; adding blinkers often helps them get out more cleanly. When a horse is donning blinkers for the first time, you should pay attention, especially if it has gotten in trouble in one or more of its recent races or has had trouble getting good position at the beginning of a race.

Pads and Bar Shoes

Aluminum pads and bar shoes are often used with horses that are experiencing minor foot problems. An aluminum pad is just that, an aluminum pad put over a tender roof. A bar shoe is a horseshoe with a bar across it, often used when the horse has a slight crack in its hoof. When a horse is adding a pad or a bar shoe, it should be downgraded—but only a bit. In the past you could virtually eliminate such a horse, but not any more. Both equipment and veterinary care have improved in recent years, and horses with bar shoes and aluminum pads are not at the obvious disadvantage they once were. When such equipment comes off, it signals that the horse is in better health, although this factor should not play that much of a role in your handicapping. If running with a modern bar shoe is not such a disadvantage, removing it will not necessarily signal any major improvement.

Mud Caulks

Special horseshoes have been developed for use on wet and deep tracks. My experience is that shoes like mud caulks, or stickers (which have pieces of metal attached that give better traction, especially on a sloppy track, although they are not permitted on turf), are a distinct plus when the going is wet. For the life of me I cannot understand why they are not automatically used by every trainer whenever the track is wet or the footing is tricky. The fact that they are not is to the advantage of the good handicapper. A horse wearing such a shoe on an off track should be upgraded.

Wraps and Bandages

Front leg wraps or bandages can mean several things. They can signal soreness, in which case you would want to toss out the horse. They can also signal that the horse is an off-the-pace horse who just dislikes having dirt kicked back on its legs. Since you don't know why the horse has them on, don't pay a lot of attention to leg wraps. Back wraps are not important since many horses run with them all the time. It's the dirt-kicking problem again, in this case from their own front hooves.

Medication

Some states allow both Lasix (furosemide) and Butazolidin (phenylbutazone); some do not. Lasix is a diuretic prescribed in cases of pulmonary bleeding; "Bute" is an antiinflammatory drug. Some trainers claim that neither is a performance-enhancing drug; others aren't so sure. There have been several inconclusive studies of the effect these drugs have on performance. Nevertheless, many trainers will use the discovery of even the tiniest drop of pulmonary blood as an excuse to treat an animal with Lasix. Either they believe it helps or they are hedging their bets on the grounds that it probably can't hurt.

How should a handicapper deal with these drugs? This is a complicated question. There are wide individual differences in how horses react to these drugs. Some may be helped by them, others unaffected, and others, perhaps, hindered. There's no way to know in advance how a given horse will be affected. Also, Lasix, being a diuretic, can be used to mask the presence of other drugs, and there are suspicions that some unscrupulous trainers use Lasix to cover up other drugs that do have performance-enhancing properties. Finally, a horse getting Bute may not be in the best of shape, since evidence of inflammation is needed before the drug can be administered.

There are two considerations in determining how to deal with the presence of these drugs: judging the effect of first-time use, and evaluating the impact of running drug-free after one or more races with medication. Some horseplayers will upgrade a horse getting one of these drugs, especially Lasix for the first time. They argue that first-time Lasix users typically run better, either because of the direct effects of the drug or because of its ability to prevent detection of some other drug that is also being administered. It may, in fact, be reasonable to upgrade a horse that is getting Lasix for the very first time, particularly if there has been a recent drop-off in performance. The diuretic effects of Lasix can improve the breathing of a horse by clearing liquid from the lungs. However, not all horses getting Lasix for the first time have such physical problems, and not all horses are going to react in the same way to the medication. The "first-time-Lasix" angle, which will be noted in the track program, is there to use, but I wouldn't get carried away with it.

There are also horseplayers who will similarly downgrade a horse running for the first time *without* its usual drugs. It is reasonable to assume that a horse running without Lasix for the first time might have problems either in breathing or because of bleeding—if it really needed the drug. Unfortunately, you won't know whether it did or not. My experience is that if these drugs do have performance-enhancing effects, they are small and variable, and running without them is not a particularly strong predictor. I give the drug angle little weight in my handicapping, although I wish that there were some kind of coherent national policy rather than the crazy quilt situation that allows each state to set its own regulations.

Age

All horses have the same birthday regardless of the day on which they were born. On January 1 every horse gets one year older. Horses start to run as two-year-olds, and there is no upper limit, although it is rare to find horses still competing after about eight or nine. Here are some pointers:

Two-Year-Olds

Two-year-olds are really just babies. Although the economics of racing makes such a suggestion untenable, I would prefer to see them not race at all. At the very least, I would favor a cap on the number of races they can run and strict rules specifying the time between them. But reforms such as these are only for those who love horses, not for those who own and train them. So, let's get to the question of how to handicap the young 'uns. First off, in the spring and summer, when the two-year-olds first step onto a track, some of them are as much as four or five months older than others. The *DRF* publishes the month of birth. This can be useful information, with an edge going to the older horses. Second, the horse's breeding and its connections (its owner and trainer) are important. Pay attention here; classy outfits don't waste their time and money on horses that are unlikely to develop as they grow.

Generally speaking, two-year-olds are green and untested. They run short races full tilt until they either run out of gas or reach the finish line, whichever happens first. So, the single most important element in handicapping two-year-olds is front speed. Second is staying power, which becomes more important as young horses gain experience and begin running longer distances. There is not a lot of tactical stuff in racing babies.

Three-Year-Olds

A three-year-old horse is not fully grown. It still has a year to go before it reaches maturity and fills out physically. As a result, a good handicapper needs to ask some of the same questions that were asked of the two-year-olds. Can the horse carry its speed into the classic distances? Can the horse negotiate a race around two turns? How will the horse react to being pressed on the lead? Questions like these are legit and need to be asked about the three-year-olds, particularly when they are making their first couple of starts early in the year.

Generally, the public's eye each year is on the three-year-olds, since horses from this crop will run in the Triple Crown races, beginning with the Kentucky Derby in early May. Fascinating as the focus on each year's crop of potential champions is, the fact remains that top-ranked three-year-olds are a most distinct minority. The regular handicapper will see them only a couple of times at best and must spend the rest of the time dealing with the thousands of ordinary three-year-olds. With these run-of-the-mill critters, there is a problem that keeps popping up: how to handle all the mid level claiming and allowance races that are listed "for three-year-olds and up."

There are no simple answers here, but there are guidelines. The class of the competition is important. Classy three-year-olds can certainly handle older horses. Recent outstanding three-year-olds such as Best Pal and Holy Bull were able to dominate fields of top four-year-olds, and many of the track records that Secretariat set as a three-year-old still stand. But when dealing with "ordinary" horses, the older horse often has an edge. A four-year-old is fully grown in both bone structure and musculature, and a handicapper needs to respect the older horse when matched with the younger.

But age must be adjusted along with other factors. Four-year-olds that have never run a lick in their lives should be tossed even when they are running against a full field of three-year-olds. But the age factor changes as the year goes by; by the time autumn rolls around, this element becomes less important.

Four-Year-Olds and Up

By its fourth year, a horse is fully grown and mature. There's no reason to differentially evaluate horses' ages from this point on—until they start getting into their eighth or ninth years, when they begin to lose some speed and, this is important, become more variable.

Age and Layoffs

Age is an important factor when you're trying to handicap a horse returning from a layoff. Young horses are still growing, and as a result they tend to improve during a layoff simply by virtue of the growth process. When assessing two- and three-year-olds who have been away, expect that their typical speed figures will increase by 1 to 2 points for each month of layoff. However, do not expect such natural improvement in fully mature horses.

Weight

The ratio between words used to talk about a topic in racing and its importance is greater for weight than for any other element of the game. Everyone talks about it. Everyone worries about it. Owners risk thousands of dollars in claiming prices to get a couple of pounds off. Trainers sign up budding young apprentice jockeys to get an additional break in the weights. Races are run at weight for age or gender where younger horses carry less than older ones and fillies and mares carry less than colts and horses. In handicap races, horses with more talent and better records are saddled with more weight than horses with lesser ability. Trainers put smaller claiming tags on horses to gain a couple of extra pounds. It goes on and on. Yet, in the midst of all of this flurry, there is precious little evidence that weight makes all that much difference.

The average thoroughbred weighs over a thousand pounds. If a horse weighs 1,100 pounds and the jock plus equipment goes 115, the total is 1,215. If the horse is asked to carry an additional 5 pounds, that amounts to adding on four tenths of 1 percent of the original total. I'm not convinced that this minuscule impost has a consistent, detectable impact on the outcome of a race, even though many handicappers regard an additional 5 pounds as a significant factor.

Steven Crist, racing writer, handicapper par excellence, and hotshot administrator with NYRA, once carried out an analysis of the New York Fall Highweight Handicap race. He compared the times of horses saddled with extremely heavy weights with their times in races of similar class run with much lower imposts. He found no difference in running times or speed figures. The high weights apparently had no effect on the horses' performance. I was not surprised.

Andrew Beyer recently carried out a more extensive analysis of weight by looking at shifts in performance when a horse either added or dropped weight from one race to another. His findings do nothing to clarify matters. Horses that added weight had lower Beyers the next time out (a little, anyway; they dropped by .79 per pound added). However, horses that *dropped* weight also had lower Beyers (though less dramatically so, with an average of .20 lower per pound dropped). Weight is not a simple factor, folks! In Beyer's analysis of his own data, he decided to accept the former finding as real but dismissed the latter as a statistical aberration. Sure.

In my handicapping, about the only time that weight emerges as a factor worthy of a closer look is when, by virtue of the conditions of the race, one of two horses I am considering is taking a substantial drop in weight relative to its opponent, whose weight is going up. But even here, my emphasis on this aspect of handicapping is only minor.

What may be more important than weight is the material the jockey's silks are made of. Several trainers and owners have taken to using tight, slick silks that have much less wind resistance than the traditionally loose, floppy silks. Given what we already know about wind resistance from studies with speed skaters, skiers, and other athletes, I suspect that this factor may be more important than weight. And, unlike weight, it is under the complete control of the trainer.

There is one more factor commonly raised by experts who emphasize weight: the pounds awarded to the apprentice jockey. Handicappers point to hotshot apprentices who set the world afire when they get weight breaks but revert to rather ordinary form when they lose their "bug" (the asterisk in the program denoting the apprentice's weight reduction). This oft-observed pattern, they argue, shows the importance of weight. Well, yes and no. If trainers believe weight is a factor, they will look for hot apprentices for their good horses, since they believe the bug gives them an additional advantage. So, the hot apprentices get good mounts. But after they lose the bug and must ride at comparable weights, the (believing) trainers no longer offer them mounts—preferring, instead, the journeyman jocks with solid reputations. The ex–bug boy's record takes a dive, and the cognoscenti nod and murmur about the importance of weight. Alas, in these cases weight is confounded with class, and it is far from clear which one is really significant.

The Key Race

Occasionally a race will turn into a key race in the sense that you can use it to predict future performances. Such a race is one in which each horse that did reasonably well improves in its next outing. This suggests that each horse that was competitive in the race was in good shape and even those who lost are likely to run well next time out. If you can spot such a race—say, one where the first- and third-place finishers each went on to win next time out with improved Beyers—look for the next race for the horse that finished second, or even fourth if it was a decent fourth. They will likely improve as well, and often will be good underlays.

Horses for Courses

Sometimes, particular horses seem to thrive under the conditions at a given track. In recognition of this, the *DRF* and many track programs publish a horse's lifetime record at that track. Frankly, I am of two minds on this. While it certainly seems sensible that there might be a match between a track and a horse, it is not at all clear that this is a factor you can use effectively. The typical horse's lifetime record usually looks pretty similar to the one for the individual track the *DRF* is focusing on. The problem is that there typically aren't enough data to reveal any patterns that might be there. Are there "horses for courses"? Maybe. Easy Goer was unbeatable at Belmont, where the wide sweeping turns were perfect for his off-the-pace kick. But he was a damn good horse elsewhere as well. Some people play this angle; I think it's real, but I don't pay much attention to it.

Reading the Horse

There are some folk who maintain that they can look at horses during the saddling, the post parade, and the warm-up and tell who is ready to run and who is not. I don't put a great deal of stock in this form of handicapping, but you might want to watch for a couple of things that may turn out to be of use. First, trainers who are cavalier and disinterested in their horses in the saddling ring often don't think much of their horses in the race. Second, horses that are nervous and erratic during saddling and the post parade often are not ready to run. Unfortunately, sometimes horses that behave this way are, in fact, at the peak of their training and just itching to run. It isn't easy to tell which of these two states is the correct one. One hint is that horses that are all lathered up with a soapy-looking foam on their shoulders are usually (but not always) the nervous, overwrought ones that are not going to run well. Third, some experts maintain that horses that move cleanly and alertly during their warm-ups are ready to run a solid race while those that seem to lag about in a disinterested manner are not.

These visual clues may be of some help to handicappers, and I recommend taking time out to look over the horses, to watch the post parade and the warm-ups. Even if you don't pick up useful handicapping information, you get to look at horses, and they are beautiful animals.

Heuristics Summary

How're we doing? If you're a rank beginner you are probably feeling a bit overwhelmed. If you're a moderately experienced horseplayer you should have learned something that will help you in the future. If you're a real pro you are probably thinking about the various angles I neglected to mention. That's all right. As I noted at the outset, my goal was to present an overview of handicapping that would give the novice or the experienced loser a deeper understanding of the game by identifying various factors whose importance might not have been appreciated. It's pretty much like the approach we took to blackjack and poker. The goal is to turn the inveterate loser into someone who can approach thoroughbred racing as a break-even proposition. Remember, handicapping is an art. There are no magical formulas, and there is no simple mechanical algorithm that will unerringly uncover the winner. If anyone approaches you with a system that is guaranteed to produce winners, run the other way, fast.

However, handicapping with all its complexities is still only a piece of the pie. There are other elements to the game that must be mastered before you can really approach horse racing with positive expectation.

BETTING AND BANKROLL MANAGEMENT

Finding the best horse is the easy part. Finding the best bet is much tougher. In order to play the ponies with positive expectation, you must learn how to control your betting and manage your bankroll. Here's some pretty good advice.

Pick Your Spots

The most common mistake made at the track is to bet too many races. In fact, most of my buddies bet every race and look at me as though I were nuts for passing as often as I do. They say things like "Whaddya come here for, to bet or eat lunch?" Well, actually, I like to do both. The point is simple: The game is tough enough without tossing away your money in races where you don't think you have an edge. Of course, judging when you have an edge is not easy to do. The difficulty is that there is always going to be a winner and hence always a potentially profitable payoff, and it's often difficult to stay out. But there are times when you just have to. Here are a couple of my rules of thumb for passing a race.

- In maiden races with two- and three-year-olds, if three or more horses are first-timers with decent connections and/or workouts, I usually pass. Frankly, it's just too tough to figure out how these babies are going to run. And even all my handicapping tricks just don't seem to give me an edge in the long run. Once in a while I'll venture into such a race, but generally, I just watch 'em run.

- However, let me tell you about the Buzzy Special, named in honor of my good friend and "partner in crime," who first spotted this wrinkle. A Buzzy Special is a horse racing for the second time who looked just awful the first time out but had an excuse, such as getting out of the gate slowly or being bumped badly by another horse. Buzzy Specials take on additional allure when they are dropping from a maiden special weight into a maiden claiming race or are adding equipment like blinkers or breaking from a more favorable post position. A classic case is a horse adding blinkers who finished eighth some ten lengths back with a Beyer around 30 or 40, but where the comment line shows evidence of its having been troubled. The horse is now facing others who either had much more impressive first races, with Beyers in the neighborhood of 50, 60, or even 70, or are first-timers with good breeding and connections. Buzzy Specials are always long shots. Over the years Buzzy and I have done quite well with horses that fit this profile, not infrequently hitting a horse with serious double-digit odds.

- When everyone likes the horse(s) you like. One of this game's more diffi-cult lessons is to stay out of a race when it seems pretty clear that your picks are everyone's picks. The problem is that even though it looks like you've found the likely horse (for a straight win bet) or horses (for exactas and doubles), the short prices make the proposition an unbettable one. When the public makes the horse or horses you like short-priced favorites, it is time to sit back and watch a race for the pure aesthetics of it.

- When you feel confused. This happens to me all the time. In fact, in talk-ing with lots of the local characters who hang around the track, this feel-ing of confusion about a race is the dominant state of affairs. But most of my buddies plunge in anyway, grasping at straws and hoping for some minor miracle. I take the feeling of confusion about a race as an impor-tant signal that I don't really have a grip on it and that, consequently, any money invested is likely to become money down the old toilet.

I know it seems simplistic, but frankly, the preceding paragraph rep-resents the single most important piece of advice in this chapter. It's a lot like what happens in poker when you are suddenly gripped by the feeling that you don't really know what is going on in a hand, that your read is likely wrong. When this happens in poker you should check or fold; when it happens in racing you should pass. These are tough games, and it doesn't make sense to toss in your cash when you suspect that you don't have the best of it.

Finally, the expansion of simulcasting and the opening of many race books in casinos have given the astute horseplayer a great deal more flex-ibility than in the past. Rather than being stuck at the track with a bunch of essentially hopeless races on the card, the handicapper can simply take a look at what is happening at another track, where races with legit-imate opportunities may be being run.

Trust Yourself

Once you've begun to get a sense of the game, you must learn to trust your judgment and stay with your picks. I don't mean that you shouldn't talk with your friends. Most good handicappers have buddies who are also good handicappers, and by exchanging opinions on a race you can profit from the insights and perspectives of others. I usually sit with several of my friends, and no race goes by without a serious exchange of opinions about who likes whom and why. Then, once I've come to a conclusion about just how I think the race will shape up and where the best investments are, I go and make my bets.

Alas, this is not the way most horseplayers behave. They study, think, discuss, agonize, finally zero in on their picks, and then get knocked off their horse by some snake oil salesman who slithers by and whispers nonsense in their ears. They go up to the window prepared to key the 5 horse with the 3 and 7 and overhear some character at the next window make a $600 bet on the 6 horse, and then some lowlife sidles up and tells them that "they" love the 6. They abruptly change their bets to key on the 6. A couple of minutes later the 5 horse wins with the 7 second and the 6 somewhere back up the track and they rip up tickets, kick trash cans, and throw programs to the floor.

My good friend George—or, as we all know him, Giggi—is one of the very best handicappers I know. He has an almost uncanny ability to unpack the complexities of a race and find the horses with real value. Giggi hates favorites. But it's not a blind hate, he simply has the kind of understanding of the game that enables him to spot the false favorite and dismiss it.

Unfortunately, for reasons that completely escape me, Giggi is weak. After cleverly analyzing a race, on the way to the window he will bump into some addlepated tout who says something like, "Hey, Gig, you know the 4 horse has been taking serious money and Louie and his guys are keying it." Now, Giggi has already tossed the 4 out as a money burner, but jeez, if Louie is keying the horse, well, maybe . . . So Giggi suddenly finds himself laying all kinds of folding green on a horse that he (properly) dismissed—all because some tout he doesn't respect told him that some character he knows to be a fraud has bet it. You can write the end of this little scene yourself.

Giggi and I talk about this problem of his endlessly. He always laughs and admits that he is weak. He always has this lingering sense that somebody has an in, a hook, some inside information on the race. Well, once in a very unusual while this happens, but to play this game you've got to be able to differentiate reliable sources of information from random noise. The thing to remember is that while there may, indeed, be some good inside dope on the race, you sure as hell aren't going to hear it on your way to the window. Ask yourself, if you had solid information on a horse, would you tip it around the track? I sure as hell wouldn't, since the only thing that can happen is that the price will get depressed. If I were a trainer and I knew my horse was ready, I wouldn't tell a soul. I'd simply bet it myself—and at the very last minute.

Once you have begun to develop decent handicapping skills, you should begin to settle into a kind of groove where you know you can trust your judgment and you stay with the horses you have selected. Okay? Okay! Now let's get into the various kinds of bets and the pluses and minuses of each.

Straight Bets, Exactas, and Doubles

The basic wagers are straight bets, when you pick a horse to win, place, or show; exactas (or perfectas), when you must pick the first two finishers in a race in the right order; and doubles, when you must pick the winners of two successive races. Most tracks take out a smaller percentage of these bets than for the so-called exotics, which we will discuss later.

Straight Bets

Once upon a time, the win bet was the proper one to make in most situations. Alas, that was then and this is now. In days gone by (and we're not talking ancient history here, folks, you only have to go back some ten years), overlays were common and a good handicapper who made four or five well-judged, solid win bets on an average day could grind out a decent profit. These days, maybe one in four or five races has a horse that warrants a serious win bet. (See page 268, "Why the Game's So Tough," for an explanation of how and why this happened.)

My recommendation on the straight bet is simple: When you can find a horse you strongly believe is an overlay, bet it. This can mean a horse you judge to be a virtual lock going off at 6 to 5, or a horse you feel just might have a shot if everything goes just right and is on the board at 25 to 1. The point is to limit yourself to situations where you judge yourself to have an edge. If your handicapping is correct you will have a small but real positive expected value for these wagers.

Exactas

The exacta (or perfecta), when you must pick the first two finishers in order, has become today's dominant wager. There are two basic reasons for this shift. First, the payoffs are larger than on straight bets; and second, the opportunity for finding clear overlays is greater. There are lots of ways to bet exactas; the most common is to identify three or four horses and "box" them—that is, bet them in all combinations with each other. For example, a three-horse box using horses numbered 1, 2, and 3 is composed of six separate bets (1-2, 1-3, 2-1, 2-3, 3-1, 3-2), a four-horse box is composed of twelve bets (1-2, 1-3, 1-4, 2-1, 2-3, 2-4, 3-1, 3-2, 3-4, 4-1, 4-2, 4-3). The formula for figuring out how many bets are in a box with n horses is n $(n-1)$.

Frankly, I don't recommend this course of action for a lot of reasons, the most obvious being that it spreads your investment among all possible combinations when your handicapping tells you that not all are equally likely to occur. There are several other approaches to betting exactas. The one I recommend is to key on one or perhaps two horses and build your exactas around them. Suppose I like the 3 horse best and give the 7 a decent shot in the race. I also like two long shots (the 1 and the 10), who look like they could get up for second depending on how the race shapes up. If I were to box all four horses at a deuce a pop, it would cost $24. I would rather focus my money on the more plausible combinations. Suppose that the 3 is the lone speed and the 7 is an off-the-pace runner who has some back class, a decent last race, and a couple of recent works that make him look like he is ready to return to form. It seems unlikely that neither of them would run, so I want to include at least one of them on all tickets. So, depending on the odds and the projected exacta payoffs, I might distribute my $24 in something like the following manner: an $8 exacta on 3-7, $4 on 7-3, $3 exactas on 3-1 and 3-10, and $3 on 7-1 and 7-10. If the race goes anything like I suspect, I will win more money than the player who blindly boxed all four horses and wasted money on wildly improbable outcomes. Sure, I'll have to tear up my tickets if one of the long shots miraculously wins, but hell, I've torn up a lot of tickets in my time.

Try to narrow your focus in a race and go with the scenario that your analysis tells you is the one with the greatest value. In addition, narrowing your betting interests has a purely mathematical component to it. The more horses you use, the more difficult it becomes to beat the vigorish. To see this principle, suppose you used the maximally broadest strategy: You simply bet every possible combination in each race. Every now and again you would hit a huge exacta, but in the long run you would lose some 17 to 20 percent (plus breakage) of money wagered. Logically, every time you increase the number of bets in a race without solid handicapping reasons for doing so, you move closer and closer to this rather unpleasant bottom line. The way to play exactas is pretty straightforward: Don't waste bets.

Exactas present a good handicapper with better opportunities than virtually all other forms of betting. Hitting an exacta is dependent on your being able to properly handicap a single race. Most of the other forms of betting we will discuss below are based on being able to dope out what is going to happen in two or more races. Obviously this becomes increasingly difficult.

Daily Doubles

Doubles should be treated pretty much like exactas except that you need to handicap each race separately. As a result, doubles are a bit tougher to catch, since you've got two chances for your scenarios to fail rather than just one. My approach to playing doubles parallels that for exactas. Find key horses in each race and focus on them. Distribute your bets about so that you gain maximum advantage of odds and projected payouts.

With both exactas and doubles, I rarely, if ever, bet the top two horses, and my advice is to stay away from using only the "chalk."* An awful lot of favorites are false favorites; they don't really deserve the short prices they are going off at. Similarly, exactas and doubles involving two short-priced horses are usually bizarrely overbet by the public and don't give anything near long-term positive expectation. Even though each of the two short-priced horses looks pretty good on paper, the likelihood that both of them will run their race is usually much smaller than the payoff. It is quite likely that one will get caught in traffic, get a bad ride, get burned in a speed duel, get stuck running against the bias, or just have a bad day. Remember, favorites win less than one

---

* This term for the favorite comes from the early days, when all money was bet with bookmakers, who posted the odds on chalkboards. As more and more money was bet on a horse, the odds dropped over and over again and more chalk had to be used.

third of the time, so the odds that two favorites will capture the double are only about 8 to 1. The key to the game is finding the overlay; betting the chalk won't work in the long run.

The Exotics: the Triple, Pick-Three, and Pick-Six

The term "exotic" is used for any wager that involves picking three or more horses, either within a single race (the triple, or trifecta) or across races (the pick-three and pick-six). More and more, the racing public is turning toward these bets. The exotics have a couple of positive points to recommend them—and a couple of negative points that should give the average punter pause.

On the positive side, the payoffs are larger than anywhere else at the track. If no one has hit the pick-six for a couple of days, the potential payoff becomes lottery-size. In addition, since so few players know how to bet these propositions, there is a lot of stupid money floating about, which gives the expert an edge. Most interestingly, some of these bets, like the pick-six, actually have an overall positive expectation for the player under the right circumstances. This most extraordinary happening occurs when these propositions are not hit for several days, so that even after the track takes its vig off the top there will be enough money in the pot from previous days that the payoff will exceed the money bet that day. If you have not contributed to the pot with losing wagers on previous days but get in only when there is a carryover, you are playing a game with positive expectation. The situation is much like when a progressive jackpot for the slots or video poker gets large enough to change the expectation of the game from negative to positive. Of course, you've still got the problem of picking six consecutive winners, but at least you know you're playing a game with a positive statistical expectation.

On the negative side, the vigorish on these bets is ghastly, averaging around 25 percent and running as high as 30 percent. On days when there is no carryover, it is doubtful that the reasonably skilled low- to mid-stakes handicapper can beat this kind of rake. In addition, the larger payoffs are subject to federal and state tax takeouts that cut further into the player's payout. Finally, in order to play the most exotic of the exotics on anything other than a wing and prayer, you need to invest serious amounts of money. The typical small bettor who puts $10 to $12 into the pick-six is unlikely to turn a long-term profit on these wagers. Let's go into these bets in more detail.

Pick-Six

This bet involves picking the winners of six consecutive races. For starters, it is essential to understand that the way most players bet the pick-six is seriously counterproductive. The typical bettor makes out a single ticket using each of the horses that he or she thinks has a shot. However, by virtue of the mathematics of the wager, the optimum investment is one based on several tickets, one of which is built on the handicapper's primary picks and the others organized around these key horses plus the "maybe-they-got-a-shot" horses. Steven Crist was the first to make public this approach to the pick-six (although Andrew Beyer claims the technique was developed by California horseplayers who first carried out systematic analyses of the bet). For our purposes, it doesn't matter who was first. Serious exotics players quickly appreciated both the logic and economics of this approach. Let's look at an example to get a feeling for how it works.

Suppose you've zeroed in on the following horses as having a shot in each of the six races. Notice that I've marked them as either primary horses (bold type) or backups.

Race	Horses
1	**1**, 3
2	**1**, 4, **9**
3	2
4	3, **6**, 7
5	**1**, **2**, 3, 4, 6, **8**
6	**8**, **9**

If you were to build a single ticket that used every horse you thought had a shot, it would cost you $432 (2 × 3 × 1 × 3 × 6 × 2 = 216 × $2). However, by constructing a set of tickets around your key horses with the backups used in a more sparing fashion, you can give yourself a good shot at the pick-six for considerably less money. First, break your choices down into primary and backup horses, as follows:

Race	Primary Horses	Backup Horses
1	1	3
2	1, 9	4
3	2	—
4	6, 7	3
5	1, 2, 8	3, 4, 6
6	8, 9	—

Take the primary horses and make up a ticket using these. It will cost $48. Then write additional tickets that use the primary horses with the backup horses from each race starting from the first race, as follows:

Race	Horses (First Race)
1	3
2	1, 9
3	2
4	6, 7
5	1, 2, 8
6	8, 9

Like the first ticket, this will cost $48. Now do it again using the backup horse(s) in the second race.

Race	Horses (Second Race)
1	1
2	4
3	2
4	6, 7
5	1, 2, 8
6	8, 9

This will produce a $24 ticket. There will be no backup ticket for the third race since there is no backup horse there. For the fourth race, the procedure will yield another $24 ticket.

Race	Horses (Fourth Race)
1	**1**
2	**1, 9**
3	2
4	3
5	**1, 2, 8**
6	**8, 9**

And finally, for the fifth race we get another $48 ticket.

Race	Horses (Fifth Race)
1	**1**
2	**1, 9**
3	**2**
4	**6, 7**
5	3, 4, 6
6	**8, 9**

There will be no backup ticket for the sixth race. These five tickets will cost only $192, or less than half of what a single ticket using all of your horses would cost. Now, it's true that if two or more of those long shot backup horses come in you won't hit the pick-six, but the fact that you've cut your investment by more than 50 percent pays off in the long run. What you have accomplished is to maximize the chances of hitting the pick-six if most of your key horses win and one of those "one-timers" gets the perfect trip and comes home in front. To appreciate why this strategy is so powerful, you need to understand the scenarios that frequently develop and that make the pick-six so tough.

One fairly common occurrence is where all or nearly all of the obvious horses lose and each race is won by a horse going off at odds greater than 3 to 1 or 4 to 1. Since the pick-six gets just too expensive to play without singling (using just one horse), one or two races, days like this usually have no winner. The other common occurrence is the day when weird things happen. Some oddball horse who once showed a smidgen of speed suddenly gets an uncontested lead and wires the field at 30 to 1, or three top horses kill each other off in a suicidal speed duel and some basically hopeless plodder slips through on the rail at 22 to 1. Surprisingly, days where one or two of these unlikely outcomes occur often produce a winner or two. The folks who cash these tickets are usually those who followed the advice given above, since the astute pick-six player will, from time to time, have just these fluky horses on one or more tickets.

So, you should approach the bet in one of three ways. First, you're just having some fun and are willing to toss in a couple of bucks on the off chance of making a score. This is fine; have fun and don't get hurt. Who knows, you could get lucky. Second, you are a serious horseplayer, do some intense handicapping, and would like to play the pick-six for profit. If this is your approach, you can make it pay, but you must be prepared to invest serious dollars. The example given above is a minor play—$192 is not much to put into the pick-six, especially if there is a carryover. The dedicated pick-six player will often have six or seven horses in one or two races if he or she has got a pretty good bead on the other races. This kind of play starts getting expensive. The third approach is to hook up with friends and form a syndicate. If you get four or five dedicated handicappers together, you can each put some $40 or $50 up each day and become serious pick-six players.

Pick-Three

Pick-three is partway between a double and the pick-six, since it requires picking the winners of three successive races. There is really only one basic approach to the wager. Treat it like a reduced pick-six where you key in on particular horses in one or two of the races. Toss in a few long shots that just might give you a good race, and use them in other tickets with your keys. Remember, however, that unlike the pick-six, where the basic wager is fixed at $2, in the pick-three you can make different-size wagers with each combination. It is often wise to make a larger bet on the ticket with your primary horses and smaller bets on those using the backup horses.

Triple (or Trifecta)

This wager is basically an extended exacta in that the first three finishers must be picked in the correct order. However, unlike the exacta, the bet is treated as an exotic and is burdened with the larger takeout. Handicapping a trifecta is pretty much like handicapping an exacta; you should try to create a mental picture of how the race will likely shape up and get a feel for who will be left at the end. Betting a trifecta is a different kettle of fish altogether, however, because almost everyone uses their horses in boxes. That is, if someone likes the 1, 3, and 5 horses, he or she will box them, giving bets on the six possible combinations of these three horses' coming in first, second, and third. If the bettor also likes the 7 a little, he or she may box all four, giving twenty-four separate bets.

This manner of wagering sharply skews the kinds of payoffs that will occur should these horses all hit the board. Suppose the 3 is the strong favorite but gets out of the gate badly, and its late rush gets it up for only third, with the 5 and 7 finishing first and second. You would think the payoff would be relatively large. Surprisingly, however, the payout won't be all that much more than it would have been had the horses come home 3, 5, 7 or 3, 7, 5. The reason is that all those boxed bets produce just as many tickets with the 5, 7, 3 order as with the 3, 5, 7 order. Similarly, having two short-priced horses finish first and second with a long shot in third usually produces a relatively small triple, since a lot of players will use the two favorites on top with all the others in third. The best payoffs in the triple come when the shortest-priced horses finish out of the money; the favorite wins and two long shots finish second and third; two short-priced horses finish first and third and a long shot gets up for second: or the favorites finish second and third and a long shot wins the race. The first of these, of course, is the toughest to handicap; the others are much easier to catch.

The best opportunities in the triple occur in races with what you believe to be a false favorite. When you spot such a race, toss the chalk out and spread your bets around among the remaining horses you think have a chance. In races where the favorite looks strong and likely to win, don't make boxes with it. Instead, key it on top with long shots who look like they have a chance to get second and third. If there are two solid horses in the race, key them both and use them in combinations with viable long shots who look like they may be able get up for second. That is, use some cheap speed if the bias is running that way, or a couple of plodders if it looks like they may be able to benefit from a speed duel. If it looks like there are really only three or four playable horses in the race, pass. The payoff won't make it worth the bet even if you hit. The worst relative payout at the track is a triple with all chalk on the board.

Place and/or Show

There are at least three situations when it makes sense to look closely at the place or show slots: the serious long shot that you believe has a chance of coming in second or third, the bridge jumper's special, and the Hausch and Ziemba guaranteed lock. Let's look at these.

Long Shots with a Shot at Second or Third

In many races there will be horses that don't have a snowball's chance in hell of winning but that, provided the right things happen, might get a piece of the pie. Because they invariably go off at long odds, they make for big exacta and triple payoffs and can provide good betting opportunities. To spot them, look for horses with weak records and low Beyers but that have a chance for some other reason.

- A plodder might be able to get on the board after a speed duel.
- Blinkers are being added for the first time.
- The horse is using mud caulks for the first time, especially if the track is wet (although the *DRF*, infuriatingly, does not note whether a horse wore caulks or any other special equipment in previous races).
- The horse has a mundane dirt record but is running on the turf for the first time—or the other way around.
- The horse drew a decent post position after being stuck way on the outside the last couple of times out.
- Lasix is being used for the first time.
- The horse showed a bit of early speed in sprints and is now racing in a route for the first time, even if it folded up like an accordion in the sprints (especially if it is adding blinkers and even more especially if the track is very wet).
- A horse coming back from a long layoff, even if it looked just dreadful before the layoff, that has had a series of not unreasonable workouts in preparation for its return.

The trick is to use these horses in exactas and triples under the logical horses in the race, or occasionally in the win position if the price warrants it. Straight place or show bets are generally not worth it since the payoff is dependent on who else hits the board.

The Bridge Jumper's Special

Every now and again, a horse runs in a situation where it just seems beyond the pale that it cannot finish somewhere in the money. Under such conditions, it may be reasonable to make a sizable show wager on the horse. Tracks are obligated to pay a minimum of five cents on the dollar (in some states, ten cents) no matter what the true odds dictate. Even though there may be a minus pool (more money paid out than is collected), the player will still receive $2.10 (or $2.20) for every $2.00 wagered.

The people who make these bets often put mind-bending amounts of money into them—wagers of $100,000 and $200,000 are not unheard of, and I know folks who routinely bet as much as $30,000 or $40,000 on such propositions. These bets are called "bridge jumper's specials" because if something should go wrong (don't forget, Holy Bull broke down in his last race), the first thing that crosses your mind is to do a swan dive off the local span. In order to sustain a profit on these wagers, your horse has to finish in the money about 96 percent of the time. For whatever it's worth, historically speaking, such bets have the highest positive expectation of any bets at the track. Prohibitive favorites, those with odds of 3 to 10 or less, finish in the money with such stunning regularity that the bridge jumper bet has a high, long-term, positive expected value. Of course, if you decide to make these plays, you must be prepared to take the occasional, most serious bath.

The Hausch and Ziemba Guaranteed Lock

Here it is, sports fans, the only absolutely guaranteed, can't lose bet in horse racing. I mean it; this one is the real McCoy. Indeed, because it is an absolute, can't lose proposition, it is becoming increasingly difficult to find. Many tracks have taken to eliminating show betting when it looks like the proper money circumstances that make it work may emerge.

It was bruited about back in 1979 in an article by Myra Gelbard in *Sports Illustrated*, but the mathematics of the lock were first presented in 1990 by Donald Hausch and William Ziemba in the journal *Interfaces*. The Hausch and Ziemba lock takes advantage of a situation that occurs occasionally when there are only a few horses (five or six) in a race and one of them is so outstanding that it has attracted the attention of several bridge jumpers. The lock requires that something in the order of 95 percent of the show money has been wagered on a single horse. To see how it works let's use the same example Hausch and Ziemba use, the

Alabama Stakes at Saratoga Race Track, August 11, 1979. Here's how the show money was distributed.

Horse	Show Money	Percentage of Show Pool
Davona Dale	$435,825	95.5
It's in the Air	7,901	1.7
Mairzy Doates	4,518	1.0
Poppycock	4,417	1.0
Croquis	3,873	.8

You now wager something like $10,000 to show on Davona Dale and $200 to show on each of the other horses for a total wager of $10,800. If Davona Dale finishes in the money, you will get back $10,500 on Davona Dale and $210 on each of whichever two horses finish second and third, for a total income of $10,920 and a profit of $120. If Davona Dale finishes out of the money, you will have $200 wagers on each of the three horses that do finish in the money and a *huge* show pool to split up, which is guaranteed to provide you with a profit—although the size of your profit will depend on which horses hit the board. Hausch and Ziemba give the formulas for calculating exactly how much you must bet on each horse in order to guarantee a profit should the favorite end up off the board. These formulas are quite complex, so I won't give them here, but any interested reader can find them in *Efficiency of Racetrack Betting Markets,* edited by Hausch, Victor Yo, and Ziemba. The H & Z guaranteed lock doesn't come up very often, but when it does, feel free to mortgage the house and take advantage of it. If you have carried out the calculations properly, you absolutely cannot lose!

ADDITIONAL POINTERS

In addition to being able to handicap and maintain control over your bankroll, there are a couple of other elements of the game that you will need to understand if you want to play the ponies even semiseriously.

The Bounce

A good deal of fuss has been made about the so-called bounce, when a horse's next outing after a terrific race is mundane at best. The debates focus on such factors as the physiological toll the outstanding perfor-mance took on the horse, how much improvement signals an impending bounce, whether the bounce is more likely to happen after one or after two above-average performances, whether particular trainers are "bounce proof," and whether or not bounces are more likely following an outstanding race after a layoff. While each of these components of the analysis has virtues, the bounce issue can be viewed from a much more simple perspective. A bounce is really nothing more than another example of the principle of regression to the mean. If you recall from chapter 2, regression to the mean is expected following extreme obser-vations. In a nutshell, unlikely events are unlikely. A horse that throws an inordinately high Beyer and romps home lengths ahead of its com-petitors is likely to bounce simply because its stunning performance is probabilistically unusual and unlikely to occur next time out. In short, the horse will tend to regress to its normal (mean) level of performance.

This principle points to another important angle, the return to form after an uncharacteristically bad race. Many handicappers downgrade a horse because of a particularly poor previous outing. Again, while it is always possible that something has gone amiss and the horse is now off form, it is more likely that it was just a fluke—we all have bad days. If so, the principle of regression to the mean suggests that the next race is likely to find our horse back at its usual level of performance. Pay attention.

Touts and Tip Sheets

There are three kinds. The first is a service through which tips are transmitted by modem to your computer or by a voice telephone call. These services are expensive and, frankly, I have no real insight into how valuable the advice is. I have a friend who subscribes to one and he loves it, but I don't think he does better than I do in the long run—especially since he has to cover the cost of the service. However, I will tell you one thing: Don't trust outfits that guarantee to give you the winner in a par-ticular race free of charge. What these con artists do is give a different horse to everyone who calls. The ones who get the winner by blind chance think this tipster must really know what he is doing, and they then sign up for the paid (and worthless) service. Let's face it, folks. If anyone absolutely knew the winner of a race, do you think he or she would give it out to just any slob who dropped a quarter into a pay phone?

The second type is the tout sheets that are sold at the track. There are several of these, such as Lawton, The Beard, The Wiz, and so on. They provide tips on each of the day's races.

Finally, there are the pickers who give their choices in the daily newspapers, the *DRF*, and the track program. All of these touts have their followers; so much so that they can have a dramatic impact on the tote board, often depressing the price on a horse they have picked as their best bet. There are many players who don't even buy the *DRF*, relying only on their favorite tip sheet or the touts in the local paper. While it will come as no surprise that I do not recommend such a course of action, the question is: How should you deal with tip sheets and touts? Remember, their opinions will have an indirect impact on you because their advice will affect the movement of money.

One thing to recognize is that all the advice given by touts and tip sheets is based on information from either the previous day or, in the case of the *DRF*, two days ago. As such, it cannot take into account late changes in weather, shifts in the track bias, jockey changes, equipment changes, late scratches, and the like. Clearly, at least some of the time, the tip sheets and touts must be giving flawed advice. For example, if there were two solid speed horses in a race and a tip sheet was using this fact to recommend a closer, the advice is near worthless if one of the speed horses is a late scratch. Similar homilies apply to recommendations of horses with poor off-track form after a heavy morning rain, grass horses with no dirt track figure when the race is taken off the turf, and so on.

However, it is possible for you to use the touts to your advantage, simply because you can get a sense of which horses are likely to be bet even though there are good reasons for downplaying their chances. While I do not use the tip sheets or the newspaper handicappers, I do like to know who they are picking—if for no other reason than to identify false favorites who will take more money than they should.

Why the Game's So Tough

Make no mistake about it, handicapping the thoroughbred horse has become tougher over the last two decades. There's a whole bunch of reasons why this has happened, and it's worth taking a look at some of them.

First, racing has been seriously cut into by casinos, lotteries, and sports betting, and fewer people are playing the game. Those who left for these other venues tended to be hunch players, the ones who bet birthdays and horses' names and cute jockeys rather than handicapping. These folks were the ones whose money we were all taking! They made ill-judged bets galore, drove down the prices on horses with no chance, and filled the cards with excellent opportunities for handicappers with a modicum of skill. Alas, the ones who stayed behind were the dedicated, inveterate handicappers, the ones who study hard and understand the nuances of the game. I fondly recall the days when I would go over the *DRF* the night before going to the races and confidently spot a solid horse that looked like it would (and did) go off at 5 or 6 to 1. Nowadays when I spot such a horse, I'm not surprised to see it go off at an unbettable 6 to 5. This situation is worst at the major tracks, especially those in New York. At smaller tracks and in places where large numbers of unskilled players still come out, things are not quite so grim. The winter scene in Florida is still pretty good, as is racing in the newer venues like Texas, and the California tracks haven't yet been distilled down to the hard core. Fortunately, if you are within reach of a simulcasting parlor you may be able to wager on horses at these tracks.

Second, there is just too damn much information available these days. I know that sounds like an ungrateful whine when earlier I was complaining about all the things that the *DRF* still failed to provide the horseplayer, but it is one of the reasons why the game has gotten tougher. With the expanded *DRF*, the sheets, various sophisticated computer services, and the like, there are phalanxes of players out there who have a rather deep understanding of the game. These players also tend to be pretty high rollers. As the number of unskilled players has gone down, the impact these skilled handicappers have on the tote board has become magnified. If there is a bright spot here for the good handicapper, it is that when serious money shows up on a horse, it attracts other money and the horse quickly becomes an underlay. When this happens, it means that opportunities exist with other choices in the race.

Third, cash-hungry state governments have been upping the takeout. Each time the state increases the vigorish, it cuts dramatically into the player's edge. In previous chapters we saw how compelling a shift of just a few tenths of a percentage point can be in games like blackjack and baccarat. The takeout for straight bets, exactas, and doubles, which used to be in the neighborhood of 12 or 14 percent, now runs between 15 and 20 percent. For exotics it averages around 25 percent, and on occasion you can find greed driving the vig up to 30 percent! While it's possible to play the horses as a Type W game, it's not easy with a rake like this.

However, increasing the takeout has not produced the long-term increase in revenues state governments anticipated. The reason is obvious: As the vig goes up, the game gets tougher. As the game gets tougher, players leave for other forms of gambling. As players leave, the handle goes down and revenues drop. To get their money back, the states up the takeout again.

This vicious circle has been brought to the attention of state legislatures time and time again, so the above paragraph is not some great revelation. However, no one seems to have the guts or the long-term patience to do anything about the situation. The typical politician looks at today's bottom line, not tomorrow's. A long-range plan that accepts short-range decreases in revenue in anticipation of increases in the future is not going to fly in statehouses these days. But it is the only thing that is going to save racing in this country. Recently, the New York State Racing Association boldly went where no one had gone before. It appointed a skilled horseplayer, Steven Crist, as its director of communications and development. Crist understands these problems better than anyone, and I and many other lovers of the game are holding our collective breaths, hoping that his counsel will find receptive ears in the places that count.

Angles

Racing has been around long enough to attract hundreds (if not thousands) of characters who claim to have some special kind of insight into the game. I can hardly begin to describe the array of books, newsletters, pamphlets, videos, flyers, and services that are designed to give the punter an edge in this difficult game. Some of them are pretty good; most are worthless. The ones that are worthless are usually easy to spot: They present a single line of play that some dedicated horseplayer has uncovered. For example, after sifting through thousands of race records, it is revealed that particular trainers have startling success with horses the second time back after a layoff, or that horses with a particular pattern of workouts win with otherwise unaccountable frequency, or that a combination of weight, blinkers on, and shifts from a route to a sprint heralds a top performance.

The difficulty with these "angles" is that they "postdict," they don't "predict." Their authors found the patterns by exhaustive searches of the data base, where they emerged as seemingly significant factors, but —and this is the key—there is no reason to believe that they will predict future performance. Search around in a mass of data long enough and you are certain to find what seem to be significant and meaningful patterns. Some of them will, of course, be "real" in the sense that using them *does* predict future performances. These are the ones I have outlined in this chapter. But none of them is simple, and none involves using only one or two factors to predict performance.

If you wish to go beyond the material presented in this chapter, there are several excellent places to turn. *Beyer on Speed* is very good. Also worth reading is James Quinn's *Figure Handicapping Revisited*. For the academically inclined with some background in mathematics, look at *Efficiency of Racetrack Betting Markets*, edited by Donald Hausch, Victor Yo, and William Ziemba; and for those who want to try the truly arcane mathematics of pace handicapping, see Tom Brohamer's *Modern Pace Handicapping*.

The Bottom Line

After all my grousing about how tough the game has gotten, about how shortsighted legislatures have fouled up the system, and about how devastating the vigorish has become, the bottom line is that handicapping the horses is still a Type W game. The reason for this is, of course, because the game is based on a pari-mutuel system, where the odds and payouts are set by the betting public and each handicapper is arrayed against all the others. Hence, the ultimate bottom line is simple: Are you better than the average bettor by a margin sufficient to cover the vigorish? If your answer is yes, the game belongs in the Type W category for you.

In the next chapter, we will look at sports betting, where the underlying foundation of the game is different because the basic line is set by linemakers, who, of course, are experts in their own right. We shall see that although the sports bettor need only beat a vigorish in the neighborhood of 4.5 percent, the game is probably tougher to beat than the horses.

8

SPORTS BETTING

I must confess that this chapter differs from all others in this book in that my appreciation of this game is largely secondhand. While I know a good bit about sports and sports betting, I rarely wager on these events. Sports betting is tough, and beating it requires a serious investment of time and energy, more than I have to give it. It's also illegal where I live. While I feel that the reluctance of most states to legalize sports betting is silly, I don't like putting myself in positions that could jeopardize my reasonably comfortable and stable life. Hence, a good bit of the advice I offer comes from professionals on both sides of the game, including Roxy Roxborough and Lem Banker; the writings of experts like Arne Lang and David Sklansky; and two old friends whose identities, alas, I cannot reveal.

These last two people are, of course, illegal bookies. Their clients include a number of fairly high rollers and people who, one might think, given the amount of money they routinely wager, should have a pretty solid understanding of the game. However, these two bookies have, between them, three—maybe four—clients who beat them with any consistency at all, and at best maybe two who are ahead of them over the years. Hence, the theme of this chapter will be that while it is possible to beat your bookie, doing so is a tough proposition.

For the most part we can forget local guys. For obvious reasons we need to focus not on where sports betting is illegal but on where it is legal—specifically, Nevada. Nevada is the only state that allows betting on the myriad forms of sporting events. Other states, like Oregon, have restricted forms of legal sports betting, but Nevada lets it all hang out. Accordingly, this chapter is written to benefit the resident of or visitor to Nevada (which more often than not means Las Vegas) who has gotten interested in wagering on sporting events, lost more than he or she has won, and would like to reverse this trend. In this sense it follows the pattern established by chapters on other Type W games we have covered—only this chapter involves geographic restrictions.

But it would be naive in the extreme to imagine that only in Nevada do people actually wager their hard-earned cash on the outcomes of sporting events. Ever since the tortoise first lined up against the hare there has been some joker willing to put a deuce on one of them and another just as ready to book the bet. There isn't a place in this far-flung land of ours—from the genteel New England farmlands to the crowded neighborhoods of Chicago to some backwater whistle-stop in the Southwest—where you couldn't find someone willing to book your bet on this Saturday's game. It is surprisingly easy to find a bookie. If you live in a town or city of modest size, begin to frequent a popular sports bar. After you become a familiar face and get to know the regulars, you will easily find yourself a bookie; in fact, the guy sitting next to you at the bar is likely to be one. If you live in a large metropolitan area, a good place is a sports bar in the financial district, since many stock, bond, and commodities brokers are serious sports bettors. If you live near a racetrack, the contacts you make there will almost always be able to help you get in touch with one of the local bookies. Having dispensed that piece of practical advice, I'll assume that all the sports betting you'll be doing will take place in licensed sports books in Nevada.

If you take a close look at sports betting, you should be struck by a distinct paradox. By all accounts, it is easier to beat the track, with its vig ranging from 15 to 25 percent, than to beat the sports book, with its "juice" (as it's also known as) in the neighborhood of 3 to 5 percent. This holds despite the fact that, in addition to the small rake, you are wagering on the performances of human beings, who give press conferences, tell you how they feel, think about their situation, get emotionally psyched for a game, respond to factors like revenge, defend their own territory, and all manner of other stuff that we can understand and fold into our handicapping because we are also human and see ourselves and our own beliefs and emotions reflected in those of the athletes. You can't ask a horse how it feels about a race; you can't discern whether it is psychologically up to the task of taking on others with higher speed figures or better breeding, or how it plans to deal with being stuck in an outside post. So why is sports betting so tough?

Here's the answer: In horse racing the odds and payoffs are set by the flow of money through a pari-mutuel system; in sports betting, the terms of the wager are set by the linemaker and the oddsmaker (terms I will now use interchangeably). The tracks couldn't care less what the odds are on old Beetlebaum, and it is irrelevant to them whether he romps home in front or is an "also ran." As does a poker room, the tracks take their rake off the top and let the players split up what is left. If you as a handicapper typically have a better read on selected races than the public, you are in a good position to beat the vig in the long run. In sports betting, on the other hand, the line and/or odds are set by people who are deeply knowledgeable about the sport, and they are very tough to beat.

By the way, don't think there is one single person who makes the odds and sets the line. These operations are complex processes that involve the input of various experts and advisers before final decisions are made. In addition, many sports books seek the advice of independent consultants in setting lines and dealing with special circumstances. The most influential linemaker and consultant in Las Vegas these days is

Michael Roxborough, who is the founder and president of the independent Las Vegas Sports Consultants (LVSC). While a line may appear under his name ("Roxy's line"), it is actually worked out in close conjunction with a variety of individuals whose input is carefully filtered before a final decision is made. Because of the nature of the enterprise, a linemaker necessarily works with two distinct but interactive principles in mind. For want of better terms, let's call these the reality and the psychology principles.

The Reality Principle

The linemaker needs to set the line on a game so that it reflects the actual competitiveness of the teams. If Dallas is established as a four-point favorite playing at home over the Giants, this figure should mirror reality. Dallas should really be about four points better in the sense that were they to play a very large number of games under these conditions, you would expect Dallas to score, on average, 4 points more than the Giants. This is called the true line. This element involves the linemaker's pitting his or her skills against those of the bettors. If the bookie's line differs significantly from the true line, the real pros will shower the book with bets.

The Psychology Principle

The linemaker also needs to take into account what the betting public believes—which may or may not jibe with reality. Since the ultimate goal is to establish a line that will attract approximately half of the action to each side of the wager, the linemaker may have to loosen his or her commitment to reality and factor in beliefs about the public's beliefs.

If the sports book manages to attract exactly half the money onto each side of a wager, it cannot lose. It pays off the winners with the losers' money and keeps the juice. This is why the line will often move as money starts to come in. If too much money begins to show up on Dallas as a four-point favorite (which will be posted as "DALLAS –4"), the linemaker will shift the line to something like $-4\frac{1}{2}$ or -5, which will attract more money on the Giants.

Unlike pari-mutuel systems, where you are paid off in accordance with the final odds, in sports betting you get the line that was in effect when you made your wager, no matter how it moved afterward. If you took Dallas at -4 you will win your bet if Dallas wins by five, even if the line had moved to $-5\frac{1}{2}$ by game time. This principle allows a bettor to occasionally be in a situation where he or she can make two bets, one on each side of a game, and win them both. This is known as "middling," or "catching a middle."

SOME PRELIMINARIES: GAMES, LINES, AND SPECIAL WAGERS

Games

While lots of folks like to wager on hockey and boxing and even golf and tennis, the big three—football, basketball and baseball—attract some 92 percent of the action. So I'll be focusing on them in this chapter. My aim is to present a sufficiently sound foundation so the punter (as they like to call bettors in Britain) can wager on any of these games with positive expectation.

Lines

A line is a proposition, a way of stating the terms of a bet. There are two basic lines, a pointspread line and an odds line. The odds line is also known as a "money line," and has a peculiar variation known as the "East Coast line." Let's look at the forms of the line.

The Pointspread Line

The pointspread line is easy to understand. Your Grandma Sadie, who never even thought of laying some loose change on the Bears, could probably explain it to you. It represents the number of points that one team is favored over the other. The Bills might be listed as $-3\frac{1}{2}$ at home over the Dolphins, which means that if you bet on the Bills they must win by four or more points for you to collect. Note: If you bet on a line that is given in half points, there cannot be a "push," or tie. Standard notation in posting a line is to put the favorite first and the home team in capital letters. The Bills-Dolphins example would be posted as either "BUFFALO $-3\frac{1}{2}$; Miami" or "BUFFALO; Miami $+3\frac{1}{2}$," with the former being more common. When you bet the favorite, you give the points (you effectively start out minus three and a half points). When you bet on the underdog, you take the points (you've got a three-and-a-half-point cushion to work with).

When betting the pointspread, you lay 11 to 10. That is, for every $10 you hope to win, you must put up $11. If you lose the bet, you are out the $11. If you win, you get back $21. The extra 10 percent (the eleventh dollar of the losing bets) that the book keeps is called the "juice." It's the book's take for running the game.

Overall, the sports book has an edge in the neighborhood of 3 to 5 percent. When betting into the pointspread, it is 4.55 percent. Many sports bettors actually think it is 5 percent, since they figure they are giving up 10 percent when they lose and nothing when they win. But this is not the way to calculate it. The calculation must be made on the basis of money wagered. Suppose you make two bets for $100 each, win one, and lose one. You will have shelled out a total of $220 and gotten back $210. Hence, you have lost $10 out of $220, or 4.5454 percent of money wagered.

Since you are laying 11 to 10, to beat the book when betting against the pointspread you need to win more than eleven out of every twenty-one games you bet, or more than 52.38 percent of your wagers. This may not seem like a big number, but it is. Consider football, which is the largest draw in sports betting, currently accounting for over 40 percent of the money wagered in Nevada. As David Sklansky pointed out, if your handicapping is accurate, each point in the line is worth roughly 2.5 percent. Thus, if the true line is off by only a point from where the bookie has set it, there is no way a bettor can win in the long run. Only if the line is off by at least a point and a half or two points from the true line can the astute handicapper gain an edge.

The Money Line

The money (or odds) line is about as difficult to understand as the pointspread line was easy, but stay with me here, I'll try to make it comprehensible. The money line is used in sports like baseball, where the teams are relatively even and the scoring isn't high enough to give or take runs. There are several money lines to look at. Let's first examine what is called the 10¢ line, or the "dime" line.

When a book is using the 10¢ line, as virtually all do these days, a game will be posted in the following fashion: "YANKEES −1.20; Red Sox +1.10." The "10¢" refers to the difference between the two numbers and is often called the "straddle." As with the pointspread line, the favorite is listed first and the home team is printed in caps. This notational system means that players who wish to bet on the favored Yanks must put up $1.20 for each $1.00 they hope to win. Those who wish to go with the underdog Red Sox put up $1.00 for each $1.10 they hope to win. Many books will post these lines without the decimal point: "YANKEES −120; Red Sox +110." It doesn't matter which is used. They mean the same thing and I'll use them interchangeably.

When you see a game listed as "pick" or "pick 'em," it means that it is really −1.10; −1.10. That is, the game is considered an even match; you pick your team and put up $1.10 for each $1.00 you hope to win. This situation is precisely what we saw in our discussion of the pointspread line, where, of course, the points function to make the game "pick 'em."

If one team is regarded as a strong favorite, the money line will reflect this by moving further and further from the even-money, pick 'em point. In the Yanks–Red Sox example, the Yankees are a moderate favorite. If you see a line like "BRAVES −1.80; Mets +1.60" you are looking at a more lopsided affair. Here, to win $1.00 on the heavily favored Braves you must put up $1.80, while each $1.00 on the Mets will produce a profit of $1.60 should they win.

Several interesting things happen with the money line that are not entirely obvious from scanning these examples. First, the closer the favorite and the underdog are posted to each other, the smaller the book's vigorish. The book's vig in terms of money wagered on a game posted at −1.50; +1.40 is less than on one posted at −1.50; +1.30. Similarly, the further the line is from pick 'em, the smaller the juice becomes—in terms of money wagered. The house's percent edge on a game posted at −1.40; +1.30 is smaller than on one posted at −1.20; +1.10. This shows that the pointspread line, where the player is always laying 11 to 10, is, in fact, the maximally disadvantageous one for the player. These two points reflect essential aspects of the economics of sports betting that are of sufficient importance for us to take a longer look at them.

The dime line has been routinely available to the player only in the past couple of years. The 20¢ line, where the difference between quotes for the favorite and the dog was twenty, was the norm until a number of books began using the 10¢ line as a way of attracting customers in the 1980s. To remain competitive, the other books began offering the dime line. To see why the dime line is better for the player, compare a game posted at −130; +120 with one at −130; +110. In each case let's assume two bettors, each backing one of the teams and using a base bet of $100. The book will be taking in a total of $230 in both situations; $100 from the bettor who backs the dog and $130 from the one betting on the favorite. In either case, if the favorite wins the book pays out $230 for no profit. However, if the dog wins, the book pays out $220 in the first case but only $210 in the second.

Strong favorites produce similar circumstances. If a game is posted at −130; +120 and then drifts to −140; +130, the house's raw bottom line remains the same in the sense that it theoretically holds the same number of dollars. But in terms of percent of money wagered, the house's vig is reduced. In the former case it holds $10 out of $230, but in the latter it holds $10 out of $240.

Trying to maintain a profit using a dime line with strong favorites is extremely difficult, and the bookies began making adjustments. It is not uncommon to see books offering lines that shift from 10¢ through 15¢ to 20¢ and even higher, depending on the extent to which one side or the other is favored. For example, when one team is a prohibitive favorite, a line like +300; −250 may be posted. This is a 50¢ line where betting the favorite requires laying $300 to win $100 and betting the dog calls for an outlay of $100 to win $250. We can get a better feeling for this by taking a look at some numbers. The following table gives the book's "in principle" vigorish on each of a select series of lines as the favorite becomes a stronger and stronger favorite. All numbers are in percent of money wagered.

Line	10¢	15¢	20¢
Pick 'em	2.3	3.5	4.5
−120	2.1	3.2	4.3
−140	1.8	2.7	3.6
−160	1.5	2.3	3.1
−180	1.3	2.0	2.7

Clearly, the circumstances that put the player at a maximum disadvantage are the even game using a 20¢ line, which is the case when the money line is equivalent to the standard bet with the pointspread line. The dime line is much to be preferred. The player should look for books that use the dime line and maintain it longer as one team becomes a stronger favorite.

Before leaving this topic, it's worth getting a hint here of how line movement places the book in jeopardy. Suppose the game opens "YANKS −140; Red Sox +130." You walk in and put $140 on the Yanks. You are not alone; more and more money appears on the Yanks. The book must now move the line to make a bet on the Red Sox more attractive. Let's say it goes to −150; +140. But money still keeps coming in on the Yanks, and the book moves it again until it reaches −155; +145. Now you jump back in and put down $100 on the Red Sox. You now have a lock on the game. You have put up a total of $240; if the Yanks win, you will get back your $240 from your first bet for a push; if the Red Sox win, you will get back $245 on the second bet, giving you a profit of $5. Obviously, moving the line cuts into the book's percentage hold and provides the player with opportunities. By the way, don't expect to see this kind of movement in a line from a single book these days. It used to happen more often when a big bettor who had lots of "followers" could manipulate the line. Today, if the Yanks were to be bet that heavily, the book would slide into using a 15¢ and, if necessary, a 20¢ straddle to prevent the lock situation from occurring. But by shopping around at various books, a genuine lock can occasionally be found. If you find one, get a hammer and give that old piggy bank a whack.

Just how much does line movement cut into the book's juice? The following table gives the theoretical percent holds of a sports book for the same lines and favorite sizes as used above but with line movement factored in. These figures come from *Race and Sports Book Management* by Michael Roxborough and Mike Rhoden.

Line	10¢	15¢	20¢
Pick 'em	1.2	1.9	2.3
−120	1.0	1.6	2.2
−150	0.8	1.1	1.6
−180	0.6	0.9	1.3

Notice that at the extreme of a 10¢ line and a strong favorite, the book is working with an edge that is lower than the edge in such table games as baccarat and craps. The house's edge in games like baseball, where the money line is used, is pretty small. It is easier to bet against a money line, especially with a dime straddle, than to bet into a pointspread line.

The East Coast Line

This line is nothing more than a cumbersome and inelegant way of presenting the money line that is used in many newspapers, particularly on the East Coast. Rather than post a game as "TORONTO −1.30; Red Sox +1.20," it will be posted as "TORONTO–Red Sox; 6–6½." In this notation, the line is always quoted as against $5, with the higher of the two numbers linked with the favorite. That is, if you wanted to bet the favored Blue Jays, you would put up $6.50 for every $5 you hoped to win. If you wanted to bet the Red Sox, you would put up $5 to win $6. To translate an East Coast line into the standard (Las Vegas) line, simply double the number and then multiply by 10. Doubling the 6½ on the Blue Jays gets you 13, and multiplying by 10 yields 130. Multiplying by 20 will, of course, yield the same result.

Notice that the example I've used here translates into a Vegas dime line. Watch out for odds posted using the East Coast line that hide a 20¢ line. If this game were posted as "TORONTO – Red Sox; 5½–6½," you are looking at a bet into a 20¢ line, which is to your disadvantage. For the rest of this chapter I will use only the money line, since it is used in virtually all Las Vegas books.

Some Special Wagers

We will be focusing on the primary bet, wagering on one team to either win (against a money line) or beat the spread (against a pointspread line). But a vast array of other bets can be made. Here are some reasonable wagers that should be considered by the serious sports bettor, as well as several less reasonable ones that should be avoided.

Over/Under (or Total)

This is a bet made against a posted total of points or runs scored in a game. The bettor wagers that the two teams will cumulatively score more or less than the posted line. The bet can be made in any sport, although it is particularly popular in football. It is treated like a pointspread bet, with the player putting up $11 for every $10 he or she hopes to win. Scores in overtime or extra innings count toward the total.

Halftime Bets

In football, separate bets can be made at halftime. On these wagers, anything that happened in the first half is irrelevant; only scores during the second half count.

Futures

These are wagers that are made before a season is over. The typical futures bet is made before the first game has been played, but virtually all books will continue to post versions of the futures bet as a season progresses. Futures bets are found in every sport. For example, in professional football you may wager on the team you believe will win a division title, a conference title, and even the Super Bowl before training has even started.

The typical futures book has a huge vigorish built into it, often running 40 to 50 percent. The reason is simple: The high vig protects a book's action. It's tough enough for a sports book to get balanced action with only two teams, and it's virtually impossible to get it when there are over twenty teams. So to protect against getting "sided" (when a disproportionate amount of the money is on one team), the books build in a huge vig as a cushion. Naturally, this makes futures bets difficult ones for the player.

Parlays

The basic parlay is a combined bet on the outcomes of two or more games. You can bet a parlay by specifying your teams or you can use what is called a "parlay card." In either case, you must win all of your bets to collect. Parlays can be played against a pointspread line or a money line. When betting with a football parlay card against a pointspread, first check the rule the book uses for handling ties. Some parlays are set up so that ties lose, some so ties win, others so a tie is a push; and some post only half-point lines—so there can be no ties. Although this may make a difference in terms of whether the bet looks more or less appetizing, you can be sure of one thing: The payoffs are always appropriately adjusted. If you look closely at the lines offered on football parlay cards, you will notice this subtle but nasty aspect: On "ties lose" cards, an inordinately high number of lines will be posted at what are known as "key numbers," while on "ties win" cards, there will be a distinct paucity of such lines. Key numbers are numbers, like three and seven in football, that frequently decide the outcome of games.

You can play parlays yourself; take all your winnings from the first game and bet them on the second, and so forth—unless, of course, two of the games are being played at the same time, in which case you need a bookie. The attraction of parlays is the big payoff. The typical parlay card allows for bets on as many as ten teams with payoffs for hitting all ten as high as 600 for 1.

Teasers

A teaser is a kind of parlay used with a pointspread line, but the bookie gives you some extra points to play with. Suppose the lines on two games are Broncos −4 over the Saints and 'Skins −2 over the Rams, and you want to bet the dog in each game on a six-point teaser. You could take your six points and divide them up, giving each of your teams three points. This would produce two bets in which you take the Saints +7 and the Rams +5. Or you could put five points in one game and one in the other and have Saints +9 and Rams +3. The payoffs are adjusted to take into account the extra points. Unlike some parlays, with teasers ties always lose for you.

HEURISTICS FOR SPORTS BETTORS

I'm going to give you three different kinds of heuristics. The first will present general strategies you need to understand, the second covers more specific handicapping tips, and the third deals with economic and statistical issues.

General Strategies

Don't Bet Too Many Games

Some pros will tell you that the secret to success is to bet a modest amount of money on each of a large number of games. Others will argue that the optimum approach is to focus your bets and place large wagers on games where you believe you have a substantial positive expectation.

The first approach is generally favored because it has less volatility. A bad run using the focusing strategy can be devastating to your bankroll. Legendary sports bettor and occasional writer Lem Banker, who has been making a living betting sports for more years than he likes to admit, favors the first approach—although Lem's "modest" bets would seem quite large to the average bettor. His argument is that careful handicapping and systematic line shopping can gain you a small overall edge, and by betting lots of games you can work a decent living out of the game. This situation is akin to that of the professional blackjack player who plays with a small positive expectation and counts on grinding out a profit by playing many hands.

If that's true, why do I recommend that you don't bet too many games? Because playing the sports betting game this way requires a serious investment of time and energy, which isn't feasible for most occasional bettors. The professional player is functioning at a different level altogether. As when weak players play too many hands in poker, and when the typical horseplayer bets too many races, there aren't going to be that many opportunities when the recreational bettor can do the necessary deep handicapping and find a line that is off by the necessary amount. Betting games without these elements can only hurt you in the long run.

Here's a quick way to limit the number of games you bet: Stay away from games you're emotionally involved in. True fans (remember, the term is a shortened form of "fanatic") often let their emotions get in the way of their handicapping skills. Sure, devoted fans know the players on their team well, but they also tend to think they are better players than they are. Sports betting is a game that is best played by using logic, proper play, and sophisticated handicapping—not emotion.

Pick a Specialty

Concentrate at first on a single sport and preferably a single domain within that sport. If you like football, focus on football; if you like the college game, make that your specialty. After you've learned that game well and are playing it with positive expectation, you can branch out. The linemaker has to set a line on all the games. You can pick your spots. Become an expert on the Pac-10 or the Southwest Conference. It will become more likely that you will find the misposted line, because in this area, you will know more than the linemakers.

Bet Only "Bettable" Games

This heading sounds kind of stupid, but it makes sense. If the bookie's line is correct, the game is not bettable. I don't mean you can't put down a bet; of course you can. But you won't be wagering with a positive expectation. When betting against the pointspread you need to win more than 52.38 percent of your bets to be playing with positive expectation. If the bookie's line is right, the game will fall too close to the stated line to make it a sensible wager. What makes a game bettable? Read on.

Respect the Linemaker

This piece of advice was given to me by Lem Banker. If you're not a sophisticated sports bettor, it may seem an odd idea, but it is absolutely fundamental. Linemakers are real pros. They know their stuff and they do their homework. If the average Southern California Joe looks at the Lakers-Pistons game and thinks the Lakers are at least twelve points better than Detroit, but the line is a "mere" Lakers −5, he'd better think again. Las Vegas books are virtually never off by seven points on NBA games. What you should be looking for are games where the line is off by two or three points. Appreciate that when the line does appear to be this far off it is typically because the money coming in has forced the movement.

But here's an interesting angle: If you're using an illegal bookie, regional action will often push a line in a particular area of the country off by a significant margin from the Las Vegas line because of the action of fanatical fans. When this happens, trust the Las Vegas line and bet against the movement.

Interpreting Line Movement

Money makes the line move—that's pretty obvious. But where is the money coming from? If the money is what is known as "wise guy" money or, in the modern vernacular, "syndicate" or "combine" money—it is often very smart money. This kind of money tends to land heavily on a team because the pros have spotted a line that, in their judgment, is seriously off. If, on the other hand, the money is tourist, or "square," money, it has virtually no predictive value. Syndicate money tends to move the line closer to the "true" line; tourist money, if anything, tends to move it further away. The problem for the recreational bettor is to know which is which.

There are no unfailing answers, but here are a couple of factors that may help. First, sudden, heavy money landing on a game is usually smart money. If a betting syndicate spots a line that is off by a significant margin, it tends to make several large bets and often at several different sports books to get in before the line shifts. Tourist money, on the other hand, tends to trickle in. Second, the sport itself can be a clue. Smart money makes up a larger proportion of the total handle in basketball than it does in the other major sports. Hence, line movement in basketball is more often movement toward the true line than away from it. Finally, take a clue from the time of year. Playoffs, the NCAA tournament, bowl games, and the Super Bowl attract large amounts of tourist money. This "not-so-smart" money makes up a larger proportion of the handle and tends to move away from the true line.

The Early Line

In these days of intense competition, linemakers are hanging lines earlier and earlier to get more action and, in principle, make more money. However, since determining the proper line on a game is not an easy task, early lines are occasionally patched together without the proper research. An astute handicapper can do quite well by carefully charting early lines and looking for those that seem out of whack. When the bookie does make a mistake with an early line, it will show severe shifts over the next couple of days, which can provide opportunities for pointspread middles and money line locks.

Because the early lines are not infrequently flawed, most illegal bookies will not permit their customers to bet them. For a Sunday NFL game, in Las Vegas you can sometimes get a bet down as early as the preceding Sunday night or Monday morning. My consultants in New York tell me they won't take a bet until Tuesday at the earliest—and often not until Wednesday. They are waiting for the sharp handicappers to force the Las Vegas books to adjust the line before they permit their customers to bet. Chalk up one more reason for the serious gambler to live in Las Vegas.

Line Shopping

Line shopping is, literally, shopping for the best line you can find on a game. It takes place after you have handicapped the game and have a reasonably good feel for it. According to such storied gamblers as Lem Banker and David Sklansky, it is the single most important factor in successful sports betting. Suppose you have concluded that the true line is Dallas −4 over the Giants. In order to bet this game, you need to find a book that has the game at Dallas −2½ or Dallas −5½ or anything more extreme. Without a line like either of these, you don't have a bet. When line shopping, either track movement in the line at a particular book or shop around among the approximately 100 legal sports books currently operating.

Line shopping is damn near impossible if you're betting with an illegal bookie somewhere other than Nevada. But if you have access to bookies in different parts of the country you can occasionally get serious line shifts. In the Dallas-Giants example above, illegal bookies in Dallas are likely to have Dallas at −6, while those in New York may have the game at −2. If you're in Dallas or know some way to get a bet in down there, take the points; if you're in New York, give. If you can get bets down in both places, do it. A four-point spread makes for a middle situation with a high likelihood of success.

Getting and Evaluating Information

Accurate information is one of the keys to successful sports handicapping, just as it is in horse racing. However, there is a very big difference between the two games. Betting on the horses, largely because it is so legally widespread, has spawned a number of sources of critical information, most notably the *Daily Racing Form*. Sports betting, by virtue of being legally restricted to but a few venues, has no equivalent sources. Most serious handicappers rely on specialized publications like Mort Olshan's *The Gold Sheet*, which provides "power ratings" that rank teams in terms of overall strength, and compilations of statistics such as the *Elias Baseball Analyst*. You can also buy stat and log books, and publications that lay out trends in play over extended periods of time. Any reader who is serious about getting into sports betting should call the Gambler's Book Club and ask for its latest catalog of publications on these topics.

However, these sources still do not provide the serious sports bettor with the detail necessary to beat the vig. Trends are statements of past performance; they do not necessarily predict future performance—particularly when a factor like team personnel changes. Ditto stat and log books. Power ratings are useful but are not sensitive to critical elements such as individual matchups (more on this below) and the impact of emotional factors on particular games. Serious sports bettors subscribe to periodicals that specialize in sports, they watch games every chance they get, they pay attention to injury reports, they follow the fortunes of specific teams and individual players, and they try to project future performance based on current conditions. They zero in on knowledgeable sports writers and, importantly, they develop contacts in various cities who can supply them with critical information about upcoming contests.

Is it really necessary to do this to play this game? It is if you plan to bet sports professionally, but for the average bettor who wants to stay roughly even or gain a small edge over his or her bookie, such deep analyses are not necessary. You simply need to pay attention, handicap wisely, and follow the basic guidelines presented in this chapter. Careful reading of your local tabloid can provide you with all kinds of insights into upcoming games.

Specific Handicapping Tips

Matchups

Individual team and personnel matchups are important elements in sports betting. Handicapping begins by using some metric that ranks teams in terms of their overall strength. These include very basic measures such as each team's overall win/loss record and related figures such as win/loss at home or on the road or within the team's own conference, as well as more sophisticated measures like the power ratings published in *The Gold Sheet*. Using metrics like these is not a terrible way to handicap, but in the long run weaknesses in the method will become obvious. It's like trying to use the Beyer Speed Figures to handicap the horses without taking into consideration factors like pace or post position. These rankings can fail to detect situations where, to use a term borrowed from mathematics, transitivity fails.

What is transitivity? It's easiest to explain with an example. Suppose we know that Bill is taller than Max and that Max is taller than Andrew. We now also know that Bill is taller than Andrew. Apply this notion to the question of which team is better than another. If Team A regularly beats

Team B and B regularly beats C, the relationship between all three would show transitivity if Team A were to beat Team C on a very regular basis.

But while we expect to find transitivity in the first case, we may or may not expect to find it in the second. The scale for measuring height is unidimensional and linear. With complex entities like sports teams, we are dealing with multidimensional, nonlinear scales. Here it may be a mistake to expect to see transitivity, because while there is only one way to be tall, there are a lot of different ways in which teams can be better than other teams.

The individual matchup is one of these. David Sklansky calls it the most important aspect of successful sports handicapping. He uses basketball to make his point. Suppose you are considering wagering on an excellent basketball team (Team A) that is anchored by a strong defensive center. If Team A is playing an opponent (Team B) whose center is also defensively minded and is not a significant factor in the overall offense, then Team B should be seriously considered a possible bet— even if its overall record were poorer than Team A's and even if it had already lost to teams that A had beaten easily. The reason? Team A's overall record is based in large measure on the ability of its star defensive center to keep offensively minded centers from scoring. But when playing opponents like Team B, whose center is not an integral part of the offense, the skills of Team A's center are going to be largely wasted. On the other hand, if Team A is playing against Team C, whose offense is built around the scoring of its aggressive center, Team A becomes a legit consideration since Team A's center is likely to disrupt Team C's tempo. This analysis holds even if Team C has an overall better record or has beaten teams that have beaten Team A.

Similar cases can be made in any sport. In football, downplay a passing team when playing a team with an exceptionally strong pass defense but upgrade it when playing a team whose forte is stopping the run. In baseball, look for matchups like a sidewinding left-handed pitcher going up against a team whose offense is provided almost entirely by left-handed batters.

Dogs Make for Better Bets; Small Dogs Often Make the Best Bets

This is akin to the general principle that you should often go against public opinion. The average player overbets favorites. This is partly due to the sense that one or another team is "unbeatable" based on earlier performances. It is partly due to a bandwagon effect, where people see money flowing toward one team, make the assumption that someone "has inside info," and jump on board. If this is a temptation for you, consider the following:

- Underdogs typically have much more invested in a game (psychologically speaking) than favorites. An underdog is trying to *win* the game—just like the favorite. But when betting the dog on a pointspread line, *you don't have to win*—you've got the points on your side. When betting the dog with the money line, your team must win, but you are getting a higher price. Backing the underdog will put you in better financial shape than shoveling your money onto the favorites.

- In football and basketball, when the favorite is ahead toward the end of the game, it will often shift into a defensive mode. It doesn't particularly care if its opponent scores a couple of points so long as it still holds on to the lead. But those couple of points are often enough to cover the spread.

- But be careful. These principles apply primarily to small dogs. Mismatches don't typically work out quite so well because the underdog often acts like a lamb being brought in for slaughter. I would avoid betting huge mismatches. The books usually can't figure out where to put the line—and you won't be able to either.

Should You Root, Root, Root for the Home Team?

It is universally recognized that the home team has a distinct advantage. Home team players get to stay in their own homes, live with their wives or girlfriends, and drive their own cars to the park or stadium. It is a distinct disadvantage to have to fly into a city, live out of a suitcase in a hotel, and have to take the team bus. Traveling is tiring, especially through time zones. By the way, traveling west to east is more disruptive of normal bodily rhythms than going from east to west. West Coast teams heading east suffer more from jet lag than East Coast teams heading west. But before you jump on the East Coast home team, make sure you know exactly when the team flew in. The effect is strong only if the flight was in the previous day or two. The general rule is: When traveling west to east, it generally takes one day to recover for each time zone passed through; when traveling east to west, it takes about half that.

For the home team, the fans are its own fans. The impact of the home crowd is strongest in college sports, though it also plays a role in the pros.

Also, at least some of the time the visiting team must play on a surface different from the one it is used to. And, finally, the officials, no matter how hard they try to be neutral, frequently tilt just a tad in the direction of the home team. The impact of the crowd can be considerable, and officials, despite the opinions of many sports bettors and coaches, are quite human and subject to the crowd's emotional pounding.

Does all this mean that you should automatically lean toward betting the home team? Not really. These ingredients are well-known and are usually reflected in the line or the odds. In professional football, a three-point home field factor is included in the posted line. However, if you feel that the line is off because the book has not taken a home field advantage sufficiently into account or has perhaps overemphasized it, you may have found yourself a good bet. It is a matter of careful handicapping.

Playing Surface

In football and baseball, the extent to which you have to consider the fact that a team is going from artificial turf to grass (or vice versa) is far from clear. There used to be a general rule of thumb for football: A team that played its home games on turf and moved to grass gained a point. Teams that went from grass to turf lost a point. But careful analyses of the outcomes of NFL games over the past several decades (see Arne Lang's *Sports Betting 101*) suggest that these estimates are no longer valid. While the shift in playing surface seemed to be a significant factor back in the 1970s, when artificial turf was still a bit of a novelty, it doesn't seem particularly important these days. Most teams, both college and pro, practice on both surfaces and are sufficiently familiar with both so that shifting from one to the other is not a major factor.

However, in baseball, some teams are sculpted for a particular surface. A team like Saint Louis, which plays at home in a large stadium with a very fast rug, will often emphasize speed and defensive ability over sheer raw power. When such a team plays on natural grass in a small park, it is going to be at a disadvantage. Unfortunately, the bookies know this and the posted line will reflect this factor. Still, keep your eye peeled for cases where the line appears to be off.

Catching Middles

Catching a middle is the sports bettor's ultimate fantasy. The situation occurs when you are betting a pointspread and, by virtue of the differential in two lines, you can make bets on opposite sides of a game and win both. Here's a football example. The game opens at Patriots −4 over the Jets. You give the points. Two days later you notice that the line has shifted so that it is now Pats −6. You jump in with a bet on the Jets. The Patriots win by 5, which is in the middle of the two bets you have made. You collect on both.

Middles make up a significant part of the serious sports bettor's game, since relatively little money is risked for rather considerable gain. In the above example, suppose you have put down $110 on each bet for a total outlay of $220. If you lose one bet and win the other, you get back $210 and are out only $10. However, you've got a decent shot at catching your middle, which will bring you $420 and a profit of $200— and there's an even better shot at winning one bet and pushing on the other, which will leave you $100 in the black. Middles don't happen all that often, but they don't have to for the astute player to make a profit from them.

Here's a rule of thumb: If you find a differential of two points or more around what you take to be the true line on the game, take a shot at hitting a middle. In fact, in football even one and a half points may be enough, especially if it is around a key figure—one of the frequently occurring margins of victory, such as three or seven points. If lots of games are decided by exactly three points, then catching a middle when the two lines straddle three is a lot more likely than catching one when the lines straddle a number like five.

When betting on a money line, there is an analog to the middle: It is a set of circumstances when the line differential is sufficiently great that you have a lock. However, these two situations differ. When you go for a middle with a pointspread line you have a small chance at a large win. When you hit the parallel situation with a money line, you are certain to win, but only a little.

Looking for middles can get pretty sophisticated. Indeed, it resembles what on Wall Street is known as arbitrage. For example, you judge the true line as Chiefs −4 over the Raiders. Early in the week you find a book that has the game at Chiefs −3 and give the points. Now, like a trader anticipating movement in the value of the yen against the German mark, you wait for the line to move to something like Chiefs −5 or −5½ so you can bet the other side. Can you get hurt doing this? Of course. The line can move in the other direction. But if your handicapping was correct you've still got a good bet—just not the one you were hoping for.

The opportunity for catching middles has recently increased, owing to the establishment of sports books that operate offshore, with offices in places like Antigua and Bermuda. These books use a Las Vegas line and are not sensitive to regional variations. However, unlike bookies in Las Vegas, they can be reached via telephone from anywhere in North America. As we noted earlier, regional effects often drive local lines. If the Bulls are playing the Knicks, the bookies in Chicago and New York will typically offer lines that differ significantly from each other and from those in Las Vegas. An astute bettor in Chicago or New York will often find a significant differential between the line offered by a local bookie and that offered by the offshore sports book. Under these conditions the probability of catching a middle is enhanced.

Injuries

Most linemakers overvalue the impact of an injury to a key player. Well, that's not quite right; they don't really overvalue it, they know that injuries to important players are not nearly as critical as many bettors think they are. But this is a situation where the psychology principle overrides the reality principle. Since the average bettor *believes* that an injury to a key player is more important than it actually is, the books adjust the line to take into account these beliefs. A couple of years back when 49er quarterback Joe Montana got hurt, bettors shied away from the 49ers and lost. The 49ers had a superb but then unappreciated backup in Steve Young, and more important, it was a terrifically deep team with classy players in virtually every position. Hence, it was able to handle the loss of its star quarterback.

Good teams are hurt less by the loss of key players than poor teams. Poor teams are often poor not just because of a lack of players of star caliber but because of factors like poor coaching, fragile team chemistry, or weak backups in key positions. When teams like these lose a key player, they tend to fall apart. Good teams are much more resilient and can typically overcome the loss of their stars. The typical bettor doesn't understand this point, and the line will often shift in ways that a sophisticated handicapper can exploit.

The impact of an injury to a key player differs from sport to sport. It is a relatively insignificant factor in baseball (except for pitchers). It is a slightly more important factor in football, though it depends on the position, with quarterback being most important—although you shouldn't underestimate the loss of a key offensive lineman. In basketball, because there are fewer players on the court and team chemistry is of such importance, the loss of a key player is generally more significant.

The bettor needs to take notice of situations that threaten to disrupt the team's rhythm or basic style of play. For example, if a team suffers several injuries to players in the same positions or in different positions that depend on timing and coordination, it can present a real problem. Most football teams can withstand the loss of one of their defensive backs, but losing two can be problematic. In baseball, losing both the starting shortstop and the second baseman can be critical since defensive weakness up the middle is a serious liability. Most basketball teams can deal with a power forward's being hurt, but if his backup is also injured, they are likely in trouble.

Betting the Schedule

It's important to look at not just an individual game but at each team's overall schedule. Often the next opponent is a big one, and the team is not really concentrating on the current contest. Here's an example first pointed out by David Sklansky: A nationally ranked team is playing a modestly talented team on the underdog's home field or court. For the ranked team, this is just another game. For the home team, it can make the season and the team will be all out for it. Taking the points in games like this has historically been a good bet. However, you cannot just reflexively bet the dog against a visiting ranked favorite. Backing the dog is not recommended when it is hopelessly overmatched, home crowd notwithstanding. The team has got to have some talent and some legitimate hope of an upset or it will be psychologically out of it from the beginning.

Here's another well-known example, called the "sandwich": A good team has three games coming up. The first and third are against tough opponents, the second is against a weak team. If the team wins the first game against the tough opponent, bet the dog in the second game.

You've got two factors working for you here: the inevitable letdown that follows a tough game against a tough opponent; and the tendency for the good team to take the mediocre team for granted while looking past it toward the upcoming tough opponent.

Emotion and Motivation

Emotion and motivation are integral parts of all sports, but are not of equal importance in each. Emotions run highest in football (especially college football), somewhat less so in basketball, and least in baseball. Ever since Notre Dame "won one for the Gipper," bookies have been wary of the impact of emotional and motivational factors. Like most of the factors we've been looking at here, there are no simple principles, but there are some guidelines.

- In games between historical rivals when one team is posted as a modest favorite, take the points. Dogs in these highly charged games tend to play way above their typical level.

- In college football bowl games, look closely at serious dogs, even those that are in double figures (ten or more points). I noted earlier that mismatches rarely made for good betting situations. Well, here's one case when they do. Few things fire up a team like being taken for granted in an important contest like a bowl game—remember, it may be the posted dog but it's still a good team, otherwise it wouldn't be in a bowl game. Historically, double-digit dogs in the college postseason have done very well against the spread.

- Be wary of teams that seem to be going into a game on nothing but emotion. In psychology, there is a principle known as the Yerkes-Dodson Law, which says that there is a complex interaction between emotional arousal and performance of various kinds of tasks. If emotional arousal gets too high, the ability to perform the skilled tasks that are central to success becomes compromised. A team that gets absurdly cranked up may succeed in the physical aspects of play but is prone to miscues in the more complex and subtler elements of the game. And should it fall behind, there is usually a terrible psychological letdown that leaves the players, for all practical purposes, dead in the water.

The Postseason

Betting the postseason games in any sport involves factors that are not necessarily germane during the regular season. Experience in postseason play, maturity, and solid coaching staffs become more important.

But the key to the postseason is that tourist money makes up a larger portion of the handle. The lines become less stable and postseason play begins to resemble pari-mutuel wagering, which is where the skilled handicapper has the clearest edge. Here are some tips for dealing with postseason play:

- Again, tilt toward the dogs. You have to pick your spots, but underdogs generally do better during postseason play than favorites. One reason is the emotional factor noted above. Few things fire up a good team more than being considered an underdog. Another is that favorites are sometimes not as good as their records indicate. This is particularly true in the college ranks, where low-class teams will run up the score during the season against less-talented opponents and look better on paper than they actually are. Not infrequently, such teams get their butts handed to them by a solid but unspectacular opponent in postseason play.

- Be careful, though, because this angle can cut both ways. The dog's record may make it look better than it actually is, particularly if it is one of those "low-class teams" that ran up the score against weak opponents during the season. Such a team can get killed by a really class team in a postseason game.

- Lean toward teams with playoff experience and maturity. The players won't be awed by the circumstances and put off their game by the hype. Young and untested teams typically don't do well in postseason play. Take them more seriously next year.

- Lean toward teams with superior and tested coaching staffs. Because of the additional preparation time, teams with solid coaching staffs are better prepared than their rivals. Also, a good coaching staff does a better job of making appropriate adjustments during the game, especially at halftime.

Financial and Statistical Principles

Regression to the Mean

The principle is simplicity itself: Unlikely events are unlikely. A relatively weak team that played way over its head the last time out is not likely to be able to perform at that level again and will likely regress to its typical level. Similarly, a good team that played hideously and lost to a much weaker team is likely to rebound from that performance and return to its usual high level of play. This statistical principle can provide an astute player with strong betting opportunities. When a poor team finally plays a good game or two, people tend to think it has turned a corner or finally found its rhythm. It is, in fact, more likely that it was just playing over its head for a bit and will quickly regress to its typical level of dreadfulness. The same argument goes for excellent teams that looked ugly for a game or two. Bettors who fail to understand the principle of regression to the mean will force the line to move in inappropriate ways, making for good betting opportunities for the statistically sophisticated.

Most experts who write about sports betting recognize the importance of this principle but fail to appreciate its underlying statistical nature. They look for arcane and often peculiar rationales for why these patterns emerge in the data. In *Sports Betting 101*, Arne Lang notes that baseball teams that have lost a disproportionately large number of one-run games in a year are likely to improve significantly the next year. He tries to link this with the team's record in exhibition games because the statisticians at the Elias Statistical Bureau spotted this angle. In fact, he presents it as though the exhibition season's record was the critical factor. This analysis is almost certainly wrong in that the link with the exhibition season is an example of what statisticians call a Type I error—that is, one concludes that something is statistically real when it is not. It's much more likely that in the previous year the team was actually better than its record indicated and didn't do all that well because of the statistically unlikely outcome of losing so many one-run games—an outcome that is not likely to repeat itself this year, exhibition season notwithstanding.

This example indicates how the principle of regression to the mean can be used in betting futures. Look for teams who had fluky kinds of seasons (either bad or good) to respond with performances more in keeping with their overall skill levels.

Angles and Trends

Here's a topic closely related to the preceding, since it has more to do with statistics and fallacious reasoning that anything else. In sports betting, people are always findings angles, quick statistics that seem to reveal trends that can be profitably bet. Here's one that was recently touted: Bet against any NBA team that last played in Denver. The angle here was that playing at Denver's high altitude took so much out of a team that it would not be at its best in the next game. But if the altitude angle had any merit, the Nuggets themselves ought to be a bad bet in the first game or two of a road trip—unless you want to argue that the team had become adapted to playing at altitude. Don't bother checking Denver's record; the trend evaporated soon after it was "identified."

Here's another: Bet against any team that played in overtime (basketball) or extra innings (baseball) the previous night. Like the altitude angle, this fatigue angle faded away like the colors on a cheap rug placed in the sunlight of careful analysis.

What's wrong with these angles is that they don't predict, they only "postdict." If you sift though the mountains of data in the records of all of the major betting sports, you will find what appear to be patterns and trends—even ones that seem to have a certain logic behind them. But the vast majority are merely the glitches and detritus that are bound to pop out of large amounts of data. In science, taking the outcomes of such retrospective analyses as real is an error of logic called the "a posteriori fallacy." My advice is simple: Be wary of simple, single-factor angles. Sports betting is complex, and proper handicapping requires deep analysis. Very few single-factor angles or trends have proven to be reliable in the long run—and when they have, they've quickly been incorporated into the line.

Touts and Tipsters

Touts and tipsters come in two flavors: the basically honest, hard-working characters who handicap games for their clients for a fee, and frauds. The guys in the first category study hard, do their homework, and have reasonable reputations and substantial numbers of customers who follow their selections. Of course, one could ask: If these guys really know what they are doing, why don't they just bet their own picks rather than selling them? For one, they might be unable to handle the emotional turmoil of the life of a sports bettor. The tremendous volatility of these games can take its toll on your psyche. For another, they might be good handicappers but lousy bettors. Patience, picking your spots, backing away from games where you don't feel you have a good read, and bankroll management skills are essential, and many good handicappers just don't have them. Finally, as Arne Lang points out, expert handicappers could get into the business because they are sick of handing out free tips to "friends."

So these guys may be legit, but are they any good? It's very hard to tell. Studies of the picks of the more open and aboveboard typically don't show hit rates anywhere near what is needed to turn a profit. And these studies are flawed because it's not always clear what line is being used to judge them. For example, suppose your tout service gives you the Bulls −4 over the Cavs. You stop by your favorite book and bet the Bulls, giving four points. However, after the dust has settled, the line ends up at Bulls −6. The Bulls beat the Cavs by five points. You won your (touted) bet, but did the service score a hit or not? It's not clear; it depends on how and when the data were collected. If you do decide to use a service, remember to figure in its cost as part of your investment. To be useful, tout services have to do more than just beat the vig; they have to beat the vig plus their own cost.

The touts in the second category are a different breed altogether; they tend to be either tapped-out sports bettors trying to stay afloat or outright thieves. The easiest way to spot these guys is by their outrageous advertising and impossible claims. Nobody, and I mean nobody, routinely hits 65 or 70 percent of their picks. Any tout who claims that this is what his or her record shows is to be avoided like the plague. Also stay away from services that tell you to call up and get a free tip on a game. These guys tell half their callers to back Team A and the other half get touted onto Team B. That way, half their callers think they are geniuses and sign up for their (expensive and worthless) future tips.

My advice? Do your homework, work hard, learn about the game, and trust your own choices. The game is supposed to be fun. Playing somebody else's picks is no fun.

How Good Do You Have to Be?

To be able to handle sports betting as a Type W game you need to win a sufficient proportion of your bets to cover the vigorish. The exact proportion changes with the odds. The following table shows the percentage of bets you need to win to break even for the most commonly occurring odds. They're in the form of a money line table for maximum flexibility. For a pointspread line or over/under bets, the percent of winners you need is found under −110, which is the money line equivalent.

Line on the Favorite		Line on the Underdog	
Odds	*Percent*	*Odds*	*Percent*
−110	52.38	+110	47.62
−120	54.55	+120	45.45
−130	56.52	+130	43.48
−140	58.33	+140	41.67
−150	60.00	+150	40.00
−160	61.54	+160	38.46
−170	62.96	+170	37.04
−180	64.29	+180	35.71
−200	66.67	+200	33.33
−220	68.75	+220	31.25
−250	71.43	+250	28.57

This table reveals a couple of things. First, you need to win a larger percentage of your bets when backing favorites than when betting on underdogs. Second, backing favorites starts to look pretty iffy—especially backing heavy favorites. For example, a baseball team needs to win in the neighborhood of 60 percent of its games to take its division. If you're looking at making bets that require that you win 65 or 70 percent of the time just to break even, you're talking about situations that are not going to pop up all that often. This is one of the reasons why I have been counseling you to lean toward the underdog. But be careful. There are situations when the favorite may be the proper bet—even the prohibitive favorite. In boxing, promoters will often overhype an outclassed opponent to try to sell tickets even though the bloke is really nothing more than an ambulatory punching bag. In baseball, a quality pitcher may be matched against an untested rookie. This situation gains even more significance if it is toward the end of the season and the favorite needs the game in its push for the playoffs.

How good are the pros, the ones who bet sports for a living? Well, of course, this will depend on how many games they bet, whether they are betting into a pointspread line or a money line, and their average bet size. But it's pretty clear they are going to have to hit at least some 55 percent of their bets in order to turn a decent profit. Lem Banker tells me his average win rate has been running between 58 and 60 percent for decades, with his best years around 65 percent and the worst down around 52 percent. Lem also tells me that he puts between fifty and sixty hours a week into his "job." Nobody said it was easy.

Where Does the Money Go?

Here are the latest data from the folks at Los Vegas Sports Consultants:

Sport	Percentage of Total Money Wagered
Football	41
Basketball	29
Baseball	22
Hockey	2
All others	6

It wasn't always this way. Baseball wasn't always a weak third. Back in the 1930s and 1940s when it was truly "the American pastime," baseball accounted for the lion's share of wagering. Slowly the mix shifted, with basketball and football becoming more and more popular. By the 1980s, football had taken over as the dominant betting sport. In 1990 it accounted for 36 percent of the total handle, in 1994 over 40 percent. But, interestingly, football betting provides legal sports books with about 50 percent of their profits. There are two reasons for this. First, the majority of people who bet on football are tourists who, for all practical purposes, are flipping coins. This is not true in baseball and basketball—especially basketball. Second, the basic bets in football require the bettor to lay 11 to 10, making the juice a relatively high 4.55 percent.

That about wraps up our look at the general principles that apply to all sports betting. Let's now look a bit more closely at each of our three main sports.

FOOTBALL

Football has become wildly popular as a betting sport. Interest focuses primarily on the NFL and a few dozen major college teams. Betting on football has also become a bit like craps in that there are one or two basic bets and a smorgasbord of special wagers the bookies have cooked up to stoke interest. Not surprisingly, many of these oddball propositions have a large vig built into them and are strictly advantage book. Let's do a quick overview of some of these special bets and see which ones are worth your consideration and which are not.

Special Bets in Football

Special wagers run from the really nutty ones, posted only during the feeding frenzy that occurs over Super Bowl weekend, to others that are worth consideration. The screwball ones include over/under on fumbles or intercepted passes, which team will kick the first field goal, and my favorite, who will win the coin toss (yup, books have been known to take bets on this at 11 to 10). There is no sense trying to make sense out of these propositions, and if you have ever bet one of them, you must swear an oath that you will never do so again.

There are some special bets that can be handicapped and bet sensibly (over/under), others that could be at one time but are no longer (teasers), and others that cannot be (parlay cards).

Over/Under

The totals bet in football can be beat because it can be handicapped. Factors such as weather, field condition, injuries, and scheduling can be used to identify good betting situations. Also, if the line keeps moving in one direction you are generally advised to bet the other side. Remember one of our most important heuristics: The linemaker is right more often than the public. If it looks like tourist money is driving the line in one direction, the true line is likely closer to the one originally posted.

Also, for reasons that escape me, in NFL games there is a key number in the total. It is thirty-seven. More totals have landed on this number over the years than on any other. In fact, this number pops up more than 5 percent of the time, and no other number occurs more than 4 percent. Since the over/under can be played for middles, finding two lines that straddle thirty-seven is something for the careful line shopper to keep an eye out for.

Halftime

Halftime bets should be handicapped using the same general principles as regular bets—with appropriate adjustments for how the first half of the game went. A book will not post a halftime line on a game that was not televised and watched by its people. Critical factors such as injuries, player or coach ejections, shifts in momentum, and changes in weather conditions can have considerable impact on second-half play. The books do not want to get hurt by wise guys who have been paying attention when they have not.

Here are some things to look for in halftime bets on NFL games. If the underdog is ahead (but not by too much), the favorite is likely to close the gap by outscoring its opponent in the second half. Several factors promote this outcome. First, the favorite is usually a better team, and eventually its superiority will exert itself. Second, the favorite is often a better *coached* team, and its staff will find ways to exploit weaknesses in the opponent's play spotted during the first half. Third, the underdog will often go to the prevent defense. If the dog is still ahead going into the final quarter, it will typically shift away from the style that has gained it the lead and go into the prevent. The prevent defense mainly prevents winning. But even if it enables the dog to hold on to win the game, it often allows the favorite to score enough points to cover the halftime line. Finally, look for factors such as experience and maturity to manifest themselves in the second half. Often young underdogs will play an outstanding first half, only to be slowly ground down in the second half by the more mature and more skilled favorite.

But, as always, be careful. There is another scenario that might be playing itself out in the first half of a game. Your dog may actually be a better team than anticipated, which means the score in the first half was no fluke. In such a situation you actually would want to increase your bet on the dog. It's not easy to know which of these alternatives is correct. I don't recommend halftime bets unless you've been watching the game—closely.

Here are some other things to look for in halftime bets. Run-oriented teams that have fallen behind are typically in trouble and will likely not score much in the second half. Because they need to catch up in a hurry, they will often overemphasize the pass, which is unlikely to work particularly well. Favorites who jump out to a big lead will hunker down and play conservatively. Conservative play helps to maintain a lead, and the favorite doesn't want to run up the score. This is particularly true when it is playing a conference foe it will have to meet again. These guys have long memories and won't forget being embarrassed the last time out. Look for regression to the mean situations. Teams that scored points on fluky plays like fumbles or tipped passes are statistically unlikely to have such good fortune continue.

Another reason why halftime bets can be good ones is that the line must be composed and hung very quickly. Linemakers like to take their time, think things through, and post a line only after they have had a chance to accumulate information and check with their consultants. With the halftime bets there is no time, so the bookies are more likely to make mistakes. The bettor is under the same kind of time constraints, but the book has to post the line on a number of games at roughly the same time; the player can specialize.

Most of the above advice doesn't always apply to the college game. Often the first half is quite different from what was anticipated because of particular matchups that turned out to be more critical than expected. When this happens, it would be unwise to expect to see a reversal of fortunes in the second half, and the suggestions given above should likely be ignored.

Parlays

Parlay cards are to be avoided. You can't line shop and the juice is virtually insurmountable. Here's an example of the parlay card payoffs from a randomly selected Las Vegas casino for a weekend's NFL play. The true odds have been added for your enlightenment.

Number of Games	Payoffs	True Odds
3	6 for 1	8 for 1
4	11 for 1	16 for 1
5	20 for 1	32 for 1
6	40 for 1	64 for 1
7	80 for 1	128 for 1
8	150 for 1	256 for 1
9	300 for 1	512 for 1
10	600 for 1	1,024 for 1
Special Bonus: 9 out of 10 pays 20 for 1		

It's clear that, as Roxborough and Rhoden note, "Parlay cards have a large theoretical hold built into the payoffs."

There are, however, lots of other ways to bet parlays. You could bet the outcome of a game and the over/under in a parlay. Some books will even allow cross-sport parlays for example, Broncos +3 over the Colts and the Knicks −8 over the 76ers. These parlays are better plays because the wagers can be handicapped separately and the bettor can choose games with favorable lines. But when you make such parlays, the book will extract a price. The payout will be less than what you would get were you to parlay the bets yourself. In a two-bet parlay (where the vig is lowest), the books typically pay 13 to 5, but you can get odds of approximately 13.2 to 5 if you bet the parlay yourself by taking your winnings from the first bet and putting them down on the second.

Teasers

The teasers most commonly used in football involve from two to six teams and from six to seven points, although some books have been known to accept bets using up to fourteen points. The two factors are balanced. As the number of points in the teaser goes up, the payoff odds go down; as the number of teams involved goes up, the odds go up. A teaser is a variant on the parlay bet in which all your teams must win for you to collect; in teasers, ties lose. Using the LVSC recommendations, most books offer the following payoffs:

Number of Teams	6 points	6½ points	7 points
2	10 to 11	5 to 6	10 to 13
3	8 to 5	3 to 2	6 to 5
4	5 to 2	2 to 1	9 to 5
5	4 to 1	7 to 2	3 to 1
6	6 to 1	5 to 1	9 to 2

At one time the payoffs on some of these propositions were higher; specifically, the two-team, six-point teaser was paid at 1 to 1. The bookies took a bath on this one because players who did their home-work discovered an interesting angle. NFL home teams over a period of several years were covering the spread (with the six points) nearly 71 percent of the time. Since $.71^2$ is greater than .5, you didn't even have to handicap to make money on this bet. And if you did handicap and ferreted out the best situations, the two-team, six-point teasers were extremely profitable.

Can teasers be played with positive expectation today? I'm not sure anyone knows the answer. Since the volatility of the game becomes a significant factor when playing teasers with more than two or three teams, it is unlikely that the higher payoffs can compensate. When I checked with one of my unnamed consultants, he smiled at me and said, "Artie baby, [only by these guys do I get called that!] I love my customers who play teasers." I think that says it all.

Futures

The problem with futures in football is that the juice is too high. The one situation that can be exploited is when a book offers a futures bet involving a relatively small number of teams and a correspondingly low vigorish. The best places to look are the division championships, where only four or five teams are involved. When exploring these bets make sure you calculate carefully the total juice. If it's above 5 percent or so, the bet starts to get tough to make.

Key Numbers

Not surprisingly, the most important key number in football is three, followed by seven, and, in decreasing order of frequency, four, six, ten, and one. More games are won by exactly three points than any other number, the last-second field goal being the primary reason. With the two-point conversion, one has become a more important key number, since teams will attempt it when success will give them a one-point win (and failure a one-point loss).

An astute player looks for games that are posted at or near these key numbers. We noted earlier that a movement of a point in the line was worth something in the order of 2.5 percent in expected value to an astute bettor. This number is an average, and when the line is posted on or near a key number, the value of a shift in the line of a single point is magnified significantly. The main things to look for are games that move around a key number. A game with the favorite at $-2\frac{1}{2}$ that then moves to $-3\frac{1}{2}$ is an ideal situation for catching a middle.

Don't think that the bookies aren't aware of this situation; they are very reluctant to move a line around a key number. However, this can work to the player's advantage, since the line may stay far off the true line. A bookie who is trying to keep from getting middled can end up getting sided. To find these kinds of opportunities you are going to have to do a bit of line shopping. And don't forget the NFL's key number of thirty-seven in the over/under. It is possible to look for a middle by finding books with an over/under that straddles this key.

Money Line Bets

Quite a few books offer a money line on football games. It is usually hung toward the end of the week after the pointspread line has settled, and is generally posted using a 20¢ line—though a larger straddle, up to $1 and more, will be used when one team is a strong favorite. If you wish to bet into a money line rather than a pointspread line, the first thing you need to do is get a feeling for the rough equivalents between the two lines. Here's the pattern recommended by the folks at Roxborough's LVSC:

Pointspread Line	Money Line (NFL)	Money Line (College)
Pick	−110 −110	−110 −110
1	−115 −105	−115 −105
1½	−120 EVEN	−120 EVEN
2	−130 +110	−130 +110
2½	−140 +120	−140 +120
3	−155 +135	−155 +135
3½	−175 +155	−175 +155
4	−200 +170	−185 +165
4½	−220 +180	−200 +170
5, 5½	−240 +190	−220 +180
6	−270 +210	−240 +190
6½	−300 +220	−270 +210
7	−330 +250	−300 +220
7½, 8, 8½	−360 +280	−330 +250
9, 9½	−400 +300	−360 +280
10	−450 +325	−400 +300

When the spread is one, there will be occasions where you might find a dime line. Clearly such postings are to the bettor's advantage. Money lines tend to be more variable than pointspread lines, and the dedicated line shopper can find books that differ from each other significantly.

The Bottom Line

Can football be beat? Absolutely. It isn't easy because the bettor must overcome the vig of 4.55 percent, but it can be done. When a sport becomes as popular as football has with the betting public, it means that the line will not infrequently get shoved around by untutored money and produce opportunities for the sophisticated handicapper.

BASKETBALL

Basketball has historically attracted the most sophisticated sports bettors, folks who are more knowledgeable about the game than those who bet football and baseball. So one of our most effective heuristics, betting against public opinion, is of less value here than elsewhere in the sports betting world.

Why do so many good handicappers focus on basketball? For one thing, counting the college games as well as the NBA, there are a lot more games in a given week than in football (one game a week) and baseball (no college game to speak of). By the sheer press of numbers, an astute handicapper will find more solid betting situations. Second, when the books have so many games to set lines on, the chance of their making a mistake is magnified. This situation makes specializing particularly useful. If you become an expert on a particular conference or two you will know more about them than the bookie, who has to handicap all the games from all the conferences. Third, basketball is played more true to form than other sports. The short-term luck factor is much less important than in either football or baseball (although, since the 3-point shot was introduced, this is not quite as true a statement as it once was). The main reason is that there is so much scoring. Points are cheap in basketball, whereas they are quite dear in football and baseball. In football, a poorly thrown pass into the end zone can lead to a swing of as much as 14 points in a game that typically sees less than 40 scored. In baseball, a bad bounce with the bases loaded can turn an inning-ending double play ball into a run-scoring single and open up the floodgates in a game where only seven or eight runs are scored on average. But in basketball, a bad pass or a fluky bounce causes a maximum swing of 4 or 5 points in a game where well over 200 points are typically scored. Since flukes play a much smaller role in the outcome of basketball games than in other sports, good handicapping has greater predictability. Hence, the pros show up in large numbers.

Special Bets in Basketball

Although the NBA playoffs and the NCAA's "March Madness" can bring out the worst in some bookmakers, I won't go into the weird wagers. The basics are the over/under, parlays, teasers, and futures. All are handled in essentially the same manner as in football. The over/under is bet against a totals line with the player laying 11 to 10. Teasers are offered at 4, 4½, and 5 points, with payoffs corresponding to those used in football for 6, 6½, and 7 points, respectively. Parlays and futures are handled just as in football.

Generally, avoid teasers and parlays since the vig compounds and works against you. The over/under can be handicapped just as the point spread, and basic good sense and logic should be applied. Note that in basketball there are no key numbers. Games are won by from 1 to roughly 13 or 14 points with virtually equal frequency. Futures are tough. Basketball runs truer to form than any other major sport, and the vig is high.

Matchups

In basketball, more than any other sport, this factor looms large. Because each team puts only five men on the floor at one time, the impact of a single individual is great. This is particularly true in the NBA, where the zone defense is (more or less, anyway) illegal, forcing players to guard one-on-one. An astute handicapper can find good betting opportunities by looking closely at the makeup of each team and how the teams match up against each other.

Injuries

Injuries are more important in basketball than in other sports—although they're still not as important as many bettors think. There are a couple of factors that determine how damaging an injury is. First, how good is the backup? The better the backup player, the less the loss to the team. Second, how important was the injured player to the rhythm and tempo of the team? Losing your point guard can be serious, usually more serious than losing a power forward. Third, how strong is the coaching staff? Good coaches can develop alternative strategies that will compensate for the loss of individual players.

Notice that injuries and matchups can interact. For example, an injury to a solid defensive forward can be a serious liability when going against a team whose main scoring comes from its inside power men, but not so damaging if playing a team whose primary offense comes from its outside shooters.

Trends

Since basketball is less fluky than other sports, there is a strong tendency to peruse the available data closely, looking for any kind of trend that might give the bettor an exploitable edge. And if you read the vast literature available on the game, you will discover various "experts" forever identifying and touting angles based on apparent trends. Arne Lang calls these folks "trendvestites." Stay away from the crazy angle and the trend guys. As examples of what to avoid, here are a few phony trends that have been put forward in recent years.

In college basketball, a line you will often hear touted is, "Always bet on the home dog." The "dog-at-home" angle has been around forever, and while it is recognized as having no predictive value in football and baseball, you will still hear it promoted in basketball, especially at the college level. However, two fairly large studies have shown that it just doesn't work. The first was carried out in the early 1980s using data from the *Blue Ribbon Basketball Yearbook* and *The Gold Sheet*; the second in 1991 using the data from the two previous years' games as compiled in the *Basketball Scoreboard*. In the early study it was discovered that the home dog won 368 games against the spread and lost 356, for a winning percentage of .508. A decade later the home dog was winning 461 and losing 458, for a win rate of .502. Since you need to be winning at better than a 52 percent clip just to break even, this angle is worthless as a betting heuristic.

Here's another highly touted trend: Bet against any team that played an overtime game the previous night. This one looked good in a retrospective study but failed miserably in predicting future games. One more: Bet against an NBA team that just won a hard-fought game on the road, especially if the team was the dog in that game. *This is actually a good angle*. It incorporates some psychological and physiological components (that last game took a lot out of the team) as well as simple statistical ones (good old regression to the mean—the team had to play way over its head to pull off that win). Alas, the bookies figured it out too, and it is now factored into the line. But if the book shifts the line too much in an attempt to compensate for the wise guys who are pushing this angle, you may be able to come in on the game on the other side.

Backing Dogs

Yup, here we go again. In basketball, as in football, you should lean toward the underdog. Again, you cannot blindly back every dog on the board; you have to be selective. One place to look closely is the NCAA tournament, where underdogs fare quite well, especially double-digit dogs and dogs from the smaller conferences.

The NCAA Tournament and the NBA Playoffs

Both the NCAA tournament and the NBA playoffs attract lots of tourist money. Tourists, as we keep pointing out, tend to tilt toward favorites and are highly subject to bandwagonlike effects. When tourist dollars become a significant proportion of the total wagered, odd things can happen to the line. Hence, the astute player has a better chance of finding lines that are off during the playoffs and the tournament than during the regular season. Careful line shopping is important. You need to look at the lines posted in various establishments as well as keep track of line movement within individual books. There are also some handicapping principles that are useful here. Let's look at the college game first.

The NCAA Tournament

Look for such factors as maturity in the players, experience in playing at this level, good coaching staffs, and good physical conditioning. Being a good free-throw shooting team doesn't hurt, either—especially since so many of these games come down to foul-shooting contests at the end. Also look to see how well each team played against its toughest opponents. This will give you a better sense of the strength of the team than simply looking at its overall record. Lots of teams get fat by playing a bunch of patsies during the year, and you do not want to be deceived by a team's overall record. When crunch time comes, lean toward teams that have fared well against tough opponents.

NBA Playoffs

The factors noted above apply here as well. But by virtue of the playoff format, other components of handicapping come into play. For example, the home court advantage cannot be neglected. Historically, a good bet has been to back the home dog that has just lost the first two games away from home. This bet is good, not because the bookies don't know about the angle but because the line gets set and moved to attract balanced action, and tourist dollars tend to come in on the visiting favorite that has just won two in a row.

There is also a well-known gimmick called the "zigzag theory." Bet against the team that just won convincingly if the line has shifted significantly from the previous game. Suppose the Bulls were -2 over the Knicks and then won in a blowout by 25 points. If the next game pops up with the Bulls -6 over the Knicks, take the points. The public has overreacted to the blowout and is undervaluing the Knicks—remember our old friend, regression to the mean?

The zigzag theory also applies to the over/under bet. If one game is a high-scoring affair, the public often forces the totals line too high for the next game. Bet the under. The same goes for low-scoring games and a total that appears to be inordinately low. Note, however, that in the playoffs the totals tend to be lower than they were during the regular season; the players play harder and with greater intensity, which tends to keep the scores down. Don't be surprised when you see a totals line that is several points below where it was when these same teams played during the season.

The Bottom Line

Can the game be beat? Yup, but it's no snap, since you're still bucking that 4.55 percent vig. The key, as always, is finding the line that is off. The best approach is to become expert in one or two aspects of the sport—really get to know, for example, the Big Sky Conference or the Big East. If you know your component of the game better than the bookies, you have a good shot at finding the misposted line. Another strategy is to focus on the NBA playoffs and college basketball's March Madness, when tourist money starts to show up and pushes the lines in ways that a careful handicapper can exploit.

BASEBALL

Despite the fact that less money is bet on baseball than on football or basketball, the smaller vig associated with the dime money line makes it the easiest to beat. Take a look at the tables on pages 280 and 281 to appreciate how small the vig is here compared with the 4.55 percent facing anyone who bets into a pointspread line. But in baseball, the short-term luck factor is more important than it is in other sports. The more luck enters into a game the more the advantage tilts toward the house. The book can live with the smaller vig and still turn a profit.

Special Bets in Baseball

There are lots of special bets that you can make in baseball, but we'll focus on the futures bets, the parlay, and the over/under.

Futures

Futures bets have had a most intriguing history in baseball. Compelling long shots have brought home the bacon often enough to make them worth serious consideration. In 1969 the "Miracle Mets" were 100 to 1 or higher with virtually every book in town; in 1991 two teams (the Braves and the Twins), each posted as high as 200 to 1, made it to the World Series. Such outcomes are seen only rarely in football and virtually never in basketball.

Start by finding books that have posted odds with at least a semireasonable vigorish. To do this you have to know how to calculate the total vig. A sports book's futures will look something like the following (of course, without the percentages being given):

Team	Odds to Win World Series	Percentage
Atlanta Braves	6 to 1	14.29
Toronto Blue Jays	7 to 1	12.50
New York Yankees	7 to 1	12.50
.	.	.
.	.	.
.	.	.
Minnesota Twins	125 to 1	.79
New York Mets	150 to 1	.66

To calculate the total juice on the proposition, add up all the percentages. I've given only five teams as examples, but the book will list all teams. The total will be considerably in excess of 100 percent, the amount over 100 percent being the vig. For baseball, the juice often runs as high as 40 percent, 50 percent, or even 60 percent. As Roxborough and Rhoden put it: ". . . the opening odds are usually rigged with a healthy house edge." (There's a line that ought to get your attention!)

It can be a good bet to take a flyer on a long shot with potential. But not just any old long shot and not always before the season has begun. Here's how to do it. First, if you are looking to make a "true" futures bet (one made before the season has begun), the teams to focus on should have the following characteristics. They should be young teams, usually overseen by an experienced manager. They should have a balance between young, still essentially untested, first- and second-year players mixed with older, stable veterans with postseason experience. In addition, they should have what looks like potentially good pitching. Be on the lookout for young upcoming pitchers on the staff, ones who haven't yet let the whole world know they are good. If one or two of them blossom the team will have an excellent chance. Finally, it helps if the team plays in a weak division. This last angle often goes unrecognized, but it is very important. Winning the division is the key. Once a team is in the playoffs, the short-term luck factor looms greater than during the long 164-game season. A young untested team in a weak division in a weak league will look really weak but may, in fact, have the component parts to get into the playoffs.

The best opportunities for solid futures bets come after the season is already in progress. You are still looking at the same types of teams, but there will be additional information available. The key is that the betting line often lags behind current results. For example, if a team that opened at 100 to 1 wins eight or nine of its first ten games or goes sixteen and four in the first twenty, it may signal that it is a legit contender. The line is unlikely to still be hanging at 100 to 1, but even if it has dropped to something like 50 to 1 or 30 to 1 you are looking at a serious overlay.

So, have some fun. Make a couple of wagers each year on some serious long shots. Pick those that fulfill the criteria I've pointed out and, most important, look for the overlays that can emerge as the season progresses because the action is light and the lines haven't yet moved to reflect reality.

Individual team futures: Many books will post a futures bet on the number of games a given team will win. While there is typically a large vig built into these, there's an angle I want to draw to your attention: Young teams improve. Look for a young team that struggled the year before, particularly one that lost a disproportionate number of one-run games. And look also for the reverse: Teams full of aging players tend to fade as Father Time does his inexorable thing.

Parlays

Parlays can be played in baseball with less risk to the bankroll because you are betting into a money line and not a pointspread line. As a result, you are getting honest odds for your wager. Your payoff will reflect the odds posted on each game at the time of the bet rather than a set odds payout. Calculating what your payoff should be on a winning parlay, however, can get a bit hairy. I suspect that an awful lot of veteran sports bettors don't really understand how money line payouts are figured; they just take their winnings and assume the book handled it right.

Here's how to calculate the payout on a money line parlay. Let's use a three-team parlay, although the same principle holds for all parlays no matter how many teams are involved. Suppose you made a $10 three-team parlay bet. Team A was a dog posted at +120, Team B was another dog posted at +130, and Team C was a decided favorite at −140. Mirabile dictu, all three won. To calculate the payout for the parlay, calculate the payout for each individual bet based on a wager of $1. Multiply these, and then multiply the product by the size of the bet. To calculate the payout on each wager, use the following formulas calculated against $1:

> Underdogs: Payoff = 1 + underdog price
> Favorites: Payoff = (1 + favorite price)/favorite price

For Team A, our payoff is 1 + 1.20 = 2.20; the payoff for Team B is 1 + 1.30 = 2.30; and the payoff for Team C is (1 + 1.4)/1.4 = 2.4/1.4 = 1.71. Our parlay bet was $10, so the payout is 2.20 × 2.30 × 1.71 × 10 = $86.53, for a profit of $76.53. (By the way, unlike in horse racing, the book doesn't keep breakage. This payout actually works out to $86.526, but the book will usually round properly.)

Over / Under

Unlike football and basketball, this bet for baseball is typically posted using a money line, but, unlike the line on the game itself, it is usually a 20¢ line. Thus, a game might be posted "Yankees – Orioles 7 over +110, 7 under −130." Here the expectation is that fewer than seven runs will be scored. To bet the under, you put up $13 for every $10 you hope to win; on the over you invest $10 for each $11 you hope to win. In principle, the book could change either the odds or the total as money comes in. However, almost invariably the books move the odds and leave the total alone.

The total bet in baseball is tricky. Since nearly 45 percent of all games end up with between six and ten runs scored, there isn't a lot of play. I would suggest that you look for specific situations such as betting the over in Wrigley Field when the wind is blowing out, or taking the under in Houston when one or more sinkerball pitchers are working. The problem is that everybody knows these angles—including the bookies. The total bet in baseball is tough and is best handicapped by looking closely at the pitchers. (By the way, the over/under bet is taken off the board if either of the scheduled starting pitchers doesn't play.)

Pitching

In handicapping baseball, pitching is of paramount importance. So let's take a look at the basics.

The Starters

The starting pitchers are so important that the basic money line bet is posted with them specified. For example, say the Yanks are starting someone named Smith against the Orioles, who are starting some guy named Jones. A bettor basically has four choices:

1. Both pitchers specified. You bet the game with both starting pitchers as scheduled; if either Smith or Jones fails to start, there is no action. The bet is off.

2. Your team's pitcher specified. You might take the Yanks with Smith against the Orioles as a team. If Smith doesn't start, there is no action. If Smith does start but Jones doesn't, you will still have a bet—although the line may be adjusted depending on which other starting pitcher is named.

3. Your team against a specified pitcher. You might bet on the Yanks as a team against the Orioles, but only if Jones is their starting pitcher. If Jones fails to start, there is no action. If Jones starts but Smith doesn't, you still have a bet, but the line may change depending on the Orioles' starter.

4. Pitchers not specified. You bet your team independent of starting pitchers. If one or both scheduled starters don't play, you still have a bet, but the line may change.

My advice is straightforward: Bet only under the first condition. If you are handicapping sensibly, a major hunk of your thinking has gone into the starting pitchers and the manner in which each opposing manager has structured his lineup to best counteract the opposing pitcher's strengths and exploit his weaknesses. Any other bet just doesn't make sense. You don't know who the so-called off pitcher will be, and you don't know what the adjustments in the odds will be. These are not the kinds of circumstances a sensible handicapper should be in.

Now admittedly, some people argue that a given pitcher may seem to "have another team's number" and that so long as he is the starter his team should beat the opponents no matter whom they pitch. Others maintain that a particular team routinely roughs up a particular pitcher and when he is scheduled to start you should bet against that team no matter whom your team starts. While these arguments make a certain superficial sense, I don't like them for betting purposes. These patterns are known to the books, so the line usually reflects them. You still have to deal with the off pitcher and whatever his impact on the game will be. And you must still face a possibly unhappy shift in the odds.

Pitchers Coming off the DL

In horse racing we cautioned against betting a horse that had been away for an extended period of time in its first time back. For a starting pitcher coming off the disabled list (DL), the same principle holds. It usually takes a starter a game or two to get back in rhythm, and an angle worth close scrutiny is to bet against the returning pitcher. You can occasionally find a favorable line, especially when the returning pitcher is a frontline star. The reason is that the public overestimates the impact of the pitcher on his first, and often his second, start after coming off the DL. In general, the longer a starting pitcher was on the DL, the more likely it is that he will perform below his standard on the first and second games back. But when playing this angle, be cautious. You must take into account what kind of injury the pitcher suffered, how serious it was, and how long he was on the DL.

The Bullpen

In order to prosper these days a team must have a closer, a relief pitcher with ice water in his veins who can come in and preserve a lead under the most trying of circumstances. And all good teams have such a player. But what does the rest of the bullpen look like? A significant drop-off in talent after the stopper can make for an interesting betting proposition. Most managers are reluctant to use their bullpen ace more than two days in a row. As a result, in games where the closer has worked several days in succession and is unavailable, you can gain a small edge by betting against a team when the rest of the relief corps is ordinary at best. Some handicappers forget how important the bullpen can be in determining the outcome of games.

Favorites and Dogs

In baseball, like our other sports, the small dog continues to be the place to look for value. The public tends to overbet favorites, setting up bets with positive expectation on the underdogs. In baseball, by virtue of the mathematics of the money line and the nature of the game, the bettor is advised to handle strong favorites with kid gloves. The problem in a nutshell: The best teams win only some 60 percent of their games. If you are betting on teams that are posted at −150, you must win 60 percent of your bets just to break even, and as the odds get higher so does the required winning percentage (look back at the table on page 301). The percentage of games you need to win when betting on prohibitive favorites can be sobering. The exception is when you're dealing with a topflight starting pitcher. While the team may not win 60 percent of all its games, it may well win well over 60 percent of those in which the star is the starter.

Nutty Angles to Ignore

Two aspects of the weird and nonsensical have trickled into baseball betting: astrology and biorhythms. While no serious player pays any attention to the former, biorhythmic handicapping has garnered a number of adherents. You are supposed to be able to spot individual players who will or will not be at their best on any given day given the date of their birth and the physiological cycles their bodies follow. Biorhythms are a prime example of junk science. There is absolutely no evidence to suggest even a smidgen of validity here. Never make a bet based on biorhythmic analysis.

The Bottom Line

Baseball is probably the easiest of the big three for the astute sports bettor to learn to play with positive expectation. Baseball is, to use Malmuth's phrase, "the most statistical of all sport," so you don't have to worry so much about the subtle aspects of handicapping. You only need to crunch numbers. And the dime line provides a comparatively small vig. Put these two factors together and you have the best game for the punter.

CAN YOU MAKE A LIVING AT SPORTS BETTING?

Sports betting is a Type W game. If you do your homework, pick your spots, and manage your bankroll with care, you will do just fine. Making a living at it is a different proposition. Mike Lee, legendary sports handicapper and writer, claims that the astute sports bettor should be able to find something like 280 games a year worth playing if he or she bets all three major sports. My salary as a professor has reached the stratospheric level of $79,000 per annum. Suppose I want to quit my day job and become a professional sports bettor but not suffer any loss in income. If I were to make Lee's recommended 280 bets, I would need to win an average of $285 on each to achieve my goal. Only the very best win at rates above 55 percent, but since I'm supposed to be an expert, let's assume I can win an average of 60 percent of my wagers each year. What does my average bet size need to be so I can maintain an average of $285 profit per bet (assuming a standard bet size and that all bets were made against a pointspread line at 11 to 10)? A shade under $1,900.

That seems workable. But do I have the bankroll to make this feasible, given the volatility of the game? Lem Banker has had *entire years* when he won only 52 percent of his bets. What would this do to me? Answer: A loss of $2,660 for the year. Hey, wait a minute. If I've just dropped over two and half grand on the year, how do I pay my mortgage, my car payments, my insurance, buy clothing, food . . . I'm not just two grand in the hole, I'm short $81,000! That's why I haven't quit my day job.

The real bottom line on sports betting for the sensible player is the same as for all Type W games. Get involved, study hard, work at the game, enjoy yourself, don't get hurt, stay even, and maybe turn a small profit. What more could you want? But if you do decide to start playing the game seriously, here's a quote from Arne Lang to think about: "Handicapping is intellectually satisfying. Chasing around from one book to another in search of the best lines is a grueling ordeal."

PART IV

PROTECTING YOUR MONEY

9

CHEATING

Wherever there's a game of chance, you can be sure there's some lowlife busily at work figuring out how to get an illegitimate edge in it. Cheating is nowhere near the problem it once was, when con artists and card sharps worked the Mississippi riverboats and mechanics with loaded dice and funny decks fleeced innocent marks in craps and card games across the land. But it is an issue that concerns anyone who gambles.

Today cheaters come in a variety of forms. For our purposes, they can be divided into two categories: those who attempt to beat the house, and those who try to beat their fellow players. From the point of view of yours truly, the latter is a far more dangerous category of beast than the former, although I certainly appreciate that casino executives like my friend Danny Montagna at TropWorld might take a slightly different view. We, the players, do not need to worry overly about the third form of possible cheating: the casino that is ripping off its customers. The typical modern casino is scrupulously honest, and it's very much in its best interests to be so. Remember, in virtually every game, the house already has an edge. There's no need to cheat, and any casino that got a reputation for playing fast and loose with its games would quickly find itself either empty or closed.

Obviously, it's also very much in a casino's best interests to prevent cheating and/or to catch cheaters. The next time you are in a casino, look up. You will notice half spheres of reflective glass projecting from the ceiling at regular intervals. These spheres are made of one-way mirror glass, and behind each is a sophisticated video camera panning the area below it. The camera is monitored by security agents who can directly control it, focusing on a particular part of the action below and, if necessary, zooming in to pick up the smallest dust mote within its range. This system, known as "the eye in the sky," can spot irregularities at any table game and at any slot machine and, moreover, it can pick up the dastardly, nongambling-related deeds of pickpockets and purse snatchers working the casinos.

Before the development of today's sophisticated video systems, security people used to walk back and forth on catwalks above one-way-mirrored ceilings and watch the action below. This was regarded as about the worst job the casino had to offer. It was cramped, hot, and unpleasant up there, and for the most part all those poor bastards did was watch somebody pick his teeth. In many ways the primary gain was psychological; the knowledge that there might be someone up there watching was enough to prevent some of the grosser scams from taking place. Nowadays, the only time people venture up into this area is to repair one of the cameras.

In addition to spotting various forms of cheating, the modern video monitoring systems can be used to resolve disputes between a player and the house. Some years back, I was playing blackjack, had a $50 wager on the table, and won the hand with a twenty to the dealer's nineteen. However, in the rush to collect the cards, pay winners, and pick up checks from the losers, the dealer failed to pay me off—acting as though the hand were a push. When I pointed this out to her, she said that she had, in fact, paid me—implying, of course, that I had taken back the $50 and was lying. I got rather annoyed, reiterated my claim that she owed me $50, and suggested that she had perhaps made a simple mistake. As is typical in these situations, the pit boss was called over to mediate. It was clear that it was my recollection of what happened versus the dealer's and there was nothing to be gained by simply arguing. When this kind of thing happens with a $5 bet, the house will usually just give the player the benefit of the doubt (provided it happens only once!), but this was for $50. I suggested the pit boss ask to see if the monitoring system had caught the hand and could help in discerning what had actually happened. To my surprise and delight, about ten minutes later a phone call came into the pit. The tape verified that the dealer had, indeed, neglected to pay me on the hand in question. I got my $50 and a heartfelt apology from the dealer, who, it was clear, really had made an honest mistake.

In addition to the "eye in the sky," casinos use a variety of procedures to keep track of the action on the floor. Pit bosses and floorpersons keep track of the play at all tables within their pit. They rate the play of each individual at each table, keeping a rough track of typical bet size, whether the players are winning or losing, and roughly how much. Any abrupt shift in a pattern of wagering or in an apparent bankroll will bring closer scrutiny. The pit crew is responsible for turning in rating sheets that provide the casino brass with a record of the play at each of the tables in its pit during its shift. Shifts and pits are compared with each other and matched against the known typical PC for that game and that pit. Systematic drifts in the PC for a given table or pit area will bring very close scrutiny upon the players and the dealers.

Security people in plainclothes will occasionally patrol the casino floor. Looking perfectly ordinary, they scan the casino, the pits, the dealers, the players, and the hangers-on. From time to time, some oddball will get into a really desperate state and try something weird, like grabbing a few thousand dollars' worth of checks from a table and heading for the exit. Security people, plainclothes and uniformed, invariably tackle such culprits before they get past the first row of slot machines.

There is another army of people who are involved directly or indirectly in security behind the scenes. They include guards, who transfer money, markers, and chips; counters, who count and record cash intake; and accountants, who scrutinize the casino's books to make sure that everything is "kosher."

Casino security people will go to great lengths to tell you about the many scams they have broken up and the many cons they have exposed. They are justifiably proud of their record and the subtle techniques they have developed over the years to spot cheating. But they cannot tell you about the ones they haven't caught, the scams they haven't cracked. I had one security chief tell me that cheating had been virtually eliminated in his casino because they had caught them all. Of course, they only caught the ones they caught. Who knows whether there are cheaters they haven't caught. The history of the gaming industry suggests that no matter how careful and how thorough the security systems are, there are always going to be scams and con artists, cheats and thieves.

The easiest way to cover the various forms of cheating is to look at them from the perspective of the games involved. As we go through these you will start to see patterns emerge; for example, collusion between a player and a dealer is a form of cheating that pops up in various gaming contexts. Let's begin where we started this book, with casino games.

CASINO GAMES

Roulette

Several forms of cheating occur in roulette, and all of them involve cheating the house. The simplest is the "capping" of one's bet. Capping a bet is adding to the initial wager after the result has become known. In roulette, the capper will make several wagers, at least one of which must consist of a stack of at least a couple of chips. When the dealer looks away or is distracted by something or someone (cappers often work with a confederate who will make a fuss, knock over a stack of chips, drop something onto the floor, and so forth just as the ball lands in a slot), the capper quickly adds several chips to his or her stack, placed on what's now turned out to be a winning bet. It helps if the capper is someone with large bodily movements, loud and invasive, so that the move to cap the stack looks like the player's typical bodily movements. It takes only one or two successful caps to produce a fairly sizable profit. If the capper manages to put a single extra $5 check on a number, he or she will take out of the game an additional $175. If the capper is wagering "blacks" ($100 chips) on, say, the dozen bets that pay off at 2 to 1, an extra two chips on a stack can yield a $400 profit. Cappers depend on not arousing the suspicion of the dealers and prefer busy games with many players.

Another form of cheating at roulette involves collusion between the dealer and a player. The dealer pays off his or her partner more than a bet is worth, or pays off a bet that wasn't even made. The two meet later and divide up the winnings. It seems simple, and more than a few dealers have fallen afoul of this practice. However, it's a good deal harder to get away with this scam than it first appears. First of all, the floorperson and the pit boss are always watching the game and may spot such inappropriate payoffs. If they are spotted more than once or twice, the dealer is going to come under suspicion and close scrutiny. Second, if a dealer's table drop is out of line with other tables in the pit, and systematically so over a period of time, the house will become suspicious. It is tough to get away with this kind of collusion for any length of time, but it's likely that it takes place on a minor level.

In the old days, there were stories about wheel mechanics who would doctor the wheel itself to increase the likelihood that particular numbers would come up. Today, such a scam is virtually impossible. Roulette wheels are carefully constructed and regularly checked for any imbalance or imperfection. They are also locked tighter than a drum when they are not in use. One of the more intriguing episodes of what I guess we should call "semicheating" occurred some years ago when a group of scientists used a miniature camera and computer to record the position of the ball when it was released relative to the wheel. After calculating its speed and location relative to the wheel during the first couple of spins, they estimated the quadrant in which the ball was most likely to come to rest. The projections were calculated using basic principles of physics, rather like those used to compute the orbits of spacecraft. The tale of this group of entrepreneurs was written up in the book *The Eudaemonic Pie*, by Thomas Bass. Although the principles on which the system was based were sound, the group was never quite able to get the system working properly.

For anyone who contemplates such a program, be warned that the casinos regard the use of artificial devices such as video cameras and computers as cheating, and they will bar (if not prosecute) anyone caught

using them. In any event, even if such devices became workable and con-
cealable, the casinos could neutralize them simply by changing the rules
of play so that no bets could be made once the ball was in motion.

Baccarat

From everything I can gather, cheating is virtually nonexistent in
baccarat. In this game, there are three dealers at each table. There are
always at least two floorpersons about, and a pit boss. Cappers can operate at roulette (and occasionally at blackjack), where a single dealer is
typically running the game, but any attempts at capping will be spotted
in baccarat. For similar reasons, it is virtually impossible for a dealer and
a player to be in collusion. There are just too many people around who
will spot the inappropriate payoff.

Other standard gimmicks like marking the cards with daub or a
crimp are ineffective because knowing the identity of the cards once
they are dealt is irrelevant. Palming and switching cards is nearly impossible, since there are so few cards on the table and the player must hand
over those dealt to the dealer. If there is a way to cheat at baccarat, I
haven't heard about it—which, of course, doesn't mean it doesn't exist.

Craps

Here cheats are legendary. Prehistoric ruins have revealed gaming
cubes that were weighted to give their owner an unfair advantage. Modern cheats run the gamut from dice mechanics who have perfected ways
to hold and throw the dice so that particular numbers are more likely to
come up than others, to dice switchers who introduce loaded dice into a
game, to bet cappers, to "one-time Charlies" who make a phony verbal
bet and expect a payout. By and large none of these will hurt you, the
player. Their larceny is directed toward the house. Let's take a quick
look at some of these.

The Blanket Roll

The blanket roll is named for the blankets on which private games
are often played. It consists of holding the dice with a particular set of
numbers face-up, and rolling the dice in a controlled manner so those
numbers are more likely to land face-up. Typically, the blanket roller
tries to control only one die, by causing it to spin rather than tumble; the

other is rolled in a normal fashion. The blanket roll has been pretty much eliminated in casinos by the requirement that both dice must bounce off the specially designed wall of the craps table.

Dice Mechanics

There are a few folks who have, by dint of years of practice, learned to control the flight of the dice so that they land cleanly in the groove between the table and the wall. By tossing them with the right force and angle, they claim they can control to a significant degree the outcome of the roll. I've never seen one of these fellows in action, but I have read of them. I guess the only thing I can recommend is that if you find yourself at a table with one of these characters, bet the way he is betting.

Dice Switchers

A relatively simple sleight of hand is all that is required to introduce a set of loaded dice into a game. The most common kinds of loaded dice are weighted slightly so that small (or large) numbers are more likely. With a set of such dice biased, say, toward large numbers, the probability of establishing and then making high points (eight, nine, and ten) goes up. Actually, only one die needs to be loaded to accomplish the cheater's goals. And, indeed, this is what is often done. Having only one die biased produces a seemingly more balanced sequence of numbers so the pit personnel are less likely to become suspicious. But the shooter still has a huge statistical upper hand. Again, it is the house that needs to be concerned with these guys, not you.

Slots

Slots, perhaps because they sit by themselves and are not directly patrolled by a dealer or a supervisor, have been the objects of more concentrated and creative larceny than any other casino game. For the slot thief, the game is man against machine. The earliest and most primitive assault on the slot was the use of a naked drill bit, when the "mechanic" would drill a hole in the machine, insert a tool, and turn the wheels until they came up a winner. Today, this kind of heavy-handed assault is rarely used, having been replaced by more subtle devices like wires that can be slipped up the coin payout slot to hold it open, or a coin soldered to a thin wire that is lowered down the coin slot to release the wheels and is then pulled back up. Some of the more sophisticated thieves actually purchase a slot machine, take it apart in the comfort of their workshop, and examine it until they can find its weak spots.

Ever since Charles Fey built the first slot, mechanics have been working on ways to cheat these machines. There is more cheating in the slots than in any other area of the casino, and not surprisingly, there is more energy and creativity on the part of casino management invested in stopping the slot thief than anywhere else. None of this, of course, remotely concerns us, since the slot thief is not out to get the player and we are all too honest to engage in such lowly endeavors as ripping off an innocent slot.

Blackjack

For the most part, cheating is on the part of the player trying to beat the casino. These folk use the standard array of gimmicks, including capping winning bets, card switching, daubing and marking cards, and working in collusion with dealers who overpay them on wins or conveniently miscount their cards. Casinos have introduced a variety of procedures for dealing with these situations. Most casinos now use a shoe and deal the game face-up. Not permitting the player to touch the cards eliminates card switching, daubing, and marking. Dealers working in collusion with players are typically caught because over time the PC on their tables is out of line with the rest of the casino. These, however, are not our problems. What concerns us are the rare situations when the house is cheating the player.

My read on this form of cheating is that it is pretty rare these days. Some feel otherwise: Lance Humble and Carl Cooper, in their book *The World's Greatest Blackjack Book*, maintain that cheating is rampant in Nevada casinos, particularly those that still use the hand-held deck. I think they are wrong, simply because the risk is too great. If a casino were caught having its personnel deal seconds (deal the second card in a deck rather than the one on the top), stack decks, use false shuffles, or any of the many other gimmicks in the card mechanic's armamentarium, it would suffer heavy fines and could lose its license. Since casinos have the upper hand against anyone other than a highly skilled card counter, it hardly makes sense for them to take such a risk for the small additional gain it would provide. It's easier to simply have a player barred. Nevertheless, if you suspect that you are being taken to the cleaners by a cheating dealer, simply get up and leave. Go to a casino that uses a shoe.

POKER

Here is where the individual player needs to start worrying: The poker cheat is after your money, not the casino's. In organized settings like poker rooms in modern casinos, cheating is rare and not really a problem. The greatest safeguard against cheating is the honest dealer hired by the house. Problems can emerge, however, in a couple of ways. First, if the dealer is a cheat and is working in collusion with one or more of the players, you can be at a distinct disadvantage. A good card mechanic is almost impossible to spot. I have watched people deal seconds when they told me they were doing it, and I was still not able to detect it. The only clue was a slight swishing sound when the card was pulled out, but in a crowded card room you would never hear it. Most poker rooms rotate dealers every half hour so that no dealer sits with the same players over an extended period of time, making partnerships with specific players unlikely. If, however, you have watched one player pull seemingly weird cards on a series of hands with a particular dealer —cards that seem a bit too much even given the volatility of the game —you might just want to take a break until the dealer moves on to another table.

Second, you need to be concerned about the player who can palm a card and remove it from the game only to reintroduce it later when needed. The best safeguard against this is the routine counting of the deck. The dealer should count the deck after every couple of hands and not deal if there is a card missing. However, many dealers get sloppy and may go for dozens of hands without a count. Again, if you suspect you are being cheated, just get up and leave. Unless you are playing in the higher-limit games, there's always another game down the road a piece.

One final note. If you really do think there is cheating going on, you could have a chat with the poker room manager. If a casino gets to be known as one that tolerates cheaters, it will quickly lose its customers. The casino will do everything possible to straighten out the situation. Similarly, if you spot someone in a casino whom you know to have been caught cheating elsewhere, inform the manager immediately.

Partnerships

Players who work partnerships in poker like to pretend that they aren't really cheating. Players who have been taken by a partnership, not surprisingly, take a different view of the practice. Two players can work in a partnership with each other in a manner that can squeeze a third player, and it goes like this. Suppose Players A and B are in a partnership. Player A holds a very strong hand, and a third player, C, has a strong hand, while Player B has rags. Player C bets and is raised by Player A, who signals his partner that he has what is likely to be the winning hand. Player B now reraises even though he knows he has rags and no chance at the hand. His purpose is to force additional bets out of Player C. Even though the casinos impose a limit of three raises when there are more than two players in a hand, a partnership can coax up to three additional bets out of the other player on each round of betting. If you think something like this is happening to you, inform the manager about what has happened and make sure you don't play with those guys again.

Player-Dealt Games

There are card mechanics who can make a card jump out of a deck and spit tobacco juice in your eye. My rule is simple: I don't play in games where the players deal the cards unless I know all the players.

THE THOROUGHBREDS

The situation here is pretty good these days, although that hasn't always been the case. There have been all kinds of wild and crazy scams in racing, including bribing jockeys to stiff horses and then betting on the others in the race, swapping a classy stakes winner for a hopeless nag and engineering a betting coup, using illegal drugs to improve a horse's performance, and so on. Once in a while some evidence is gathered that makes it look like a race has been fixed, but in recent years this has tended to take place with the trotters and not with the thoroughbreds. Trotters are easier to fix since it is easy for a driver to give an asymmetric tug on the reins that will cause a horse to break stride and effectively take it out of the race. Since horses often break stride, it is unlikely that anyone is going to call foul. The indication that a race was fixed usually shows up as a stunningly small triple payout relative to the horse's straight prices. If you get a triple where the winner went off at 22 to 1, the place horse at 25 to 1, and the show horse at 33 to 1, but the triple pays only $1,520, the state racing authority is going to get *very* suspicious.

I approach the horses with the presumption that everything is above-board, and until persuaded otherwise I suggest you do so as well. The only marginal situation we need to be alert to is the unscrupulous trainer who may be using illegal drugs to improve a horse's performance.

SPORTS BETTING

As with horse racing, the past was pretty ugly, but things look pretty clean these days. Lem Banker points out that in recent years there have been many more cases of insider trading and other scams on Wall Street than betting scandals in organized sports. As in racing, the price paid if you are caught is so great that it is usually just not worth the attempt. I treat the games as clean and recommend that you do so as well. Besides, if the fix is in, you sure aren't going to hear about it.

HUSTLING

Hustling occurs when one individual is considerably more skilled than another but only one of them knows it. Is hustling cheating? I don't know. I don't think so. Here's a little story that gives you a sense of just how fascinating gambling can be, especially when skill is involved and, well, a hustle is there to be exploited.

I had never in my life thought of one-wall handball as much of a gambler's game until one day I happened to pass by the courts at Coney Island in Brooklyn. Two guys were playing handball against each other for $5 a game. They were clearly friends and had come down to get some exercise and enjoy the competition and whoever won had to buy lunch. There was this big guy in a suit watching them—he reminded me of the Big Julie character in *Guys and Dolls*. Julie starts kibitzing with the two, who do the only polite thing. They ask him if he would like to play. Julie proceeds to play a decent-enough game, losing by just a couple of points. One thing leads to another, and pretty soon Julie's also putting up $5 a game. He wins a couple and he loses a couple. I can smell this one coming a mile away.

After about twenty minutes Julie has taken off his jacket, shirt, and tie but is still playing in street shoes. He is also now playing singles against the other two guys and the stakes are up to $20 per person per game. Julie is winning about two out of three games, but usually only by a point or two. The stakes move to $50 for the last game. It is strictly no contest: Julie is a master. Fade shots fall like a dying quail untouched, spin shots twist off the wall at unreachable angles, power shots fly by. Julie pockets the $100 (along with the other $100 or so he has already won), puts on his shirt, his tie, his jacket, thanks the two guys for a terrific set of games, and leaves. They're left trying to figure out what hit them.

It was a masterful performance. You can watch similar little dramas in bowling alleys and pool halls, on golf courses and at chess boards, on basketball courts, squash courts, and a dozen other venues. There is always the question of whether someone is cheating you, hustling you, or merely outsmarting you. The lore of gambling is filled with rich and varied stories of the exploits of weird and wondrous characters. One of the true legends of this genre was "Titanic" Thompson, a man of considerable wealth who had an insatiable appetite for a wager. Thompson reportedly was the first to suggest what has now become the prototype of the totally nutty bet: which of two raindrops would get to the bottom of a windowpane first. Thompson, who in his long career concocted and won some of the most bizarre wagers imaginable, habitually tiptoed along the line that separates a clever con artist from a flat-out cheat. He once bet a golfing buddy that he could drive an ordinary golf ball over six hundred yards off an ordinary tee. Thompson waited until winter to execute the wager, when he smacked a ball across a frozen lake, where it skidded and bounced for nearly a mile.

The granddaddy of all gambling gambits took place in a small logging town in the Oregon woods. Somewhere around the turn of the century, a sleazy-looking character, known to history only as Sammy, met up with Mr. James McTavish, the meanest, most ornery, most unsavory man in town. Sir James, as he was referred to by the locals, was the owner, bartender, chief cook, bottle washer, and bouncer at McTavish's Saloon and House of Illicit Pleasure.

Well, one day Sammy, our protagonist, a diminutive and scrofulous man, rides into town. After keeping pretty much to himself for a day or two, Sammy startles everyone by strolling into Sir James's establishment followed by the full membership of the town council, seven gentlemen who, at least by reputation, had never seen the inside of this infamous tavern.

Sammy pulls himself up top a bar stool and calls Sir James over. "Sir," he says while flashing two hundred in American green, "I hear you are a man who likes a wager. I will, if you are agreeable, wager you the fine sum of two hundred dollars that I can bite my eye."

"Bite your eye?" queries Sir James. Being by nature a suspicious man, he looks carefully at Sam, tugs at his beard once or twice, and finally reaches into this pocket and puts $200 on the long, oaken bar next to Sam's $200. Sammy, with a sly smile, removes his false eye from its socket on the port side of his wizened face, cradles it carefully to his mouth, gives it a gentle chomp, and picks up the money. Sir James, a man who does not like to be cheated, reaches down over the bar, grabs our hero, and pulls him damn near out of his underwear. "Listen, you puny little runt, nobody cheats James McTavish and gets away with it. I'm going to separate your ugly little head from whatever it is you call your body."

"Hold, hold," cries small Sam, hands splayed outward to protect his less than admirable face. "I do not wish to offend you, sir, for you are clearly too clever to be conned by such a wretch as I. I tell you what I will do. I will wager you double or nothing that I can bite my *other* eye." Sir James drops the dusty bundle of rags and looks at him askance. "No cane, no helpers, no nothing . . . clearly the little creep can see," he mutters under his breath. Out comes $400 of Sir James's hard-earned cash. With a flourish and a smile so evil that even Sir James is caught by surprise, Sammy takes out his false teeth and bites himself on his good right eye.

This is more than poor McTavish can stand. He leaps over the bar and lunges at Sammy, who scurries under a table. "Hold, hold," he calls out, clutching a chair in front of him. "I don't mean to cheat you, fine sir. I am so sorry, so terribly sorry. I just cannot resist this little joke of mine. You, sir, are a good sport and a fine fellow and I'll offer you one more chance. Again, double or nothing on the full eight hundred dollars." Sir James backs off a bit. He is out some serious change and thinks that perhaps this last bit will work in his favor. "What's the deal this time, runt?"

"Well," says our sleazy con artist, "put a shot glass up there at the end of your bar. I'll bet you I can stand over here on this table and piss into that glass, fill it up, and not get one drop on your bar." Sir James measures the distance from the table to the bar, thinks for longer than anyone has ever seen him think before, goes to the strongbox under the bar, and pulls out another $800.

Sammy stands up on the table, unbuttons his fly, and proceeds to urinate in a long and glowing yellow arc across the room. He barely touches the glass, instead fully drenches the bar from one end to the other.

Sir James howls with delight, slapping his thighs. "I knew you couldn't do it, you scummy little bastard. Gimme my money back." But as he puts his money into his pocket he turns and looks at our hero, who is roaring with laughter and hopping up and down in delight.

"What the hell is so funny? You just blew sixteen hundred dollars on that stupid stunt."

"Oh, indeed I did, sir, indeed I did," chuckles Sammy. He gestures to the members of the city council standing about in disbelief. "You see, my friend, earlier today I bet these fine fellows one thousand dollars each that I could walk in here, piss all over your bar, and you'd do nothing but laugh."

Is this story true? It really doesn't matter, does it?

10

INTUITION, HUNCHES, AND VAGUE FEELINGS

*T*here is a lot of loose and unsupported talk these days about using one's intuition to make choices, solve problems, and formulate decisions. People use the term "intuition" as though there were some kind of mysterious element to it, as if some folks had more of it than others, as if it were some kind of special power or ability. Many people seem to believe that intuition is somehow akin to something paranormal, like ESP. I was surprised to discover several recently published books on gambling with whole chapters devoted to this topic. Alas, these authors claim that you can learn to use your ESP-like, intuitive powers to win at various Type L games, and their books seem to appeal most often to slot aficionados and people who play games like keno and the lotteries, which are based on picking numbers.

Sadly, there is no truth to any of these claims. Indeed, the very idea of precognition is utterly implausible, but being able to make intuitive judgments is a perfectly normal faculty of the human mind. Research clearly indicates that there are times when you should indeed trust your intuition and there are times when you should not. I'll explain the difference and outline how such intuitive judgments can be made in various gambling situations.

Parapsychology, or the study of psychological processes that lie outside of normal psychological function, has been around as a subject of scientific debate since the 1880s, when the Society for Psychical Research was established in London, England. The field had its heyday during the 1930s, 1940s, and 1950s, when Joseph Banks Rhine (who, interestingly, was trained as a botanist and not a psychologist) was the director of the Parapsychology Laboratory at Duke University in North Carolina. One of his most engaging claims was that everyone possessed the potential for paranormal function but that most people had simply not discovered or developed it.

There was, however, a glaring problem with this claim. Casinos around the world were and are still doing just fine, winning at rates that correspond quite nicely with the predictions of probability theory. Were Rhine's claims true, various individuals should have been wreaking havoc on the casinos. But the only people who were regularly beating them were ordinary cheats with loaded dice, card daubers, and bet cappers—all strategies most decidedly within the bounds of the ordinary. Similarly, roulette wheels were not being beaten by people who showed supposedly psychokinetic abilities, and baccarat and blackjack tables seemed to be similarly immune from those with precognitive capacities.

On the other hand, intuition is a very real psychological phenomenon. There is nothing paranormal about it. We have a pretty good understanding of how intuitive knowledge is acquired and how it can be used. Good gamblers use intuitive knowledge all the time, and it's important to understand what they do and how they do it.

People are extremely astute at picking up on patterns and trends in the world around them. A simple study will help you understand what

I'm talking about here. Participants in the study are presented with a number of strings of letters that look like TPPPTXVPS or VXPTTVV and are asked to memorize them. The letter strings are formed using an extremely complex set of rules, although the participants in the study are not told this until later. After the memorization phase is complete, participants are presented with new letter strings, some of which conform to the rules and some of which do not, and they are asked to classify them. Although the participants have little or no knowledge of the rules, they are quite effective in detecting which of these novel strings follow the rules and which do not. When asked why they made these decisions, they typically respond, "I don't know. I just had this vague sense that some of them were okay and others just kind of felt wrong."

This phenomenon has been dubbed "implicit learning," in that what is learned is implicit and lies largely outside of consciousness. What we are calling "implicit" is very close to what, in nontechnical language, is referred to as "intuitive" or "instinctive." In common language, we often talk about people acting "intuitively" or "instinctively." A good shortstop is described as making an "instinctive" move to his left to knock down a bouncer that looked like it was headed up the middle. A boxer is said to have "instinctively" ducked out of the way of a sharp left hook that looked like it was going to deck him. A sensitive office manager is characterized as having "intuitively" sensed that one of the people under his or her supervision is having a difficult time coping with an assignment.

In all these cases, the individual is engaging an ability for implicit learning. Such people have had considerable experience with the various events that occur within their area of interest—be it baseball, boxing, or a business office—and they have learned something about the patterns and structures of events that occur in those settings. As a result of this experience, they have acquired a large amount of knowledge about those situations. A lot of this knowledge is held outside of consciousness.

"Very interesting," you say, "but what's all this stuff got to do with gambling?" Well, while we may not have precognition or psychokinesis, we do have the capacity for implicit learning and it is going on all the time —including in various gaming forums. As you play poker or handicap the ponies, you are picking up all kinds of information based on the patterns of events that surround you. In poker this will involve the patterns of betting and play, the talk, the shifts in tones of voice of various players, their physical mannerisms, their idiosyncrasies—indeed, anything that happens in the game that is reflective of some underlying pattern. At the track it will revolve around complex relationships among the many factors we identified in chapter 7.

Anyone who has become even semiexpert in a particular game is familiar with the feeling that he or she just has a sense of what is going on in a hand or a race, although the person usually cannot explain it very well to someone else. In poker you may look at your opponent and know in some inexplicable way that he is bluffing. It's not as though there's a simple tell or some obvious mannerism. There's just something about the way the hand developed, the way your opponent has bet, the manner in which he or she reacted to the cards, that gives you this intuitive, ineffable sense that you know what is going on. A reasonably seasoned poker player will have learned to trust these intuitive feelings. When they are strong, call that last bet.

Similar situations pop up in horse racing when, after handicapping a race, you find yourself feeling turned off by the favorite though the objective record suggests that he is the best horse in the race. There's something about the nature of the race, the opponents, the trainer, the conditions; something that whispers in your ear "This horse isn't going to like this track today." When this happens, you usually find it difficult to articulate just why you feel this way. It just seems intuitively right. When this implicit mental state emerges, trust yourself. Toss the horse.

But—and here's the important part—this sense of knowing intuitively doesn't come cheap. Building up the kind of knowledge and understanding of a complex game that allows you to begin to make these kinds of intuitive judgments reliably takes a good deal of experience and practice with the game.

So, when should gamblers trust their intuition and when not? Let's consider both types of games.

INTUITION IN TYPE W AND TYPE L GAMES

Type W Games

When you are dealing with a Type W game that is based on complex patterns of play and action with an underlying structure and logic, the experienced and successful player should trust his or her gut feelings.

There *really are* patterns in these games, in your opponents' behaviors, in their manner of reacting to particular situations, in the myriad factors that go into making a horse race, in the various elements that play themselves out in athletic contests. If you have been exposed to these patterns over a period of time you have likely been picking up on them without being aware of what it is you have learned. You can use this tacit knowledge profitably.

However, if you are still a novice, without sufficient experience in a particular game, you should be less confident in any vague intuitive sense you might have. People get these loose and ill-defined feelings of knowing something all the time, and, for the most part, they are unreliable. If you sat down at a poker table for the very first time and experienced a kind of nebulous sense that the guy who just raised your bring-in bet is bluffing, you're likely on a blind guess. Without extensive experience in the game, you just haven't built up the (unconscious) knowledge base to make such a judgment in a manner that reflects reality.

In passing let me note that these intuitive abilities have no place in blackjack. To play blackjack as a Type W game, you must resolutely follow the principles of basic strategy plus the count. There are no options.

Type L Games

When you are dealing with a Type L game, where there are no underlying patterns or structures, do not trust any vague feelings that may offer themselves to you. There is, quite simply, nothing to trust! There's nothing emanating from a slot machine that reliably indicates that it is about to pay out a jackpot. There is nothing about a roulette wheel or a pair of dice that can provide you with useful information about what to bet. These situations are as different as they can be from those in poker or horse racing, where there are patterns and structures; in Type L games there are none. Trust your intuitions in the former case; do not trust vague feelings of immanent futures in the latter.

Of course, since the negative expectations of Type L games will not be changed by any beliefs you may have, you may wonder why I'm counseling you against using any nonrational strategy. The answer is simple: People often follow nonrational impulses with higher bets. Increasing the amount of money you put into play in these games will hurt you in the pocket in the long run. Casinos provide paper and pencil for baccarat and roulette players. Though casino owners know there are no patterns, they understand that people love to search for them—and, of course, "find" them to do. When they think they have done so, they do exactly what the casino wants them to do. They increase their bets.

So what's the bottom line advice? The next time a slot machine winks at you seductively, just walk on by. But when your cognitive unconscious tweaks you with the compelling sense that you are a pathetic second-best on a hand, you probably want to quietly fold. No mystery here, just good old cognitive psychology.

11

BANKROLL
MANAGEMENT

*N*ow that you know almost everything you need to know in order to at least stay out of trouble, here comes the last but hardest lesson of all: how to manage your bankroll—or, as most gambling books put it, how to manage your money. Here, there are no simple probabilistic analyses to clue you into which games to play and which plays to avoid, no cluster of heuristics that will give you the upper hand. There are no secrets to money management—with the possible exception of that ancient line carved into the temple of Apollo at Delphi: "Know thyself."

Watch out for books that recommend particular rules such as setting "loss limits" or "win limits" either in absolute amounts or amounts relative to your initial bankroll. Such advice is simplistic and, in the long run, counterproductive.

Money management is too subtle an issue to be dealt with in such trivial ways. Mason Malmuth has called it an "extremely silly topic," and in some ways it is—at least in that a lot of extremely silly things have been written about it. Malmuth also recommended that this chapter be called "Bankroll Management" rather than "Money Management," on the grounds that one is really trying to maintain control over one's gambling bankroll, not one's money in any absolute sense. He is, of course, correct. Bankroll management is an essential element of gambling. Let's see if we can say some nonsilly things about it.

First off, what do I mean by your "bankroll"? Your bankroll is your gambling money. It is not your rent money or the car insurance payment or the fund for the kids' braces. Remember, it's critical that you never bet scared money, money you cannot afford to lose. You should view your bankroll as money that you can afford to lose—you won't like it if you lose it, but it won't devastate you to do so.

The overwhelming majority of casual gamblers, the ones who fly into Las Vegas for a vacation once or twice a year or who take in a day at the races once a month or so, do not really put aside a cache of coins that they label their bankroll. The typical recreational gambler, like yours truly, merely plays with available cash. I take what I calculate I will need for the games I plan to play. That becomes my bankroll for the day, weekend, week, or whatever length of time I plan to play. Nevertheless, it is my bankroll and it needs managing. So far, I've never lost it in the sense that I've had to slink home dead broke (although it's been nip and tuck once or twice). Let's hope you never lose yours.

That's a bankroll. Managing it means handling it so that you lose as little as possible in losing situations, add as much as possible in winning situations, and keep your head about you at all times. Bankroll management means knowing what your expectation is in the game you are playing and having a good sense of the variance that you can expect. Even when you have the best of it statistically, you are going to experience a good deal of session-to-session and day-to-day variability. You must be prepared, financially and psychologically, for brief or extended losing sessions.

Bankroll management involves mastering dozens of different sets of circumstances. It means not betting the triple on the last race to try to "get out for the day" when you don't see a clear case for one or two horses with value. It means picking up what few chips are left after a disastrous three hours of blackjack when you busted on every 12 and the dealer caught nothing but 5's and 6's on 14's and 15's and going home— not because you've lost but because you're depressed and confused and making playing errors. It means taking your $500 win at $5/10 hold 'em, thanking the players for their company, tipping the dealer an extra $5, and going out for a well-earned dinner—not because you think the cards are going to "turn against you" but because you're hungry and it feels like time for a break. Bankroll management means passing up the temptation to "cover yourself" by betting the other four horses in the second race that you don't have "live doubles" on. It means not getting suckered in on the "over" just because you overheard a couple of blowhards remarking about how porous Miami's defense really is. Bankroll management means knowing your limits, knowing what level of play you feel comfortable with, and recognizing when it is time to quit—whether you are ahead or being taken to the cleaners. It is the toughest lesson of all.

WHEN TO QUIT

There are no simple rules to follow, no magic formulas, no easy answers. Many authors will tell you to set a clear upper limit on the amount of money you will permit yourself to win or lose, and if you hit that mark, retire. There are occasions when that may not be bad advice, but it is also *very* hard to do, and in many cases it might not even be the best advice. I've been around this gambling racket a long time, and I really don't know anyone who follows such a regimen with any regularity. It's much more complicated than that. I've had days playing poker when I got "jobbed" at every turn. I remember (all too poignantly) a recent evening at $15/30 hold 'em. On an early hand I picked up pocket aces in late position, caught a third ace on the flop, bet like a genius, built a huge pot, and got nailed on the river by a small straight who never should have called the first bet. Over the next half hour or so there were three more hands with similar fates, and I suddenly found myself down in the neighborhood of $800, which was about a third of the bankroll I had for the weekend. Should I have quit? I don't think so. I was playing properly, I just got snookered by the short-term volatility of the game. So far as I could figure I still had the edge on this crew. I hung in there, caught a couple of decent hands later on, and eventually walked out some four hours later down a shade under a hundred—which I consider to have been a clear victory.

Yes, it's true that you should not put yourself in a position where you could lose serious amounts of money and, to be perfectly honest, I certainly could have dropped another eight hundred. This would not have felt real good, but I could have lived with it. What is important is knowing yourself, knowing your game, knowing the overall expectation. If you know these things, you will know when to stop playing and do something else.

When do I quit? I quit when I'm not having fun any longer! Sometimes that means quitting when I'm down a couple of hundred dollars. Sometimes it means quitting when I'm even. And, yes, sometimes it means quitting when I'm up. Not too long ago I was playing in a loose, passive $10/20 seven-stud game where I definitely had the best of matters. After about six hours of play I was ahead some $900. At that point I got up, thanked everyone at the table for their play, and headed back to my room. I really don't know why—except, for some reason, I just wasn't having fun. I was tired, the game had become somewhat routine, the whole atmosphere was kind of dull and uninteresting. Most people would think me weird to get up and leave in such a situation, but it seemed like the only thing to do. I do like winning, and I was glad to be ahead as much as I was, but that wasn't really the point. Of course, if you play professionally, you can't leave a situation like this. It's what you do for a living.

So I can't subscribe to the advice that you set clear dollar or percent-of-bankroll win or loss limits. There have been many times that I've kept on playing when I've been behind more than I would like, and there have been many times that I've quit when I'm up and would likely continue to win were I to stay. If I can't adhere to the notion of a "cut point," how could I advise others to?

BET SIZE?

Should you change your basic bet size? Yes and no. This is a complex topic, and to do it justice we need to see it in the context of Type L games and Type W games.

Type L Games

Here, I have some strong and clear advice to impart. Do not increase your level of play no matter what is happening to your bankroll. If you are shooting craps with a base bet of $10 because that's what feels right given your financial situation and your willingness to take risks, then make sure you stay a $10 player even if you are down a couple of hundred dollars (which can happen all too easily). Quit if you're no longer having fun, or if you've reached the point where you can't afford to lose any more. Play on if that's what you feel you would like to do, but don't increase your basic bet. Don't go "on tilt." Don't start steaming. Don't try to get even in a hurry.

Remember our discussions of probabilities and the expected value of particular wagers in chapter 2? In Type L games the odds are still against you, just as they were when you made your first bet. If you increase your average bet you will only incur a larger expected loss in absolute dollar terms. There is nothing you can do about this; the probabilistic nature of the game is fixed and the edge is with the house. The more you play, the more likely it becomes that the house will "grind you down," and if you increase your basic bet, it is a dead certainty that, in the long run, you will end up further in the hole.

Lots of self-appointed experts will advise you to increase the size of your bets when you are ahead because "now it's their money you're betting with." But nothing could be stupider. It's *not* their money anymore; it's yours. You just won it, and now it's yours. If anything, *decrease* your average bet when you get ahead; this will increase the probability that you will get out at the end of your session with some of "their money" in the sense that your future expectation is less negative. Don't forget the principle of regression to the mean, discussed in earlier chapters. Winning at a Type L game in the long run is statistically unlikely. Hence, the most likely thing to happen is that your play will regress toward the mean, which, given the nature of Type L games, is a negative value.

The reason many so-called experts tell you to increase your basic bet when you're ahead is that they are thinking about that psychologically lovely "big score," when you win some serious money. But the search for the "big score" only produces increases in variance. Players who jump up their basic wager in Type L games when they're ahead increase the likelihood of large wins *and* of large losses. But in the long run they do not alter the expected value of the gamble one iota.

Type W Games

Here the situation changes slightly. If you are using the advice given in earlier chapters, you are likely playing with a positive expectation. However, you must be wary still of increasing your basic bet, since the psychology of most Type W games changes as you do and your edge can vanish in a twinkling of an eye. Each game needs to be approached differently. In blackjack your decision should be based on the size of your bankroll. Review the section on the gambler's ruin in chapter 5 before determining whether it makes sense to increase your basic bet. Remember, although you increase the expected value of your play, you also increase the probability of losing serious money. If your bankroll can't withstand an extended negative run, you must not increase your average bet. Ditto in horse racing and sports betting. Only when you feel comfortable that a larger base bet won't put you in a situation where you might jeopardize your bankroll should you step up your average bet.

With poker, things are a little trickier. Movement to a higher-stakes game should be done with caution, since these games are often tougher games. If you have been winning consistently, you may wish to move to a higher-stakes game because your success may be taken as an indication that you are playing the game properly. However, the step upward should take place *across* sessions, not *within* a session. If you've been winning semiregularly at $5/10 and feel comfortable with the game, you might want to move up to a $10/20 game the next time you play. I'm against hopscotching up in a single session. For myself, such shifting makes sense only after I have thought about the game, understood that such a move will increase the variability of my bottom line, and am psychologically (as well as financially) prepared to deal with this. Generally, the higher-stakes games are tougher games. Just because you have been routinely beating the $5/10 games doesn't mean you'll have a similar edge on the folks in the $10/20 games.

Should You Split Your Bankroll?

What about the advice that you should never risk your entire bankroll in a single session of play? Well, on one hand this isn't terrible advice. If you carve your bankroll into small packets and make each last for a whole session by making small bets, you can keep playing for a long time. But if you are playing a Type L game like craps or baccarat, remember two important principles. First, the house edge doesn't change no matter how much or how little money you have on the table. Second, by virtue of the fact that the house edge operates on each and every separate bet you make, making many small bets yields a lower long-term expectation than making a few big bets. Suppose you have a bankroll of $100 and decide to play craps at $5 a roll by making pass line bets only. Each bet you make has a negative expectation of −1.41 percent, or about −7 cents. If you continue to play for any significant length of time, you will constantly be churning your money and the house edge will grind you down. The longer you play, the more certain it becomes that you will lose your entire $100 bankroll.

However, suppose you put the entire $100 on a single pass line bet. The expected value of this bet is a mere –$1.41 and you have close to a 50 percent shot of doubling your bankroll. However, the key to this strategy is to make only this single bet. No matter what happens, you must quit. If you win, go have dinner; if you lose, go for a walk. This strategy actually protects your bankroll better than the former—but it's not much fun.

Which one should you use? Should you split your bankroll and play the long slow grind, or should you become the ultimate plunger? This decision is one of personal preference. It's your money, of course, so it's up to you. The "ultimate plunger" strategy makes more financial sense, but I must confess that I don't know anyone who would choose it. People who like to gamble like the action and they like it to continue. I have a friend who is the ultimate "bankroll splitter." She plays the nickel slots. She gets $20 or $30 worth of nickels and plays until she has either won a like amount or has lost it all. Sometimes she wins; usually she loses. She regards the occasional win plus the fun of it all to balance out the long-run loses. If you are playing Type L games, this is a perfectly sensible strategy.

VARIANCE, VOLATILITY, AND YOUR BANKROLL

I know I keep worrying over this topic like an old dog with a treasured bone, but I do so for two reasons. First, it is of fundamental importance in gambling, and second, most gambling books neglect it completely. So, let's take a look at what lessons can be gleaned from understanding the variance and volatility of the games we've covered.

The life of a gambler is a roller coaster ride. There can be stunning and almost unbelievable swings in one's fortunes. If you are in a downswing, it is crucial that you recognize that such awful doldrumlike spells are an inevitable element of any game that follows complex statistical principles. The swings can *feel* unbelievable, but they are, in fact, very believable.

In his *Gambling Theory and Other Topics*, Mason Malmuth examines the theoretical fortunes of an excellent middle-stakes poker player who wins at a rate of $30 an hour with a standard deviation of $650. This means that this player will have a mean positive expectation of $30 per hour but that his fortunes will vary dramatically. Roughly 68 percent of the time he can expect to end each hour somewhere between being down $620 and being up $680. Some 95 percent of the time, he will end up between $1,240 in the hole or $1,360 to the good. A question: How long would a player of this level of skill have to play in order to be reasonably assured (95 percent sure) of turning a profit? The answer turns out to be a staggering 2,841 hours. A depressing number indeed.

However, suppose that our expert plays a tight, conservative game. His swings of fortune are much smaller, and he has managed to reduce his standard deviation to $500 per hour. Now only 747 hours of play are needed to produce a 95 percent chance of coming out ahead. If he really battens down the hatches and manages to keep his standard deviation down to $250, only 187 hours of play are needed for a 95 percent chance at a win. Variability has a huge, and much greater, impact on your bankroll than most players (and many experts) appreciate. Even though you may have the best of it, the gods of chance can still play havoc with your bankroll.

All of the games we have discussed in this book have high volatility, and the impact of the standard deviation on your bankroll is going to be marked and substantial. What this calls for from you is simple but critically important. You need to have a bankroll large enough to withstand these swings in your karma, and you absolutely must be prepared to deal with them psychologically. When things start to go bad, people get a little nuts; when they go really bad, they can just plain lose it. They start "steaming" and they go "on tilt."

THE PLAYER "ON TILT"

One of the scariest things in gambling is when a player loses all sense of the value of his or her play and starts to "steam" or goes, as they say, "on tilt." As a psychologist I have found such episodes oddly riveting. It's like watching an auto accident in slow motion. I was playing in a modest $5/10 game of seven-stud, and about an hour into the session a young man, let's call him Howie, had been beaten out of two decent-size pots back to back. In the first, his two pair lost to trip sevens. Howie looked over at the guy with the trips and snarled, "Caught the damn seven on the river, didn't you?" The guy simply smiled at him.

On the very next hand, Howie got hammered by the same guy, who this time really did catch a flush on the river. The pot was very large, and Howie lost out with a high straight. With daggers in his eyes, he looked at the guy and said, "You bastard, you did it again, you caught that damn heart on the river."

There were now two nails in Howie's coffin. The third came about a half hour later, and this one was a legit bad beat. Howie had filled aces up on sixth street. This was well hidden with pocket aces, and he was betting with both hands. There was only one other player, who was showing nondescript cards—10♣, 8♥, 6♥, and 2♠. But this guy raised on third street and called Howie's reraise; he raised again on fourth street. I put him on rolled-up tens. On the river Howie bet, the guy raised, Howie reraised, and they went back and forth till Howie, now in agony, figured out what was going on and called. Sure enough Howie's aces full went down to quad tens caught on the river.

Howie was now toast. For the next twenty minutes or so—or however long it took for him to run out of money—he stayed in to the river on every hand. He raised at every opportunity and called any raise sent his way. He swore, muttered, grumbled, and moaned about every card, every hand, and mostly about the bastards who had screwed him on the river three times. He had been down about $400 before he started steaming, and he went through at least another $500 in less than half an hour —quite a sum in a $5/10 game.

This is not the only time I've seen someone on tilt; it was just one of the more dramatic times. Any gambler who's been around for any length of time has seen similar episodes. In poker, it can have several manifestations. Sometimes, it's chasing with hands that the player normally would throw away, or calling bets with marginal hands and hoping for the magical card that will make the hand. In casino table games, it's marked by much grumbling and swearing and substantial increases in the player's basic bet. At the track, it's characterized by an increase in bet size and a search for long shots to "get out on the day." In sports betting, there's an irrational affection for parlays and teasers that have large payouts but dreadful expected value. In all cases, a player on tilt is marked by one common feature—his or her judgment is totally shot.

The best advice I can give any player is: Don't go on tilt! Great, that's a lot of help. It reminds me of when I was a Boy Scout (it really is amazing to look back at what we've done in our lives, isn't it) and this kid cut his hand on his knife. The scoutmaster was going nuts trying to set up camp, pitch twelve tents, cook dinner, and all the rest. When this kid came up crying and holding his sliced finger, he just lost it and screamed at him, "Damn it, Charlie, stop bleeding!" Sometimes it is really difficult to stop the bleeding.

Have I ever been on tilt? Sure. Who hasn't? One evil day at Belmont Racetrack, I was in the throes of a truly wretched run. I hadn't cashed a single ticket the last three times out! It had been a stunning run of hideous luck. My sleeper 7 to 1 shot got nipped at the wire. I watched $1,200 disappear when my $120 cold exacta on which I had $20 was taken down because my key horse bore out in the stretch and got disqualified. My can't-miss favorite got stuck in the gate. And the final nail in my coffin, the jock on my key horse in the second half of the early double *lost his irons coming out of the gate.* He rode all the way around the track sitting upright on the horse, trying his damnedest to boot him home. The horse, unbelievably, finished fourth—which just goes to show how much better he was than all the others. My buddies started asking which horses I liked in each race so that they would know which ones to throw out.

A little while latter, I lost it. I began increasing my wagers by 50 to 100 percent. I began finding all sorts of reasons to play long shots that any sensible handicapper knew had virtually no chance. I even played a demonstratively hopeless triple in the ninth race to try to "get out for the month." At the end of the day I was nearly broke and furious. I slammed down my paper and kicked over a chair. The kick of the chair got everybody around me looking at me like I was, well, like I was Howie. That was the last time something like this happened to me.

It isn't easy to stop the bleeding and it isn't easy to keep from going on tilt. Remember, not all such episodes have the memorable elements of Howie's whining or my kicked chair. You've got to learn to spot your own particular signs and do some mental work on yourself before you lose it. As with fatigue, learn to spot the situation before your judgment gets contaminated. Take a walk, a nap, a meal—anything, just get away from the situation until you have calmed down and understand what is going on. Remember, in pinball "tilt" means the game's over.

SOFT STEAMING

This is a term that I've coined for the less-dramatic but financially unhappy state in which players are not really on tilt but are misplaying situations and costing themselves money. Soft steaming is a symptom of a mildly pathological state of mind. Like real steaming, it tends to occur to players in Type W games like poker, horse racing, and sports betting. It's marked by a tendency to play hands that should have been folded, bet races that should have been passed, and wager on teams that are not worth the bet. It is not like real steaming, when the player is hemorrhaging cash from every pore; it's more like a nagging, dripping faucet.

It occurs most often in poker, when you are in the throes of a long, seemingly interminable run of mediocre cards. The mediocrity of the cards is the key element. When the cards are truly dreadful, when you haven't seen an overcard or a high pair in ages, virtually everybody knows that you just have to toss your hands into the muck and bleed slowly. The danger comes when you have been in a long dry spell and then start catching mediocre cards that entice you to play them, or reasonable starting hands that improve just a little. Were you not in this pathological state of mind, you would fold. But because you are so sick to death of not playing *anything,* you have lost your judgment. You toss in another bet to test the waters, to try to improve a little, to see what will develop. You start looking for some action; you try to force a hand that can't stand up to the situation.

Here's an example. It's seven-stud and you are dealt [A♦, 6♦], 6♠. You call the bring-in along with one other player. On fourth street you get 8♦, but you look out and see two A's, a 6, and three diamonds. You have no realistic drawing chances and the pot is small, but it's been so long since you went past fourth street that you suddenly find your fingers (acting almost as though they belonged to someone else) tossing in the checks to call a bet from the first A. Now you catch 9♣ and think, "Gee, a three straight; maybe this hand's got real potential." You can write the end of this script yourself.

Many good and even very good players get sucked into soft steaming on occasion. They probably don't even think they are doing anything terribly wrong. They feel they are just "taking a shot" at a hand that still has some potential or making a call on the basis of marginal pot odds. But two, three, or four mistakes like this can cost you dearly. Resisting the temptation to soft steam is an essential part of managing your bankroll.

LEAKS

Lots of really good gamblers don't do as well as they should because they spring "leaks." Here's a case. There's a guy who plays very good poker in several Atlantic City casinos and thinks he knows something about the horses. Alas, he doesn't, and he isn't about to listen to me or anyone else. He sits at the poker table with the *DRF* folded up on his lap and whenever he is out of a hand he takes a couple of quick glances at it and tries to handicap. Every half hour or so he gets up and goes over to the simulcasting room and places a bunch of bets. Off and on for some time now, I have been watching this guy systematically piddling away his not insubstantial poker winnings on the horses. The man has a serious leak. He is not alone. Las Vegas is full of players who are good at one game, like sports betting or poker, but who bleed profusely from self-inflicted wounds at the craps tables or baccarat or even the slots.

Do I have any advice here? Sure. Stick to the games you know, those where you have a positive expectation. I've counseled throughout this book the need to know yourself and to maintain a sensible and coherent stance with respect to gambling. I recommended learning but one or at best two games of poker before trying others. I suggested sticking with one sport and mastering it before betting others. You want action? Get it within the confines of a game that you know. Developing a leak is one of the surest ways to erode your bankroll.

THINKING ABOUT THE BOTTOM LINE

Everyone likes to talk about the "bottom line," but it is not entirely clear what this concept really means. Of course, the only *real* bottom line is the one that moves along with you throughout your gambling life. Are you up on your life? Or down? But players who go to a casino for several days or a week tend to think of their bottom line in terms of how much they won or lost during that particular visit. The IRS, which takes a close look at those who gamble, looks at your annual bottom line. Whether or not you owe Uncle Sam taxes is based on whether or not you turned a profit within a calendar year. But a year is just as arbitrary a time unit as anything else.

Restricting one's focus is a mistake and encourages poor bankroll management. By thinking within single-day units you focus too much on what has happened in a relatively short period of time and with a relatively small sample. It takes a lot of time and a large number of events before things can be expected to start evening out. If you are a high roller small samples are even less useful since variance goes up with bet size, making day-to-day fluctuations larger.

By focusing on the single-day or single-session bottom line, the player can get seduced into making bad plays in order to "get out." The last race of the day at virtually every race track offers a triple or trifecta—what better way for the horseplayer to try to get even? The typical outcome, of course, is an even greater loss on the day, since the last race is often one for, to use my friend Buzzy's line, "confused horses" that specialize in being unpredictable. If you can get yourself to stop thinking in terms of single-day or single-session results and start thinking in terms of longer time units, you ought to improve your overall bottom line because you won't be making stupid plays at the end of a session or a day.

One useful trick is to keep an accurate record of your wins and losses. Such a record has several virtues, the most obvious of which is that it keeps you honest with yourself. You will need to keep track of the games played, the stakes, how much you won (or lost), and the length of time you played or the number of races or games you bet. This will provide you with a clear record of your ongoing bottom line. It will also enable you to get a good sense of how well or poorly you are doing in terms that make sense, since you will be able to calculate, following the formulas given in chapter 2, both your mean win/loss and your standard deviation across each standard-length session. If you become seriously successful, you will need such records for Uncle Sam. The following table is an example for the ponies:

Date	Number of Races Bet	Average Wager	Total $ Invested	Win/Loss on Day	Cumulative Win/Loss	Cumulative Win/Loss per Race
6/12/95	6	25	150	− 35	− 35	−5.83
6/19/95	5	28	140	+130	+105	+9.55

More details, of course, can be listed, such as keeping straight bets separate from doubles, exactas, and exotics; or listing sprints separate from routes, and the like. For poker, a record might look something like this:

Date	Game Played	Stakes	Hours Played	Total Hours Played	Session Win/Loss	Win/Loss per Hour	Total Win/Loss	Total Win/Loss per Hour
7/10/95	hold'em	10/20	4	4	+120	+30	+120	+30
7/11/95	7-stud	10/20	6	10	−150	−30	−30	−3

Again, you can use a more detailed system. You can keep separate records for different games, or you might want to add a column listing your win/loss in terms of "big bets per hour," which will give you a measure of your overall level of play independent of the exact stakes of each game.

Record keeping is similarly straightforward in blackjack or sports betting. When playing blackjack, you base your analyses on the size of your average bet (or bet progression, if you have moved up to the level of expert play), and log hours of play and the win or loss for each session. With sports betting, keep track of wins and losses on each day of wagering and use average bet size in the same way as you would with the horses.

By the way, I strongly recommend that you also keep such records if you are primarily playing Type L games. Finding out exactly how much you are losing at these games can be sobering, and will perhaps encourage you to move in the direction of the Type W games, where your expectations can be significantly improved.

The point of all this is to encourage you to get a sense of how and where your money is coming from (or, alas, going to). You need to pay attention, not only to the bottom line but also to the variability of your play, and view both in the context of your standard wager. Proper bankroll management requires attention to all of these factors.

PICKING YOUR SPOTS

One of the best pieces of bankroll management advice I can offer is the simplest: Look for the best games to play. If you are playing poker, look for games with weak, loose players; in sports betting, look for the best line on a game; in blackjack, look for the casino with the most favorable rules and the deepest deck penetration; in horse racing, bet the tracks that have the lowest takeouts; in video poker, go for the full-pay machines or the largest progressive jackpots. At TropWorld in Atlantic City, the blackjack game is the most favorable in town, with late surrender and doubling allowed on split pairs. The craps tables allow five-times odds. Here I feel I am playing table games overall virtually even; what I give up in craps I get back in blackjack. This is not where I play poker, though; the poker room is small, the games tighter than a miser's purse strings, and the atmosphere stultifying. There are better poker rooms up and down the boardwalk. When I gamble, I look for the best situation I can conveniently find for each game.

BETTING SYSTEMS

Wherever you turn in the sharp-edged world of punters and players, you are sure to find some smooth talking, statistic-flashing promoter of a new (or recycled) betting system that is guaranteed to turn a hefty profit. These systems are designed to be used in Type L games such as roulette, craps, and baccarat; they are not proposed for Type W games. Some go by exotic names such as Martingale and d'Alembert; others, lacking a connection with a European aristocrat, remain nameless or carry the moniker of the local inventor.

But no matter, named or otherwise, none of them is going to leave you in better straights than making a consistent, standard bet. And, for some of the worst . . . well, you are better off buying snake oil from your local traveling carny than in committing your hard-earned cash to these systems (at least the snake oil can be used as a laxative). Betting schemes can be grouped into three general categories: those that produce normal distributions; those that produce distributions with a negative skew; and those that produce distributions with a positive skew.

Normal distributions are those with a bell-shaped curve such as that shown in figure 11-1a. From our gambling perspective, a session-to-session distribution with this shape indicates that the most frequently occurring sessions are those with an outcome close to the overall mean. Sessions with an outcome above and below the mean are balanced, and the distribution, accordingly, is symmetric. Of course, if you are playing a Type L game, the mean will be below zero and losing sessions will be more common than winning sessions. Negatively skewed distributions have a sharp peak around the mean but a long tail off to the left, as in figure 11-1b. A frequency distribution with this shape indicates that the player is enjoying many sessions with small wins but suffering occasional sessions with large losses. Positively skewed distributions, such as the one in figure 11-1c, are the opposite. They are characterized by many sessions with small losses and occasional blockbuster sessions with large wins. Let's look at some examples of each of these and analyze what the impact on your bankroll of using them would be. While these systems are applicable to any Type L game, I'll use craps as the example here since, typically, craps players have been most likely to implement them.

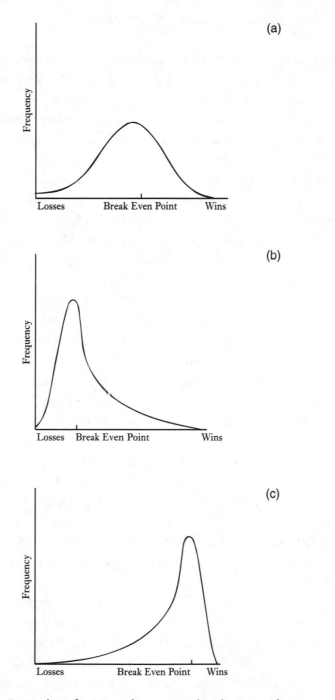

Figure 11-1 Examples of various frequency distributions. The top curve (a) shows a normal distribution, (b) a negatively skewed distribution, and (c) a positively skewed distribution.

Systems that Produce Normal Distributions

Betting systems based on a single bet size that is not adjusted will produce normal distributions. For example, suppose you follow the advice given in chapter 3. You are making a one-unit wager on the pass line and taking double odds, and that is all you bet. Your session-to-session distribution of wins and losses will resemble a bell-shaped curve, with a mean slightly below zero (the house has an edge in the game). The tails of the distribution will be symmetrical, meaning that sessions above and below the mean will occur with roughly equal frequency. A simple variation on this system calls for the player to make two additional come bets and take double odds on these. This system is known as the Ponzer. It produces a normal distribution, although, by virtue of the increase in the amount of money that is wagered, there will be a larger negative expectation and an increase in the standard deviation.

But these two approaches are not really what we think of as "systems." When people talk about using a betting system they typically refer to some wagering scheme where there are systematic increases and/or decreases in bet size depending on the circumstances. An example of such a betting system is one known as the Patrick Basic Right.

This system is a particularly bad one that can cost the player serious money. It goes like this: An initial $5 bet is made on the pass line, and after a point is established, $6 place bets are made on 6 and 8—unless, of course, either 6 or 8 is the point. If either 6 or 8 is the point, the other place bet is made on the 5 or 9, respectively. A progressive bet schedule is used whenever any of the bets wins. On the pass line bet it goes: 5, 5, 10, 10, 15, 15, 20, 20, 25, 25. On the place bets: 6, 6, 12, 12, 18, 24, 30. Minor adjustments are made to accommodate place bets when they need to be moved to either the 5 or 9, since these bets are paid at 7 to 5. If a bet is lost, the progressive schedule begins again. If you begin to win big, you can, of course, start the progression over again. But this time you up the foundation bet to $10 and double all wagers in the progression.

Anyone who recalls the material in chapter 3 can immediately see why this system is counterproductive. First, it involves making place bets, where the house has a larger edge than it does with betting the pass line and taking the odds. Second, it calls for systematic increases in bet size, which will increase both your total loss in dollars and your session-to-session variance.

Let's look at another progressive betting strategy that yields a normal distribution. It was presented by Edwin Silberstang in an otherwise excellent chapter on craps in his *Guide to Casino Gambling*. The player begins with the Ponzer, using a base bet that is divisible by three. Make this three-unit bet, follow it with two come bets of three units each, and take the odds on all. If your point comes up and you win, increase the next bet to five units and again take maximum odds. If you win again, increase the come bet to six units and, with each successive win, add three more units. Take maximum odds on all bets. If you seven-out, start the sequence over again.

Siberstang's system has the advantage of producing large wins when the shooter is "throwing numbers." It has the disadvantage of producing occasional sessions with rather large losses. If the shooter sevens-out early in the sequence several times, it gets very expensive.

Systems that Produce Negatively Skewed Distributions

The original and most vulnerable of these is known as the Martingale, which is based on a doubling of your bet after each loss. You start with a bet of one unit. If you lose, you double to two units; if you lose again, double to four units, and so forth. When you finally hit a winner you will be left with a profit of one unit and you begin again. Not bad, eh? Looks like you can't lose. So where's the problem? Simple, the table limits. Suppose you start with a $5 bet and hit a losing streak. Your bet size goes up quite rapidly. It will be $10 on the second roll, $20 on the third, $40 on the fourth, and so forth, until on the eighth it will $640. If the table has an upper limit of $1,000, a run of eight losing bets will wipe you out. The casino will not allow you make the next bet the system requires. If the limit is $500, a mere seven losses in a row brings about ruin. You can see how the Martingale produces a negatively skewed distribution. You will have many days where you will win a little and a few days where you will suffer devastating losses.

Another system that also yields a negatively skewed distribution is known as Oscar's Grind, or simply Oscar, and was first described by Allan Wilson. It goes like this: Start with a bet of one unit. If it loses, make a bet the same size as the one just lost. If the bet wins, the next bet is increased by one unit unless you win a bet that would produce a profit in excess of a single unit. If this happens, reduce the bet so that if you win you are ahead exactly one unit. Thus, each successful sequence terminates with a win of exactly one unit. Each time this happens, begin a new sequence.

Oscar's Grind is like a conservative version of the Martingale. A successful sequence yields a profit of a single unit, and the probability of achieving that end is quite high. And, as with the Martingale, eventually you will run into a hideous run of luck and suddenly find yourself at the table limit and unable to make the bet necessary to recover your losses— although this level is reached much more slowly.

Let's look at one more system that produces a negatively skewed distribution, the d'Alembert. This system involves increasing your wager one unit after each loss and decreasing by a like amount after each win. You start with a bet of one unit. If you lose, you bet two units; if you lose again, bet three units; and if another loss ensues, four units. If you win this last bet, drop your wager to three units. If you win again, drop it to two units. Anytime you hit zero, start over with a single-unit wager. This system, like Oscar's Grind, is safer than the Martingale, although there's the same small probability of catastrophic loss.

All these systems have the advantage of being relatively safe, in the sense that on the vast majority of your visits to the tables you will win a modest amount of money and you will rarely go home a loser. The problem is that when you *do* go home a loser, you go home *one hell of a loser*. And the bottom line hasn't changed a bit.

Systems that Produce Positively Skewed Distributions

The first of these was the Anti-Martingale. It uses similar logic to the Martingale, but in reverse. Each time you win, you leave your winnings on the table until you hit a certain number of wins in a row—you pick the number. For example, you might decide to continue doubling until you win seven times in succession. Anytime you lose before hitting the required run of wins, you have lost only a single unit. The Anti-Martingale system has the advantage of being less ruinous than the Martingale, and adds a certain measure of excitement when a winning run gets going. The system produces many sessions with small losses and occasional ones with large wins.

Another oft-touted system that produces a positively skewed distribution is the Contra-d'Alembert. Start with an initial bet of one unit. If you win, increase the bet by one unit. Any loss is followed by a decrease of one unit, unless, of course, you are at the table minimum, in which case you simply make the same-size bet. Like the Anti-Martingale, it primarily produces sessions with small losses and occasionally ones with large wins.

Many more systems have been proposed from time to time. There are several so-called hedge systems, where you balance one bet (like a pass line bet) against another (a don't pass bet), and there are rather complex systems like the Labouchère, which is based on arcane patterns of addition and/or cancellation of particular sequences of numbers. None of these work, in the sense that they can't change the bottom line. If you use any of them in a Type L game like craps, your negative expectation stays exactly the same.

Recently, Ken Elliott carried out a Monte Carlo analysis of about a dozen betting systems, carefully choosing examples that produced each of the three distributions. A computer was programmed to shoot craps, using each of the betting systems, for the equivalent of up to 800 rolls of the dice. Here's a quick overview of the results for the systems we've covered, using a base bet of $5. These data are given for 100 roll sessions, which, while small in terms of stable statistical estimates, correspond nicely with the typical crap shooter's average session.

System	Mean Net Loss After 100 Rolls
Simple pass line	$1.52
Oscar's Grind	2.60
Ponzer	3.31
d'Alembert	3.57
Contra-d'Alembert	3.91
Anti-Martingale	4.86
Martingale	5.26
Patrick Basic Right	7.10

No surprises here. All systems cost the player significant amounts over the straight pass line bet. Notice that even the Ponzer, which lowers the house edge by taking double odds, still costs the player in the long run because it calls for making two additional come bets. Patrick's system is clearly the worst, since it calls for making place bets that seriously diminish the player's expected return. Silberstang's system was not included in Elliott's analysis, but I'd guess it would produce a mean net loss somewhat above the Ponzer, since it is based on it but calls for progressive increases in bet size. Oscar's Grind is the least damaging of the genuine systems, which is not surprising since it is the most conservative.

Why are all these systems around, and why do players use them? There are two psychologically interesting angles operating here: the love of the big score, and the fear of the big loss.

The Big Score

A lot of gamblers like the big score, the knockout punch, the home run. They are attracted to a "break-the-bank" mentality. These folks don't go home and tell their buddies about the time they won $75 shooting craps, but do they *ever* get conversational mileage out of the time they won $12,000. People with this kind of personality are attracted to systems that produce positively skewed distributions. If you're a modest bettor using a simple pass line bet, you aren't ever going to win that kind of cash. But with a progressive system like Silberstang's or the Anti-Martingale, you could. These betting systems have the same kind of seductive element found in progressive slots and lotteries.

Another factor that boosts the attractiveness of these systems is that people have wonderfully convenient memories. The emotional residue of the big day at the casino lives on in their minds, becoming one of life's markers and assuming mythic proportions. My friend's wife, a fan of Siberstang, went on one of those magical tours around a craps table one glorious weekend in Vegas and won $23,000. She loves to tell the story of driving home to California with her winnings tied up in twenty-three stacks of $1,000 each and spread across the backseat of the car, of turning around every couple of miles to talk to her little stacks. She has apparently forgotten all about the many thousands of dollars she lost before and after that big score—many thousands more, her husband assures me, than she won.

She is not alone. Most of us tend to recall the pleasant events in our lives and push the unpleasant aside. When done in moderation, such a defense mechanism is psychologically healthy. To dwell unnecessarily on episodes of misfortune is neurotic and obsessional. The big win, the serious score, serves an important psychological role in our lives. But it is critical to remember one simple fact: How much you remember winning and/or losing has no impact on the size of your bankroll. Progressive betting systems may occasionally provide you with an episode of psychological significance, but in the long run, they will cut the very heart out of your wallet.

Individuals attracted by the "big score" tend to be risk takers. When they see the possibility of considerable gain, they are not put off by taking great risks that might jeopardize their bankrolls. Other people tend more toward the risk-aversive end of the scale and feel uncomfortable at the possibility of large losses no matter what potential gains might exist. For the risk-aversive person, with a fear of losing, there is a deep attractiveness in betting schemes that produce negatively skewed distributions. Oscar's Grind is popular with the risk aversive. Moreover, if they have a decent measure of self-control, they don't have to play the full "grind." If they've lost a couple of bucks and don't like the way things are going they can just pick up their checks and go home. These folks won't ever have the "big score." But they'll also never go bust.

The Final Word on Betting Systems

So what practical advice should the player take from this discussion? First of all, avoid really nutty systems like the Martingale and the Patrick Basic Right; they have nothing to recommend them. They don't guarantee wins and they can cause you to take a serious beating at the tables. As for others, such as Oscar's Grind and Silberstang's, well, the decision really depends on your personality and your style of life. If you are basically risk aversive, conservative, hate big losses, and get really unhappy when they happen, a system like Oscar's is ideal. However, if you get a real charge from a big win, if you are one of those folks who lives for the "big score" and you are willing to live with the occasional catastrophic loss, a system like Silberstang's is your cup of tea. It won't alter your expected value in terms of the percent of money wagered that you will lose in the long run, but it will give you the (unlikely, but real) opportunity for a really big day at the tables. It's your call.

TIPS AND TOKES

This final aspect of bankroll management concerns your expected outlay for tips and tokes. In casino parlance, the term "tip" is used for gratuities to waiters, waitresses, carhops, and the like; "toke" is for those given to dealers.

By design, most employees of casinos are poorly paid in terms of their base salaries; some earn only minimum wage. They derive the majority of their income from tips. A dealer's hourly income from tokes can run from a low of about $5 to $6 an hour up to a high of $12 to $15; waiters and waitresses average in the middle of this range; bellhops and busboys are near the bottom. The higher levels tend to come from the larger casinos in Atlantic City and on the Las Vegas Strip; the lower from the smaller downtown Vegas casinos and those in more remote areas where gambling is new, such as the riverboat casinos in the Midwest. The best estimate is that between 50 and 75 percent of the income of casino employees is derived from tokes. Since this has now become the financial culture of the casino, the player needs to take into account the impact that adhering to it has on his or her bankroll.

Playing Table Games

When playing table games like roulette, blackjack, or craps, you should tip dealers when they have been pleasant and understanding and done their job properly. Most people tip primarily when they win, but it's nice to tip when losing, especially if a dealer has gone out of his or her way to make your time at the table as enjoyable as possible. There are three ways to do this, depending on the game you are playing and how you play it. First, you can place a bet for the dealers; second, you can tip them outright as you are playing; third, you can wait until you are ready to leave and then tip.

Blackjack

One accepted way to toke the blackjack dealers is to place a bet for them. Put a chip in front of your regular bet, and if you win, the dealer wins; if you lose, of course, the dealer will get nothing. Many players ask the dealer if they'd prefer the toke straight up or if they'd like to play it. They virtually always say play it—which shows you that dealers are just as silly as the rest of us. I usually put down a $1 bet for the dealer every thirty minutes or so of play. Generally, if the hand turns into a double-down or split hand, I double the dealer's wager as well. At this rate, I give up a tad less than $3 per hour of play in tokes.

Craps

I generally don't tip while playing. Since I only play the pass line and take maximum odds, it's awkward to place a bet for the dealers on the table. I wait until I am ready to leave, then toss the dealers between $2 and $5, depending on how long I've played. Players who are fond of "proposition" bets will often place one or more of these for $1 or $2 for the dealers. Once, I watched a hot high roller place a $25 check on the yo for the dealers, who were delighted to watch a clean 5 on one die and 6 on the other put $400 into their toke box.

Baccarat

Here, where I am a relatively small-stakes player, I wait until I am leaving the table to toke the dealers. However, many high-stakes players toke the dealers after a particularly large win or after a winning streak of several hands.

Roulette

If I played roulette where the American wheel is used, I would toke the dealer after a decent win, like on a single number with a couple of chips on it, or when leaving the table. It is possible to bet for the dealer, but it gets complicated with all the different colored checks littering the table.

Poker

There is an established protocol here. The winner of a hand has the option to tip the dealer. In modest-size games with stakes from $5/10 to $15/30, fifty cents to $1 is the standard toke. In higher-stakes games, the size of the tip may go up a bit. In the very highest stakes games, toking is rare. Professionals tip less than tourists and recreational players.

The Racetrack

I do not tip the ticket clerk who punched out my winning wager. Some people do, but usually only when they had a very large payout. Tipping at the track is not part of the standard culture. The base salaries of racetrack ticket clerks are higher than for most casino employees, and clerks are not expected to derive a majority of their income from tips. On the other hand, if I have gotten a good tip from a ticket clerk, a tip is perfectly legitimate. But you should know the clerk first, and make sure that he or she knows what he or she is talking about. Some clerks give out random tips to try to increase their income when one of them hits.

Related Workers

In casinos and other palaces of chance, there are lots of other folk whose livelihood is intimately woven with the tipping culture.

Waiters and Waitresses

I generally tip whoever brings me a drink in a casino $1 for each drink. Many players only tip waitresses who smile at them or flatter them, but I disagree with this. It's reasonable not to tip surly or uncooperative waitstaff, but insisting that they fawn over you is inappropriate.

Carhops and Bellhops

Treat these folks as you would similar staff at any hotel.

Maids

I usually leave $2 for the hotel maid for each night I have stayed in my room. Of all the people who work to make your stay a comfortable and pleasant one, maids are the lowest paid and the most often forgotten. I leave the money on the night table the day I check out.

Tipping and Its Impact on Your Bottom Line

Most of these gratuities involve people who are part of your gambling operation and, as such, need to be taken into account when you figure your bottom line. Over a typical three-day stay at a casino hotel, during which I take my car in and out twice, eat two dinners in casino restaurants, and play various games for perhaps thirty hours, I shell out about $100 in tips. How much of a bite in your bankroll is this? Well, if you have a dinner for two in a good restaurant the bill can easily come to $60 to $100 (if you live in New York, like me, it can go this high for one). The standard tip on this would come to $10 or $20. Given that over this three-day period you've been wagering many thousands of dollars, $100 doesn't seem like that much.

Is it reasonable to shell out these kinds of dollars? Yes and no. Because casinos have maneuvered us into supporting their personnel just as restaurants have manipulated us into paying for their waitstaff, it is reasonable. Otherwise these folks couldn't make a decent living. On the other hand, consider your bottom line. Suppose you are playing blackjack for a base bet of $10 in a moderately crowded casino with four other people at the table. Under these conditions you are wagering in the neighborhood of $350 an hour. If you are a good basic strategy player, you are probably playing in the neighborhood of −.4 percent or −.5 percent. This means that you should expect to lose some $2 an hour at worst. If you toke the dealer $3 an hour, your tokes are the biggest single component of your bottom line!

Suppose you are a decent middle-stakes poker player in the $10/20 to $15/30 range where the rake is a time charge of between $10 and $14 an hour. If you are tipping dealers $3 to $5 per hour, the erosion of your bankroll starts to approximate half a small bet per hour. It takes a pretty good player to consistently win at a rate of one big bet per hour, so toking at this rate will have a dramatic impact on your overall expectation. Some players have worked this out and, as a result, no longer tip the dealer. I understand the problem, but I'm bothered by asking people to deal eight hours a day for only minimum wage. I recommend a compromise: Tip fifty cents for each winning hand (other than an ante steal, of course).

That's the tipping/toking story. I think my recommendations on tipping are appropriate, though I am (painfully) aware of their impact on the player's bankroll. In the final anaysis, tipping/toking is a personal thing and players will ultimately find the level they feel comfortable with.

*T*his book was written for the recreational gambler, and one of its messages is that gambling is fun. Alas, not everyone who gambles has fun at it. Many people get too involved, become stressed out, lose too much money, and lose their way. I've tried to teach you how to play these games so that you come out on top—one way or another. If you play Type L games, you are going to lose in the long run. I've showed you how to minimize your losses, but there will be losses. You don't have to walk out a loser, though—not in the larger scheme of things. Money is but one line in the ledger; the other logs the psychological aspects of the experience. This one should always be in the black. One nice thing about knowing the expected value of various games is that you won't be upset should you lose. You'll see it as one of the inevitabilities of life. Try to think of it as money spent on a vacation. If you play Type L games, make sure you have your play rated by your casino. The comps you will receive will add to the psychological side of the ledger.

If you play Type W games and use my advice, the situation is even better, since you will be playing with positive expectation. But here, as well, there are elements besides money. If you are playing blackjack, play with friends. Form a small syndicate and work together. In addition to the pleasure of being with others, teaming up diminishes the volatility of the game and reduces the swings in your bankroll. If you play the horses, go with friends. Sit in the restaurant, have a good meal, enjoy the day whether you win or lose. If you play poker, get to know some of the regulars. Make new friends and feed, psychologically, off your time at the tables.

Of all the forms of gaming, the ones I most enjoy are poker and horse racing. Poker fascinates me because, win or lose, there is the psychological intrigue of the game, the battle of wits and guile, the exchange of subtlety and bravado. These aspects provide an element of pure pleasure that is not easy to find elsewhere. In horse racing, something special awaits. It has an aesthetic quality, a special beauty at its heart that is not found elsewhere. Making a big score at poker or riding the crest of a crapshooter with hot dice may produce euphoria, a visceral sense of satisfaction. But if there is beauty in these kinds of emotional experiences, it is very different in kind from the sublime beauty of the racehorse. Do not miss this element of the game. Go down to the paddock and watch the horses being saddled. Follow them through the post parade and onto the track. Admittedly, you'll get a better view of the race on the televisions dotted all around the track, but sacrifice that view from time to time. Go down to the rail on the stretch as the horses turn for home and battle each other to the wire. Feel the power and beauty of these animals as they drive past you. Learn to appreciate the thoroughbred for its own sake, as a splendidly sculpted running machine, a world-class athlete.

There is more to life than dollars and cents and whether or not you're involved in a game with positive or negative expectations. Enjoy yourself, enjoy your comps, appreciate the aesthetics of the games you play, make new friends, eat well, sleep soundly, and always look for the game where you have an edge.

We covered a lot of ground, and not surprisingly, there is more lurking behind the material presented. For those who want to take a deeper look into any of the games covered, the following sources are good ones. You can find most of these titles in your local bookstore, or for hard-to-find books, try the Gambler's Book Club. Their toll-free line is 1-800-522-1777.

CASINO TABLE GAMES

Oddly, there really aren't any books I could recommend here in terms of play, since no better strategies exist than what I've given you. However, there are a couple of general books that are terrific. Specifically:

Welcome to the Pleasure Dome by David Spanier. Spanier is a British correspondent who has been a longtime follower of and writer on gambling.

Comp City: A Guide to Free Las Vegas Vacations by Max Rubin. How to survive in and take advantage of Las Vegas. Good fun.

VIDEO POKER

There are several places to turn for extremely detailed information on playing these machines. I recommend:

Winning Strategy for Video Poker by Lenny Frome. It presents the tables and formulas necessary to work out the optimal choice for every situation that occurs on several dozen machines.

Professional Video Poker by Stanford Wong. This book is just what it says it is: a how-to for those who wish to play the game professionally.

BLACKJACK

There are literally dozens of good books on blackjack. My favorites are:

Professional Blackjack and *Blackjack Secrets,* both by Stanford Wong, and *Blackbelt in Blackjack* by Arnold Snyder. These books lay out the High-Low system in detail and give excellent advice on how to use it.

Million Dollar Blackjack by Ken Uston. Uston's innovativeness, boldness, and just plain ballsiness make the book a delight. His "Plus/Minus" and "Advanced Point Count" systems, however, are more difficult to learn than Wong's High-Low and provide no significant gain.

The World's Greatest Blackjack Book by Lance Humble and Carl Cooper. This book presents the Hi Opt systems, both I and the more advanced II. The Hi Opt system is similar to the Wong High-Low, but it pits three, four, five, and six against the tens and ignores twos and aces. It is less efficient than Wong's, though it produces a more accurate metric for taking insurance.

Blackjack Essays by Mason Malmuth. A terrific collection of essays on the nuances of blackjack.

Beat the Dealer by Edward O. Thorp. This is the original book that first laid out the principles of card counting.

POKER

There must be a hundred books on poker on the market. Of those that I've read, the ones that stand out are those written by the crew at Two Plus Two Publishing, specifically:

Hold 'em Poker for Advanced Players by David Sklansky and Mason Malmuth, and *Seven-Card Stud for Advanced Players* by David Sklansky, Mason Malmuth, and Ray Zee. These two will take you past the material I've covered on these two games.

High-Low Split Poker, Seven-Card Stud and Omaha Eight-or-Better for Advanced Players by Ray Zee. An excellent source for these games that I did not cover.

Sklansky on Poker by David Sklansky. A superb general source of insight, including coverage of the game of razz, or seven-stud lowball.

Winning Concepts in Draw and Lowball by Mason Malmuth.

The Body Language of Poker by Mike Caro. Terrific for learning about tells. But don't believe Caro's estimates of how much spotting each tell is worth.

Super System by Doyle Brunson. One of the classics. A must read.

HORSE RACING

Again, the breadth of literature is huge. I recommend you start with:

Beyer on Speed by Andrew Beyer.

Figure Handicapping Revisited by James Quinn. An excellent advanced approach.

Modern Pace Handicapping by Tom Brohamer. The place to turn for the truly arcane mathematics of pace handicapping.

SPORTS BETTING

Most available material is specialized. Of general books, I'd suggest:

Sport Betting 101 by Arne Lang. The best general book on the subject.

Race and Sports Book Management by Michael Roxborough and Mike Rhoden. Provides insight into the "other side" of the game. It is important to know what the bookies are thinking.

BANKROLL MANAGEMENT AND OTHER ISSUES

A couple of thoughtful and insightful books go beyond just outlining how to beat one or another game. I recommend:

Getting the Best of It by David Sklansky. This book covers a wide range of topics, all organized around circumstances when you have the best of it and those when you don't.

Gambling Theory and Other Topics by Mason Malmuth. Deals in-depth with a variety of topics based on the statistical and mathematical principles underlying gaming.

ABOUT THE AUTHOR

Arthur S. Reber, a professor of psychology at Brooklyn College and the Graduate Center of CUNY, has been a gambler since his uncles introduced him to the wonders of the racetrack as a kid. He is expert at most forms of gaming and is especially fond of poker and handicapping the thoroughbred racehorse.